Lecture Notes in Computer Science

Lecture Notes in Artificial Intelligence   14378

Founding Editor

Jörg Siekmann

Series Editors

Randy Goebel, *University of Alberta, Edmonton, Canada*
Wolfgang Wahlster, *DFKI, Berlin, Germany*
Zhi-Hua Zhou, *Nanjing University, Nanjing, China*

The series Lecture Notes in Artificial Intelligence (LNAI) was established in 1988 as a topical subseries of LNCS devoted to artificial intelligence.

The series publishes state-of-the-art research results at a high level. As with the LNCS mother series, the mission of the series is to serve the international R & D community by providing an invaluable service, mainly focused on the publication of conference and workshop proceedings and postproceedings.

Andrei Ciortea · Mehdi Dastani · Jieting Luo
Editors

Engineering Multi-Agent Systems

11th International Workshop, EMAS 2023
London, UK, May 29–30, 2023
Revised Selected Papers

 Springer

Editors
Andrei Ciortea (iD)
University of St.Gallen
St. Gallen, Switzerland

Mehdi Dastani (iD)
Utrecht University
Utrecht, The Netherlands

Jieting Luo (iD)
Zhejiang University
Hangzhou, China

ISSN 0302-9743   ISSN 1611-3349 (electronic)
Lecture Notes in Artificial Intelligence
ISBN 978-3-031-48538-1   ISBN 978-3-031-48539-8 (eBook)
https://doi.org/10.1007/978-3-031-48539-8

LNCS Sublibrary: SL7 – Artificial Intelligence

This Springer imprint is published by the registered company Springer Nature Switzerland AG
The registered company address is: Gewerbestrasse 11, 6330 Cham, Switzerland

Paper in this product is recyclable.

Preface

The International Workshop on Engineering Multi-Agent Systems (EMAS) was formed in 2013 as a merger of three long-running workshops: Agent-Oriented Software Engineering (AOSE), Programming Multi-Agent Systems (ProMAS), and Declarative Agent Languages and Technologies (DALT). This merger established EMAS as a reference venue for work that is broadly concerned with the engineering of agents and multi-agent systems.

The three parent events have a long history of association with the International Conference on Autonomous Agents and Multi-Agent Systems (AAMAS). Since its inception, EMAS has been co-located with AAMAS as well. EMAS 2013 took place in St. Paul (with post-proceedings published as Springer LNCS/LNAI volume 8245), EMAS 2014 in Paris (LNCS/LNAI 8758, and a special issue in the International Journal of Agent-Oriented Software Engineering, IJAOSE Vol. 5 No. 2/3, 2016), EMAS 2015 in Istanbul (LNCS/LNAI 9318, and a special issue in IJAOSE Vol. 6 No. 2, 2018), EMAS 2016 in Singapore (LNCS/LNAI 10093, and a special issue in IJAOSE Vol. 6 No. 3/4, 2018), EMAS 2017 in São Paulo (LNCS/LNAI 10738), EMAS 2018 in Stockholm (LNAI 11375, and a report in Software Engineering Notes), EMAS 2019 in Montreal (LNAI 12058), EMAS 2020 in Auckland (LNAI 12589), EMAS 2021 in London (LNAI 13190), and EMAS 2022 in Auckland (a special issue is to appear in AMAI). From 2020 to 2022, because of the COVID-19 pandemic, AAMAS and its co-located workshops (incl. EMAS) were organized as online events in a fully virtual format.

EMAS 2023 aimed to build on this tradition by bringing together researchers and practitioners interested in the theory and practice of engineering autonomous agents and multi-agent systems. The overall goal of the workshop was to facilitate the cross-fertilization of ideas and experiences in the various fields to:

- advance our knowledge and the state of the art of the theory and practice of engineering intelligent agents and multi-agent systems;
- demonstrate how MAS methodologies, architectures, languages, and development tools can be used in the engineering of deployed large-scale, open, and data-driven MAS;
- define new directions for engineering MAS by drawing on results and recommendations from related research areas; and
- encourage Ph.D. and Master's students to become involved in and contribute to the area.

EMAS 2023 was the first edition since 2019 to be held in person and was organized as a 1.5-day workshop[1]. We received 25 submissions, each of which was reviewed (single-blind) by three reviewers. In total, 18 papers were accepted for presentation at the workshop (11 regular papers, 5 short papers, and 2 demonstration papers)—and

---

[1] The complete workshop programme is available online: https://emas.in.tu-clausthal.de/2023/program.html, accessed: 13.09.2023.

were invited after the workshop for submission to the post-proceedings. In addition to these 18 papers, the workshop programme featured two invited talks, "Learnable and Interactive Autonomous Agents through Reinforcement Learning" by Shihan Wang (Utrecht University) and "A New Solid Web for Agents that Rock" by Pierre-Antoine Champing (W3C). On the second day, our invited speakers were joined by Terry Payne (University of Liverpool), Ganesh Ramanathan (Siemens), Alessandro Ricci (University of Bologna), and Munindar P. Singh (North Carolina State University) in an engaging panel discussion on "Learning Agents, the Web, and Industrial Applications".

Last but not least, a novelty of the workshop programme for EMAS 2023 was the organization of an informal and interactive session for demonstrators at the end of the first day. This session was meant to encourage discussions and creative thinking—and was organized in one of the coffee break areas with the support of the AAMAS 2023 local organizers. A total of 9 demonstrators were registered and presented in this session.

We would like to thank: the authors and all participants to the open demonstration session for their valuable contributions to the workshop programme; the members of the Program Committee for their work in ensuring a high-quality reviewing process, and the members of the Steering Committee for their guidance; Pierre-Antoine Champin and Shihan Wang for their insightful keynotes; our invited panelists Terry Payne, Ganesh Ramanathan, Alessandro Ricci, and Munindar P. Singh for creating a vibrant discussion at the workshop; the AAMAS 2023 Local Arrangement Team and especially Enrico Gerding for their support in organizing the open demonstration session; TU Clausthal and especially Tobias Ahlbrecht for their support in hosting the workshop website.

We look forward to the next edition of the EMAS workshop!

September 2023   Andrei Ciortea
                                                           Mehdi Dastani
                                                            Jieting Luo

Organization

Program Committee Chairs

Andrei Ciortea	University of St.Gallen, Switzerland
Mehdi Dastani	Utrecht University, The Netherlands
Jieting Luo	Zhejiang University, China

Program Committee

Natasha Alechina	Utrecht University, The Netherlands
Matteo Baldoni	Università di Torino, Italy
Luciano Baresi	Politecnico di Milano, Italy
Cristina Baroglio	Università di Torino, Italy
Olivier Boissier	MINES Saint-Étienne, France
Daniela Briola	University of Milano-Bicocca, Italy
Rafael C. Cardoso	University of Aberdeen, UK
Moharram Challenger	University of Antwerp, Belgium
Amit Chopra	Lancaster University, UK
Andrei Ciortea	University of St.Gallen, Switzerland
Rem Collier	University College Dublin, Ireland
Stefania Costantini	Università degli Studi dell'Aquila, Italy
Fabiano Dalpiaz	Utrecht University, The Netherlands
Mehdi Dastani	Utrecht University, The Netherlands
Maiquel de Brito	Federal University of Santa Catarina, Brazil
Davide Dell'Anna	Delft University of Technology, The Netherlands
Louise Dennis	University of Manchester, UK
Angelo Ferrando	Università di Genova, Italy
Lars-Ake Fredlund	Universidad Politécnica de Madrid, Spain
Stéphane Galland	UBFC – UTBM, France
Jorge Gomez-Sanz	Universidad Complutense de Madrid, Spain
Zahia Guessoum	Sorbonne Université and Université de Reims Champagne-Ardenne, France
James Harland	RMIT University, Australia
Vincent Hilaire	UTBM/IRTES-SET, France
Koen Hindriks	Vrije Universiteit Amsterdam, The Netherlands
Tom Holvoet	Katholieke Universiteit Leuven, Belgium
Jomi Fred Hübner	Federal University of Santa Catarina, Brazil

Joao Leite	Universidade NOVA de Lisboa, Portugal
Yves Lespérance	York University, Canada
Jieting Luo	Zhejiang University, China
Viviana Mascardi	Università di Genova, Italy
Simon Mayer	University of St.Gallen, Switzerland
John-Jules Meyer	Utrecht University, The Netherlands
Roberto Micalizio	Università di Torino, Italy
Luis Gustavo Nardin	Mines Saint-Étienne, France
Enrico Pontelli	New Mexico State University, USA
Wishnu Prasetya	Utrecht University, The Netherlands
Alessandro Ricci	Università di Bologna, Italy
Luca Sabatucci	ICAR-CNR, Italy
Valeria Seidita	Università degli Studi di Palermo, Italy
Jaime Sichman	University of São Paulo, Brazil
Tran Cao Son	New Mexico State University, USA
Jørgen Villadsen	Technical University of Denmark, Denmark
Danny Weyns	Katholieke Universiteit Leuven, Belgium
Michael Winikoff	Victoria University of Wellington, New Zealand
Vahid Yazdanpanah	University of Southampton, UK
Neil Yorke-Smith	Delft University of Technology, The Netherlands
Rym Zalila-Wenkstern	University of Texas at Dallas, USA
Yingqian Zhang	Eindhoven University of Technology, The Netherlands

Steering Committee

Matteo Baldoni	Università degli Studi di Torino, Italy
Rafael Bordini	PUCRS, Brazil
Mehdi Dastani	Utrecht University, The Netherlands
Jürgen Dix	Technische Universität Clausthal, Germany
Amal El Fallah Seghrouchni	Sorbonne Université, France
Brian Logan	Utrecht University, The Netherlands
Jörg P. Müller	Technische Universität Clausthal, Germany
Alessandro Ricci	Università di Bologna, Italy
Danny Weyns	Katholieke Universiteit Leuven, Belgium
Michael Winikoff	Victoria University of Wellington, New Zealand
Rym Zalila-Wenkstern	University of Texas at Dallas, USA

Contents

Agent-Oriented Software Engineering

Towards Forward Responsibility in BDI Agents

Rafael C. Cardoso[1]([:envelope:])([iD]), Angelo Ferrando[2]([iD]), Joe Collenette[3],
Louise A. Dennis[3]([iD]), and Michael Fisher[3]([iD])

[1] University of Aberdeen, Aberdeen, UK
`rafael.cardoso@abdn.ac.uk`
[2] University of Genova, Genova, Italy
`angelo.ferrando@unige.it`
[3] The University of Manchester, Manchester, UK
`{joe.collenette,louise.dennis,michael.fisher}@manchester.ac.uk`

Abstract. In this paper, we discuss forward responsibilities in Belief-Desire-Intention agents, that is, responsibilities that can drive future decision-making. We focus on individual rather than global notions of responsibility. Our contributions include: (a) extended operational semantics for responsibility-aware rational agents; (b) hierarchical responsibilities for improving intention selection based on the priorities (i.e., hierarchical level) of a responsibility; and (c) shared responsibilities which allow agents with the same responsibility to update their priority levels (and consequently commit or not to the responsibility) depending on the lack (or surplus) of agents that are currently engaged with it.

Keywords: forward-looking responsibility · task responsibility · BDI agents

1 Introduction

A recent "Blue Sky Ideas" paper [27] discussed existing research and new research opportunities in the application of responsibility for trustworthy autonomous systems. They describe many research themes and challenges, but of particular interest to us is the challenge of using responsibility "to ensure system reliability and fault tolerance in the technical software development context".

We refer to rational agents as cognitive programmable entities that perform autonomous decision making by reasoning about events, capabilities, and knowledge of the world. Recent literature reviews on agent-oriented programming have highlighted the need for safer and more reliable agents [6,9,17].

In this paper we focus on *forward-looking* (as opposed to *backward-looking*) responsibilities [19]. In the context of rational agents, the former uses responsibilities to aid in the process of task selection, while the latter is related to the notions of accountability, liability, and blameworthiness. Many concepts of responsibility exist, see [27] for a more comprehensive discussion.

A. Ciortea et al. (Eds.): EMAS 2023, LNAI 14378, pp. 3–22, 2023.
https://doi.org/10.1007/978-3-031-48539-8_1

We illustrate these different concepts of responsibility in Fig. 1. Besides the dimension regarding its meaning, when considering responsibility-aware agents we also have to consider if the view of responsibility that was chosen is centralised or decentralised. A centralised view of responsibility in autonomous agents occurs when the information about responsibilities (either backward or forward-looking) is stored in a shared environment (e.g., organisation, electronic institution), which makes it easier for any agent to access the responsibilities of other agents. On the other hand, a decentralised view usually requires communication between agents in order to obtain access to other agents responsibilities (e.g., stigmergic behaviour). Whereas previous literature about responsibility in agent systems have often focussed on organisations or some other centralised model of responsibilities [2,3,25,26], in this paper we focus on forward-looking responsibilities where our agents reason about their own individual responsibilities and have an individual (decentralised) view of responsibilities. We achieve this by extending well know formal theories for agent computational models.

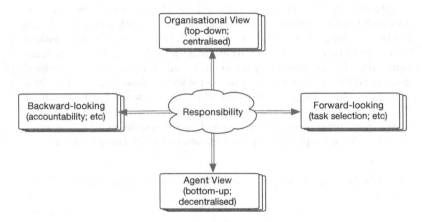

Fig. 1. Different dimensions when considering responsibility for rational agents. Directions of arrows and axes have no additional semantic meaning, an axis simply represents a different dimension.

Formal agent theories, such as those based on the Belief-Desire-Intention (BDI) model [8], do not include the notion of responsibility. Models where responsibilities (and the similar concept of agent roles) have been described predominantly take a centralised/organisational view. We propose extending agent models and theories with forward-looking, decentralised responsibility and instantiate this by considering their computation in the reasoning cycle of agents. As previously mentioned, we are interested in improving the reliability of rational agents through reasoning of responsibilities. In particular, we extend the standard syntax and operational semantics of rational agents to support responsibility-aware agents. We focus on two concepts to improve the reliability and flexibility of the agents: *hierarchy of responsibilities* and *shared responsibilities*. The hierarchy is formed by attaching priorities (the hierarchical level) to the responsibilities which guides the agents during their intention selection; this also improves flexibility since it provides agents with a new way of selecting their intentions to be executed based on the priorities of the responsibilities that they are committed to performing. Agents that have shared responsibilities need to be aware of the status of these responsibilities in order to take over from other agents that can no longer perform them (this is achieved by manipulating the associated priorities), and thus, effectively improving the reliability of the system.

Our concept of forward-looking responsibilities is distinctively different from concepts of beliefs and organisational roles, and as such it would not be possible to flatten our representation to either of these concepts without losing some of our contributions and still maintain the original identity of beliefs and organisational roles. Most notably, one of these contributions is the direct impact that responsibilities (in particular their hierarchy) causes in the reasoning cycle by guiding the intention selection of rational agents.

The paper is structured as follows. Section 2 discusses the differences between our work and existing approaches for responsibility-aware agents. In Sect. 3 we present some of the basic operational semantics for rational agents and extend it to allow for responsibility-aware agents. Sections 3.1 and 3.2 contain extensions of the theory to include the concepts of hierarchy of responsibilities and shared responsibilities (respectively). In Sect. 4 we discuss how our approach can be applied in practice. Future work and concluding remarks bring the paper to a close in Sect. 5.

2   Related Work

The work in [26] presents a strategic reasoning approach for tackling backward-looking responsibility in rational agents. They specify the system as a Concurrent Epistemic Game Structure (CEGS), and apply formal verification of strategic properties (Alternating-time Temporal Logic in particular) to conclude the responsibility of the agents w.r.t. the occurrence of some bad event (e.g., applied to an example where some agents want to poison a certain agent, and when the agent dies, they want to know who was responsible for it, and in which amount). In further extension of their work a task coordination framework is proposed, TasCore [25], which is a dynamic task coordination method for multi-agent strategic reasoning. There are two main parts of TasCore: task allocation and a retrospective mechanism for ascribing responsibilities to agents. The latter is based on their previous work of assigning degrees of responsibilities based on past history, which in this case relates to the tasks that have been allocated and how they have been fulfilled. Both works are based on the notion of backward-looking responsibilities. This paper explores forward-looking responsibilities, where agents adopt responsibilities and tasks are then attributed to the agent.

A series of research papers have tackled the notion of accountability in multi-agent organisations as a means to improve robustness of the system [1–3]. In these papers, the definition of responsibility is closely related to that of roles in multi-agent organisations. That is, a responsibility is a collection of tasks that should be performed within a society of agents. Agents are assumed to be autonomous, and therefore must explicitly commit to responsibilities that they want oversee. Accountability is represented through accountability agreements between a pair of agents, where one agent can ask for an account about a particular task to the other agent. Robustness is obtained by connecting failed accounts to recovery strategies, which in turn can trigger treatment tasks that eventually lead to new commits to responsibilities. The main difference between their work and ours is that they take an organisational view of responsibilities rather than our individual agent view.

Another approach to accountability was suggested for sociotechnical systems where a metamodel exploits accountability requirements based on the legal concepts of commitments, authorisation, and prohibition [10]. The authors suggest that their approach can be operationalised using a normative language to express the accountability requirements. As we previously discussed, accountability falls within the sphere of backward-looking responsibilities, and as such, do not directly relate to the concept of forward-looking responsibilities that we explore in our paper.

Other works that are tangential to ours include: the missions in the organisational layer of the JaCaMo multi-agent programming framework [5] that resemble our notion of forward-looking responsibility in that they also serve as triggers for adding a collection of goals, but provide no means of automatically reasoning about them, and their use requires a centralised organisation; maintenance goals [15] seek to maintain a particular state of the world, which share some similarities with our work, but in our case we are more interested in the overall behaviour of the agent and its impact in intention selection; and a set of requirements for accountability in autonomous agents [12] with a strong focus on organisational norms. However, none of the above consider the concept of forward-looking responsibility reasoning in rational agents with an individual agent view.

3   Responsibility-Aware Agents

We formalise responsibility by extending the syntax and operational semantics of BDI agent languages such as AgentSpeak(L) [21], AgentSpeak$^-$ [13], and Jason [7]. Note that we do not present the complete syntax or formal semantics for these languages, we simply report the necessary rules and extensions for obtaining responsibility-aware agents. Further considerations may be necessary when trying to implement it in these (and other) agent languages. Nonetheless, the observations about the implementation details that we provide in Sect. 4 may be of some help.

We focus on BDI because it is the most traditional implementation of rational agents with a rich selection of programming languages (Jason, JaCaMo [4], ASTRA [11], CAN [24], Gwendolen [14], etc.) and has been shown in recent surveys [6,9,17] to have many open research problems that still need to be solved.

The BDI model of agency [8, 20] revolves around three main attitudes: *beliefs* is the knowledge that the agent has about the world; *desires* are goals that the agent wants to achieve; and *intentions* are the means of achieving the goals that the agent has committed to. BDI agents have a reasoning cycle that follows the 'sense-plan-act' methodology. The sense phase consists of receiving perceptions from the environment and messages from other agents. The plan phase starts with the generation of events, which can come from the addition/deletion of beliefs or goals. These events trigger the plan selection mechanism, which consults the plan library for relevant and applicable plans and then selects one to be added to the intention stack. The act phase removes and executes the top intention in the selected intention stack.

We add the notion of task responsibility (henceforth referred to simply as responsibility) in the reasoning cycle of the agent. Informally, responsibility is a task containing a collection of goals that relate to an overarching topic (e.g., responsibility for safety). When an agent adopts a responsibility, an event is generated that triggers the associated plan to start pursuing the goals that it is now responsible for achieving. An overview of the resulting reasoning cycle for responsibility-aware agents is shown in Fig. 2.

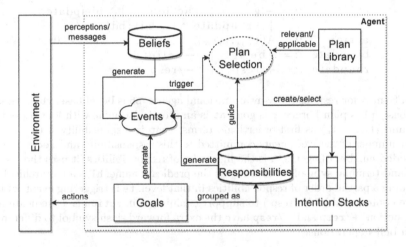

Fig. 2. Responsibility-aware BDI agent reasoning cycle.

We show the syntax for rational agents with responsibilities in Fig. 3. The differences from the traditional syntax found in most BDI-based agent languages are the addition of a responsibility base along with the notion of responsibilities and the respective triggering events from adopting/dropping responsibilities, as well as adding support for updating the responsibility base inside the body of a plan. Note that the dynamic creation of responsibilities is not supported in this paper, the update simply refers to adopting or dropping a responsibility. We also support expressing responsibilities in the context of a plan, even thought this is not used directly in our theory, it can be useful in practice when building an agent program.

$$
\begin{array}{lll}
\texttt{agent} & ::= & \texttt{bb}\quad\texttt{rb}\quad\texttt{pl} \\
\texttt{bb} & ::= & \texttt{belief}_1\ \ldots\ \texttt{belief}_n \qquad (n \geq 0) \\
\texttt{rb} & ::= & \texttt{resp}_1\ \ldots\ \texttt{resp}_n\quad\texttt{h} \qquad (n \geq 0) \\
\texttt{pl} & ::= & \texttt{plan}_1\ \ldots\ \texttt{plan}_n \qquad (n \geq 1) \\
\texttt{belief} & ::= & \texttt{at} \\
\texttt{g} & ::= & \texttt{at} \\
\texttt{at} & ::= & \texttt{P}(t_1,\ldots,t_n) \qquad (n \geq 0) \\
\texttt{resp} & ::= & \texttt{P}([g_1,\ldots,g_n],\texttt{na},\texttt{rec}) \qquad (n \geq 1) \\
\texttt{h} & ::= & \texttt{hierarchy}([\texttt{hl}_1\ \ldots\ \texttt{hl}_n]) \quad (n \geq 1) \\
\texttt{hl} & ::= & [\texttt{P}_{resp_1}\ \ldots\ \texttt{P}_{resp_n}] \qquad (n \geq 1) \\
\texttt{plan} & ::= & \texttt{te}\ :\ \{\texttt{context}\} \leftarrow \texttt{body} \\
\texttt{te} & ::= & +!\texttt{g} \quad\mid\quad +\texttt{belief} \quad\mid\quad -\texttt{belief} \\
& & \mid\quad +/\texttt{resp} \quad\mid\quad -/\texttt{resp} \\
\texttt{context} & ::= & \texttt{ct1} \quad\mid\quad \top \\
\texttt{ct1} & ::= & \texttt{belief} \quad\mid\quad \neg\texttt{belief} \quad\mid\quad \texttt{resp} \\
& & \mid\quad \neg\texttt{resp} \quad\mid\quad \texttt{ct1}\wedge\texttt{ct1} \\
\texttt{body} & ::= & \texttt{bd1},\top \quad\mid\quad \top \\
\texttt{bd1} & ::= & +!\texttt{g} \quad\mid\quad \texttt{action} \quad\mid\quad \texttt{bbupdate} \\
& & \mid\quad \texttt{rbupdate} \quad\mid\quad \texttt{bd1};\texttt{bd1} \\
\texttt{action} & ::= & \texttt{A}(t_1,\ldots,t_n) \qquad (n \geq 0) \\
\texttt{bbupdate} & ::= & +\texttt{belief} \quad\mid\quad -\texttt{belief} \\
\texttt{rbupdate} & ::= & +/\texttt{resp} \quad\mid\quad -/\texttt{resp}
\end{array}
$$

Fig. 3. Syntax for responsibility-aware rational agents. **bb** is belief base. **rb** is responsibility base. **pl** is plan library. **g** is goal. **at** is an atomic formulae with **P** as a predicate name and $(t_1,\ldots,t_n)$ as first-order logic terms. **resp** is responsibility with **na** as the current number of "active" agents committed to this responsibility and **rec** as the recommended number of agents. **h** is the hierarchy of responsibilities, it uses the reserved word (and terminal symbol) **hierarchy** as the predicate name. **hl** is a hierarchical level containing a partial order of responsibilities in that level. **te** is triggering event. **ct1** and **bd1** are context and body (resp.) to support chaining. **A** in **action** is a predicate name for the action. $+/\texttt{resp}$ and $-/\texttt{resp}$ have the extra forward slash symbol to differentiate it from belief operations.

The main purpose of adding a recommended number of agents for a responsibility is to facilitate the reasoning around shared responsibilities (this is further explored in Sect. 3.2). Nevertheless, we note that the relevance of such feature may be subject to domain specific information, where some domains may not require a lower bound in the number of agents. This will be explored in future work when we deal with more complex and diverse examples.

The responsibility base is there to provide a clear separation from the belief base. Each agent has its own individual responsibility base. An agent is capable of handling any responsibility in its base, but it does not initially commit to any of them by default. Adopting and dropping responsibilities have to be manually inserted in the agent program, since the best moments at which to do this will require domain specific information. A responsibility that is dropped remains in the responsibility base because the agent can decide that it needs to adopt it again in the future.

A key difference between responsibility and belief bases is that responsibilities can only be defined at design time. Nevertheless, the following changes can occur to them at runtime: an agent can decide to adopt or drop a responsibility, thus altering the number of agents currently committed to it (i.e., active agents); and the priority that the agent has for a responsibility can be changed depending on specific circumstances at runtime related to shared responsibilities. Priorities and how they are used to guide intention selection are presented in Sect. 3.1. Shared responsibilities and how they can alter the priority that an agent has for a responsibility through agent communication are covered in Sect. 3.2.

To illustrate a typical responsibility, let us consider an example where a domestic robot is embedded with a rational agent that performs the high-level decision making. This agent has the following responsibility in its responsibility base:

$$cleaning([clean(bathroom), clean(bedroom)], 0, 1)$$

where the responsibility name is cleaning, the associated goals are to clean the bathroom and the bedroom, the current number of active agents committed to this responsibility is 0, and the recommended number is 1. Because we only have one responsibility in this example we omit the hierarchy (this is discussed in Sect. 3.1).

Each responsibility also has a corresponding plan that triggers once the agent has decided to adopt the responsibility. For the previous example we would have the following plan:

```
+/cleaning : { T }
  ←  +!clean(bathroom),
     +!clean(bedroom),
     −/cleaning.
```

The context of the plan is always true and the body of the plan contains the goals associated with the responsibility. Note that the body of plans usually follow a sequential composition, which means that the order in which the goals appear here is the order that they will be attempted to be achieved. At the end of the plan the cleaning responsibility is dropped.

The syntax from Fig. 3 does not cover plan selection or the way that intention stacks work since these are not elements that can be expressed by the user of the language. Instead, these elements are controlled internally by rules and functions in the language. Next, we describe the standard operational semantics for these rules, since they are required to introduce our new extensions for adopting and dropping a responsibility, as well as to better understand where the contributions that are presented later on fit in the reasoning cycle of the agent. Due to space constraints we omit the cases for most of the rules where we would need an additional rule for when there are no elements to consume/handle, in which case the reasoning cycle would simply skip to another phase of the reasoning cycle. For example, rules that deal with empty elements in plan selection would skip to the intention selection phase. To improve readability we also omit the use of unifiers.

The inference rules that define the operational semantics represent transitions between agent configurations in the reasoning cycle of an agent. An agent configuration is denoted as:

$$Conf = \langle agent, C, M, T, rule \rangle$$

where $agent$ is the agent program composed of a belief base, a responsibility base, and a plan library; C is an agent's current circumstance represented by the tuple $\langle I, E, A \rangle$, respectively the set of intention stacks (sometimes referred to as intended means), set of events, and set of actions; M represents the asynchronous communication between agents as a tuple $\langle In, Out \rangle$, respectively the mail box and outgoing messages to be sent; T is an auxiliary structure that stores relevant temporary information that can be useful within a cycle, it is a tuple $\langle Rel, App, ev, ie, si, res, pl \rangle$ with Rel the set of relevant plans, App the set of applicable plans, ev, ie, si, res, and p a particular event, intention associated with event, intention selected for execution, responsibility, and plan (respectively); and $rule$ is the current step in the agent's reasoning cycle, representing which inference rule will be used in that step. To refer to sub-elements of an element in a tuple, such as the set of intentions in a circumstance we use C_I, similarly, C_E for set of events C_A for set of actions, and so on.

Plan selection is often separated into four phases: (1) selection of an event; (2) obtaining relevant plans; (3) obtaining applicable plans; and (4) selection of a plan.

Selection of an Event. We need to select an event from the events that are currently active. The following inference rule is used for selecting an event[1]:

$$(\text{SelEv}) \frac{SelectEvent(C_E) = te}{\langle agent, C, M, T, SelEv \rangle \rightarrow \langle agent, C', M, T', RelPl \rangle}$$

$$where \quad \begin{aligned} C'_E &= C_E \backslash \{te\} \\ T'_{ev} &= te \\ T'_{ie} &= GetIntention(te) \end{aligned}$$

This rule says that the *SelectedEvent* function uses the event set in the circumstance C_E to select a triggering event te. Usually implementations of this function will simply select an event following the ordering method first in, first out. The rule updates the event set in the circumstance by removing the selected event from it, as well as assigning the event to the respective auxiliary structure to be used in further rules. The get intention function returns the intention

---

[1] In subsequent inference rules we assume that elements of the state remain unchanged unless explicitly stated in the rule.

associated with the selected event if that event was generated from previous executions of other plans (i.e., internal event), or $\top$ if it was generated from a perception (i.e., external event).

Obtaining Relevant Plans. It is necessary to obtain the relevant plans that match the selected event, which can be obtained with the rule:

$$(\text{RelPl})\ \frac{RelevantPlans(T_e) \neq \varnothing}{\langle agent, C, M, T, RelPl \rangle \rightarrow \langle agent, C, M, T', AppPl \rangle}$$

$$where \quad T'_{Rel} = RelevantPlans(T_e)$$

The relevant plans function is straightforward since we simply have to match the previously selected event with the triggering event of plans in the plan library.

Obtaining Applicable Plans. To obtain the applicable plans we need to compare the set of relevant plans to the belief base:

$$(\text{AppPl})\ \frac{ApplicablePlans(agent_{bb}, T_{Rel}) \neq \varnothing}{\langle agent, C, M, T, AppPl \rangle \rightarrow \langle agent, C, M, T', SelPl \rangle}$$

$$where \quad T'_{App} = ApplicablePlans(agent_{bb}, T_{Rel})$$

The applicable plans function will iterate over each relevant plan while checking the context of the plan against the belief base. If the result of this check is true, then the plan is applicable.

Selection of a Plan. A plan is selected for execution from the applicable plans:

$$(\text{SelPl})\ \frac{SelectApplicable(T'_{App}) = plan}{\langle agent, C, M, T, SelPl \rangle \rightarrow \langle agent, C, M, T', UpdtSt \rangle}$$

$$where \quad T'_{pl} = plan$$

The function for selecting an applicable plan usually picks the first in a top to bottom order from where they appear in the plan library.

Once a plan is selected, then a new intention stack for the instance of that plan is created if the intention associated with the triggering event is external:

$$(\text{CrtSt})\ \frac{T_{ie} = \top \wedge T_{pl} = plan}{\langle agent, C, M, T, CrtSt \rangle \rightarrow \langle agent, C', M, T, SelInt \rangle}$$

$$where \quad C'_I = C_I \cup \{plan\}$$

Otherwise, with an internal event we use rule *UpdtSt* to update an existing stack of intentions:

$$(\text{UpdtSt})\ \frac{T_{ie} = intention \wedge T_{pl} = plan}{\langle agent, C, M, T, UpdtSt \rangle \rightarrow \langle agent, C', M, T, SelInt \rangle}$$

$$where \quad C'_I = (C_I \backslash \{intention\}) \cup \{intention[plan]\}$$

In this case, we update the intention by adding the selected plan at the bottom of the associated intention stack (represented by $intention[plan]$).

Plans can be instantiated into separate intention stacks, i.e., at any moment we can have more than one intention stack. Therefore, it is necessary to have a way to select the next intention stack to be executed:

$$(\text{SelInt}) \frac{C_I \neq \varnothing \wedge SelectIntention(C_I) = i}{\langle agent, C, M, T, SelInt \rangle \rightarrow \langle agent, C, M, T', ExecInt \rangle}$$

$$where \quad T'_{si} = i$$

The implementation of the select intention function usually attempts to select an intention stack based on fairness to avoid starvation. For now we assume a similar behaviour, but in Sect. 3.1 we discuss a different implementation that will instead prioritise intention stacks related to responsibilities based on the existing partial order in the hierarchy.

In practice, an intention stack is composed of the bodies of selected plans (or subplans), and as such can include the following (see body in the syntax from Fig. 3 for a complete list): an action, a belief update, a new goal, etc. Each of them will have their own individual rules that are activated when $ExecInt$ is called. For the sake of brevity we only show the new operational semantics inference rules for executing intentions that are related to updating the responsibility base (i.e., adopting or dropping a responsibility), the remaining rules are all unchanged and thus similar to past work [7,13,21,23].

If the head (topmost) intention in the selected intention stack is the adoption of a responsibility, then the following rule applies:

$$(\text{AResp}) \frac{T_{si} = i[head \leftarrow +/resp; body]}{\langle agent, C, M, T, AResp \rangle \rightarrow \langle agent', C', M, T', ClrInt \rangle}$$

$$where \quad \begin{aligned} agent'_{rb} &= (agent_{rb} \backslash resp) \cup UpdateAdopt(resp) \\ C'_E &= C_E \cup \{+/resp\} \\ C'_I &= C_I \backslash \{T_{si}\} \\ T'_{res} &= resp \end{aligned}$$

The function to update a responsibility after it has been adopted is used to update the number of agents currently committed to it (it simply performs arithmetic addition by increasing it by 1). Note that in practice this would require some form of communication for these numbers to be useful, but for now let us assume that this is being done inside $UpdateAdopt$ function (communication is added to the semantics later in Sect. 3.2. More importantly, the set of events is updated to include a new event about this responsibility, which will eventually trigger (when the event is selected) the corresponding plan containing the list of goals related to it. Lastly, the selected intention is removed from the set of intentions ($C'_I = C_I \backslash \{T_{si}\}$).

Otherwise, if the head is the dropping of a responsibility:

$$(\text{DResp})\frac{T_{si} = i[head \leftarrow -/resp; body]}{\langle agent, C, M, T, DResp \rangle \rightarrow \langle agent', C', M, T', DInt \rangle}$$

$$where \quad agent'_{rb} = (agent_{rb} \backslash resp) \cup UpdateDrop(resp)$$
$$C'_E = C_E \cup \{-/resp\}$$
$$C'_I = C_I \backslash \{T_{si}\}$$
$$T'_{res} = resp$$

In this case, the function to update a responsibility decreases the number of agents currently committed to it by 1 (i.e., it performs arithmetic subtraction), similar to the *AResp* rule, communication is added to the semantics later in Sect. 3.2. The selected intention that was just processed is removed from the set of intentions. Additionally, this rule leads to the rules for dropping an intention about a responsibility. Rule *DInt1* is used when the drop is invoked from the body of the responsibility plan:

$$(\text{DInt1})\frac{T_{res} \subseteq T_{pl}}{\langle agent, C, M, T, DInt1 \rangle \rightarrow \langle agent, C, M, T, ClrInt \rangle}$$

This means that the responsibility is dropped because it came to a natural conclusion and there are no additional operations to make.

Rule *DInt2* deals with the opposite condition:

$$(\text{DInt2})\frac{T_{res} \nsubseteq T_{pl}}{\langle agent, C, M, T, DInt2 \rangle \rightarrow \langle agent', C', M, T', ClrInt \rangle}$$

$$where \quad C'_I = C_I \backslash DropIntention(T_{res})$$

This means that the responsibility is dropped from a plan outside the original plan, which means that the agent has autonomously decided to stop being responsible for it (e.g., something has failed, or another responsibility with a higher priority that conflicts with this one has been adopted). The drop intention function drops the intention associated with the responsibility by performing some parsing over the responsibility information stored in the auxiliary structure T_{res}, which in this case will drop the corresponding plan along with its subplans (plans for the goals listed within the responsibility).

Rules *AResp*, *DInt1*, and *DInt2* lead to the *ClrInt* rule, which we omit because it simply removes empty stacks of intentions and then proceeds to the beginning of a new cycle.

3.1 Priorities and Hierarchy of Responsibilities

Each agent has it own individual responsibility base which includes not only the responsibilities that the agent can adopt but also a hierarchy that determines the priority of a responsibility in relation to others by categorising them into different hierarchical levels. Responsibilities and the hierarchy are defined at design time and our theory does not (yet) provide support for them to be changed dynamically at execution time. The only exceptions are when the current number of agents committed to a responsibility changes (as shown in the rules *AResp* and *DResp* with the *UpdateAdopt* and *UpdateDrop* functions), and when an agent tries to adopt a shared responsibility which can cause the hierarchy to change (this defined later in Sect. 3.2).

Recall function SelectIntention(C_I) from rule *SelInt*; we now provide a pseudo-code implementation for it in Algorithm 1 where an intention stack is selected based on the priority defined by the hierarchical levels in the agent's hierarchy.

Algorithm 1: Selects an intention stack given a set of intentions stacks as input (C_I).

---

1 **Function** *SelectIntention(C_I)*
2     $i \leftarrow \varnothing$;
3   **if** $C_I \neq \varnothing$ **then**
4        $RespStacks \leftarrow GetRespStacks(C_I)$;
5        $hlevel \leftarrow 0$;
6   **while** *there exists* $\{stack\} \in RespStacks$ **do**
7           $slevel \leftarrow GetHLevel(stack)$;
8   **if** $slevel > hlevel$ **then**
9              $hlevel \leftarrow slevel$;
10             $i \leftarrow stack$;
11          $RespStacks \leftarrow RespStacks \setminus \{stack\}$;
12   **if** $i = \varnothing$ **then**
13          $i \leftarrow SelectIntentionFairness(C_I)$;
14   **return** i

First, we initiate the return variable with null. Next, we check if the set of intention stacks is not empty, i.e., there is at least one active intention stack. If that is the case, then we use the function $GetRespStacks(C_I)$ from line 4 to get all intention stacks that contain a responsibility (we then call these the responsibility stacks). Because each responsibility has a corresponding plan, then whenever that plan is selected a new intention stack is created, and any subplans (e.g., from the associated goals) originated from it are attached to the same stack. We initiate the variable that holds the most prioritised hierarchical level (*hlevel*) with 0. Hierarchical levels are implicit within the hierarchy, and as such can be extracted with an appropriate function. The last hierarchical level starts at 1, and increases by 1 as it goes up the levels of the hierarchy.

The *while* loop (lines 6–11) iterates over each element in the set of responsibility stacks. In this loop we first get the hierarchical level of the responsibility attached to the stack (stored in variable *slevel*), and then check if that value is greater than our currently most prioritised hierarchical level. If it is then we update the related variables accordingly. Note that we do not test if the level is equal, since there is no priority between responsibilities within the same hierarchical level. Thus, it will simply pick the stack with the responsibility that it processed first. At the end of the loop we remove the stack that was processed from the set of responsibility stacks.

It is possible for the set of intention stacks to not be empty while the set of responsibility stacks is. In this case, the if condition on lines 12–13 is triggered, which calls an intention stack selection function based on fairness. Our view of responsibilities in this work is that they should be intentionally prioritised over intentions belonging to other plans. This may lead to starvation of plans, especially any plans not related to a responsibility (such as plans for belief updates that come from the environment or other agents). An efficient implementation of our function requires to incorporate some level of fairness to attempt to avoid starvation while still preserving priority of hierarchical levels of responsibilities as much as possible. Fairness and starvation of threads/processes/resources are extensively researched topics in Software Engineering, and as such we do not tackle these concepts here.

To illustrate the use of the hierarchy of responsibilities, let us expand the previous example of a domestic robot by adding a few extra responsibilities and building a hierarchy:

```
cleaning ([ clean ( bathroom ) , clean ( bedroom )] , 0 , 1 )
safety ([ locks ( frontdoor ) , search ( triphazards )] , 0 , 2 )
cooking ([ cook ( breakfast ) , makelist ( grocery )] , 0 , 1 )

hierarchy ([[ safety ] , [ cleaning , cooking ]])
```

Note that the responsibility base above is of a single agent, other agents in the system may have different configurations in their responsibility bases. In this extended example, we now have three responsibilities: cleaning, safety, and cooking. Safety is recommended to have up to two agents being responsible for it, while the others remain at only one. We provide a visual representation of the hierarchy for this example in Fig. 4.

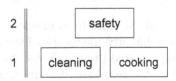

Fig. 4. Visual representation of a hierarchy.

The hierarchy has two levels, the bottom starts at 1 and contains the cleaning and cooking responsibilities (recall that responsibilities within the same hierarchical level have no relation of priority between each other), then the level above is 2 and contains safety. Effectively this means that safety has priority over (i.e., its hierarchical level is greater than) both cleaning and cooking. Note that the hierarchical levels do not need to be represented as numbers, for example we could also use "Low Importance", "Medium Importance", "High Importance" by limiting the hierarchy to three levels (there is always one special level called "idle" which we present in the next section). In this visual representation and in our algorithm we used $\mathbb{N}^*$ to represent each level with larger numbers being higher up in the hierarchy. This is an implementation abstraction, and the information can be easily extracted from the hierarchy definition and transformed as preferred (some necessary small updates would need to be made to Algorithm 1 if not using numerical values).

3.2   Improving Reliability with Shared Responsibilities

An individual view of responsibilities requires some form of communication between the agents in order to keep track of shared responsibilities. Shared responsibilities are responsibilities that appear in more than one agent's responsibility base. Our mechanism to improve reliability in shared responsibilities is based around the recommended number of agents to commit to a responsibility. Once that number is met, then any agents that try to commit to it will become "backup" agents in the sense that they alter their responsibility hierarchy to place this responsibility in a special hierarchical level which we call "idle". If at any point this situation reverses (i.e., the number of agents committed to a responsibility drops below the recommended) then the backup agent has to revert the position of the responsibility in its hierarchy back to the original one.

An extensive discussion on the formal semantics of speech-act communication in BDI agent languages is available in [23]. In their semantics, messages were defined as a tuple $\langle mid, id, ilf, cnt \rangle$ where mid is a unique message id, id is the sender (when the message is being received M_{In}) or the receiver (when the message is being sent M_{Out}), ilf is the illocutionary force, and cnt is the content of the message. To simplify notation and since we are not changing the semantics of communication, here instead we use a simple speech-act $tell(adopt(resp))$ or $tell(drop(resp))$ for sending information about a responsibility that the sender has in its own responsibility base to all other agents (i.e., a broadcast). Note that $tell$ would be mapped into ilf and $adopt(resp)$ or $drop(resp)$ into cnt in the original semantics.

We need to update some of the rules from previous sections to now account for communication and the reliability mechanism for shared responsibilities. In particular, the $AResp$ rule presented previously has to be split into two. First, is the standard case of when the recommended number has not been achieved yet:

$$(AResp1)\frac{T_{si} = i[head \leftarrow +/resp; body] \wedge resp_{na} < resp_{rec}}{\langle agent, C, M, T, AResp1 \rangle \rightarrow \langle agent', C', M', T', ClrInt \rangle}$$

$$where \quad agent'_{rb} = (agent_{rb} \backslash resp) \cup UpdateAdopt(resp)$$
$$C'_E = C_E \cup \{+/resp\}$$
$$C'_I = C_I \backslash \{T_{si}\}$$
$$T'_{res} = resp$$
$$M'_{Out} = M_{Out} \cup tell(adopt(resp))$$

Here we simply add an extra condition to our premise in the original rule to check that the number of agents committed to the responsibility ($resp_{na}$) is less than the number of agents recommended ($resp_{rec}$). Additionally, since we are now also concerned about updating other agents' information about the number of agents committed to a responsibility we add the performative $tell(adopt(resp))$ to the outgoing messages of the agent. Upon receiving such a message, if the agent has the responsibility mentioned in the message, then the agent calls the $UpdateAdopt(resp)$ function to update the number of agents that are committed to it.

Otherwise, if the recommended number of agents has already been met then this agent becomes a "backup" agent:

$$(AResp2) \frac{T_{si} = i[head \leftarrow +/resp; body] \wedge resp_{na} \geq resp_{rec}}{\langle agent, C, M, T, AResp2 \rangle \rightarrow \langle agent', C', M, T', ClrInt \rangle}$$

$$where \quad C'_E = C_E \cup \{+/resp\}$$
$$C'_I = C_I \backslash \{T_{si}\}$$
$$T'_{res} = resp$$
$$agent'_{rb[hierarchy]} = UpdtH(agent_{rb[hierarchy]}, resp)$$

Apart from the addition of the extra condition in the premise, this rule also modifies the agent's hierarchy. Because the agent has adopted the responsibility in a "backup" capacity, it calls the function $UpdtH(agent_{rb[hierarchy]}, resp)$ which changes the hierarchical level of ($resp$) to idle. Note here that because this is a backup agent, we no longer update the number of active agents nor do we use the communication performative that are present in the previous rule. These two things are only done when the agent changes from backup to active, which is explained later on.

Similarly, we also have to update $DResp$, but in this case we only need one rule so we simply overwrite the previous one:

$$(DResp) \frac{T_{si} = i[head \leftarrow -/resp; body]}{\langle agent, C, M, T, DResp \rangle \rightarrow \langle agent', C', M', T', DInt \rangle}$$

$$where \quad agent'_{rb} = (agent_{rb} \backslash resp) \cup UpdateDrop(resp)$$
$$C'_E = C_E \cup \{-/resp\}$$
$$C'_I = C_I \backslash \{T_{si}\}$$
$$T'_{res} = resp$$
$$M'_{Out} = M_{Out} \cup tell(drop(resp))$$

The only difference here is the addition of the communication performative $tell$ which will broadcast the message that an agent has dropped a responsibility, and therefore any agent that has the same responsibility will use this as a triggering event to call the *UpdateDrop(resp)* function, which works the same as before and simply decreases the number of agents currently committed to a responsibility.

Due to space constraints, we do not show the rules for processing the agent's outgoing messages or for processing incoming messages in the mail box, and instead refer to the work in [23] for a complete list. A couple of straightforward extensions are required in particular for processing incoming messages about responsibilities:

tell(adopt(resp)) message

- call function *UpdateAdopt(resp)* to increase by 1 the number of agents committed to the responsibility (only if present in the responsibility base).

tell(drop(resp)) message

- call function *UpdateDrop(resp)* to decrease by 1 the number of agents committed to the responsibility (only if present in the responsibility base);
- if the result of the *UpdateDrop(resp)* function causes the number of commitments to drop below the recommended number, then call the function *RestoreH(agent$_{rb[hierarchy]}$, resp)* to restore the responsibility to its previous hierarchical level (only if it had been changed to idle in the first place);
- call function *UpdateAdopt(resp)* to reflect that the backup agent has now become active; and
- send the broadcast *tell(adopt(resp))* so that other agents update their information accordingly.

We also need to add support for discarding intention stacks for idle responsibilities in Algorithm 1. This is straightforward as we can simply extend the function *GetRespStacks(C_I)* to return only non-idle responsibility stacks.

Note that we do not explicitly deal with coordination of shared responsibilities. By default, multiple agents adopting the same responsibility will perform all the goals associated with that responsibility. In practice, this could be solved in various different ways, such as through communication, organisations, argumentation, task allocation, etc. In this paper we are concerned with providing the basis for reasoning in responsibility-aware agents, which allow for these extensions to be developed in future work.

Furthermore, we define how the agent can drop a responsibility and what happens when it is dropped, and not the specification of when the agent should drop the responsibility (apart of course from when it believes its responsibility has come to a natural end) or why (e.g., non-conformance due to time-sensitive deadline or failure). Deciding when to drop a responsibility, and the reasoning behind the decision, is specific to the domain the agent is implemented in. Therefore being out of scope of this paper.

4   Towards Implementation

The agent languages that are based on AgentSpeak(L) are natural candidates for incorporating our extensions, especially those that have not extensively modified the original AgentSpeak(L) semantics. Two options that fit well in this category are Jason [7] and Gwendolen [14]. Other languages may be viable alternatives, but may also require additional implementation considerations. We limit this discussion to be about the most difficult challenges in implementation.

Note that a pure implementation approach without any changes to the operational semantics of AgentSpeak could achieve similar results by compiling the notion of responsibilities into other BDI concepts (such as beliefs and goals). However, it would be increasingly difficult to extend such an approach with additional responsibility-related concepts if reasoning about responsibilities is not part of the reasoning cycle of the agent.

To implement our selection intention stack function from Algorithm 1 is relatively straightforward. In the Jason language this can be altered in the `TransitionSystem` class which represents most of the agent's reasoning cycle; in particular function `selectIntention` (part of the `Agent` class) which is called from the `applySelInt` method. Similarly, in the Gwendolen language this could be done in the `selectIntention` from the `AILAgent` class by extending the `SelectIntentionHeuristic` interface. The most challenging part is trying to incorporate some level of fairness in order to prioritise the hierarchy of responsibilities while still avoiding starvation of intention stacks. There are different ways of tackling this scheduling problem, and one option would be to look at this as a multi-resource allocation problem (e.g., the work in [16]) where different types of stacks (intended means created from responsibilities, environment reaction, proactive goals, etc.) can be seen as different types of resources.

Another important aspect is the communication between agents that is required for keeping the agents' responsibility bases up to date. This is particularly important if in the application domain the number of recommended agents for a responsibility is strict (i.e., it has maximum limit). A direct implementation of our approach requires some level of centralisation about updates to agents responsibility bases or a period of negotiation/argumentation to ensure that the information is consistent across all agents. This is especially important when backup agents receive a message about a responsibility being dropped, since otherwise without some synchronous behaviour it can be possible that multiple backup agents will become active at the same time (same time here refers to the period of time before these agents receive a message from each other updating the number of active agents). Again there are many ways to solve this which depends on the constraints of the application domain, but for example one possibility is to add a centralised shared list of active agents for each responsibility as well as a backup list, and then consume from the backup list in FIFO order.

5   Conclusion

In this paper we have extended the traditional operational semantics of rational agents to include an individual agent view of forward-looking responsibilities. This improves the reliability of responsibility-aware agents on two fronts: (i) introducing a hierarchy of responsibilities allows us to reason about the partial order relation by extending the intention stack selection function to prioritise more important responsibilities, which leads to improving the reliability of the system; and (ii) adding the notion of shared responsibilities which is realised through agent communication and it is used to coordinate agents so that if an active agent drops a responsibility and as a result the number of recommended agents is not met, then one of the backup agents will become active.

There are many different ways of extending our approach in future work. In this paper we focussed on a rather explicit definition of how rational agents reason about responsibilities, but much freedom is left to the user of the language (e.g., when to adopt a responsibility); it could be interesting to investigate reasoning about responsibility at a more meta level in regards to how responsibilities relate to each other, such as conflicts; perhaps exploring recent advances in argumentation for agents [18,22]. Such feature would also better justify adding support for the dynamic creation/deletion of responsibilities at runtime, which we did not consider for this paper. An efficient implementation in existing agent-based programming languages would also serve to better demonstrate the usefulness of our approach in practice.

References

1. Baldoni, M., Baroglio, C., Micalizio, R.: Fragility and robustness in multiagent systems. In: Baroglio, C., Hubner, J.F., Winikoff, M. (eds.) EMAS 2020. LNCS (LNAI), vol. 12589, pp. 61–77. Springer, Cham (2020). https://doi.org/10.1007/978-3-030-66534-0_4

2. Baldoni, M., Baroglio, C., Micalizio, R., Tedeschi, S.: Implementing business processes in JaCaMo+ by exploiting accountability and responsibility. In: Proceedings of the 18th International Conference on Autonomous Agents and MultiAgent Systems, pp. 2330–2332. AAMAS 2019, International Foundation for Autonomous Agents and Multiagent Systems, Richland, SC (2019). https://dl.acm.org/doi/10.5555/3306127.3332102

3. Baldoni, M., Baroglio, C., Micalizio, R., Tedeschi, S.: Robustness based on accountability in multiagent organizations. In: Proceedings of the 20th International Conference on Autonomous Agents and MultiAgent Systems, pp. 142–150. AAMAS 2021, International Foundation for Autonomous Agents and Multiagent Systems, Richland, SC (2021). https://dl.acm.org/doi/10.5555/3463952.3463975

4. Boissier, O., Bordini, R., Hubner, J., Ricci, A.: Multi-Agent Oriented Programming: Programming Multi-Agent Systems Using JaCaMo. Intelligent Robotics and Autonomous Agents Series. MIT Press, Cambridge (2020)

5. Boissier, O., Bordini, R.H., Hübner, J.F., Ricci, A., Santi, A.: Multi-agent oriented programming with JaCaMo. Sci. Comput. Program. **78**(6), 747–761 (2013). https://doi.org/10.1016/j.scico.2011.10.004

6. Bordini, R.H., El Fallah Seghrouchni, A., Hindriks, K., Logan, B., Ricci, A.: Agent programming in the cognitive era. Auton. Agent. Multi-Agent Syst. **34**(2), 1–31 (2020). https://doi.org/10.1007/s10458-020-09453-y

7. Bordini, R.H., Wooldridge, M., Hübner, J.F.: Programming Multi-Agent Systems in AgentSpeak Using Jason. Wiley, Hoboken (2007)

8. Bratman, M.E.: Intentions, Plans, and Practical Reason. Harvard University Press, Cambridge (1987)
9. Cardoso, R.C., Ferrando, A.: A review of agent-based programming for multi-agent systems. Computers **10**(2), 16 (2021). https://doi.org/10.3390/computers10020016
10. Chopra, A.K., Singh, M.P.: Accountability as a foundation for requirements in sociotechnical systems. IEEE Internet Comput. **25**(6), 33–41 (2021). https://doi.org/10.1109/MIC.2021.3106835
11. Collier, R.W., Russell, S., Lillis, D.: Reflecting on agent programming with agentspeak(L). In: Chen, Q., Torroni, P., Villata, S., Hsu, J., Omicini, A. (eds.) PRIMA 2015. LNCS (LNAI), vol. 9387, pp. 351–366. Springer, Cham (2015). https://doi.org/10.1007/978-3-319-25524-8_22
12. Cranefield, S., Oren, N., Vasconcelos, W.W.: Accountability for practical reasoning agents. In: Lujak, M. (ed.) AT 2018. LNCS (LNAI), vol. 11327, pp. 33–48. Springer, Cham (2019). https://doi.org/10.1007/978-3-030-17294-7_3
13. Dennis, L., Fisher, M., Hepple, A.: Language constructs for multi-agent programming. In: Sadri, F., Satoh, K. (eds.) CLIMA 2007. LNCS (LNAI), vol. 5056, pp. 137–156. Springer, Heidelberg (2008). https://doi.org/10.1007/978-3-540-88833-8_8
14. Dennis, L.A.: Gwendolen semantics: 2017. Technical report ULCS-17-001, University of Liverpool, Department of Computer Science (2017)
15. Duff, S., Thangarajah, J., Harland, J.: Maintenance goals in intelligent agents. Comput. Intell. **30**(1), 71–114 (2014). https://doi.org/10.1111/coin.12000
16. Joe-Wong, C., Sen, S., Lan, T., Chiang, M.: Multi-resource allocation: fairness-efficiency tradeoffs in a unifying framework. In: 2012 Proceedings IEEE INFOCOM, pp. 1206–1214. IEEE (2012). https://doi.org/10.1109/INFCOM.2012.6195481
17. Logan, B.: An agent programming manifesto. Int. J. Agent-Oriented Softw. Eng. **6**(2), 187–210 (2018). https://doi.org/10.1504/IJAOSE.2018.094374
18. de Oliveira Gabriel, V., Panisson, A.R., Bordini, R.H., Adamatti, D.F., Billa, C.Z.: Reasoning in BDI agents using Toulmin's argumentation model. Theoret. Comput. Sci. **805**, 76–91 (2020). https://doi.org/10.1016/j.tcs.2019.10.026
19. van de Poel, I.: The relation between forward-looking and backward-looking responsibility. In: Vincent, N., van de Poel, I., van den Hoven, J. (eds.) Moral Responsibility. Library of Ethics and Applied Philosophy, vol. 27, pp. 37–52. Springer, Dordrecht (2011). https://doi.org/10.1007/978-94-007-1878-4_3
20. Rao, A.S., Georgeff, M.: BDI agents: from theory to practice. In: Proceedings 1st International Conference Multi-Agent Systems (ICMAS), pp. 312–319. AAAI, San Francisco, USA (1995)
21. Rao, A.S.: AgentSpeak(L): BDI agents speak out in a logical computable language. In: Van de Velde, W., Perram, J.W. (eds.) MAAMAW 1996. LNCS, vol. 1038, pp. 42–55. Springer, Heidelberg (1996). https://doi.org/10.1007/BFb0031845
22. Shams, Z., Vos, M.D., Oren, N., Padget, J.: Argumentation-based reasoning about plans, maintenance goals, and norms. ACM Trans. Auton. Adapt. Syst. **14**(3), 1–39 (2020). https://doi.org/10.1145/3364220
23. Vieira, R., Moreira, A., Wooldridge, M., Bordini, R.H.: On the formal semantics of speech-act based communication in an agent-oriented programming language. J. Artif. Int. Res. **29**(1), 221–267 (2007)
24. Winikoff, M., Padgham, L., Harland, J., Thangarajah, J.: Declarative & procedural goals in intelligent agent systems. In: Proceedings of the Eights International Conference on Principles of Knowledge Representation and Reasoning, pp. 470–481. KR 2002, Morgan Kaufmann Publishers Inc., San Francisco, CA, USA (2002)

25. Yazdanpanah, V., Dastani, M., Fatima, S., Jennings, N.R., Yazan, D.M., Zijm, H.: Multiagent task coordination as task allocation plus task responsibility. In: Bassiliades, N., Chalkiadakis, G., de Jonge, D. (eds.) EUMAS/AT -2020. LNCS (LNAI), vol. 12520, pp. 571–588. Springer, Cham (2020). https://doi.org/10.1007/978-3-030-66412-1_37
26. Yazdanpanah, V., Dastani, M., Jamroga, W., Alechina, N., Logan, B.: Strategic responsibility under imperfect information. In: Proceedings of the 18th International Conference on Autonomous Agents and MultiAgent Systems, pp. 592–600. AAMAS '19, International Foundation for Autonomous Agents and Multiagent Systems, Richland, SC (2019). https://dl.acm.org/doi/10.5555/3306127.3331745
27. Yazdanpanah, V., Gerding, E.H., Stein, S., Dastani, M., Jonker, C.M., Norman, T.J.: Responsibility research for trustworthy autonomous systems. In: AAMAS 2021: 20th International Conference on Autonomous Agents and Multiagent Systems, Virtual Event, United Kingdom, May 3–7, 2021, pp. 57–62. ACM, Richland, SC (2021). https://dl.acm.org/doi/10.5555/3463952.3463964

Imperative and Event-Driven Programming of Interoperable Software Agents

Giuseppe Petrosino[1], Stefania Monica[1], and Federico Bergenti[2(✉)]

[1] Dipartimento di Scienze e Metodi dell'Ingegneria Università degli Studi di Modena e Reggio Emilia, Reggio Emilia, Italy
{giuseppe.petrosino,stefania.monica}@unimore.it

[2] Dipartimento di Scienze Matematiche, Fisiche e Informatiche Università degli Studi di Parma, Parma, Italy
federico.bergenti@unipr.it

Abstract. Jadescript is a recent agent-oriented programming language conceived to support the effective development of agents and multi-agent systems based on JADE. Jadescript is designed to ease the development of agents by means of a tailored syntax matched with a programmer-friendly development environment. This paper presents a brief overview of Jadescript by describing its main features and abstractions and by comparing them with the corresponding features and abstractions advocated by other agent-oriented programming languages. Moreover, to show the applicability of Jadescript to the construction of interesting multi-agent systems, this paper concisely summarizes a case study in which Jadescript is used to implement agents that participate in English auctions. Finally, this paper is concluded with a brief overview of planned future developments of the language.

Keywords: Agent-oriented software engineering · Agent-oriented programming · JADE · Jadescript

1 Introduction

Over the past two decades [7], numerous researchers and practitioners have effectively used *JADE* (*Java Agent DEvelopment framework*) [2] for their projects. By taking the role of the reference implementation of *FIPA* (*Foundation for Intelligent Physical Agents*) [35] specifications, JADE has significantly contributed to shape the ideas, the methodologies, and the tools of *AOSE* (*Agent-Oriented Software Engineering*) [9]. In particular, JADE helped promote a peculiar view of agents that focuses on the features of agents that are considered as useful for software development. Essentially, in this view, agents are software components [4] that engage in complex interactions [24] by exchanging messages in possibly heterogeneous [1,15] and challenging [8,12,16,21,23] environments.

A. Ciortea et al. (Eds.): EMAS 2023, LNAI 14378, pp. 23–40, 2023.
https://doi.org/10.1007/978-3-031-48539-8_2

Recent trends in software engineering, exemplified by *DSLs (Domain-Specific Languages)* [22], suggested that the adoption of the peculiar view of agents that JADE advocates would greatly benefit from programming languages specifically designed to easily employ the features and the abstractions that JADE already provides in terms of a Java framework. This idea motivated the introduction of JADEL [5,11], a programming language based on Xtend [17], which is a dialect of Java designed to support the construction of DSLs. Although JADEL was intended to simplify the development of agents and *MAS (Multi-Agent Systems)*, informal experiments on its use suggested that it exhibits inherent problems that severely limit its applicability. For example, programmers who were new to JADEL often preferred to directly use JADE in Java because they disconsidered Xtend as Java plus irrelevant syntactic sugar. Therefore, the main advantage of using JADEL, which is the possibility of easily adopting the abstractions that JADE provides, was not effectively perceived during the informal experiments.

Jadescript [7,13] is a fresh start toward the objectives that motivated JADEL. Jadescript is a programming language that was designed from scratch around the view of agents and MASs promoted by JADE, and it ultimately encompasses the following objectives. First, Jadescript aims at providing a clear and simple way to implement agents and related abstractions, such as ontologies [41] and behaviours [14]. Actually, the source code of a Jadescript agent bears a resemblance to the pseudocode found in textbooks on agents and MASs (e.g., [40,42]). Therefore, Jadescript inevitably shares several similarities with popular scripting languages, e.g., Python and JavaScript, hence its name. Second, Jadescript is intended to help programmers adopt best development practices. For example, agents should not use busy-waiting to detect events, and Jadescript natively provides cyclic behaviours [27] to allow agents to suspend when no events can be processed by available event handlers [13]. Third, Jadescript is meant to enhance the overall quality of produced software, and therefore it offers a specific type system designed to natively support the features and the abstractions that characterize JADE. Actually, the Jadescript type system [30] aims at providing very high-level abstractions for effective agent programming and at promoting the development of robust and maintainable MASs. Finally, Jadescript is intended to support mainstream development, and therefore it comes with a comprehensive set of programmer-friendly development tools. In particular, a dedicated plugin for Eclipse is proposed as the official tool to effectively use Jadescript in production environments. The Jadescript plugin [29] for Eclipse provides an integrated compiler and a set of support tools that include, e.g., dedicated graphical interfaces to manage project files and launch agents and platforms. Actually, the Jadescript plugin is designed to enhance the overall development experience of Jadescript programmers by offering a streamlined and programmer-friendly toolset to help them effectively create and manage complex projects that use Jadescript in some, or even all, parts.

This paper is organized as follows. Section 2 briefly introduces Jadescript by describing its main features and abstractions. Section 3 presents a practical use of Jadescript in a classic scenario in which agents participate in English auctions.

Section 4 succinctly compares the features and the abstractions that Jadescript provides with related aspects of other programming languages. Finally, Sect. 5 concludes this paper by outlining some directions for future developments.

2   A Short Introduction to Jadescript

The major agent-oriented abstractions advocated by Jadescript are: agents, (agent) behaviours, and (communication) ontologies. The programmers that use JADE are well-acquainted with these names, and the abstractions that Jadescript provides purposely share similarities with their JADE counterparts. Note that, despite being designed for the implementation of MASs based on JADE, and despite being compiled to Java, Jadescript is not an object-oriented programming language. It does not provide ways to declare classes of objects, to construct objects, to invoke the methods of an object, or to access the state of an object. Actually, needed abstract data types can be defined in Jadescript by means of ontology concepts together with procedures and functions. Jadescript provides procedures and functions to define portions of reusable code with an associated visibility, which can be public or private. Functions are used to implement operations that compute a value while procedures are limited to the execution of commands. These and other features of the language are designed to direct programmers to reason about agents, their tasks, and their interactions, rather than concentrating on lower level aspects of the computation, like the organization of data in memory or the management of computational resources.

Agents represent the most relevant abstraction that Jadescript provides, and Jadescript agents inherit several characteristics from JADE agents. Since multiple agents in a MAS can share the same source code, a Jadescript agent declaration actually defines a family of agents [5] whose members have similar behaviours and share the structure of their internal states. The structure of the internal states of the agents in a given family is defined by a set of property declarations. Actually, a property is a named and statically typed part of the internal state of an agent, and it is always private to ensure that agents cannot directly access the internal states of other agents.

Jadescript supports the definition of behaviours to model the conducts of agents in terms of stateful and concurrent tasks. The behaviours that are active in an agent concurrently contribute to implement the conduct of the agent, and therefore they share the internal state of the agent. However, no race conditions on the internal state of the agent can occur because active behaviours in the same agent are executed one at a time using an internal non-preemptive scheduling mechanism. Similarly to agents, behaviour declarations can include property, function, and procedure declarations. Note that a behaviour can be bound to an agent family to limit its usage only to the agents of the specified family. This possibility has the advantage of making the private properties, functions, and procedures of an agent in the family freely accessible from the behaviour.

Currently, Jadescript behaviours are split in two categories: one-shot behaviours and cyclic behaviours. A one-shot behaviour is automatically deactivated at the end of its executions. Therefore, it is executed only once after its activations, and it represents a good way to implement atomic actions, e.g., the broadcasting of a start message to all agents in the MAS. Instead, a cyclic behaviour is normally kept in the pool of active behaviours after its execution, and it is repeatedly executed until explicitly deactivated. Therefore, it can be used to implement repetitive actions, e.g., continuously waiting for a start message. Note that behaviours can be explicitly activated by means of the `activate` statement, and they can be deactivated using the `deactivate` statement. The activation of behaviours can be delayed [33] to occur at a specific time or after a specified delay. Moreover, cyclic behaviours can be scheduled to be executed periodically [33]. All these scheduling capabilities are essential to let agents organize their tasks in time, e.g., to implement active monitoring tasks.

Jadescript promotes event-driven programming because agents are expected to timely react to internal and external events. The reactions to these events are implemented in Jadescript using event handlers, which can be defined in agents and in behaviours. Internal events are related to the changes in the internal states of agents and behaviours. For example, an `on destroy` handler of an agent is executed by the agent right before the agent is removed from the agent container in which it is executing. Conversely, an `on create` handler of an agent is executed by the agent as soon as the agent becomes alive in order to initialize the internal state of the agent and to activate the needed behaviours. Note that `on create` handlers can have a set of named parameters. These parameters are transparently bound to the arguments provided to the agent at construction either via the command line, when the agent is created using the command line, or via external Java code, when the agent is created using the Jadescript-Java interoperability framework [32]. Moreover, note that mentioned event handlers are also available for behaviours. Actually, a behaviour can have event handlers to react to its creation, destruction, activation, deactivation, and to its selection for execution by an agent. Finally, note that other events and associated event handlers are available for agents and behaviours to handle exceptional situations and behaviour failures [31].

Currently, external events are events associated with the reception of messages. A message is characterized by a sender agent and a nonempty set of receiver agents, and all these agents are uniquely identified by means of their *AIDs* (*Agent IDentifiers*) [3], which are texts with a specific structure directly inspired by JADE AIDs. A message is also characterized by a performative [3] and a content, which is constructed by means of the ontology used for the message. Jadescript advocates an approach to communication based on asynchronous message passing, and the exchange of messages is implemented in Jadescript using asynchronous `send message` statements and message handlers. Message handlers support pattern matching [28], which allows programmers to easily express the structure of the messages that a message handler can manage. The use of pattern matching allows unifying the parts of the received message with the free variables declared in the header of the message handler, thus providing a concise and effective way to deconstruct the received message while making the relevant parts of the message explicit and readily usable.

It is common opinion that the construction of MASs can benefit from the adoption of ontologies to formalize the target application domain and to ensure that agents have a common understanding of the messages that mention the elements of the domain. Ontologies are provided in Jadescript as one of the main abstractions of the language, and they play a central role not only in supporting communication but also in structuring the data that agents manipulate. Actually, ontologies can be associated with agents to allow agents to create and manipulate the concepts, actions, (atomic) propositions, and predicates defined in the ontology. In addition, all agents associated with the same ontology can freely exchange messages whose contents are defined using the elements of the ontology, sharing their definitions, and consequently, their meanings.

Concepts and actions are elements of ontologies used to manipulate domain-specific structured data and agent actions, respectively. They are characterized by properties, and Jadescript provides for inheritance of both concepts and actions to allow defining hierarchies of data types. Predicates and propositions are other elements of ontologies, and they are used to express facts. A predicate is associated with a lists of named and typed arguments while a proposition is not structured. Note that predicates and propositions share the `Proposition` supertype, even if programmers cannot use inheritance on these types. Finally, note that predicates and propositions are used in logical expressions, and they are also used to denote the reasons for behavior failures and exceptional situations [31].

3 English Auctions in Jadescript

This section provides a description of how Jadescript can be used to implement a MAS in which agents participate in English auctions. This example is used to show several characteristics of the language and only a few marginal details of the reported source codes were intentionally omitted. Note that this example relaxes several assumptions of ordinary toy problems, and it can be considered as genuinely more complex than the didactic examples that previous papers include to present and discuss specific features of the language.

3.1 The Scenario

In the considered scenario, an agent designated as auctioneer is first created. The auctioneer knows the item it is prompted to sell, which is normally a painting, and it also knows the opening bid for the item and the reserve price. Once created, the auctioneer waits for participants to register to the auction. When at least two participants have registered, the auction starts and the auctioneer issues an initial call for bids to all registered participants. The initial call for bids includes the description of the item together with the necessary details needed to submit valid bids, namely the opening bid, the minimum increment on bids, and the deadline for submitting bids. Note that the auctioneer considers a bid as valid only if it is submitted before the deadline and if it is higher or equal to the standing bid plus the minimum increment publicized in the last call for bids. After each successful reception of a valid bid, the auctioneer issues a new call for bids to all registered participants. The new call for bids includes the current standing bid, the updated deadline, and the name of the participant who submitted the standing bid. The auctioneer continues to send updated calls for bids until the deadline has passed and no pending bids are left. When this occurs, if the standing bid is lower than the reserve price, then the auctioneer concludes the auction without selling the item. Otherwise, the auctioneer informs all registered participants that the item is assigned to the participant that submitted the current standing bid. Note that, during the auction, participants can freely join and leave the auction. The auctioneer replies to late registrations with the latest call for bids to allow new participants to make their bids before the deadline.

3.2   The Ontology

The `EnglishAuction` ontology shown in Fig. 1 is used to describe the content of each message exchanged in the MAS. The first two elements of the ontology, namely the `Participating` and the `Leaving` propositions, are used by participants to join and leave the auction, respectively.

The `Item` concept is included in the ontology to describe an item being traded in an auction. For the sake of simplicity, generic items are described using only their names. However, the scenario assumes that the auctioneer sells paintings, and therefore the `Painting` concept is included in the ontology as a specialization of the `Item` concept. The `Painting` concept includes the `title` and the `author` properties, and when a new description of a painting is created, its name is constructed from to the title and the author of the painting.

The `SubmitBid` action is included in the ontology to be used as content for the calls for bids sent by the auctioneer to the participants. The `SubmitBid` action has several properties that specify the details of valid bids. The first property is `item`, and it is the item being traded. The second property is `currentBid`, which is either the opening bid or the standing bid. The third property is `bidMinimumIncrement`, which is the specified minimum increment. The fourth property is `deadline`, and it indicates the time at which the auctioneer will stop accepting new bids. Finally, the fifth property is `currentlyWinning`, which is the name of the participant that submitted the standing bid. If this value is the empty string, then no valid bids have been submitted yet.

The `Buy` action is included in the ontology to denote the act of buying the specified item, while the `Priced` predicate is used to associate an item with a price. The `Buy` and the `Priced` elements are both used as content of messages sent by participants to submit new bids, while the `BidRejected` predicate is used by the auctioneer to refuse a bid indicating the reason that caused the bid to be rejected. This reason is described using one of the following predicates of the ontology. The `BidTooLow` predicate indicates that the submitted bid was too low, and it includes a property that specifies the minimum value for a valid bid. The `InvalidBid` predicate is used to generically reject a bid by providing a textual explanation of what went wrong during the submission of the bid.

```
1   ontology EnglishAuction
2      proposition Participating
3      proposition Leaving
4      concept Item(name as text)
5      concept Painting(author as text, title as text)
6         extends Item with name = title+" by "+author
7      action SubmitBid(item as Item, currentBid as integer,
8         bidMinimumIncrement as integer,
9         deadline as timestamp, currentlyWinning as text)
10     action Buy(item as Item)
11     predicate Priced(item as Item, price as integer)
12     predicate BidRejected(reason as Proposition)
13     predicate BidTooLow(minimumBid as integer)
14     predicate InvalidBid(otherReason as text)
15     predicate ItemSold(item as Item, buyer as aid,
16        finalPrice as integer)
17     predicate ItemNotSold(item as Item)
```

Fig. 1. The Jadescript implementation of the English auction ontology.

Finally, two predicates of the ontology are used by the auctioneer to inform registered participants of the outcome of the auction. The `ItemNotSold` predicate includes a property to specify the item the auctioneer failed to sell. The `ItemSold` predicate includes two properties, namely `buyer`, which contains the AID of the winning participant, and `price`, which contains the price of the winning bid.

3.3   The Auctioneer

The Jadescript source code for the auctioneer is shown in Fig. 2. The properties defined in the declaration of the auctioneer constitute the internal state of the auctioneer, which equals the state of the auction for the sake of simplicity. These properties can be subdivided in three groups. The first group contains the pre-defined parameters of the auctioneer. In particular, the `minimumParticipants` property specifies the minimum number of participants required for an auction to start. The auctioneer waits until the number of participants that registered to the action reaches the specified minimum number. The amount of time that the auctioneer waits for new bids after sending a call for bids is denoted by the `waitingForBidsTime` property. The `startBid` property specifies the opening bid, and the `bidMinimumIncrement` property denotes the minimum required increment between two subsequent bids. The `reserve` property denotes the reserve price. Finally, the last property of this group is the `item` property, which denotes the item being traded.

The second group of properties that constitute the internal state of the auctioneer is used to track the dynamic state of the current auction. The `currentBid` property denotes the standing bid, and it is initialized with the mentioned `startBid` property. The `candidateBuyer` property is used to store the identity

```
1   agent Auctioneer uses ontology EnglishAuction
2      property minimumParticipants = 2
3      property waitingForBidsTime = "PT30S" as duration
4      property startBid = 80
5      property reserve = 120
6      property bidMinimumIncrement = 2
7      property item = Painting("Leonardo", "Mona Lisa")
8
9      property currentBid = startBid
10     property candidateBuyer as aid
11     property thereIsCandidate = false
12     property participants as set of aid
13
14     property doAuction = DoAuction
15     property endAuction = EndAuction
16
17     on create do
18        log "Agent "+name of agent+" created."
19        activate AwaitParticipants
```

Fig. 2. The Jadescript implementation of the auctioneer.

of the participant that submitted the standing bid when at least one valid bid has been received, which is an event that is denoted by the thereIsCandidate property. Finally, the participants property is a set of AIDs used to store the identities of all registered participants. This set is updated dynamically by the auctioneer every time a participant registers or deregisters.

The last group of properties that constitute the internal state of the auctioneer contains two properties that refer to behaviours. The first property refers to a DoAuction behaviour, and the auctioneer uses this behaviour to run the auction. The second property refers to an EndAuction behaviour, and the auctioneer uses this behaviour to finalize the auction by informing all registered participants of the outcome of the auction. Note that these two properties refer to behaviours that are explicitly activated and deactivated when needed.

The agent declaration shown in Fig. 2 is concluded with an **on create** handler. As soon as the auctioneer starts, it writes a message to its log, and then it activates an AwaitParticipants behaviour, whose source code is shown in Fig. 3. The activated AwaitParticipants behaviour performs the task of waiting for a sufficient number of participants to register to the auction. This behaviour is designed to be used exclusively by the auctioneer, and therefore its declaration uses the **for agent** clause in its header. This tight link between the AwaitParticipants behaviour and the auctioneer has two relevant consequences. First, the behaviour can refer to the properties of the agent, which are always private. In particular, the minimumParticipants and the participants properties are used by the behaviour. Second, the behaviour is transparently associated with the ontologies used by the agent. In this case, this is used to access to the **Participating** and the **Leaving** propositions.

```
1   cyclic behaviour AwaitParticipants for agent Auctioneer
2     on message inform Participating do
3       add sender of message to participants
4       if size of participants >= minimumParticipants do
5         log "Starting auction."
6         log "Selling: "+item+"."
7         activate doAuction
8         deactivate this
9
10    on message inform Leaving do
11      remove sender from participants
12
13    on activate do
14      do log "Waiting for participants."
```

Fig. 3. The Jadescript implementation of the behaviour used to wait for participants.

The **AwaitParticipant** behaviour created by the auctioneer to manage the start of the auction uses the two message handlers shown in Fig. 3. The first handler processes inform messages that contain a **Participating** proposition. These messages are sent by agents interested in participating in the auction, and therefore their AIDs are added to the set of participants. If, after this addition, the number of registered participants reaches the specified minimum number of participants, then the auctioneer changes its behaviour by deactivating its current behaviour and by activating the **doAuction** behaviour. The second handler shown in Fig. 3 processes inform messages that contain a **Leaving** proposition. These messages are sent by participants that want to leave the auction, and therefore their AIDs are removed from the set of participants. Finally, note that the **AwaitParticipant** behaviour created by the auctioneer writes a message to its log when activated.

The task of running an auction is implemented by the auctioneer using a **DoAuction** behaviour, whose declaration is shown in Fig. 4. This behaviour assumes that a sufficient number of participants is registered to the auction. As soon as the behaviour is activated, the actioneer executes the **callForBids** procedure. This procedure sends a call for proposals to all registered participants. This call for proposals contains a **SubmitBid** action that details the information needed by participants to submit valid bids. After sending the call for proposals, the **DoAuction** behaviour performs a delayed activation of the behaviour used to terminate the auction, which is referenced by the **endAuction** property. The time at which this behaviour will be activated is stored in the **nextTimeout** property, which is computed as **now + waitingForBidsTime**. Note that each call

```
1   cyclic behaviour DoAuction for agent Auctioneer
2     property nextTimeout as timestamp
3
4     on activate do
5       do callForBids
6
7     procedure callForBids do
8       nextTimeout = now + waitingForBidsTime
9       do sendCFPMessage with bidders = participants
10      activate endAuction at nextTimeout
11
12    procedure sendCFPMessage with bidders as set of aid do
13      currentlyWinning = ""
14      if thereIsCandidate do
15        currentlyWinning = name of candidateBuyer
16      send message cfp SubmitBid(item, currentBid,
17        bidMinimumIncrement, nextTimeout,
18        currentlyWinning) to bidders
19
20    on message inform Participating do
21      add sender of message to participants
22      do sendCFPMessage with bidders = { sender }
23
24    on message inform Leaving do
25      remove sender of message from participants
26      if size of participants < 2 do
27        activate endAuction
28
29    on message propose (Buy(proposedItem),
30      Priced(proposedItem, proposedPrice)) do
31      minBid = currentBid + bidMinimumIncrement
32      if proposedPrice < minBid do
33        send message reject_proposal (Buy(proposedItem),
34          Priced(proposedItem, proposedPrice),
35          BidRejected(BidTooLow(minBid)))
36          to sender of message
37      else do
38        send message accept_proposal (
39          Buy(proposedItem),
40          Priced(proposedItem, proposedPrice)
41        ) to sender of message
42        currentBid = proposedPrice
43        thereIsCandidate = true
44        candidateBuyer = sender of message
45        do callForBids
```

Fig. 4. The Jadescript implementation of the behaviour used to run auctions.

to the `callForBids` procedure resets this delayed activation, thus postponing the activation of the behaviour used to terminate the auction.

The behaviour used by the auctioneer to run auctions also handles the reception of inform messages that mention either the `Participating` or the `Leaving` propositions in order to dynamically manage the set of registered participants. In particular, when an inform message from an agent who wants to join the auction arrives, the auctioneer adds the agent to the set of participants, and it replies to the agent with a call for proposals. This call for proposals is populated with the needed information for the new participant to place valid bids before the deadline. Similarly, when an inform message from a participant that wants to leave the auction arrives, the auctioneer removes the AID of the sender from the set of participants. Note that if the number of registered participants is less than two, the auctioneer immediately terminates the auction.

Finally, note that the `DoAuction` behaviour used by the auctioneer to run the auction provides a message handler for proposals, as shown in the bottom of Fig. 4. In order for this handler to be executed, the content of the message must match against the pattern composed of a pair of types (`Buy`, `Priced`). If the received message successfully matches against this pattern, the message handler is executed and it can access the `proposedItem` and the `proposedPrice` variables. The values of these variables are transparently extracted from the content of the message during the matching against the specified pattern. Therefore, these values can be freely used to verify the validity of the received proposal. First, the auctioneer ensures that the bid is valid by checking that the proposed price is sufficiently high. In particular, the proposed price must be higher than or equal to `currentBid + bidMinimumIncrement`. If the proposed price is not sufficiently high, the bid is rejected with an appropriate reason for the rejection. Otherwise, the auctioneer accepts the bid, and the state of the auction is updated to take into account the new standing bid. In particular, a new iteration of the auction is immediately started by calling the `callForBids` procedure. Note that if no valid bids are submitted by the deadline, the delayed activation of the behaviour used to terminate the auction ensures that the auction is still terminated.

The source code of the behaviour used to terminate an auction is shown in Fig. 5. The auctioneer uses a delayed activation of this behaviour to ensure that the auction terminates at the appropriate deadline. When activated, this behaviour first deactivates the behaviour used to run the auction, which is referenced by the `doAuction` property, in order to prevent it from accepting bids submitted after the deadline. Then, it checks the final state of the auction to compute its outcome. If there is no valid standing bid higher than the reserve price, the auction is concluded with no transactions. In this case, the auctioneer informs all participants that the item was not sold. On the contrary, if a valid standing bid is available, the auctioneer notifies all participants of the successful outcome, and it indicates the identity of the winner of the auction. Finally, note that some corner cases were intentionally omitted for the sake of simplicity. For example, the auctioneer does not treat sufficiently well the case of a participant that leaves the auction while it is the current winner.

```
1  one shot behaviour EndAuction for agent Auctioneer
2    on activate do
3      deactivate doAuction
4      if not thereIsCandidate or currentBid < reserve do
5        log "No valid bid submitted. Not selling the item."
6        send message inform ItemNotSold(item)
7          to participants
8      else do
9        log "Selling item "+item+" to "+candidateBuyer+"."
10       send message inform ItemSold(item, candidateBuyer,
11         currentBid) to participants
```

Fig. 5. The Jadescript implementation of the behaviour used to terminate auctions.

3.4 The Participants

Together with the auctioneer, the MAS comprises a set of participants. Even if the Jadescript source code of participants, in the **Bidder** agent declaration, is not shown for space constraints, participants are very simple and they can be easily described. First, participants use the **EnglishAuction** ontology to share the definition of concepts, actions, predicates, and propositions with the auctioneer. Then, each participant has a **budget** property that stores the amount of money available for the auction. Once created, participants immediately activate a **ParticipateToAuction** behaviour to enter the auction and try to win it. The implemented strategy adopted by participants to try to win the auction is very simple: a participant always proposes the minimum price sufficient to make the proposal valid, and it stops bidding only if it does not have enough money to make a valid proposal.

The source code of the **ParticipateToAuction** behaviour used by participants to participate to the auction is shown in Fig. 6. This behaviour is defined by several event handlers. Upon activation and deactivation of this behaviour, the participant informs the auctioneer about its interest to participate to the auction. When a call for proposals arrives, the corresponding message handler deconstructs it and uses its parts to compute the decision on what to do. In particular, if the participant is not the one that submitted the current standing bid, and if the participant has enough money and time to propose a higher bid, then the participant proposes a higher bid by sending the corresponding message to the auctioneer. The proposal is then either accepted or rejected by the auctioneer. These two events are handled in the participant by the two message handlers that match against accept proposals and reject messages. Note

that the behaviour also handles the final outcome of the auction, providing a
message handler for each one of the possible messages sent by the auctioneer to
inform participants of the termination of the auction.

```
1  cyclic behaviour ParticipateToAuction for agent Bidder
2     on activate do
3        send message inform Participating to aid("Auctioneer")
4
5     on deactivate do
6        send message inform Leaving to aid("Auctioneer")
7
8     on message cfp (SubmitBid(item, currentBid,
9        bidMinimumIncrement, deadline, currentWinner), _) do
10       bid = currentBid + bidMinimumIncrement
11       if currentWinner != name of agent
12          and now < deadline and bid <= budget do
13          log "Submitting bid: "+bid+"."
14          activate SendPropose(item, bid)
15       else if bid > budget do
16          log "Not enough money, giving up."
17
18    on message accept_proposal do
19       log "My bid has been accepted."
20
21    on message reject_proposal (_, _, reason) do
22       log "My bid was rejected, reason: "+reason
23
24    on message inform ItemSold(item, aid of agent, bid) do
25       log "I bought "+item+" for "+bid+"!"
26
27    on message inform ItemSold(item, other, bid) do
28       log other+" bought "+item+" for "+bid+"."
29
30    on message inform ItemNotSold(item) do
31       log "Item not sold: "+item+"."
```

Fig. 6. The Jadescript implementation of the behaviour used by participants.

4   Related Work

Several *AOP (Agent-Oriented Programming)* languages have been developed in
the last few decades to provide effective tools to support a novel programming
paradigm [39] suitable to develop agents and MASs. Besides languages mostly
intended for theoretical purposes, like AGENT0 [38] and AgentSpeak(L) [36],
notable examples of AOP languages intended for practical applications are Jason,

ASTRA, and SARL. In the remaining of this section, the main features and abstractions of these three languages are outlined and compared with the related features and abstractions that Jadescript advocates.

AgentSpeak(L) [36] is a well-known AOP language that was formalized to provide an operational proof-theoretic semantics to reason on *BDI* (*Belief-Desire-Intention*) agents. In AgentSpeak(L), agent programs are expressed as logic programs, and they are composed of beliefs, goals, and plans. Jason [18], which is one of the most popular implementations of AgentSpeak(L), has gained significant popularity in recent years. Jason extends AgentSpeak(L) with several features, like a specific support for interoperability with Java. The tight link between Jason and Java is so relevant that Jason agents are expected to be situated in environments implemented in Java, and several parts of the Jason interpreter can be customized by extending the core Java classes of the interpreter. ASTRA [19,20] is another implementation of AgentSpeak(L), and it also provides specific extensions. ASTRA extends AgentSpeak(L) by introducing several features inspired by the literature on agents and MAS, e.g., a support for teleo-reactive [26] functions with encapsulated rules.

Jadescript and the mentioned implementations of AgentSpeak(L) are all AOP languages intended for practical uses. However, Jadescript has some significant differences with respect to AgentSpeak(L) and its derivates, one of the most significant of which is in the approach to programming agents. AgentSpeak(L) is a language that uses the BDI model to program agents, while Jadescript, on the other hand, is both an imperative and an event-driven programming language. Actually, while the focus in AgentSpeak(L) is on describing the mental attitudes of the agents, the focus in Jadescript is on specifying the tasks performed by the agents and on structuring the interactions among agents in the MAS. Another key difference between Jadescript and the languages that derive from AgentSpeak(L) is in the syntax and the semantics of the language. AgentSpeak(L) is based on logic programming, and it uses a syntax that is similar to Prolog. Jadescript, on the other hand, has a syntax that is closer to modern scripting languages like Python and JavaScript. Therefore, Jadescript is more accessible to mainstream programmers, who are not supposed to be familiar with logic programming and with the declarative paradigm. Finally, it is worth noting that Jadescript is specifically designed to use JADE, whereas the mentioned practical implementations of AgentSpeak(L) can be used with a variety of agent platforms. Therefore, Jadescript is a better choice for developers who are already familiar with JADE, also because its main features and abstractions are inspired by the corresponding features and abstractions provided by JADE.

Differently from AgentSpeak(L) and its implementation, SARL [37] is an AOP language that can be considered as imperative and event-driven. SARL is equipped with a syntax that is easy to understand for users of mainstream programming languages. One of its most noteworthy features is its support for holonic agents, which are agents composed of other agents. Moreover, SARL is designed to not be tied to any particular platform, although it is frequently used with Janus [37]. SARL has several similarities with JADEL, which is the predecessor of Jadescript. For example, SARL and JADEL have similar syntaxes to define agents, and they use similar linguistic constructs to handle events. Moreover, both SARL and JADEL include specific extensions of Xtend for the imperative parts of the source codes of agents. Despite these similarities, SARL and JADEL were developed independently and have distinct purposes.

The main difference between SARL and Jadescript is that SARL explicitly supports object-oriented programming, while Jadescript is a pure AOP language. Actually, SARL supports the definition of classes and the manipulation of objects alongside the declaration of agents and of their tasks. On the other hand, Jadescript purposely excludes the concepts of object-oriented programming from the language to offer agent-oriented abstractions as valid alternatives to promote reusability and composability [10].

5   Conclusion

Jadescript is a promising tool to develop real-world MASs that target mission-critical applications and services (e.g., [6, 25]). Its unique combination of simplicity and conciseness makes it a valuable addition to the toolkit of the programmers of agents and MASs. However, Jadescript is still in its early stages, with early versions of the compiler and associated tools having only recently been made available (github.com/aiagents/jadescript). Therefore, Jadescript presents significant opportunities for further developments.

One promising direction for extending Jadescript is to incorporate *IPs* (*Interaction Protocols*) [34] as a primary abstraction of the language. IPs are intended to precisely specify the possible patterns of the interactions among agents, and therefore their support in Jadescript requires linguistic constructs to allow specifying new IPs and to allow agents to enact IPs on the basis of these specifications. Actually, by defining the role of an agent within an IP, the designer of the agent is guided to design the behaviours of the agent taking into account the expected interactions of the agent in the scope of the IP. This approach to the design of agents and behaviours has the beneficial effect of improving the clarity and the modularity of the design, and it also eases the identification of reusable agents and behaviours for common communication patterns.

Finally, another possible development of Jadescript is about providing effective language-level features to enable the use of epistemic and intentional propositions in the agents. This extension is expected to provide Jadescript with a more expressive way to describe the decision making processes and cognitive abilities of the agents, thus ultimately improving the robustness, the maintainability, and the reusability of agents and MASs.

Acknowledgements. This work was partially supported by the Italian Ministry of University and Research under the PRIN 2020 grant 2020TL3X8X for the project *Typeful Language Adaptation for Dynamic, Interacting and Evolving Systems* (T-LADIES).

References

1. Adorni, G., Bergenti, F., Poggi, A., Rimassa, G.: Enabling FIPA agents on small devices. In: Klusch, M., Zambonelli, F. (eds.) CIA 2001. LNCS (LNAI), vol. 2182, pp. 248–257. Springer, Heidelberg (2001). https://doi.org/10.1007/3-540-44799-7_28
2. Bellifemine, F., Bergenti, F., Caire, G., Poggi, A.: Jade — a java agent development framework. In: Bordini, R.H., Dastani, M., Dix, J., El Fallah Seghrouchni, A. (eds.) Multi-Agent Programming. MSASSO, vol. 15, pp. 125–147. Springer, Boston, MA (2005). https://doi.org/10.1007/0-387-26350-0_5
3. Bellifemine, F., Caire, G., Greenwood, D.: Developing Multi-Agent Systems with JADE. In: Wiley Series in Agent Technology. Wiley, Hoboken (2007)
4. Bergenti, F.: A discussion of two major benefits of using agents in software development. In: Petta, P., Tolksdorf, R., Zambonelli, F. (eds.) ESAW 2002. LNCS (LNAI), vol. 2577, pp. 1–12. Springer, Heidelberg (2003). https://doi.org/10.1007/3-540-39173-8_1
5. Bergenti, F.: An introduction to the JADEL programming language. In: Proceedings of the 26th IEEE International Conference on Tools with Artificial Intelligence (ICTAI 2014), pp. 974–978. IEEE (2014)
6. Bergenti, F., Caire, G., Gotta, D.: Large-scale network and service management with WANTS. In: Industrial Agents: Emerging Applications of Software Agents in Industry, pp. 231–246. Elsevier (2015)
7. Bergenti, F., Caire, G., Monica, S., Poggi, A.: The first twenty years of agent-based software development with JADE. Auton. Agent. Multi-Agent Syst. 34(2), 1–19 (2020). https://doi.org/10.1007/s10458-020-09460-z
8. Bergenti, F., Franchi, E., Poggi, A.: Agent-based social networks for enterprise collaboration. In: Proceedings of the 20th IEEE International Workshops on Enabling Technologies: Infrastructure for Collaborative Enterprises (WETICE 2011), pp. 25–28. IEEE (2011)
9. Bergenti, F., Gleizes, M.P., Zambonelli, F. (eds.): Methodologies and Software Engineering for Agent Systems. Springer, New York (2004). https://doi.org/10.1007/b116049
10. Bergenti, F., Huhns, M.N.: On the use of agents as components of software systems. In: Bergenti, F., Gleizes, M.P., Zambonelli, F. (eds.) Methodologies and Software Engineering for Agent Systems. Multiagent Systems, Artificial Societies, and Simulated Organizations, vol. 11, pp. 19–31. Springer, Boston (2004). https://doi.org/10.1007/1-4020-8058-1_3
11. Bergenti, F., Iotti, E., Monica, S., Poggi, A.: Agent-oriented model-driven development for JADE with the JADEL programming language. Comput. Lang. Syst. Struct. 50, 142–158 (2017)
12. Bergenti, F., Monica, S.: Location-aware social gaming with AMUSE. In: Demazeau, Y., Ito, T., Bajo, J., Escalona, M.J. (eds.) PAAMS 2016. LNCS (LNAI), vol. 9662, pp. 36–47. Springer, Cham (2016). https://doi.org/10.1007/978-3-319-39324-7_4
13. Bergenti, F., Monica, S., Petrosino, G.: A scripting language for practical agent-oriented programming. In: Proceedings of the 8th ACM SIGPLAN International Workshop on Programming Based on Actors, Agents, and Decentralized Control (AGERE 2018) at ACM SIGPLAN Conference Systems, Programming, Languages and Applications: Software for Humanity (SPLASH 2018). ACM (2018)

14. Bergenti, F., Petrosino, G.: Overview of a scripting language for JADE-based multi-agent systems. In: Proceedings of the 19th Workshop "From Objects to Agents" (WOA 2018). CEUR Workshop Proceedings, vol. 2215, pp. 57–62. RWTH Aachen (2018)
15. Bergenti, F., Poggi, A.: Ubiquitous information agents. Int. J. Coop. Inf. Syst. **11**(3–4), 231–244 (2002)
16. Bergenti, F., Poggi, A.: Developing smart emergency applications with multi-agent systems. Int. J. E-Health Med. Commun. **1**(4), 1–13 (2010)
17. Bettini, L.: Implementing Domain-Specific Languages with Xtext and Xtend. Packt Publishing, Birmingham (2013)
18. Bordini, R.H., Hübner, J.F., Wooldridge, M.: Programming Multi-agent Systems in AgentSpeak Using Jason. In: Wiley Series in Agent Technology. Wiley, Hoboken (2007)
19. Collier, R.W., Russell, S., Lillis, D.: Reflecting on agent programming with AgentSpeak(L). In: Chen, Q., Torroni, P., Villata, S., Hsu, J., Omicini, A. (eds.) PRIMA 2015. LNCS (LNAI), vol. 9387, pp. 351–366. Springer, Cham (2015). https://doi.org/10.1007/978-3-319-25524-8_22
20. Dhaon, A., Collier, R.: Multiple inheritance in AgentSpeak(L)-style programming languages. In: Proceedings of the 4th ACM SIGPLAN International Workshop on Programming Based on Actors, Agents, and Decentralized Control (AGERE 2014) at ACM SIGPLAN Conference Systems, Programming, Languages and Applications: Software for Humanity (SPLASH 2014), pp. 109–120. ACM (2014)
21. Federico, B., Agostino, P.: Agent-based approach to manage negotiation protocols in flexible CSCW systems. In: Proceedings of the 4th International Conference on Autonomous Agents (AGENTS 2000), pp. 267–268. ACM (2000)
22. Fowler, M., Parsons, R.: Domain Specific Languages. In: Addison-Wesley Signature. Addison-Wesley, Boston (2010)
23. Iotti, E., Petrosino, G., Monica, S., Bergenti, F.: Exploratory experiments on programming autonomous robots in Jadescript. In: Proceedings of the 1st Workshop on Agents and Robots for Reliable Engineered Autonomy (AREA 2020) at the European Conference on Artificial Intelligence (ECAI 2020). Electronic Proceedings in Theoretical Computer Science, vol. 319. Open Publishing Association (2020)
24. Iotti, E., Petrosino, G., Monica, S., Bergenti, F.: Two agent-oriented programming approaches checked against a coordination problem. In: Dong, Y., Herrera-Viedma, E., Matsui, K., Omatsu, S., González Briones, A., Rodríguez González, S. (eds.) DCAI 2020. AISC, vol. 1237, pp. 60–70. Springer, Cham (2021). https://doi.org/10.1007/978-3-030-53036-5_7
25. Monica, S., Bergenti, F.: A comparison of accurate indoor localization of static targets via WiFi and UWB ranging. In: Trends in Practical Applications of Scalable Multi-Agent Systems, the PAAMS Collection. AISC, vol. 473, pp. 111–123. Springer, Cham (2016). https://doi.org/10.1007/978-3-319-40159-1_9
26. Nilsson, N.J.: Teleo-reactive programs for agent control. J. Artif. Intell. Res. **1**, 139–158 (1993)
27. Petrosino, G., Bergenti, F.: An introduction to the major features of a scripting language for JADE agents. In: Ghidini, C., Magnini, B., Passerini, A., Traverso, P. (eds.) AI*IA 2018. LNCS (LNAI), vol. 11298, pp. 3–14. Springer, Cham (2018). https://doi.org/10.1007/978-3-030-03840-3_1
28. Petrosino, G., Bergenti, F.: Extending message handlers with pattern matching in the Jadescript programming language. In: Proceedings of the 20th Workshop "From Objects to Agents" (WOA 2019). CEUR Workshop Proceedings, vol. 2404, pp. 113–118. RWTH Aachen (2019)

29. Petrosino, G., Iotti, E., Monica, S., Bergenti, F.: Prototypes of productivity tools for the Jadescript programming language. In: Proceedings of the 22nd Workshop "From Objects to Agents' (WOA 2021). CEUR Workshop Proceedings, vol. 2963, pp. 14–28. RWTH Aachen (2021)

30. Petrosino, G., Iotti, E., Monica, S., Bergenti, F.: A description of the Jadescript type system. In: DAI 2021. LNCS (LNAI), vol. 13170, pp. 206–220. Springer, Cham (2022). https://doi.org/10.1007/978-3-030-94662-3_13

31. Petrosino, G., Monica, S., Bergenti, F.: Robust software agents with the Jadescript programming language. In: Proceedings of the 23rd Workshop "From Objects to Agents" (WOA 2022). CEUR Workshop Proceedings, vol. 3261, pp. 194–208. RWTH Aachen (2022)

32. Petrosino, G., Monica, S., Bergenti, F.: Cross-paradigm interoperability between Jadescript and Java. In: Proceedings of the 15th International Conference on Agents and Artificial Intelligence (ICAART 2023), vol. 1, pp. 165–172. Science and Technology Publications (2023)

33. Petrosino, G., Monica, S., Bergenti, F.: Delayed and periodic execution of tasks in the Jadescript programming language. In: Omatu, S., Mehmood, R., Sitek, P., Cicerone, S., Rodríguez, S. (eds.) DCAI 2022. LNCS, vol. 583, pp. 50–59. Springer, Cham (2023). https://doi.org/10.1007/978-3-031-20859-1_6

34. Poslad, S.: Specifying protocols for multi-agent systems interaction. ACM Trans. Auton. Adapt. Syst. 2(4), 15-es (2007)

35. Poslad, S., Charlton, P.: Standardizing agent interoperability: The FIPA approach. In: Luck, M., Mařík, V., Štěpánková, O., Trappl, R. (eds.) ACAI 2001. LNCS (LNAI), vol. 2086, pp. 98–117. Springer, Heidelberg (2001). https://doi.org/10.1007/3-540-47745-4_5

36. Rao, A.S.: AgentSpeak(L): BDI agents speak out in a logical computable language. In: Van de Velde, W., Perram, J.W. (eds.) MAAMAW 1996. LNCS, vol. 1038, pp. 42–55. Springer, Heidelberg (1996). https://doi.org/10.1007/BFb0031845

37. Rodriguez, S., Gaud, N., Galland, S.: SARL: a general-purpose agent-oriented programming language. In: Proceedings of the IEEE/WIC/ACM International Joint Conferences of Web Intelligence (WI 2014) and Intelligent Agent Technologies (IAT 2014), vol. 3, pp. 103–110. IEEE (2014)

38. Shoham, Y.: AGENT0: a simple agent language and its interpreter. In: Proceedings of the 9th National Conference on Artificial Intelligence (AAAI 1991), vol. 91, pp. 704–709 (1991)

39. Shoham, Y.: Agent-oriented programming. Artif. Intell. 60(1), 51–92 (1993)

40. Shoham, Y., Leyton-Brown, K.: Multiagent Systems: Algorithmic, Game-Theoretic, and Logical Foundations. Cambridge University Press, Cambridge (2008)

41. Tomaiuolo, M., Turci, P., Bergenti, F., Poggi, A.: An ontology support for semantic aware agents. In: Kolp, M., Bresciani, P., Henderson-Sellers, B., Winikoff, M. (eds.) AOIS -2005. LNCS (LNAI), vol. 3529, pp. 140–153. Springer, Heidelberg (2006). https://doi.org/10.1007/11916291_10

42. Yokoo, M.: Distributed Constraint Satisfaction: Foundations of Cooperation in Multi-agent Systems. Springer, Heidelberg (2001). https://doi.org/10.1007/978-3-642-59546-2

$vGOAL$: A GOAL-Based Specification Language for Safe Autonomous Decision-Making

Yi Yang$^{(\boxtimes)}$ and Tom Holvoet

imec-DistriNet, KU Leuven, 3001 Leuven, Belgium
{yi.yang,tom.holvoet}@kuleuven.be

Abstract. Formal verification is a reliable approach to addressing safety concerns in autonomous applications. We have designed $vGOAL$ based on the internal logic of the GOAL agent programming language, which serves as the formal specification language of our innovative formal approach to safe autonomous decision-making. A detailed description of $vGOAL$ is necessary to present and justify our approach to safe autonomous decision-making, yet it is currently missing. Therefore, this paper aims to provide a comprehensive description of $vGOAL$, including its formal syntax, its operational semantics, a real-world robotic application, and a comparison with several comparable agent programming languages, namely, GOAL, Gwendolen, and AgentSpeak (Jason).

Keywords: Formal Specification · Autonomous Decision-Making · Safety Assurance · $vGOAL$

1 Introduction

The applications of autonomous systems have seen a remarkable increase in recent years. These systems are capable of operating without human intervention to achieve complex goals. As autonomous applications become increasingly common in industries like manufacturing and transportation, it is crucial to ensure their safety.

Safe autonomous decision-making is one of the key challenges in developing autonomous robotic applications. Agent programming languages (APLs), including AgentSpeak [2], Jason [3], Gwendolen [8], and GOAL [10], have been extensively researched for programming autonomous agents for decades, indicating two facts: (1) A multi-agent system can properly model agent-based autonomous systems; (2) APLs are well-suited for tackling the challenge of the decision-making of agent-based autonomous systems. Despite the potential benefits of APLs in the development of autonomous robotic applications, their research has not been widely used in the field. Integration with the Robot Operating System (ROS) may expand their applications to robotics, as ROS has become the de

A. Ciortea et al. (Eds.): EMAS 2023, LNAI 14378, pp. 41–58, 2023.
https://doi.org/10.1007/978-3-031-48539-8_3

facto standard for developing robotic applications. If an APL has built-in support for ROS, it would be advantageous to integrate it with ROS-based robotic applications.

The Belief-Desire-Intention (BDI) model is a popular reasoning mechanism utilized in various APLs including Jason and Gwendolen [4]. GOAL shares many features with BDI APLs, such as beliefs and goals, but it is primarily a rule-based APL that differs in its approach to action selection [4]. Specifically, while BDI APLs select actions from a plan library, GOAL derives actions based on its rules to fulfill goals, making it highly suitable for specifying autonomous decision-making.

To facilitate safe decision-making of agent-based autonomous systems, we have developed *vGOAL*, which is a GOAL-based specification language that focuses exclusively on the internal logic reasoning mechanism of GOAL, motivated by three primary considerations. First, the decision-making mechanism of GOAL is highly suitable for autonomous decision-making, but many of its specifications are irrelevant to this domain, such as environment specifications. Second, the intrinsic logic-based nature of GOAL makes it highly suitable for formal verification, which is ideal for providing safety assurance for autonomous decision-making. Third, GOAL cannot directly access ROS, which limits its applicability in robotic applications. Therefore, *vGOAL* can be highly valuable for safe autonomous decision-making used in robotic applications, as it can leverage the strengths of GOAL, ROS, and formal verification.

On the basis of *vGOAL*, we have developed a three-stage formal approach to safe autonomous decision-making: formal specification using *vGOAL*, safe decision generation using the *vGOAL* interpreter, and the verification of *vGOAL* using an automated translator for *vGOAL* and a PCTL model checker (Storm [6] or PRISM [15]). Additionally, we have integrated the *vGOAL* interpreter into ROS via rosbridge to facilitate implementation and execution. We validated our approach in a real-world autonomous logistic system consisting of three autonomous mobile robots. There are three demonstration videos accessible for viewing at [18].

In [19], we established the preliminary groundwork for the formal specification and verification of *vGOAL* by outlining how to verify a GOAL program with specific restrictions, including a stratified program, a single agent, and a single goal. Building on this initial work, we described the rationale and implementation of the three-stage formal approach in [20]. [17] presents a high-level overview of the three-stage formal approach. However, a detailed description of *vGOAL* is crucial to thoroughly describing our approach to safe autonomous decision-making, similar to the descriptions of Gwendolen in [7] and in [8], and of GOAL in [10]. Therefore, the purpose of this paper is to provide a detailed explanation of *vGOAL*.

The paper is structured as follows. In Sect. 2, we present the formal syntax of *vGOAL*. In Sect. 3, we present the operational semantics of *vGOAL*. In Sect. 4, we demonstrate how to use *vGOAL* with a validated real-world autonomous logistic system. In Sect. 5, we will discuss the essential features of *vGOAL* and provide a comparative analysis with other APLs, namely GOAL, Gwendolen, and AgentSpeak (Jason). In Sect. 6, we draw conclusions on *vGOAL*.

2 Formal Syntax

In this section, we introduce the formal syntax of *vGOAL*. Initially, we introduce the core elements of *vGOAL*, highlighting its fundamental basis in first-order logic. Next, we delve into the predefined functions and the rule construction within vGOAL, elucidating its constraints within the first-order logic framework. Finally, we present the high-level components of *vGOAL* specifications.

The first part of the *vGOAL* syntax, which includes elements like terms and predicates, conforms to the conventions established in first-order logic. Nevertheless, in contrast to first-order logic, the specification allows for the optional indication of the domains associated with universally quantified variables. Minimal model generation is required for the generation of autonomous decision-making, hence necessitating the inclusion of domain specifications for universally quantified variables.

$$
\begin{aligned}
word \quad &::= char \mid num \\
constant \quad &::= word\ constant^* \\
variable \quad &::= char\ word^* \\
constant\_list \quad &::= constant\ constant^* \\
predicate\_name \quad &::= char\ word^* \\
ground\_atoms \quad &::= predicate\_name\ '('\ constant\_list\ ')' \\
term \quad &::= constant \mid variable \\
term\_list \quad &::= term \mid term\ ','\ term\_list \\
p \quad &::= predicate\_name\ (term\_list) \\
neg\_p \quad &::= \neg p \\
Uni\_Q \quad &::= \forall\ variable \mid \forall\ variable \in D \mid Uni\_Q^* \\
Ex\_Q \quad &::= \exists\ variable \mid Ex\_Q^*
\end{aligned}
$$

The second part of the *vGOAL* syntax involves some keywords, predefined functions, and the way of constructing rules.

R represents a group of agents, with its domain consisting of three distinct elements: *all*, *allother*, and *id*. Specifically, *all* and *allother* are keywords in *vGOAL*, denoting all agents and all agents within the multi-agent system excluding the individual responsible for transmitting messages, respectively; and *id* designates a particular agent.

For describing communication among agents, *vGOAL* offers six predefined functions: *send:*, *send!*, *send?*, *sent:*, *sent!*, and *sent?*. Like in GOAL, Message specifications in *vGOAL* differentiate among three types: indicative messages, indicated by the functions *send:*(R, p) and *sent:*(R, p); declarative messages, defined as *send!*(R, p) and *sent!*(R, p); and interrogative messages, represented as *send?*(R, p) and *sent?*(R, p). A sent message is represented as msg_s and encompasses three distinct elements within its domain: *send:*(R, p), *send!*(R, p), and *send?*(R, p). Conversely, a received message is symbolized as msg_r and comprises three distinct elements within its domain: *sent:*(R, p), *sent!*(R, p), and

$sent?(R,p)$. Moreover, in a msg_s, R represents the recipients of the message, whereas in a msg_r, it signifies the sender.

Similarly to GOAL, $vGOAL$ incorporates an event processing component responsible for handling communication messages and effecting changes in goals and beliefs. To facilitate these modifications, $vGOAL$ provides four predefined functions: $insert$, $delete$, $adopt$, and $drop$. $response$ signifies the outcome of event processing, which may encompass the generation of sent messages, the alteration of beliefs and goals, or both.

The minimal model serves as the foundation for establishing the semantics of $vGOAL$. Constructing the minimal model involves employing $qrule_i (1 \leq i \leq 6)$, which enforces three constraints on first-order logic: the quantification for each variable, a finite domain for each variable, and the absence of negative recursion. Furthermore, $qrule_7$ is used to define the effects of actions, and it is not used to deduce the subsequent safe autonomous decision.

$$
\begin{array}{ll}
id & ::= constant \\
R & ::= all | allother | id \\
msg_s & ::= send{:}(R,p) | send!(R,p) | send?(R,p) \\
msg_r & ::= sent{:}(R,p) | sent!(R,p) | sent?(R,p) \\
update & ::= insert(b) | delete(b) | adopt(g) | drop(g) \\
response & ::= msg_s | update \\
b & ::= ground\_atoms \\
g & ::= ground\_atoms \\
hs & ::= True | p \wedge hs | neg\_p \wedge hs \\
lh & ::= a\text{-}goal(p) \wedge hs \\
rule_1 & ::= hs \rightarrow p \\
qrule_1 & ::= Uni\_Q\ Ex\_Q\ rule_1 \\
rule_2 & ::= lh \rightarrow p \\
qrule_2 & ::= Uni\_Q\ Ex\_Q\ rule_2 \\
rule_3 & ::= hs \rightarrow msg_s \\
qrule_3 & ::= Uni\_Q\ Ex\_Q\ rule_3 \\
rule_4 & ::= msg_r \wedge hs \rightarrow response \\
qrule_4 & ::= Uni\_Q\ Ex\_Q\ rule_4 \\
rule_5 & ::= lh \rightarrow response \\
qrule_5 & ::= Uni\_Q\ Ex\_Q\ rule_5 \\
rule_6 & ::= hs \rightarrow response \\
qrule_6 & ::= Uni\_Q\ Ex\_Q\ rule_6 \\
rule_7 & ::= hs \rightarrow hs \\
qrule_7 & ::= Uni\_Q\ Ex\_Q\ rule_7
\end{array}
$$

The final part of the *vGOAL* syntax involves the high-level components of the *vGOAL* specification. The specification includes agent specifications and system specifications.

MAS denotes all agents' specifications involved in the multi-agent system. An agent specification consists of five essential components: a unique identifier: *id*, beliefs: B, goals: *goals*, sent messages: M_S, and received messages: M_R. The beliefs of an agent B consist of B_{sensor} and B_{prior}. B_{sensor} denotes the real-time beliefs obtained from sensors. B_{prior} denotes the prior beliefs that are essential for agents but cannot be received from sensors. An agent can have multiple goals, denoted by *goals*. Each goal (G) consists of goal bases.

System specifications in *vGOAL* involve six rule sets, each with a unique designation: K represents the knowledge base, C denotes enabled constraints, A refers to action generation, S pertains to sent message generation, P concerns event processing, and E describes action effects. Moreover, *a-goal* is a predefined function to evaluate if its argument is included in the first goal base.

$$
\begin{aligned}
Agent &::= (id, B, goals, M_S, M_R) \\
MAS &::= Agent^* \\
D &::= constant\_list \\
B_{sensor} &::= b^* \\
B_{prior} &::= b^* \\
B &::= B_{sensor}\ B_{prior} \\
G &::= g^* \\
goals &::= G^* \\
M_S &::= msg_s^* \\
M_R &::= msg_r^* \\
K &::= qrulc_1^*\ ground\_atom^* \\
C &::= qrule_2^* \\
A &::= qrule_1^* \\
S &::= qrule_3^* \\
P &::= qrule_4^*\ qrule_5^*\ qrule_6^* \\
E &::= qrule_7^*
\end{aligned}
$$

Remark: Belief Base and Current Beliefs

In *vGOAL*, the belief base contains information that cannot be inferred by logical deduction. More specifically, an agent's current beliefs are obtained by combining its belief base with its knowledge base. As a result, the belief base represents a subset of an agent's current beliefs.

3   Operational Semantics

This section presents the operational semantics of $vGOAL$. Initially, we establish the semantics for high-level components in $vGOAL$. Subsequently, we explain how $vGOAL$ generates autonomous decisions through its reasoning cycle. The operational semantics of $vGOAL$ encompasses function updates and the generation of minimal models for first-order theories constrained by the $vGOAL$ syntax.

We use I to define the interpretations of high-level components in $vGOAL$. The principles to interpreters $vGOAL$ specifications are as follows.

- If $Spec ::= Agent, I(Spec) = id : (I(B), I(goals), I(M_S), I(M_R))$.
- If $Spec ::= e^*$, $I(Spec) = \bigcup_n I(e)$.
- If $Spec ::= e_1...e_n$, $I(Spec) = \bigcup_n I(e_i)$.
- If $Spec ::= goals$, and $goals ::= GG^*|Empty$, $I(Spec) = I(G)$ or $I(Spec) = \emptyset$.
- If $e ::= ground\_atom$, $I(e) = True$.
- The interpretation of logical operators, such as $\wedge$, $\neg$, and $\rightarrow$, adheres to the standard conventions of first-order logic.

Following the above interpretation principles, each high-level component of $vGOAL$ specifications, including B, G, $goals$, M_S, M_R, K, C, A, S, P, and E, is converted to a first-order theory constrained by $vGOAL$ syntax.

We use $I(Agent)$ and $I(MAS)$ as the foundation for constructing $vGOAL$'s substate and state, respectively. A substate represents an agent's state, while the state captures the autonomous system's state. A substate includes a unique identifier, beliefs, and goals, while the full information of the substate adds sent and received messages. We formally define a $vGOAL$ state and its corresponding information as follows:

$$substate :: = id : (I(B), I(goals)),$$
$$sub\_info :: = id : (I(B), I(goals), I(M_S), I(M_R)),$$
$$state :: = state \cup \{substate\}|\emptyset,$$
$$state\_info :: = state\_info \cup \{sub\_info\}|\emptyset.$$

The core component of the reasoning cycle is the generation of the minimal model of a first-order theory. Given a first-order theory T, the minimal model M of T satisfies the following conditions:

- $\forall \phi \in T, M \models \phi$,
- $\forall M' \subset M, \exists \phi \in T, M \nvDash \phi$.

The first condition states M satisfies all the sentences in T. The second condition states that there is no proper substructure M' of M that also satisfies all the sentences in T. We denote the minimal model of T as $MinModel(T)$.

3.1 Stage 1: Substate Property Generation

For one agent, each substate can only differ from either its belief base, its goal base, or both. Consequently, we define the substate property as the combination of the current beliefs and the desired goals of the agent. The current beliefs and the desired beliefs are defined as follows:

$$CB :: = I(B) \cup I(K),$$
$$DB :: = I(goals)$$

CB is a first-order theory that derives current beliefs from its belief base B and knowledge base K, while DB denotes the desired beliefs. Following the fourth principle to interpreter *vGOAL* specifications, the interpretation of *goals* is either the first goal base of the agent or empty. Substate properties involve both CB and DB through a predefined function F. F transforms the agent's desired beliefs into a new form that reflects those desired beliefs. Its formal definition is as follows:

$$F(G) ::= \begin{cases} \bigcup^{n} a\text{-}goal(g_i) & if\ G ::= g_1...g_n\ and\ n > 0, \\ \emptyset & \text{otherwise.} \end{cases}$$

The substate properties are formally defined as follows:

$$subP ::= MinModel(CB \cup F(DB)).$$

3.2 Stage 2: Enabled Constraint Generation

The constraints that constrain an agent to generate feasible actions or sent messages are referred to as enabled constraints. Constrained by the current and desired beliefs, an agent generates decisions. The generated constraints are defined as follows:

$$EC :: = subP \cup I(C),$$
$$GC :: = MinModel(EC) \backslash subP.$$

3.3 Stage 3: Enabled Action Generation

An action can be triggered only when a related enabled constraint and its preconditions are satisfied by the current beliefs. The generated actions are defined as follows:

$$EA :: = subP \cup GC \cup I(A),$$
$$GA :: = MinModel(EA) \backslash MinModel(subP \cup GC).$$

3.4   Stage 4: Enabled Sent Message Generation

During a reasoning cycle, if the decision-making module fails to generate a feasible action, it will attempt to generate enabled sent messages for exchanging information with other agents. A message can be sent only when the related enabled constraint is satisfied. The enabled sent messages are defined as follows:

$$ES :: = subP \cup GC \cup I(S),$$
$$GS :: = MinModel(ES) \backslash MinModel(subP \cup GC).$$

sub_info of the agent will be changed if GS is not an empty set. M_S will be assigned with GS, which is defined as follows:

$$M_S ::= GS.$$

3.5   Stage 5: Event Processing

In each reasoning cycle, each agent processes events including adopting subgoals to achieve the desired state, revising current beliefs, and responding to the received messages from the last reasoning cycle. The state of the multi-agent system may change as a result of the event processing altering the state of an agent. In the reasoning cycle, the received messages of an agent are denoted with M_R. The enabled event processing is defined as follows:

$$EP :: = subP \cup M_R \cup I(P),$$
$$PR :: = MinModel(EP) \backslash MinModel(subP \cup I(P)).$$

If M_R is not an empty set, the sub_info of the agent will be altered. This modification occurs because M_R undergoes reinitialization, resetting it to an empty set after event processing, which is formally defined as follows:

$$M_R ::= \emptyset.$$

3.6   Stage 6: Communication

During each reasoning cycle, agents exchange information on the basis of the information of sub_info. To define the effects of communication of the sub_info of each agent, we utilize the following functions.

We utilize three functions to convert sent messages into their corresponding received messages. First, $inst(msg_s)$ instantiates the receivers of a sent message. Secondly, $Inst(S, M_S)$ instantiates all messages sent by an agent, using $inst(msg_s)$ as the basis. Third, $MP(S, msg_s)$ converts a sent message to its corresponding received message.

$$inst(msg_s) :: = \begin{cases} \bigcup_{r} I(msg_s)[R \mapsto r], & \text{if } R = all, \text{ and } r \in \bigcup id \\ \bigcup_{r} I(msg_s)[R \mapsto r], & \text{if } R = allother \text{ and } r \in \bigcup id \backslash S, \\ I(msg_s), & \text{if } R = id, \end{cases}$$

$$Inst(S, M_S) :: = \begin{cases} \emptyset, & \text{if } I(M_S) = \emptyset, \\ inst(msg_s \bigcup Inst(S, M_S) \backslash I(msg_s)), & \text{otherwise} \end{cases}$$

$$MP(S, msg_s) :: = \begin{cases} I(sent(S, p)), & \text{if } msg_s = send(r, p), \\ I(sent!(S, p)), & \text{if } msg_s = send!(r, p), \\ I(sent?(S, p)), & \text{if } msg_s = send?(r, p). \end{cases}$$

Next, we use three functions to update the subinfo of one agent. First, $P_1(sub\_info, S, msg_s)$ defines how an agent updates its sub_info for a single sent message. Second, $P_2(sub\_info, S, M)$ defines how an agent updates its sub_info for a set of sent messages, using $P_1(sub\_info, S, msg_s)$ as the basis. Third, $P_3(sub\_info)$ describes the initialization of M_S of an agent.

$$P_1(sub\_info, S, msg_s) :: = \begin{cases} sub\_info[M_R \mapsto M_R \bigcup MP(S, msg_s)], & \text{if id=r} \\ sub\_info, & \text{otherwise,} \end{cases}$$

$$P_2(sub\_info, S, M_S) :: = \begin{cases} sub\_info, & \text{if } I(M_S) = \emptyset \text{ or } id \neq r \\ P_2(P_1(sub\_info, S, msg_s), S, M_S \backslash msg_s), & \text{otherwise,} \end{cases}$$

$$P3(sub\_info) :: = sub\_info[M_S \mapsto \emptyset)].$$

We define the *state_info* as a collective set of the *sub_info* of each agent within the multi-agent system, denoting as $(sub\_info)_{\times n}$. Moreover, we use $(id : M_S)_{\times n}$ to denote the sent messages of each agent within the system during the current reasoning cycle. After the reasoning cycle of each agent, the update of *state_info* is formally defined as follows:

$$sub\_info \xrightarrow{(id:M_S)_{\times n}} (P_3((P_2(sub\_info, id, M_S))_{\times n}))_{\times n}.$$

3.7   State Update

For a multi-agent system, agents participate in a modular reasoning cycle and communicate with other agents during the final stage of the cycle. The state of the multi-agent system is updated once all agents have completed their current reasoning cycle. The substate of a multi-agent system, i.e., the state of an agent, can only be modified by generated actions, GA, and the processed results of the event processing, PR.

An agent changes its current belief base based on the rules of action effects and the enabled actions. The action effects will change the state of the agent, subsequently changing the state of the multi-agent system.

First, we define how an action changes the current belief base of the agent. The rules on action effects E are defined by $qrule_7$, which is in the form $hs_1 \rightarrow hs_2$. Both hs_1 and hs_2 follow the construction rule of hs in syntax, and $I(hs)$: $:= I(\bigwedge_m B_m \wedge \bigwedge_n \neg B_n)$. We define a function U to describe the belief updates incurred by actions as follows:

$$U(B, GA, E) :: = \begin{cases} I(B) \cup \bigcup^m I(\{B_m\}) \setminus \bigcup^n I(\{B_n\}), \text{if} I(B) \cup GA \vdash I(hs_1), \\ I(B) \text{ ,otherwise.} \end{cases}$$

In each reasoning cycle, the agent can only generate either an enabled action or send messages, but it can handle all received messages. We define a function T to update *substate* based on action effects during each reasoning cycle, and T will not modify the substate if there is no enabled action effect.

For the generated action effect, the substate is updated as follows:

$$T(substate, GA) :: = \begin{cases} id : (U(B, GA, E), I(goals)), & \text{if } GA \neq \emptyset, \\ id : (I(B), I(goals)), & \text{if } GE = \emptyset, \end{cases}$$

$$substate :: = T(substate, GA).$$

A processed result of event processing can modify beliefs, goals, or both. Additionally, an instance of a *response* can take the form of either msg_s or *update*. It is worth noting that only an instance of *update* will modify the substate, which includes $insert(B, b)$, $delete(B, b)$, $adopt(goals, g)$, and $drop(goals, g)$.

For a processed result, the substate is updated as follows:

$$I(insert(B, b)) :: = I(B) \cup b,$$
$$I(delete(B, b)) :: = I(B) \setminus b,$$
$$I(adopt(goals, g)) :: = I(goals) \cup g,$$
$$I(drop(goals, g)) :: = I(goals) \setminus g,$$

$$H(S, r) :: = \begin{cases} id : (I(insert(B, b)), I(goals)) & \text{if } r = insert(b), \\ id : (I(delete(B, b)), I(goals)) & \text{if } r = delete(b), \\ id : (I(B), I(adopt(goals, g))) & \text{if } r = adopt(g), \\ id : (I(B), I(drop(goals, g))) & \text{if } r = drop(g), \\ id : (I(B), I(goals)) & \text{, otherwise.} \end{cases}$$

For the processed results of the event processing, PR, we define the function F to update the substate as follows:

$$F(S, PR) = \begin{cases} F((H(S, r), PR \setminus r) & \text{if } PR \setminus r \neq \emptyset, \\ S & otherwise. \end{cases}$$

Assuming a multi-agent system containing n agents ($n \geq 1$), the state is represented as $(substate)_{\times n}$. In each reasoning cycle, the substate can only be changed by the effects of enabled actions and the processed results of event processing. The effects of enabled actions corresponds to an action (Act), and the processed results of event processing involve the received messages of the current reasoning cycle (M_R). We use the $(id : (Act, M_R))_{\times n}$ to represent a transition that may change the substate, subsequently changing the state. The operational semantics of a $vGOAL$ specification is defined as follows:

$$(substate)_{\times n} \xrightarrow{(id:(Act, M_R))_{\times n}} (F(T(substate, Act), PR)_{\times n},$$

where Act represents the generated action, and PR denotes the processed results of the event processing, involving processing the received messages M_R. Although GE and PR can both be empty for an agent, if any agent has a goal, at least one agent will have non-empty GE or PR. In our setting, if an agent fails to generate any decisions based on its current beliefs, it should send messages to other agents to obtain more information to accomplish its goal.

Moreover, if any $substate$ is updated, each sub_info within the multi-agent system will be automatically adjusted, namely, the belief base and goal base will be modified to align with the $substate$.

4 Case Study

Using a real-world autonomous logistic system, we have validated our formal approach to safe autonomous decision-making. Accordingly, we use the system to explain how to use $vGOAL$.

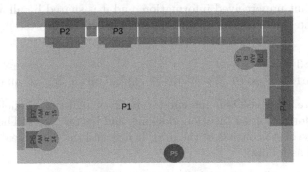

Fig. 1. Layout of the Robot Environment

The autonomous system is composed of three autonomous mobile robots, situated in the environment depicted in Fig. 1. The case study aims to perform a collaborative transportation task. Non-red areas are considered safe places, denoting from P_1 to P_8, while red areas are considered unsafe, denoting by P_9. P_2 is the destination of the delivery task; P_3 and P_4 are the pick-up station; P_5 is a waiting point for the charging station; P_6, P_7, and P_8 are the charging stations;

and P_1 is the other places except the aforementioned areas. The nine areas can be classified into four categories. Category I only contains P_1. The location of Category I is a safe place, but agents do not need permission to access it, and it has no dock. Category II includes P_2, P_3, P_4, P_6, P_7, and P_8. The locations of Category II are safe places, and agents need permission to access them. There is a dock for each location. Category III includes P_5. The location of Category III is a safe place, and agents need permission to access it, but it has no dock. Category IV only includes P_9. The location of Category IV is an unsafe place, and agents need to avoid moving there.

We demonstrate each key aspect of the $vGOAL$ specifications using a subset of the specifications that specify the case study. For a comprehensive version of the formal specification for the case study, we refer readers to [18].

First of all, we have to determine how to specify agents within the multi-agent system. We need to define four agents in the case study: three for the real-world agents, designated as A1, A2, and A3, and one for a dummy agent, denoted as C. In our approach, we utilize a dummy agent to manage competing requests for critical resources, such as permissions for locations. The specification of the multi-agent system is specified as follows:

Agents $=$ [A1,A2,A3,C] ,

where A1, A2, A3, and C are an instance of the agent class defined in the $vGOAL$ interpreter.

To facilitate real-time autonomous decision-making, an agent will take both the real-time beliefs abstracted from sensor information and the prior beliefs as the complete belief base to make decisions. As it is common that not all required information can be sensed in practical scenarios, we need prior beliefs to specify the necessary but unperceived information, and it is shared by all agents within the system. The belief base of A3 and the prior beliefs of the system are specified as follows:

```
belief_base3  =[] ,
prior_beliefs=["on(1,3)" ,"on(2,4)" ,"on(3,3)" ,"on(4,3)"].
```

Furthermore, the $vGOAL$ interpreter receives real-time beliefs abstracted from sensor information on location, docking, and battery level. The initial complete belief base of A3 consists of the prior beliefs and the initial real-time beliefs, which is listed as follows:

```
belief_base3  =["on(1,3)" ,"on(2,4)" ,"on(3,3)" ,"on(4,3)" ,
"at(8)" ,  "battery(2)" ,"docked(8)" ,"assigned(8)"].
```

An agent can have no goals, one goal, or multiple goals. Agent A3 has two goals, which are specified as follows:

```
goal_base3  =  ['delivered(2,3)'] ,
goal_base4  =  ["delivered(2,4)"] ,
goals3  =  [goal_base3 ,goal_base4].
```

Dummy agents are used to manage critical resources. Their specifications are similar to those of real-world agents, including belief bases and goals. However, while real-world agents rely on sensor information to update their belief bases, dummy agents' belief bases are not affected by sensor information. Furthermore, dummy agents have no goals to pursue. The case study only requires one dummy agent, denoted as C, whose belief base and goals are listed as follows:

```
dummy_agents=["C"]
belief_base4 = [" idle (2)" , "idle(3)" , "idle(4)" ,"idle(5)" ,
    "reserved(A1,6)" , "reserved(A2,7)" , "reserved(A3,8)"]
goals4 = []
```

The *vGOAL* interpreter provides a class for agents, whose attributes involve a unique identifier, a belief base, goals, sent messages, and received messages. The sent messages and received messages are empty by default. Therefore, users only need to specify an agent with the other three values. The specifications of Agent A3 and the dummy agent are specified as follows:

```
A3 = Agent("A3", belief_base3 , goals3)
C = Agent("C", belief_base4 , goals4)
```

A knowledge base is a collection of facts and rules that the decision-making module uses to reason about the world. In *vGOAL*, a knowledge base can contain either a first-order implication without negative recursion or a ground atom. Two representative rules in the knowledge base are specified as follows:

```
"forall w. on(w,4) implies available(w)",
"equal(charging , charging)".
```

vGOAL utilizes a set of rules, referred to as the constraints of action generation, to ensure that the generated decisions are moving towards a goal. These constraints are either related to the generation of actions or the generation of messages to acquire more information about the environment. Two representative constraints are specified as follows:

```
"forall w,y in D2 . a−goal holding(w) and docked(p) and not
holding(y) and docked(4) and available(w) implies A(w)",
"forall p,w in D2 . a−goal at(p) and not holding(w) and
                not equal(p,2) implies S(p)".
```

The first constraint pertains to the action generation, and the second constraint pertains to the generation of sent messages. As mentioned in Sect. 2, users only need to specify the domain of variables that only occur on the left side of the implication due to the implementation of the interpreter.

In *vGOAL*, feasible actions are derived using a set of rules called the enabledness of actions, which requires including a generated constraint and may impose restrictions on the current belief base. Two of the enabledness of action generation are specified as follows:

```
"forall w. A(w) implies pickup(w)"
"forall p. exists y. C(p) and at(y) and equal(y,1) and
                not equal(p,5) implies move1(y,p)".
```

The first rule only involves a generated constraint, whereas the second rule involves both a generated constraint and current beliefs.

In *vGOAL*, sent messages are derived using a set of rules, which only includes a generated constraint and may impose restrictions on the current belief base. One rule for the generation of sent messages is specified as follows:

```
"forall p. S(p) implies send!(C) idle(p)".
```

vGOAL includes rules related to event processing, which encompasses responding to received messages and adopting subgoals of the first goal base on the basis of current beliefs. Five rules for event processing are specified as follows:

```
"fatal implies drop all",
"forall z. exists x,y. sent!(x) at(y) and reserved(x,z)
                and not equal(z,y) implies insert idle(z)",
"forall x. exists y. sent!(x) idle(y) and reserved(x,y)
                  implies send:(x) assigned(y)",
"exists x,y. sent!(x) idle(y) and reserved(z,y) and
                  equal(x,z) implies delete idle(y)",
"exists x,w,p. a-goal on(w,2) and on(w,p) and at(x)
                    implies adopt at(p)".
```

The first rule states that all goals should be dropped if a fatal error occurs. The next three rules illustrate three distinct approaches to responding to a received message, including belief insertion, message sending, and belief deletion. The last rule specified how to adopt a subgoal toward the desired goal.

vGOAL employs action effects to determine how to modify the current belief base. These effects can either involve belief insertion or deletion. As a result, the associated rule may involve negative recursion, a property not shared by rules in other components. An example rule for the generation of action effects is provided below:

```
"pickup": "forall w,p,y in D2 . pickup(w) and not holding(y)
            and on(w,p) implies holding(w) and not on(w,p)"
```

Moreover, the real-time information can include error messages, necessitating error handling. We emphasize that our framework can conveniently handle errors. In another word, users can simply specify how to handle errors in the specifications without changing any implementation of the framework. In the case study, we identify four types of errors: E_1, *dock* errors; E_2, *pick up* errors; E_3, *drop off* errors; and E_4, *charge* errors. In our setting, the non-fatal errors are E_1, E_2, and E_3, and the fatal errors are E_4, which is specified in the knowledge base as follows:

```
"E1 implies nonfatal",
"E2 implies nonfatal",
"E3 implies nonfatal",
"E4 implies fatal",
```

If an agent encounters a fatal error, it should send a message to the dummy agent to report its current location. If an agent encounters a nonfatal error, we need a dummy rule to avoid any meaningful constraints. Therefore, two constraints on error handling are specified as follows:

```
"forall p. at(p) and fatal implies M(p)",
"nonfatal implies Dummy",
```

If an agent encounters a fatal error, the agent will be considered broken and will drop all goals and beliefs. If an agent encounters a non-fatal error, it will drop the focused goals and adopt new goals. After inserting new goals, it will delete corresponding nonfatal errors to enter the next reasoning cycle. The rules on error handling are specified in the event processing as follows:

```
"fatal implies drop all",
"fatal implies delete all",
"nonfatal and not goal_change implies drop all",
"nonfatal and not goal_change implies adopt located(charging)",
"nonfatal and not goal_change implies adopt at(5)",
"nonfatal and not goal_change implies insert goal_change",
"nonfatal and E1 implies delete E1",
"nonfatal and E2 implies delete E2",
"nonfatal and E3 implies delete E3",
```

5   Discussion

The motivation of *vGOAL* is the generation of verifiably safe decision-making for autonomous systems. Consequently, it is pertinent to conduct a comparison with the APLs capable of generating verified decisions. In this section, we discuss the key aspects of *vGOAL*, along with a comparison with GOAL, Gwendolen, and AgentSpeak (Jason).

vGOAL stands out from GOAL, Gwendolen, and AgentSpeak (Jason) in generating safe decisions without the need for additional computation. As discussed in Sect. 3.1, the first stage of each reasoning cycle involves generating the substate property, which links each state to a state property. Hence, we can prove that a state satisfies its safety properties by showing that all safety properties are contained within the state properties without additional computation. However, GOAL and AgentSpeak necessitate formal specifications of the original programming language and verification tools [1,13], while Gwendolen relies on the Agent Java PathFinder (AJPF) for model checking, thereby encountering efficiency problems [9].

Durative action modeling and error handling are crucial and challenging issues in autonomous decision-making. Notably, we address the challenge of error detection in a different way than GOAL, Gwendolen, and Jason. Specifically, *vGOAL* logically handles errors by separating error detection from the decision-making module and allowing users to specify how to handle errors in the specifications without modifying the implementation of the framework. In contrast, error handling is hard-coded into the implementation of Gwendolen and Jason, requiring users to modify the implementation to specify how to handle action failures [2, 16]. While GOAL does not have a specific error-handling mechanism, it can recognize action failure by comparing received perceptions with desired effects. In practice, the method involves comparing the received perceptions with the desired effects [12, 14], which can be laborious to identify all potential situations of action failure.

Despite being based on speech-act theory, the communications of all four languages have different performatives. *vGOAL* and GOAL employ the least performatives, namely indicative, declarative, and interrogative, which do not directly alter current goals [11]. In contrast, Gwendolen utilizes performatives such as *tell*, *perform*, and *achieve*, which directly affect intentions [7]. Jason employs more performatives, compared with *vGOAL*, GOAL, and Gwendolen [2]. In summary, *vGOAL* and GOAL use a simpler communication mechanism than Gwendolen and Jason, employing mailbox semantics without direct modification of goals. Notably, in *vGOAL*, the communication component is encoded in a first-order logical manner to allow automated minimal model generation.

The implementation of the interpreter for *vGOAL* is in Python, which differs from the implementation of the interpreters for GOAL, Gwendolen, and AgentSpeak in Java. *vGOAL* has the advantage that only it can be readily encoded in a decision-making node in ROS, compared with GOAL, Gwendolen, and AgentSpeak. *vGOAL* has already been integrated with ROS using rosbridge, as well as Gwendolen and AgentSpeak [5]. Additionally, there is currently no known research that connects GOAL with ROS.

6   Conclusion

To achieve verifiably safe autonomous decision-making, we have developed an innovative formal approach based on *vGOAL*. In this paper, we aim to give a comprehensive introduction to *vGOAL*, as it is pivotal in presenting and justifying our formal approach to safe autonomous decision-making. Initially, we presented its formal syntax and operational semantics, providing a solid foundation for formal verification. To demonstrate the applicability of the language, we described a real-world autonomous logistic system that has been validated using *vGOAL* and its interpreter. Finally, we compared the key aspects of *vGOAL* with comparable APLs to demonstrate its advantages. In the future, we aim to enrich the case studies of *vGOAL* with numerous complicated real-world autonomous systems. Moreover, we intend to conduct an empirical analysis to compare *vGOAL* with GOAL, Gwendolen, and AgentSpeak (Jason). We believe *vGOAL* can be highly valuable for developing safe autonomous robotic applications.

Acknowledgements. This research is partially funded by the Research Fund KU Leuven. We thank Jens Vankeirsbilck for providing Fig. 1.

References

1. Bordini, R.H., Fisher, M., Pardavila, C., Wooldridge, M.: Model checking agents-peak. In: Proceedings of the Second International Joint Conference on Autonomous Agents and Multiagent Systems, pp. 409–416 (2003)
2. Bordini, R.H., Hübner, J.F.: BDI agent programming in AgentSpeak using *Jason*. In: Toni, F., Torroni, P. (eds.) CLIMA 2005. LNCS (LNAI), vol. 3900, pp. 143–164. Springer, Heidelberg (2006). https://doi.org/10.1007/11750734_9
3. Bordini, R.H., Hübner, J.F., Wooldridge, M.: Programming Multi-agent Systems in AgentSpeak Using Jason. John Wiley & Sons, Hoboken (2007)
4. Cardoso, R.C., Ferrando, A.: A review of agent-based programming for multi-agent systems. Computers **10**(2), 16 (2021)
5. Cardoso, R.C., Ferrando, A., Dennis, L.A., Fisher, M.: An interface for programming verifiable autonomous agents in ROS. In: Bassiliades, N., Chalkiadakis, G., de Jonge, D. (eds.) EUMAS/AT -2020. LNCS (LNAI), vol. 12520, pp. 191–205. Springer, Cham (2020). https://doi.org/10.1007/978-3-030-66412-1_13
6. Dehnert, C., Junges, S., Katoen, J.-P., Volk, M.: A storm is coming: a modern probabilistic model checker. In: Majumdar, R., Kunčak, V. (eds.) CAV 2017. LNCS, vol. 10427, pp. 592–600. Springer, Cham (2017). https://doi.org/10.1007/978-3-319-63390-9_31
7. Dennis, L.A.: Gwendolen semantics: 2017 (2017)
8. Dennis, L.A., Farwer, B.: Gwendolen: a BDI language for verifiable agents. In: Proceedings of the AISB 2008 Symposium on Logic and the Simulation of Interaction and Reasoning, Society for the Study of Artificial Intelligence and Simulation of Behaviour, pp. 16–23. Citeseer (2008)
9. Dennis, L.A., Fisher, M., Webster, M.P., Bordini, R.H.: Model checking agent programming languages. Autom. Softw. Eng. **19**(1), 5–63 (2012)
10. Hindriks, K.V.: Programming rational agents in GOAL. In: El Fallah Seghrouchni, A., Dix, J., Dastani, M., Bordini, R.H. (eds.) Multi-Agent Programming, pp. 119–157. Springer, Boston, MA (2009). https://doi.org/10.1007/978-0-387-89299-3_4
11. Hindriks, K.V.: Programming cognitive agents in GOAL. Vrije Universiteit Amsterdam (2021)
12. Hindriks, K.V., Dix, J.: GOAL: a multi-agent programming language applied to an exploration game. In: Shehory, O., Sturm, A. (eds.) Agent-Oriented Software Engineering, pp. 235–258. Springer, Heidelberg (2014). https://doi.org/10.1007/978-3-642-54432-3_12
13. Jensen, A.B., Hindriks, K.V., Villadsen, J.: On using theorem proving for cognitive agent-oriented programming. In: 13th International Conference on Agents and Artificial Intelligence, pp. 446–453. Science and Technology Publishing (2021)
14. Jensen, A.B., Villadsen, J.: GOAL-DTU: development of distributed intelligence for the multi-agent programming contest. In: Ahlbrecht, T., Dix, J., Fiekas, N., Krausburg, T. (eds.) MAPC 2019. LNCS (LNAI), vol. 12381, pp. 79–105. Springer, Cham (2020). https://doi.org/10.1007/978-3-030-59299-8_4
15. Kwiatkowska, M., Norman, G., Parker, D.: PRISM: probabilistic symbolic model checker. In: Field, T., Harrison, P.G., Bradley, J., Harder, U. (eds.) TOOLS 2002. LNCS, vol. 2324, pp. 200–204. Springer, Heidelberg (2002). https://doi.org/10.1007/3-540-46029-2_13
16. Stringer, P., Cardoso, R.C., Dixon, C., Dennis, L.A.: Implementing durative actions with failure detection in Gwendolen. In: Alechina, N., Baldoni, M., Logan, B. (eds.) EMAS 2021. LNCS, vol. 13190, pp. 332–351. Springer, Cham (2022). https://doi.org/10.1007/978-3-030-97457-2_19

17. Yang, Y.: Verifiably safe decision-making for autonomous systems. In: Proceedings of the 2023 International Conference on Autonomous Agents and Multiagent Systems, pp. 2973–2975 (2023)

18. Yang, Y.: vGOAL (2023). https://kuleuven-my.sharepoint.com/:f:/g/personal/yi_yang_kuleuven_be/EjUTI-DUvkdBlBKoNWxcVgIB8GMfhyAZHSA_i1b7ovskqw?e=k6FINj

19. Yang, Y., Holvoet, T.: Generating safe autonomous decision-making in ROS. In: Fourth Workshop on Formal Methods for Autonomous Systems, vol. 371, pp. 184–192. Open Publishing Association (9 2022)

20. Yang, Y., Holvoet, T.: Making model checking feasible for GOAL. In: 10th International Workshop on Engineering Multi-Agent Systems (2022)

Agents and Microservices

Protocol-Based Engineering
of Microservices

Aditya K. Khadse[1], Samuel H. Christie V[2], Munindar P. Singh[1],
and Amit K. Chopra[3(✉)]

[1] North Carolina State University, Raleigh, USA
{akkhadse,mpsingh}@ncsu.edu
[2] Cambridge, UK
shcv@sdf.org
[3] Lancaster University, Lancaster, UK
amit.chopra@lancaster.ac.uk

Abstract. The *microservices* pattern is increasingly used in industry
to realize applications in a decentralized manner, often with the help
of novel programming models such as Microsoft-originated *Dapr*. Multiagent systems have typically been conceptualized as being decentralized. This naturally brings us to the question: Can multiagent software
abstractions benefit the enterprise of realizing applications via microservices?

To answer this question, in this paper, we show how *interaction protocols*, a fundamental multiagent abstraction, can be applied toward realizing an application as a set of microservices. Specifically, we take a
third-party application that exemplifies Dapr's programming model and
reengineer it based on protocols. We evaluate the differences between
our protocol-based implementation of the application and the Dapr-
based implementation and find that our protocol-based implementation provides an improved developer experience in terms of cleaner,
better-structured code. We conclude that (1) protocols represent a
highly promising abstraction suited to the modeling and engineering
of microservices-based applications and (2) Dapr augmented with a
protocol-based programming model would be highly beneficial to the
microservices enterprise.

Keywords: Decentralized systems · coordination · asynchronous
messaging · multiagent systems · information protocols · programming
models

1 Introduction

With the recent upsurge of cloud providers and affordable deployment solutions [20], large-scale software is increasingly written using microservices [29].
Microservices are motivated by loose coupling afforded by a decentralized application architecture. The microservices that constitute an application can be

A. Ciortea et al. (Eds.): EMAS 2023, LNAI 14378, pp. 61–77, 2023.
https://doi.org/10.1007/978-3-031-48539-8_4

independently developed and maintained, possibly using heterogeneous technologies. Further, each microservice can be deployed in its own container and scaled independently in the cloud. By contrast, the components in a monolithic application [21] are tightly coupled.

A challenge with any decentralized architecture is coordination between its components. With products increasingly adopting the microservices architecture, programming models that facilitate microservices-based application development have emerged. Dapr [14] is a leading programming model, originally conceived within Microsoft, but now an open-source project. To support coordination, Dapr provides the abstractions of state stores, pub-sub brokers, and so on. Dapr is used across different industries by companies such as Alibaba Cloud [1] and Bosch [19]. Alibaba Cloud notes that adopting Dapr helped them integrate microservices written in different languages quickly. Bosch particularly mentions how it was easy to move to event-driven microservices while using Dapr.

The field of multiagent systems (MAS) has traditionally been concerned with decentralized architectures, and the connection between services and multiagent systems has been identified multiple times over the years [2,22,23,26]. Particularly interesting are works on engineering MAS based on protocols [15–17].

Recent developments in engineering MAS have focused on the idea of information protocols [24,33]. An information protocol models a decentralized MAS by specifying declarative information constraints on message occurrence. Information protocols are enacted by decentralized agents via Local State Transfer (LoST) [25]. Programming models based on information protocols includes Deserv [9], Bungie [8], Mandrake [10], and Kiko [11]. Kiko, in particular, represents a conceptual leap because it enables viewing and implementing an agent as a decision maker, its communications being its decisions.

In this paper, we model an existing Dapr application via information protocols and implement it using Kiko to highlight the benefits of a multiagent approach to microservices development. In particular, the benefits include better system modeling via protocols and attendant benefits such as verification; better structured and more correct code; fully decentralized implementations; and more loosely-coupled components.

2   Background

We now introduce information protocols, Kiko, and Dapr.

2.1   Information Protocols

Information protocols are declarative specifications of interaction between agents. A protocol specifies the *roles* (played by agents); a set of public parameters; optionally, a set of private parameters; and a set of messages. Each message specifies the sender, receiver, and its parameters. *Adornments* such as $\ulcorner in \urcorner$, $\ulcorner out \urcorner$, $\ulcorner nil \urcorner$ on parameters provide causal structure to the protocol. *Key* parameters identify enactments. Together, they constrain when messages may be sent.

The adornment ⌜out⌝ for a parameter means in any enactment, the sender of the message can generate a binding (supply a value) for the parameter if it does already know it; ⌜in⌝ means that the parameter binding must already be known to the sender from some message in the enactment that it has already observed; ⌜nil⌝ means that the sender must neither already know nor generate a binding for the parameter. Each tuple of bindings for the public parameters corresponds to a complete enactment of the protocol. Thus, one can think of a protocol as notionally computing tuples of bindings via messaging between the roles.

Listing 1 is an example of an information protocol between a buyer, a seller, and a shipper for the purchase of an item.

Listing 1. The *Purchase* protocol [24].

```
Purchase {
   roles Buyer, Seller, Shipper
   parameters out ID key, out item, out price, out outcome
   private address, resp, shipped

   Buyer -> Seller: rfq[out ID, out item]
   Seller -> Buyer: quote[in ID, in item, out price]

   Buyer -> Seller: accept[in ID, in item, in price, out
      address, out resp]
   Buyer -> Seller: reject[in ID, in item, in price, out
      outcome, out resp]

   Seller -> Shipper: ship[in ID, in item, in address, out
      shipped]
   Shipper -> Buyer: deliver[in ID, in item, in address, out
      outcome]
}
```

Let's unpack how the protocol works. The name of the protocol is *Purchase* and BUYER and SELLER are its roles. The parameters line specifies the tuple computed by a complete enactment of *Purchase*; parameterID is annotated *key*, meaning that it identifies tuples and the other parameters in the tuple are item, price, and outcome. These parameters are *public* and may be used toward composition with other protocols. A protocol may also have *private* parameters; here, address, resp, and shipped.

Every message has a sender, a receiver, a name, and a schema. The sequence in which these messages are written is unimportant. Causality is explicitly specified via parameter adornments. Specifically, to send a message instance of a particular schema, the bindings of its ⌜in⌝ parameters must already be known; the bindings of its ⌜out⌝ parameters must be generated in sending the instance and become known thereafter; and the bindings of its ⌜nil⌝ parameters must neither be known nor generated in the sending the instance. This means that in *Purchase*, BUYER can send an *rfq* at any point since all its parameter are adorned with ⌜out⌝. Once a *Seller* has received an *rfq*, it can send the corresponding *quote* since it knows the ID and item and it can generate price. And so on.

Messages can be made mutually exclusive (thus supporting choice within protocols) by adorning the same parameter as ⌜out⌝ in the messages. In the listing, the messages *accept* and *reject* both have resp adorned with ⌜out⌝. If BUYER sends *accept*, it would have generated a binding for resp, which would mean that the sending of or *reject* would be disabled hence; and vice versa.

If *reject* is sent, the parameter address is never bound, and in effect, the messages *ship* and *deliver* will never be enabled. The enactment will be deemed as completed as all the needed parameters would be bound.

2.2   Kiko

Kiko is an information protocol-based programming model for agents. In other words, Kiko provides programming abstractions for implementing agents based on protocols.

Kiko takes to heart the idea that in a multiagent system, an agent's communications to others represent its decisions (it is in this sense that in multiagent systems, you have decentralized decision making). An agent is envisaged as running a loop in which upon the occurrence of certain events, it executes some business logic that may result in the making of new decisions, that is, the sending of messages to others.

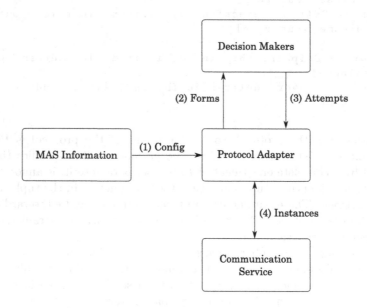

Fig. 1. The Kiko agent architecture [11].

To write an agent (Fig. 1), an agent's programmer configures the agent with the multiagent systems it is playing roles in (based on protocols). In particular, it is configured with the identities of the other agents also playing roles in those multiagent systems and how to reach them over the network. Listing 2 shows an example of how configuration can be set up for MAS based on the protocol in Listing 1. We define one multiagent system named SysName0 with one agent for each role in the protocol. *Bob* is a BUYER, *Sally* is a SELLER and *Sheldon* is a SHIPPER.

Listing 2. A configuration of a multiagent systems using Kiko.

```
systems = {
    "SysName0": {
        "protocol": Purchase,
        "roles": {
            Buyer: "Bob",
            Seller: "Sally",
            Shipper: "Sheldon"
        }
    }
}
agents = {
    "Bob": [("192.168.0.1", 1111)],
    "Sally": [("192.168.0.2", 1111)],
    "Sheldon": [("192.168.0.3", 1111)]
}
```

Kiko's main abstraction is that of a *decision maker*. The programmer also writes a set of decision makers. A decision maker is a procedure written by the agent programmer that captures business logic. It is invoked upon the occurrence of a specified trigger event; it is supplied with the *enabled* (possible) decisions given the agent's communication history; and its body contains the logic to make some decisions (possibly none) from among the possible decisions. The possible decisions are known as *forms* and are supplied by the agent's protocol *adapter*, which keeps track of protocol enactments based on the messages the agent has observed. The name 'form' captures the idea that enabled decisions have their ⌜in⌝ parameters already filled in but the ⌜out⌝ parameters are yet to be bound, which is the job of the logic in the body. The fleshed-out forms are the message instances and are emitted on the wire by the adapter when the procedure returns. Message receptions are performed by the adapter transparently from the business logic. Kiko empowers programmers by enabling them to focus on business logic.

Listing 3 shows a decision maker for BUYER Bob. Its trigger is InitEvent, which represents the start of the agent. Thus, when the agent starts, this decision maker will be invoked by the adapter. The decision *rfq* is accessible as a form via the enabled argument. *Bob* is interested in a watch and so bind item in *rfq* to watch. The corresponding message instance is sent by the adapter to Sally (based on configuration) when the procedure returns.

Listing 3. Bob sending the *RFQ* message to Sally.

```
@adapter.decision(event=InitEvent)
def start(enabled):
    ID = str(uuid.uuid4())
    item = "watch"
    for m in enabled.messages(RFQ):
        m.bind(ID=ID, item=item)
```

Let's say that Sally has replied with a *quote* message providing the value of price. Now, Bob has to decide whether to *accept* or *reject* the quote. Listing 4 explains how an agent makes a decision.

Listing 4. Bob deciding whether to accept or reject a quote.

```
@adapter.decision
def decide(enabled):
    for m in enabled.messages(Buy):
        if m["price"] < 20:
            m.bind(address="1600 Pennsylvania Avenue NW",
                resp=True)
        else:
            reject = next(enabled.messages(Reject,
                ID=m["ID"]))
            reject.bind(outcome=True, resp=True)
```

The developer is in control of what is to be done at each junction of making a decision. Kiko provides this control through the use of sets of enabled messages. If an agent attempts to send both *accept* and *reject*, the messages would fail emission as the instances being sent are inconsistent with each other.

Because of our foundation in protocols (and roles), each agent may be implemented by a different programmer, thus highlighting Kiko's support for loose coupling. The steps below summarize the steps an agent programmer follows.

1. Define the configuration of the desired multiagent system (in Python).
2. Create an instance of an Adapter for each role using the class provided by Kiko (in Python).
3. Specify decision makers based on the information protocol using the previously written instance of an adapter (in Python). This specification of the decision makers ends up as an agent.
4. Start the agent (in Python).

The following details the services and API of the protocol adapter, a generic component of the programming model.

1. The protocol adapter is initiated within every agent, with the current agent's name, the configuration of the systems as well as the configuration of the other agents.
2. Depending on the protocol and the currently available information, certain decision makers are invoked by the protocol adapter. The protocol adapter provides forms, which are message instances with unbound parameters the decision maker can fill out.

3. These filled-out message instances are processed by the protocol adapter as attempts. The protocol adapter then checks the attempts for inconsistencies. In case of no inconsistencies, the message instances are successfully emitted; otherwise, they are dropped.
4. The protocol adapter relies on the communication service for transporting messages between agents. The default communication service is UDP, which is sufficient for enacting the information protocols. The adapter receives messages from other agents.

2.3 Dapr

Dapr is an event-driven runtime that promises resilient, stateless, and stateful microservices that interoperate. Dapr provides building blocks called *components*. Some popular types of components are:

- State Store: These components can be used as a database that is accessible to any Dapr application.
- PubSub Brokers: These components provide a system that supports the publishing of messages to a topic. Applications can then subscribe to these topics and receive published messages.
- Bindings & Triggers: These components enable Dapr applications to communicate to external services without integration of respective SDKs.

Dapr also provides a new type of component called *Pluggable components*. These components are not bundled as part of the Dapr runtime and run independently of it. The primary advantage of using a pluggable component is that it can be written in any language that supports gRPC.

3 Traffic Control Application

Traffic Control [32] is a sample application that emulates a traffic control system using Dapr. Figure 2 describes the application using a UML sequence diagram. It is inspired by the speeding-camera setup present on some Dutch highways. An entry camera is installed at the start of a highway and an exit camera is installed at a certain distance from the entry camera to capture vehicle license information. If a vehicle is going faster than the speed limit, the driver of the vehicle can be fined.

The time difference between an entry camera capturing a vehicle and an exit camera capturing the same vehicle will calculate the speed of the vehicle. Based on the speed of the vehicle, there is a decision to be made about whether the driver should be fined for driving over the speed limit.

3.1 Using Dapr

To develop this system in Dapr, four applications were created:

- Camera Simulation: A .NET Core console application that simulates passing cars.

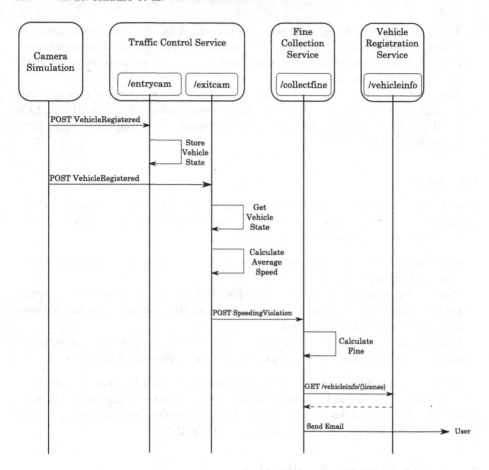

Fig. 2. A UML sequence diagram for the traffic control sample application.

- Traffic Control Service: A ASP.NET Core WebAPI application that defines two endpoints /entrycam and /exitcam
- Fine Collection Service: Another ASP.NET Core WebAPI application with only one endpoint /collectfine for collecting fines,
- Vehicle Registration Service: An ASP.NET Core WebAPI application with only one endpoint /vehicleinfo/{license-number}, which links a vehicle to its owner.

A rundown of how this system operates follows:

1. Camera Simulation generates a random license number and sends a *VehicleRegistered* message (which contains the license number, the lane number, and the timestamp) to the /entrycam endpoint of Traffic Control Service.
2. The Traffic Control Service then stores the details in a database.
3. After a random interval of time, the Camera Simulation sends another *VehicleRegistered* message, but this time to the /exitcam endpoint of Traffic Control Service.

4. The Traffic Control Service then fetches the previously stored details and calculates the average speed of the vehicle.
5. If the average speed of the vehicle is greater than the speed limit, the Traffic Control Service sends the details of the incident to the endpoint /collectfine Fine Collection Service, where the fine is calculated.
6. The Fine Collection Service retrieves the email of the vehicle's owner by sending the details of the vehicle to the endpoint /vehicleinfo/ {license-number} of the Vehicle Registration Service and sends the fine to the owner via email.

To enable the developer to focus on the business logic, Dapr provides components that are generic such as a database for storing the vehicle's information, providing an endpoint that can connect to an SMTP server that sends an email, and an asynchronous messaging queue that exchanges messages between the services.

Listing 5 shows how the /exitcam endpoint of the Traffic Control application deals with sending the fine. In particular, the endpoint is responsible for sending a NotFound() in case a vehicle that is not in the _vehicleStateRepository is detected by the exit camera.

Listing 5. The traffic control application's /exitcam endpoint.

```
1   [HttpPost("exitcam")]
2   public async Task < ActionResult >
        VehicleExitAsync(VehicleRegistered msg, [FromServices]
        DaprClient daprClient) {
3     try {
4       // get vehicle state
5       var state = await _vehicleStateRepository
6           .GetVehicleStateAsync(msg.LicenseNumber);
7       if (state ==
8         default (VehicleState)) {
9         return NotFound();
10      }
11
12      // update state
13      var exitState = state.Value with {
14        ExitTimestamp = msg.Timestamp
15      };
16      await _vehicleStateRepository
17          .SaveVehicleStateAsync(exitState);
18
19      // handle possible speeding violation
20      int violation = _speedingViolationCalculator
21          .DetermineSpeedingViolationInKmh(
22              exitState.EntryTimestamp,
23              exitState.ExitTimestamp.Value
24          );
25
26      if (violation > 0) {
```

```
27          var speedingViolation = new SpeedingViolation {
28            VehicleId = msg.LicenseNumber,
29            RoadId = _roadId,
30            ViolationInKmh = violation,
31            Timestamp = msg.Timestamp
32          };
33
34          // publish speedingviolation (Dapr pubsub)
35          await daprClient.PublishEventAsync("pubsub",
                 "speedingviolations", speedingViolation);
36        }
37
38        return Ok();
39      } catch (Exception ex) {
40        return StatusCode(500);
41      }
42    }
```

3.2　Using Kiko

To implement the Traffic Control system in Kiko, we initially need to create a protocol that can accommodate all of our requirements. Listing 6 shows an example of a protocol that would enable us to fulfill the requirements and is supported by the tooling.

Listing 6. The *TrafficControl* protocol.

```
TrafficControl {
    roles EntryCam, ExitCam, FineCollector, VehicleMngr
    parameters out regID key, out entryTS, out exitTS, out
        email
    private amount, avgSpeed, query

    EntryCam -> ExitCam: Entered[out regID, out entryTS]
    ExitCam -> FineCollector: Fine[in regID, in entryTS,
        out exitTS, out avgSpeed]
    FineCollector -> VehicleMngr: Query[in regID, in
        entryTS, in avgSpeed, out query]
    VehicleMngr -> FineCollector: Result[in regID, in
        entryTS, out email]
}
```

Let's unpack how this protocol works. The roles involved would be ENTRYCAM, EXITCAM, FINECOLLECTOR, VEHICLEMNGR. The parameters necessary for the completion of an enactment are regID which stands for registration ID, entryTS which stands for entry timestamp, exitTS which stands for exit timestamp, and outcome. Private parameters that may or may not be bound are amount, avgSpeed which stands for average speed, and query.

The first message that will be sent out is *Entered*. This denotes the ENTRYCAM alerting the EXITCAM that a vehicle has entered the highway. The next message that will be sent out is *Fine*. This is where the decision maker defined by the developer will come into play. Listing 7 shows one such implementation of the decision maker. The code is written in Python by the developer and uses the Kiko library [7]. Constants in uppercase are part of the configuration. Currently, the entry camera is simulated by a trigger event that is invoked at random times. The exit cam is simulated by adding a random amount of time to a known entry timestamp. This could easily be replaced with a blocking call to the method that would wait to observe a vehicle and continue in case the vehicle matches the registration. An observation that could be made is that it is unnecessary to explicitly store the exit timestamp as every observation is stored in the local store.

Listing 7. A decision maker for the exit camera.

```
@adapter.decision(event=VehicleExit)
async def check_vehicle_speed(enabled, event):
    for m in enabled:
        if m.schema is Fine and m["regID"] == event.regID:
            avgSpeed = DISTANCE / (event.ts - m["entryTS"])
            if avgSpeed > SPEED_LIMIT:
                m.bind(exitTS=event.ts, avgSpeed=avgSpeed)
                return m
```

We create a single decision maker for deciding whether *Fine* message should be sent next. If the Fine Collector receives the message *Fine*, it then retrieves the details of the owner of the vehicle from the Vehicle Manager and sends the email detailing the fine. The code for this implementation can be found on https://gitlab.com/masr/kiko-traffic-control. Figure 3 shows the UML sequence diagram for our implementation using Kiko.

Internal computations are omitted from the UML diagram. For example, the average speed is calculated by Exit Cam, hence a message like Exit is not explicit in the protocol.

4 Evaluation

We evaluate the implementation based on the differences in the Kiko and Dapr implementations of the scenario.

4.1 Protocol Specifications

Protocols are at the heart of both implementations. The Kiko implementation relies on the formal specification of the protocol. The protocol can be verified statically for properties such as safety and liveness. Further, an adapter takes the protocol as input (serving as a runtime) and enables implementing the agent based on the protocol. In the Dapr-based implementation, the protocol is specified only informally using UML interaction diagrams. They afford neither verification nor a protocol-based programming model.

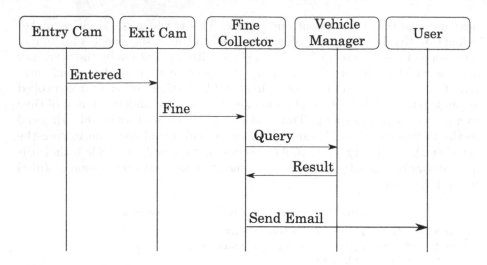

Fig. 3. A UML sequence diagram for our traffic control sample application written using Kiko.

4.2   Typing and Structuring of Agent Implementations

In Kiko, the information protocol already captures crucial domain aspects related to the interaction, such as the entry and exit identifiers, registration identifiers, and so on. These domain-related aspects are not modeled or are captured only in low-level data structures in the Dapr implementation (line 6 in Listing 5). Kiko can enforce integrity checking based on identifiers that are annotated as key. In Dapr, the agent developer has to write such integrity-checking code.

Kiko shines in structuring the agent implementation and focusing the developer on writing the business logic, with fewer possibilities for errors in decision making. Its notion of forms is particularly helpful as it provides decisions (messages) that have known information already filled in and points the developers to writing code that generates the missing information. By contrast, Dapr developers must construct entire messages by hand (line 27 in Listing 5), which introduces possibilities for errors.

The Dapr implementation contains code for getting and updating the state (Lines 5–17) that doesn't appear in the Kiko implementation because the adapter automatically maintains the state. Further, the Dapr implementation contains code for the 'error' of exit being recorded but there is no record of entry (Lines 7–9). Such error handling doesn't appear in the Kiko decision maker in Listing 7: if the exit camera doesn't hasn't received the message denoting entry, then the corresponding *Fine* form will not appear in the set of forms supplied by the adapter. Whether exits correlate with entries is something worth keeping track of as missing entries or exits may indicate problems with the cameras; however, such code need not have to be in the exit camera.

Dapr's implementation relies on the developers being responsible for integrating the endpoints. It is possible that an external agent tries to send an invalid request to an endpoint. Kiko's implementation on the other hand only relies on **agents conforming to the protocol**. Even if an external agent attempts to push a message to the agent, if the history does not match with the message, it will be ignored by Kiko.

4.3   Decentralization and Loose Coupling

Although microservices aspire to decentralization, the Dapr implementation actually relies on a shared state between the entry and exit camera endpoints. Specifically, the entry camera endpoint stores information about the entry in a shared store which is then retrieved by the exit camera endpoint to update it with the exit information and to calculate the average speed (Lines 3–15). By contrast, there is no shared state between Kiko agents. The only way for Kiko agents to share information is to transfer their local state via messaging.

Being able to independently implement and maintain endpoints is evidence of loose coupling. Since the Dapr implementation is not based on a high-level system model (the information protocol) and to interoperate the endpoint developers would have to share code, loose coupling is better supported by Kiko than by Dapr.

For asynchronous communication between microservices, the Dapr implementation relies on publish-subscribe communication via message queues. The Kiko implementation by contrast uses UDP (a lossy, unordered communication service) as the underlying communication service highlighting the fact that ordered message delivery is unnecessary. Other information protocol-based works [10] have shown how agents can deal with message loss.

5   Discussion

Based on this evaluation, we can conclude that the Kiko implementation provides a better developer experience and is better suited to decentralization and loose coupling.

Since the Kiko implementation of the traffic control application does not rely on message ordering for processing, it is possible that the exit camera agent records `VehicleExit` occurs prior to the reception of the *Entered* message. In this case, as the *Fine* message would not be enabled and therefore there is no possibility of a fine being issued. This may not be the desired effect but can be remedied by writing a decision maker that iterates over enabled messages on the reception of the *Entered* message.

Using the microservice architecture also requires a fair amount of knowledge dealing with deploying different services. A dedicated DevOps team was found to be necessary for software that followed microservice architecture [28]. With only about 10% of respondents claiming to be a DevOps specialist in the 2022 Developer Survey [27] by Stack Overflow, developers end up being the ones deploying the applications. Using Dapr, this job becomes easier to deal with when using applications written in different languages.

We posit that the conceptual integration between MAS and web architecture would facilitate the construction of multiagent systems that are widely distributed and inherit architectural properties such as scalability and evolvability [13]. The integration of Kiko with Dapr would enable the users to build a MAS that has the benefits of microservice architecture such as scalability but also the benefits of observability and secret management. Further, this conceptual integration can also lead to the resulting system being close to a Hypermedia MAS [12].

Multiagent systems need to provide an account of what happened during an abnormal situation [4,6]. Kiko would provide the protocol as a blueprint while Dapr would provide robust tooling for the observation of intercommunication of the microservices.

Microservices of the future should look at a move towards asynchronous communication [18] and this idea is supported in information protocols through their causal nature and their ability to operate on lossy, unordered protocols such as UDP. A not surprising lesson learned in an exploratory study of promises and challenges in microservices [31] was that changes that break the API should be discouraged. The use of information protocols enables the developers to version interactions between the microservices. Since the protocol file defines all valid interactions between microservices, it also defines implemented interactions between microservices of a release ready for the production environment. Timeouts within a microservice system is a problem that is remedied by using a circuit breaker [30] but has the tradeoff of requiring an update on all microservices. With the use of information protocols, we move away from synchronous communication and remove the need for timeouts and consequently circuit breakers.

5.1   Future Work

To fully obtain the benefits of Kiko under Dapr, the ideal solution would be to build a Pub/Sub–based pluggable component in Python, that uses Kiko to work on the messages. The queues that would be created as part of the Pub/Sub communication between applications, must have their messages assessed through Kiko. This way we would emulate Kiko's protocol adapter within this pluggable component and send forms to be filled out as attempts by the applications. Since Kiko can act as a verification agent, it would enable runtime verification of the developed MAS similar to existing solutions for other MASs [5]. Verification at design time [3] would also be possible as endpoints within Dapr applications are registered and known to Dapr prior to any communication between applications.

Currently, Kiko can invoke methods on the reception of a particular message or event or the enablement of a particular message. We cannot invoke a method only if multiple events are received or multiple messages are received. A future iteration could support how decision makers may be invoked when a specified set of events (i.e., messages) are received.

In cases where enactments are not fulfilled, the messages stay in the local store forever. These dangling enactments would eventually prevent storing new enactments. An automated job that gets rid of these enactments can be added to be run after a fixed time interval. As all enactments are linked via the key parameters, it is easy to identify what messages must be discarded.

Acknowledgments. We thank the EMAS 2023 reviewers and audience for their helpful comments. We acknowledge support from the UK EPSRC (grant EP/N027965/1) and the US NSF (grant IIS-1908374).

References

1. Ao, S.: How Alibaba is using Dapr. https://blog.dapr.io/posts/2021/03/19/how-alibaba-is-using-dapr/. Accessed 19 Feb 2023
2. Baldoni, M., Baroglio, C., Chopra, A.K., Desai, N., Patti, V., Singh, M.P.: Choice, interoperability, and conformance in interaction protocols and service choreographies. In: Proceedings of the 8th International Conference on Autonomous Agents and MultiAgent Systems (AAMAS), pp. 843–850. IFAAMAS, Budapest (2009). https://doi.org/10.5555/1558109.1558129
3. Baldoni, M., Baroglio, C., Martelli, A., Patti, V.: A priori conformance verification for guaranteeing interoperability in open environments. In: Dan, A., Lamersdorf, W. (eds.) ICSOC 2006. LNCS, vol. 4294, pp. 339–351. Springer, Heidelberg (2006). https://doi.org/10.1007/11948148_28
4. Baldoni, M., Baroglio, C., Micalizio, R., Tedeschi, S.: Accountability in multi-agent organizations: from conceptual design to agent programming. J. Auton. Agents Multi-Agent Syst. (JAAMAS) **37**(1), 7 (2023). https://doi.org/10.1007/s10458-022-09590-6
5. Briola, D., Mascardi, V., Ancona, D.: Distributed runtime verification of JADE multiagent systems. In: Camacho, D., Braubach, L., Venticinque, S., Badica, C. (eds.) Intelligent Distributed Computing VIII. Studies in Computational Intelligence, pp. 81–91. Springer, Cham (2015). https://doi.org/10.1007/978-3-319-10422-5_10
6. Chopra, A.K., Singh, M.P.: Accountability as a foundation for requirements in sociotechnical systems. IEEE Internet Comput. (IC) **25**(6), 33–41 (2021). https://doi.org/10.1109/MIC.2021.3106835
7. Christie, S.: Kiko. https://gitlab.com/masr/bspl/-/tree/kiko/. Accessed 15 Feb 2023
8. Christie, S.H.V., Chopra, A.K., Singh, M.P.: Bungie: improving fault tolerance via extensible application-level protocols. IEEE Comput. **54**(5), 44–53 (2021). https://doi.org/10.1109/MC.2021.3052147
9. Christie, S.H.V., Chopra, A.K., Singh, M.P.: Deserv: decentralized serverless computing. In: Proceedings of the 19th IEEE International Conference on Web Services (ICWS), pp. 51–60. IEEE Computer Society, Virtual (2021). https://doi.org/10.1109/ICWS53863.2021.00020
10. Christie, S.H.V., Chopra, A.K., Singh, M.P.: Mandrake: multiagent systems as a basis for programming fault-tolerant decentralized applications. J. Auton. Agents Multi-Agent Syst. (JAAMAS) **36**(1), 16:1–16:30 (2022). https://doi.org/10.1007/s10458-021-09540-8

11. Christie, S.H.V., Singh, M.P., Chopra, A.K.: Kiko: programming agents to enact interaction protocols. In: Proceedings of the 22nd International Conference on Autonomous Agents and MultiAgent Systems (AAMAS), pp. 1–10. IFAAMAS, London (2023)

12. Ciortea, A., Boissier, O., Ricci, A.: Engineering world-wide multi-agent systems with hypermedia. In: Weyns, D., Mascardi, V., Ricci, A. (eds.) EMAS. LNCS, pp. 285–301. Springer, Cham (2019). https://doi.org/10.1007/978-3-030-25693-7_15

13. Ciortea, A., Mayer, S., Gandon, F., Boissier, O., Ricci, A., Zimmermann, A.: A decade in hindsight: the missing bridge between multi-agent systems and the world wide web. In: Proceedings of the 18th International Conference on Autonomous Agents and MultiAgent Systems, pp. 1659–1663. AAMAS 2019, International Foundation for Autonomous Agents and Multiagent Systems, Richland, SC (2019)

14. Dapr: Dapr - Distributed Application Runtime (2019). https://dapr.io/. Accessed 14 Feb 2023

15. Desai, N., Mallya, A.U., Chopra, A.K., Singh, M.P.: Interaction protocols as design abstractions for business processes. IEEE Trans. Software Eng. 31(12), 1015–1027 (2005). https://doi.org/10.1109/TSE.2005.140

16. Desai, N., Mallya, A.U., Chopra, A.K., Singh, M.P.: OWL-P: a methodology for business process development. In: Kolp, M., Bresciani, P., Henderson-Sellers, B., Winikoff, M. (eds.) AOIS -2005. LNCS (LNAI), vol. 3529, pp. 79–94. Springer, Heidelberg (2006). https://doi.org/10.1007/11916291_6

17. Ferrando, A., Winikoff, M., Cranefield, S., Dignum, F., Mascardi, V.: On enactability of agent interaction protocols: towards a unified approach. In: Dennis, L.A., Bordini, R.H., Lespérance, Y. (eds.) EMAS 2019. LNCS (LNAI), vol. 12058, pp. 43–64. Springer, Cham (2020). https://doi.org/10.1007/978-3-030-51417-4_3

18. Jamshidi, P., Pahl, C., Mendonça, N.C., Lewis, J., Tilkov, S.: Microservices: the journey so far and challenges ahead. IEEE Softw. 35(3), 24–35 (2018). https://doi.org/10.1109/MS.2018.2141039

19. Microsoft: Bosch builds smart homes using Dapr and Azure. https://customers.microsoft.com/en-us/story/1435725395247777374-bosch-builds-smart-homes-using-dapr-azure. Accessed 19 Feb 2023

20. PwC: Cloud business survey. https://www.pwc.com/us/en/tech-effect/cloud/cloud-business-survey.html. Accessed 14 Feb 2023

21. Richardson, C.: Monolithic architecture pattern. https://microservices.io/patterns/monolithic.html. Accessed 8 Feb 2023

22. Singh, M.P.: Synthesizing distributed constrained events from transactional workflow specifications. In: Proceedings of the 12th International Conference on Data Engineering (ICDE), pp. 616–623. IEEE, New Orleans (1996). https://doi.org/10.1109/ICDE.1996.492212

23. Singh, M.P.: Distributed enactment of multiagent workflows: temporal logic for web service composition. In: Proceedings of the 2nd International Joint Conference on Autonomous Agents and MultiAgent Systems (AAMAS), pp. 907–914. ACM Press, Melbourne (2003). https://doi.org/10.1145/860575.860721

24. Singh, M.P.: Information-driven interaction-oriented programming: BSPL, the blindingly simple protocol language. In: Proceedings of the 10th International Conference on Autonomous Agents and MultiAgent Systems (AAMAS), pp. 491–498. IFAAMAS, Taipei (2011). https://doi.org/10.5555/2031678.2031687

25. Singh, M.P.: LoST: local state transfer–an architectural style for the distributed enactment of business protocols. In: Proceedings of the 9th IEEE International Conference on Web Services (ICWS), pp. 57–64. IEEE Computer Society, Washington, DC (2011). https://doi.org/10.1109/ICWS.2011.48

26. Singh, M.P., Chopra, A.K., Desai, N.: Commitment-based service-oriented architecture. IEEE Comput. **42**(11), 72–79 (2009). https://doi.org/10.1109/MC.2009.347
27. Stack Overflow: Stack Overflow 2022 Developer Survey. https://survey.stackoverflow.co/2022/. Accessed 14 Feb 2023
28. Taibi, D., Lenarduzzi, V., Pahl, C.: Continuous architecting with microservices and DevOps: a systematic mapping study. In: Muñoz, V.M., Ferguson, D., Helfert, M., Pahl, C. (eds.) CLOSER 2018. CCIS, vol. 1073, pp. 126–151. Springer, Cham (2019). https://doi.org/10.1007/978-3-030-29193-8_7
29. Thönes, J.: Microservices. IEEE Softw. **32**(1), 116–116 (2015). https://doi.org/10.1109/MS.2015.11
30. Tighilt, R., et al.: On the study of microservices antipatterns: a catalog proposal. In: Proceedings of the European Conference on Pattern Languages of Programs 2020. EuroPLoP 2020, Association for Computing Machinery, New York, NY, USA (2020). https://doi.org/10.1145/3424771.3424812
31. Wang, Y., Kadiyala, H., Rubin, J.: Promises and challenges of microservices: an exploratory study. Empir. Softw. Eng. **26**(4), 1–44 (2021). https://doi.org/10.1007/s10664-020-09910-y
32. van Wijk, E., Molenkamp, S., Hompus, M., Kordowski, A.: Dapr traffic control sample. https://github.com/EdwinVW/dapr-traffic-control. Accessed 15 Feb 2023
33. Winikoff, M., Yadav, N., Padgham, L.: A new hierarchical agent protocol notation. Auton. Agent. Multi-Agent Syst. **32**(1), 59–133 (2017). https://doi.org/10.1007/s10458-017-9373-9

Exploiting Service-Discovery and OpenAPI in Multi-Agent MicroServices (MAMS) Applications

Eoin O'Neill[(✉)] and Rem W. Collier

University College Dublin, Dublin 4, Ireland
`eoin.o-neill.3@ucdconnect.ie`, `rem.collier@ucd.ie`

Abstract. One of the key benefits of the MAMS [13,14,19] architecture is to allow agents to make use of the software engineering community's industry standard technology while being deployed in a microservices architecture. This paper is going to showcase a tool that allows MAMS agents to utilise an industry standard discovery tool to interact with a microservice based on the OpenAPI Specification document that describes the service. This interaction will be based on the "shape" of the service which is identified by the accepted HTTP verbs at the various endpoints. This tool also identifies the pitfalls associated with the current industry standard with regard to service descriptions and how they could be improved through the introduction of Linked Data and use of specifications such as *Hydra* and *Hypermedia Controls Ontology* (HCTL) to make a push from **machine-readable** towards **machine-understandable**.

Keywords: Multi-Agent MicroServices (MAMS) · OpenAPI · Hydra · Hypermedia Controls · Signifiers · ThingDescriptions

1 Introduction

One of the key concepts in a microservice (MS) architecture, is the notion of *bounded context*. This states that each MS, following the Domain Driven Design [5,7] principle, is to provide a singular 'business' functionality. With the shift in software engineering from monolithic software structures towards service-oriented architectures, the integration of microservices is a key issue. The standard specification for describing an API is currently the OpenAPI specification (OAS)[1]. These descriptions, although defined as being "machine-readable" are available in formats that provide no context. The documents themselves are geared towards the consumer having a level of tacit knowledge with regards to integrating the services and the protocols and domain knowledge associated with doing so. The main goal of this research is to allow agents to situate themselves in a microservices ecosystem, and through the use of a service-discovery tool,

---

[1] OpenAPI Specification.

© The Author(s), under exclusive license to Springer Nature Switzerland AG 2023
A. Ciortea et al. (Eds.): EMAS 2023, LNAI 14378, pp. 78–84, 2023.
https://doi.org/10.1007/978-3-031-48539-8_5

each service can make itself known on the network, describe itself to possible consumers of the service and provide a description so that any and all consumers can learn how to interact with this service solely based on it's description.

We have built a tool that allows agents deployed in a MS context to consume the OAS document of a service registered with an industry standard service-discovery tool in order to facilitate interaction between software agents and a service in a more generalised form in order to conform to the *loose-coupling* principle of a microservice architecture. Through the use of this tool, we can see that from an agent perspective, this standard is not fit for purpose as it does not provide enough context with regards to the interaction which led to the implementation of vocabularies such as Hydra [11] and Hypermedia Controls Ontology (HCTL)[2]. The paper is laid out as follows, Sect. 2 will discuss the related work in this area and why this work is relevant. Section 3 will discuss the implementation of our tool, followed by our conclusion.

2 Related Work

Roy Fielding stated in [2] *"RESTful applications are, at all times, encouraged to use human-meaningful, hierarchical identifiers, in order to maximise the serendipitous use of the information beyond what is anticipated by the original application."* If we provide semantically enriched, "machine-understandable" descriptions of services and imbue agents with the ability to integrate them how they deem fit, then we can also'maximise the serendipitous use of' the applications themselves. We present work that has been done on extending service descriptions in order to facilitate interaction and ease of integration. The research presented by Yang et al. in [20] presents a tool called D2Spec that iterates through a Web API specification and determines the number of characteristics that the specification includes. These characteristics include the Base IRI of the Application, the HTTP methods used within the application and also generates path templates to be utilised. Guo et al. [8] have established a service called *APIphany* which tries to achieve type directed program synthesis by semantically describing the types required and returned by APIs. They manage to achieve this by means of two methods; firstly, they create *witnesses* from the OAS document of the API and run a test suite in a sandbox environment and secondly, they observe live API traffic. From here, they rank the APIs suitability to that of the user's needs.

In [3], Ciortea et al. present research that proposes agents creating a mashup of services and devices as a result of their goal-driven behaviour. Agents are initialised with pre-compiled mashups and cooperate at runtime in order to achieve their goals. This work showcases a similar goal of enabling agents with enough information at runtime to achieve their goals, but in an IoT context. The research presented in [16] presents a system that parses an OAS document, generates an OWL-S ontology for each service that is present in the OAS document. This research shows the necessity for such translations and the need for a

---

[2] https://www.w3.org/2019/wot/hypermedia.

parallel standard to exist in order to establish *machine-understandability*. Furthermore, the work presented in [12] showcases a system that consumes OAS documents, stores them in a relational database and uses RDRML in order to convert the relational database entries into RDF format in order to be stored in a knowledge graph. The work detailed in [9] shows an attempt to bridge the gap between Linked Data and REST-based architectures, using the OAS document as the medium. Furthermore, Espinoza et al. [4] have implemented a system that translates from the Web Ontology Language (OWL) into OAS document (OAS document) documents in order to facilitate ease of use between web developers and users of the semantic web. These works show the level of importance being placed on introducing Linked Data concepts to API descriptions.

As mentioned by Bogner et. al in their paper entitled "Industry practices and challenges for the evolvability assurance of microservices", one of the biggest challenges with regards to building Microservices architectures and assuring their sustainability is *Microservices Integration*, according to industry practitioners. This is where we see an opportunity for agents that are able to consume service description documents, such as the OAS document, and interact with resources in an ad-hoc manner to act as a bridge between services in order to enhance loose-coupling and evolvability of individual services.

3   Demonstrating the Approach

In order to allow an agent to reason about a given service, it is essential that it first be able to develop a logical depiction of that service. The shape of a resource is created based on the IRI of each of the APIs endpoints and the HTTP verbs accepted at each of these endpoints, as described in the associated OAS document. The ``paths`` section of the OAS document provides this information, an example of which is displayed below:

```
{"paths":
 {"/game":
  {"get":
   {"tags":["Gameplay"],
    "summary":"Get the current number which
    represents the state of the game.",
    "description":"Returns a number to
    the user to guess higher or lower than.",
    "operationId":"getGameplayUsingGET",
    "responses":
     { "200":
           {"description":"OK","content":
           {"application/json":
           {"schema":
           {"$ref":"#/components/schemas/Status"}}}},
        "401":{"description":"Unauthorized"},
```

```
        "403":{"description":"Forbidden"},
        "404":{"description":"Not Found"}}}}
    }
}
```

The logical model is generated by parsing the associated OAS document for each application, should it be present. It takes the form of a series of beliefs based on the following formats:

```
    hasGET(<string>, <string>);
    hasPOST(<string>, <string>);
    hasPUT(<string>, <string>);
    hasPATCH(<string>, <string>);
    hasDELETE(<string>, <string>);
    hasNoOpenAPIDescription(<string>);
    hasOpenAPIDescription(<string>);
```

The last two belief formats are used to clarify whether or not the service has an OAS document. If it has one, then the `hasXXX(...)` beliefs are used to describe the service's endpoints. For these beliefs, the first 'string' parameter is the service's unique identifier and the second 'string' parameter is composed of the base IRI of the application, followed by the endpoint which is being described. This allows the agent to believe that the endpoint identified by a given IRI will accept a GET request.

In the context of the Web of Things, the 'shape' of a resource is described by the ThingDescription (TD) [1], which has attributes such as 'readProperty' and 'writeProperty', and is utilized widely in the Web of Things as an enabler of interoperability [10]. An OAS document can also be seen as being quite similar to the Web of Things TD. Tzavaras et. al, in [17] showcase a comparison of both OpenAPI and ThingDescriptions based on their capacity to describe Things, stating that there is a great deal of crossover between the two. Both OAS and TD give high-level static descriptions of the underlying APIs, where as Signifiers, as defined in [18] as first class abstractions in a hypermedia environment provide a more suitable solution for providing hypermedia descriptions as they can provide contextual hypermedia based on the state of the resource (see the HATEOAS principle as defined in [6]), but also the capabilities of the agent in question. This work was a move towards internalising work similar to Signifiers within the agent based on OAS documents in a Microservices environment in an attempt to bridge the gap between the current industry standard and the hypermedia rich environment we are striving for.

3.1   Experimental Setup

As a means of evaluating this approach, we propose a game of High/Low. This game will operate with the agent requesting a number and guessing whether the next number will be higher or lower than the received number. In order to achieve this we needed to not only facilitate interaction between software agents and microservices, but we also wanted to conform to the current standards of software engineering, as well as utilising components designed for and used by the microservices community. The goal of this experiment is to get an autonomous agent to participate in a game of *high-low* by identifying the correct microservice and interacting with that resource based on its **shape** that is identified by parsing the OAS documents of each service.

We created three applications and registered them with a service-discovery tool as *Application 1*, *Application 2* and *Application 3*. The purpose of this naming convention is to enforce the anonymity of the service that we are trying to allow the agent to discover and utilize. A layout of the system can be found in Fig. 1. One of these applications is an implementation of a very simple, REST compliant, game of **High/Low**. By utilising CArtAgO [15] Artifacts to implement this tool, it remains agent programming language agnostic. This system is composed of three different agents, the Main Agent queries the service-discovery instance and creates an Application Agent that is instantiated with the IRI of each application registered. Once the Application Agent been created, this agent will then visit the base IRI of the application, at the */api-docs* endpoint to view the OAS document. Once the Application Agent has determined that the application has an OAS document, it begins to create a logical depiction of the resource it has been tasked with identifying. Should this application match the *shape* of the application it will create High/Low Agent to interact with the resource. The High/Low Agent has a logical depiction of how to play the High/Low game based on the "shape" of the service. Figure 1 describes the

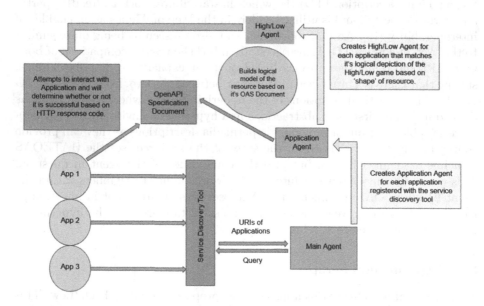

Fig. 1. System Layout

layout of the system. The code is available at the Git repo https://gitlab.com/ eoin.o-neill.3/longlivedwebopenapi with instructions on how to run it.

4   Conclusion

In conclusion, by building this tool we have identified some of the pitfalls that exist with the current standard of service descriptions when exposing them to Web-enabled intelligent software agents and the tacit knowledge that is required when integrating microservices with one another. Section 2 has identified the integration issues that face the software engineering community when building systems of decoupled services that are required to interact in an ad-hoc manner. In order to facilitate agents being able to have a profound impact, the incorporation of Linked Data within service descriptions to define domain specific knowledge, while also providing explicit interaction definitions using vocabularies such as Hydra and Hypermedia Controls Ontology (HCTL), is paramount.

The work being done on signifiers as a first class abstraction [18] shows a path forward with regards to implementing these types of systems by providing enough context for agents at runtime to determine how to utilise a service and what the request and response requirements are in order to become the integrating bodies of these environments. As microservices architectures grow and systems begin to be made up of loosely-coupled, independently evolving services, the need for continuous, contextual integration that aligns with higher level goals provides an opportunity for hypermedia enabled agents to play a significant role. The goal of this research in the future is to implement this tool in a scenario where services are being developed and managed independent of each other with hypermedia representations providing enough contextual information for autonomous agents to act as the integrating intermediaries, a context such as large scale, smart agriculture, smart building or smart city scenario which provides enough variability and change to effectively test this tool at scale.

References

1. Web of things (wot) thing description. https://www.w3.org/TR/wot-thing-description/
2. Yahoo | mail, weather, search, politics, news, finance, sports & videos. http://groups.yahoo.com/group/rest-discuss/message/3232
3. Ciortea, A., Boissier, O., Zimmermann, A., Florea, A.M.: Responsive decentralized composition of service mashups for the internet of things. In: Proceedings of the 6th International Conference on the Internet of Things, pp. 53–61 (2016)
4. Espinoza-Arias, P., Garijo, D., Corcho, O.: Mapping the web ontology language to the OpenApi specification. In: Grossmann, G., Ram, S. (eds.) ER 2020. LNCS, vol. 12584, pp. 117–127. Springer, Cham (2020). https://doi.org/10.1007/978-3-030-65847-2_11
5. Evans, E., Evans, E.J.: Domain-Driven Design: Tackling Complexity in the Heart of Software. Addison-Wesley Professional, Boston (2004)

6. Fielding, R.T.: REST: Architectural Styles and the Design of Network-based Software Architectures. Doctoral dissertation (2000). http://www.ics.uci.edu/~fielding/pubs/dissertation/top.htm
7. Fowler, M.: Domain driven design (2020). https://www.martinfowler.com/bliki/DomainDrivenDesign.html
8. Guo, Z., Cao, D., Tjong, D., Yang, J., Schlesinger, C., Polikarpova, N.: Type-directed program synthesis for restful APIs. arXiv preprint arXiv:2203.16697 (2022)
9. Idehen, K.U.: Swagger, the API economy, rest, linked data, and a semantic web (2018). https://medium.com/openlink-software-blog/swagger-the-api-economy-rest-linked-data-and-a-semantic-web-9d6839dae65a. Accessed 07 Apr 2022
10. Kaebisch, S., Anicic, D.: Thing description as enabler of semantic interoperability on the web of things. In: Proceedings of the IoT Semantic Interoperability Workshop, pp. 1–3 (2016)
11. Lanthaler, M., Gütl, C.: Hydra: a vocabulary for hypermedia-driven web APIs. LDOW **996**, 35–38 (2013)
12. Muhamad, W., Bandung, Y., et al.: Transforming OpenAPI specification 3.0 documents into RDF-based semantic web services. J. Big Data **9**(1), 1–24 (2022)
13. O'Neill, E., Lillis, D., O'Hare, G.M.P., Collier, R.W.: Delivering multi-agent MicroServices using CArtAgO. In: Baroglio, C., Hubner, J.F., Winikoff, M. (eds.) EMAS 2020. LNCS (LNAI), vol. 12589, pp. 1–20. Springer, Cham (2020). https://doi.org/10.1007/978-3-030-66534-0_1
14. O'Neill, E., Lillis, D., O'Hare, G.M., Collier, R.W.: Explicit modelling of resources for multi-agent microservices using the CArtAGo framework. In: Proceedings of the 18th International Joint Conference on Autonomous Agents and Multi-Agent Systems, Auckland, NZ, 2020. International Foundation for Autonomous Agents and MultiAgent Systems (IFAAMAS) (2020)
15. Ricci, A., Viroli, M., Omicini, A.: CArtA gO: a framework for prototyping artifact-based environments in MAS. In: Weyns, D., Parunak, H.V.D., Michel, F. (eds.) E4MAS 2006. LNCS (LNAI), vol. 4389, pp. 67–86. Springer, Heidelberg (2007). https://doi.org/10.1007/978-3-540-71103-2_4
16. Silva, S.: REST service discovery based on ontology model. Ph.D. thesis (2021)
17. Tzavaras, A., Mainas, N., Petrakis, E.G.: OpenAPI framework for the web of things. Internet Things **21**, 100675 (2023)
18. Vachtsevanou, D., Ciortea, A., Mayer, S., Lemée, J.: Signifiers as a first-class abstraction in hypermedia multi-agent systems. arXiv preprint arXiv:2302.06970 (2023)
19. W Collier, R., O'Neill, E., Lillis, D., O'Hare, G.: MAMS: multi-agent microservices. In: Companion Proceedings of The 2019 World Wide Web Conference, pp. 655–662. ACM (2019)
20. Yang, J., Wittern, E., Ying, A.T., Dolby, J., Tan, L.: Towards extracting web API specifications from documentation. In: 2018 IEEE/ACM 15th International Conference on Mining Software Repositories (MSR), pp. 454–464. IEEE (2018)

Using Multi-Agent MicroServices (MAMS) for Agent-Based Modelling

Martynas Jagutis, Sean Russell[ID], and Rem W. Collier[✉][ID]

School of Computer Science, University College Dublin, Dublin, Ireland
{sean.russell,rem.collier}@ucd.ie

Abstract. This paper demonstrates the application of the Multi-Agent MicroServices (MAMS) architectural style to Agent Based Modelling (ABM) through a prototype traffic simulator in which agents model a population of individuals who travel from home to work and vice versa by car. The simulation environment is modelled as a set of linked web resources that are deployed across a number of microservices. The agents, deployed in a separate set of microservices, connect to and interact with their environment using the REpresentational State Transfer (REST). The approach aims to take advantage of various benefits of microservices, such as loose coupling (between the agents and the environments), elasticity (the ability to add and remove environment resources at runtime) and polyglot computing (the ability to use different languages and frameworks for different parts of the application). Finally, the linking of the environment resources leads to the emergence of a simulation wide knowledge graph that can be used by suitably designed agents to supplement their local context with global knowledge of the environment.

Keywords: Multi-Agent Systems · Microservices · Traffic Simulation

1 Introduction

Multi-Agent MicroServices (MAMS) [4] encompasses both an architectural style and a prototype framework. This architectural style focuses on deploying Multi-Agent Systems (MAS) within the Microservices architecture, while the framework enables the implementation of MAMS-based applications using the ASTRA programming language [6,7].

Within the MAMS architectural style, a unique type of agent, called a *MAMS Agent*, is introduced. These agents possess a body comprising a set of web resources and are hosted on Agent-Oriented MicroServices (AOMS). Interactions between Plain-Old MicroServices (POMS) and MAMS agents occur via these resources using the REpresentational State Transfer (REST) approach. Likewise, it is expected that MAMS agents will interact with POMS in a similar manner. Importantly, the MAMS architectural style does not make any assumptions about the internal implementation of the agents themselves.

The prototype framework [13,14] combines ASTRA with a suite of CArtAgO artifacts [15] to facilitate its implementation. This integration allows Multi-Agent Systems (MAS) to be deployed as black boxes, built from AOMS, which

A. Ciortea et al. (Eds.): EMAS 2023, LNAI 14378, pp. 85–92, 2023.
https://doi.org/10.1007/978-3-031-48539-8_6

can seamlessly integrate within larger software architectures without necessitating an understanding of the underlying agent technologies. Various problem domains have already benefited from this approach, including decision support tools [3], building management [12], and digital twins for smart agriculture [10]. The source code for the framework and a number of example applications can be found on Gitlab at the following url: https://gitlab.com/mams-ucd/

This paper illustrates the use of MAMS and microservices in the domain of Agent Based Modelling (ABM) [1]. The basic idea is that a simulated environment of an ABM system could be decomposed into a set of web resources. Each of these resources becomes a kind of *"micro-environment"* that agents can inhabit and interact with. The decomposition of the environment is not constrained by the proposed approach. For example, a road network in a city could be decomposed into a number of connected districts, or with a finer granularity individual street and junction resources.

The resources can be created and accessed through standardised interfaces provided by a specially designed environment interface. Each resource has a unique URL through which it can be communicated with. As such, inter-resource relationships are modelled based on the URL associated with each resource. The interactions between resources and agents are facilitated in the same way. This requires a second set of microservices, used to implement the agents, that perform the reasoning required for the ABM and interact with the system by leveraging the MAMS architectural style.

2 Overview of Prototype

The prototype developed is a very simple traffic simulation scenario in which agents model a population of individuals who travel from home to work and vice versa by car. The environment for this scenario is decomposed into three *sub-environment* microservices. Within these three services, four types of resource are implemented: home resources, work resources and the street and junction resources that model the road network. The road network resources design is based on best practices drawn from established traffic simulators such as MATSim [17] and SUMO [11].

Figure 1 illustrates the set of microservices that were created to implement the simulation. They have been built using a combination of *Java* and *Spring Boot*[1]. The figure includes the three sub-environment microservices described above. The **Road Network** service is the most complex of the three and is underpinned by a *Neo4J database*[2] which maintains a graph of the road network. The transport network is represented as a collection of cells that the vehicles can inhabit and move between, an approach called Cellular Automata [16]. This limits the level of detail that can be modelled, but simplifies the process of calculating the movement of vehicles.

---

[1] http://spring.io.

[2] http://neo4j.com.

The **Home** and **Work** services provide a minimal model that includes access to the current time and a single activity (e.g. *Watch TV* or *Work*). These services are included as a way of showing multiple sub-simulations integrating and working together rather than to provide and real need for reasoning or actions on the part of the agents.

A **Clock Service** provides a discrete time model for the overall simulation. The **Traffic Lights Service** implements an algorithm to control traffic lights within the **Road Network** service. The **Management Service** supports the configuration and execution of a simulation run, this includes initialising services in the correct sequence and distributing URLs to the services to enable communication. Finally, the **Driver Service** implements the agent part of the system which is described next.

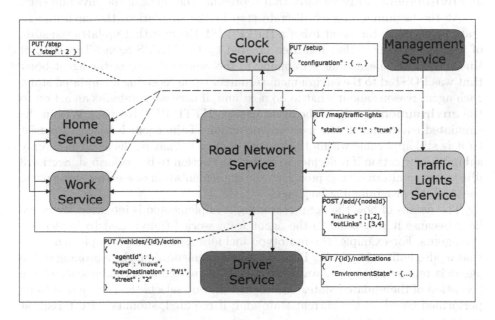

Fig. 1. Overview of Simulation Architecture

2.1 Expected Agent Behaviour

This prototype is our first attempt to implement an ABM using MAMS. As a result, the implemented behaviour of the agent is somewhat limited. Specifically, agents are initially created and linked to home sub-environments. While in this sub-environment, they watch TV or sit idle until it is time to go to work. At this point, the agents transition from the home sub-environment to a linked junction sub environment within the road network. The agents then use a built in route planner to identify their route to work. The route planner is implemented using a shortest path algorithm provided by Neo4J. The agents then drive to work view the road network, transitioning between junction and street sub0-environment resources as is necessary. Upon reaching the junction that is linked to their place of work, the agent again transitions from that junction to the associated work environment where it stays until it is time to return home. Once it returns home, the same behaviour is repeated.

2.2 Integrating Agents with the Environment

Based on the MAMS architectural style, agents connect to the simulation by registering with an environment microservice based on the resource they wish to interact with. The microservice can reject the request, but if accepted, it creates an **environment body** resource that represents the agent in the environment[3].

At the beginning of each discrete step in the simulation, the environment state is passed to the agent using a HTTP PUT Request that updates the state of a **state resource** that has been created by the MAMS agent. The URL of this resource is specified as a webhook in the representation of the agent body that was POSTed to the environment resource. Upon receiving an updated state, each agent reasons about what to do next and, if necessary, submits an action to the **environment body** of the agent using a HTTP PUT Request. Within the simulated environment, the most recent action of the agent is taken to persist (if it is still applicable within the current context). That is, the agent need only submit a new action if it decides to change the action to be performed. Section 3 illustrates an alternative approach to the implementation of a driver agent using the ASTRA programming language.

The details of how the agent reasoning is implemented is intentionally vague here because it is specific to the agent framework (if any) used to implement the agents. For example, the prototype includes a Java Driver implementation that is also built using Spring Boot. In this implementation, the reasoning of the agent is represented by a Java method that is invoked as a consequence of the reception of the updated state. The algorithm used selects the next action to be performed based on the current state and, if required, submits a PUT request containing the next action.

The environment microservice(s) tracks which resource an agent is associated with. When an agent moves to another resource, for example by moving between districts or from a junction to a street (depending on the granularity of the sub-environments), the microservice registers the change. If the agent moves to a resource that is located on a different microservice, its body is transferred to the new microservice via a HTTP POST Request. Further details can be found in [9]. The source code is available on Gitlab[4].

---

[3] This is not the same as the MAMS agent body described in Sect. 1.

[4] https://gitlab.com/mams-ucd/examples/microservice_traffic_simulator.

```
agent Driver extends mams.PassiveMAMSAgent {
  module ObjectAccess oa;

  inference atIntersection(EnvironmentState state) :-
      oa.isFalse(state, "atIntersection") &
      oa.getInt(state, "vehicleSpeed") > 0;

  inference isStopped(EnvironmentState state) :-
      oa.getInt(state, "vehicleSpeed") > 0;

  rule +!main(list args) {
    MAMSAgent::!init();
    MAMSAgent::!created("base");
    PassiveMAMSAgent::
        !itemResource("notifications", "EnvironmentState");
  }

  rule +!updatedObject(EnvironmentState state) {
    !decide(state, oa.getString(state, "type"), string action);
    !act(state, action);
  }

  rule +!act(EnvironmentState state, string action) {
    !put(oa.valueAsString(state, "webhook"),
        "{ 'action':''"+action"'}", HttpResponse response);
    if (!httpUtils.hasCode(response, 200)) system.fail();
  }

  rule +!decide(EnvironmentState state, "traffic", string action)
      : time(t) & atIntersection(state) {
    action = "move";
  }

  rule +!decide(EnvironmentState state, "traffic", string action)
      : time(t) & isStopped(state) & canAccelerate(state) {
    action = "accelerate";
  }
}
```

Fig. 2. ASTRA-MAMS Implementation

3   Using MAMS to Implement Agent Behaviours

A simplified version of the driver agent implementation that is has been
built using the prototype MAMS framework is shown in Fig. 2. The associated resource is specified as part of the !main() rule. This rule registers
the agent to the underlying MAMS framework via the MAMSAgent::!init()
goal; creates a body via the MAMSAgent::!created(''base'') goal that is
exposed via the /{agent-name} URL; and finally creates a state resource
that is exposed via the /{agent-name}/notifications URL. This resource
is defined as a passive resource whose state is defined by the field specified in
the EnvironmentState Java class. As described in [13], a passive resource is a
resource that can be updated by external services without oversight from the
agent. The agent detects changes to its resources via custom events that are
handled by the PassiveMAMSAgent code and transformed into goals, such as the
!updatedObject() goal.

The driver reasoning behaviour is defined over a set of plan rules that begins
with the handling of the !updatedObject(...) goal in the second rule. This

goal is adopted by the agent upon receipt the PUT request from the environment microservice containing the updated environment state. The argument of this goal is a Java object representation of the environment state that was used above to create the **notifications** resource. The plan part of the plan rule defines two sub-goals !decide(...) and !act(...) which must be achieved in sequence. The last two plan rules in the program highlight two possible sub-plans for achieving the !decide(...) goal. The agent will choose only one of these options based on the current state of the environment. For example, the last rule requires that the agents' vehicle be stopped. This is expressed by the isStopped(...) belief which is evaluated based on the second of the inference rules at the top of the code snippet (denoted by the inference keyword).

The ObjectAccess module provides a generic mechanism for the agent to query the internal state of Java objects. In ASTRA, modules provide a standardised extension mechanism for agents. In effect, they are Java classes whose methods are annotated as actions, sensors, formulae, terms, or events [6]. An annotated method can be referenced directly in the ASTRA code based on the annotation used. For example, a formula annotated method can be used as an atomic formula, while an action annotated method can be used as a step in a plan body. The code in Fig. 2 uses one formula annotated method from the ObjectAccess module: isFalse(...) which returns true if the value of the specified field is false (and false otherwise). It also uses two term annotated methods from this module: getInt(...), which returns the value of a field of the object as an integer; and valueAsString(...) which returns the value of a field of the object as a string. All of these methods use Java's Reflection API. In the first inference rule, the isFalse(....) formula is used to check whether or not the atIntersection field of the EnvironmentState object is true or false and the getInt(...) term is used to retrieve the value of the vehicleSpeed field. The !act(..) goal sends the getInt(...) term using the low level !put(...) goal provided by the MAMS. This low level goal constructs a HTTP PUT Request that is sent to the webhook field of the environment state. This field contains the URL required to set the next action of the agent.

4   Conclusions

This low level goal constructs a HTTP PUT Request that is sent to the webhook field of the environment state. This field contains the URL required to set the next action of the agent. This paper presents an early prototype that demonstrates what we believe to be an novel approach to Agent Based Modelling (ABM) that combines the use of microservices and the MAMS architectural style. The motivation for this is to take advantage of various benefits offered by microservices, such as loose coupling (between the agents and the environments), elasticity (the ability to add and remove environment resources at run-time) and polyglot computing (the ability to use different languages and frameworks for different parts of the application).

The prototype presented is a traffic simulation that decomposes the environment into four types of web resource that are hosted across three microservices.

Each resource acts as a "micro-environment". Agents interact with a resource by registering a "body" with the corresponding microservice, indicating which resource they wish to be associated with. Hypermedia links are used to relate resources to one another, for example, a junction resource in the road network can be linked to a home or work resource. A key part of the approach is the design of mechanisms to allow agents to transition between different parts of the environment which is achieved by transferring their "body" between the source and target environment resources either internally or via a HTTP POST request.

While reflecting on a number of shortcomings of this prototype [9], another idea emerged; that the linked representations of the environment resources can be used as a building block to implement a distributed knowledge graph [8] of the simulation. Such a knowledge graph could be used by the simulation agents to better understand and explore the environment. For example, in the current prototype, route finding is implemented using a shortest path algorithm provided by Neo4J. In a knowledge graph centric environment, the agent could perform route finding by simply exploring the knowledge graph following the URLs connecting streets to junctions and vice versa. An example of such an approach can be found in [2] where agents are implemented that use Reinforcement Learning to explore a semantically defined maze environment.

Knowledge graphs can not only enable discovery of the structure of the environment, but also can be used to provide additional knowledge necessary for the agents to operate effectively in the environment. For example, a more complex work environment could include descriptions of the main tasks associated with each role. This offers the potential for an agent with no prior knowledge of that particular workplace learning how to perform a given job. Here we use the term "learn" in its most general sense which can be realised through some form of plan sharing, the application of reinforcement learning from first principles or even some form of transfer learning. Details of this proposed approach can be found in [5].

References

1. Abar, S., Theodoropoulos, G.K., Lemarinier, P., O'Hare, G.M.: Agent based modelling and simulation tools: a review of the state-of-art software. Comput. Sci. Rev. **24**, 13–33 (2017)
2. Beaumont, K., O'Neill, E., Bermeo, N., Collier, R.: Collaborative route finding in semantic mazes. In: Proceedings of the All the Agents Challenge (ATAC 2021) (2021)
3. Carneiro, J., Andrade, R., Alves, P., Conceição, L., Novais, P., Marreiros, G.: A consensus-based group decision support system using a multi-agent microservices approach. In: Proceedings of the 19th International Conference on Autonomous Agents and MultiAgent Systems, pp. 2098–2100 (2020)
4. Collier, R., O'Neill, E., Lillis, D., O'Hare, G.: MAMS: multi-agent microservices. In: Companion Proceedings of The 2019 World Wide Web Conference, pp. 655–662. ACM (2019)

5. Collier, R., Russell, S., Ghanadbashi, S., Golpayegani, F.: Towards the use of hypermedia mas and microservices for web scale agent-based simulation. SN Comput. Sci. **3**(6), 510 (2022)
6. Collier, R.W., Russell, S., Lillis, D.: Reflecting on agent programming with agents-peak(L). In: Chen, Q., Torroni, P., Villata, S., Hsu, J., Omicini, A. (eds.) PRIMA 2015. LNCS (LNAI), vol. 9387, pp. 351–366. Springer, Cham (2015). https://doi.org/10.1007/978-3-319-25524-8_22
7. Dhaon, A., Collier, R.W.: Multiple inheritance in agentspeak (L)-style programming languages. In: Proceedings of the 4th International Workshop on Programming based on Actors Agents & Decentralized Control, pp. 109–120 (2014)
8. Hogan, A., et al.: Knowledge Graphs. No. 22 in Synthesis Lectures on Data, Semantics, and Knowledge, Springer (2021). https://doi.org/10.2200/S01125ED1V01Y202109DSK022. https://kgbook.org/
9. Jagutis, M., Russell, S., Collier, R.: Simulating traffic with agents, microservices & REST. In: Braubach, L., Jander, K., Bădică, C. (eds.) IDC 2022. Studies in Computational Intelligence, vol. 1089, pp. 89–99. Springer, Cham (2022). https://doi.org/10.1007/978-3-031-29104-3_10
10. Kalyani, Y., Collier, R.: Towards a new architecture: Multi-agent based cloud-fog-edge computing and digital twin for smart agriculture. In: Braubach, L., Jander, K., Bădică, C. (eds.) IDC 2022. Studies in Computational Intelligence, vol. 1089, pp. 111–117. Springer, Cham (2023). https://doi.org/10.1007/978-3-031-29104-3_12
11. Lopez, P.A., et al.: Microscopic traffic simulation using sumo. In: 2018 21st International Conference on Intelligent Transportation Systems (ITSC), pp. 2575–2582. IEEE (2018)
12. O'Neill, E., Beaumont, K., Bermeo, N.V., Collier, R.: Building management using the semantic web and hypermedia agents (2021)
13. O'Neill, E., Lillis, D., O'Hare, G.M.P., Collier, R.W.: Delivering multi-agent microservices using CArtAgO. In: Baroglio, C., Hubner, J.F., Winikoff, M. (eds.) EMAS 2020. LNCS (LNAI), vol. 12589, pp. 1–20. Springer, Cham (2020). https://doi.org/10.1007/978-3-030-66534-0_1
14. O'Neill, E., Lillis, D., O'Hare, G.M., Collier, R.W.: Explicit modelling of resources for multi-agent microservices using the cartago framework. In: Proceedings of the 18th International Joint Conference on Autonomous Agents and Multi-Agent Systems, Auckland, NZ, 2020. International Foundation for Autonomous Agents and MultiAgent Systems (IFAAMAS) (2020)
15. Ricci, A., Viroli, M., Omicini, A.: CArtA gO: a framework for prototyping artifact-based environments in MAS. In: Weyns, D., Parunak, H.V.D., Michel, F. (eds.) E4MAS 2006. LNCS (LNAI), vol. 4389, pp. 67–86. Springer, Heidelberg (2007). https://doi.org/10.1007/978-3-540-71103-2_4
16. Shang, X.C., Li, X.G., Xie, D.F., Jia, B., Jiang, R., Liu, F.: A data-driven two-lane traffic flow model based on cellular automata. Phys. A **588**, 126531 (2022)
17. Axhausen, K.W., Horni, A., Nagel, K.: The Multi-Agent Transport Simulation MATSim. Ubiquity Press, London (2016)

Strategy, Reasoning, and Planning

Dynamics of Causal Dependencies in Multi-agent Settings

Maksim Gladyshev$^{(\boxtimes)}$ (ID), Natasha Alechina (ID), Mehdi Dastani (ID),
and Dragan Doder (ID)

Utrecht University, Utrecht, The Netherlands
{m.gladyshev,n.a.alechina,m.m.dastani,d.doder}@uu.nl

Abstract. In this paper we discuss how causal models can be used
for modeling multi-agent interaction in complex organizational settings,
where agents' decisions may depend on other agents' decisions as well as
the environment. We demonstrate how to reason about the dynamics of
such models using concurrent game structures where agents can change
the organisational setting and thereby their decision dependencies. In
such concurrent game structure, agents can choose to modify their reactions on other agents' decisions and on the environment by intervening
on their part of a causal model. We propose a generalized notion of interventions in causal models that allow us to model and reason about the
dynamics of agents' dependencies in a multi-agent system. Finally, we
discuss how to model uncertainty and reason about agents' responsibility
concerning their dependencies and thereby their choices.

Keywords: Causal models · Interventions · Multi-agent systems

1 Introduction

The complex interactions between agents in multi-agent systems can be
described in terms of organizational structures that determine the dependencies between agents' decisions [1,6,9,15]. Such dependencies can be described
in a causal manner, allowing us to reason about the cause of agents' decisions
and explain what causes a given agent's decision in terms of the organizational
structure and the decisions of other agents on which it depends. For example, in
an organisational setting such as banking system, the decision of a loan officer to
accept or reject a mortgage application may depend on the decision of her manager. It is also clear that in multi-agent systems the agents interact not only with
each other, but also with their shared environment, which is also governed by
causal relations. In our simple example, accepting a mortgage application may
cause a new contract to be added to the administration database, which in turn
may cause a notification to be sent to the mortgage applicant. In general, agents'
decisions may have a causal effect on each others decisions' and their shared environment, which in turn may have causal effect on the agents' decisions. In order
to study such causal interactions between agents and/or the environment, we
use causal models developed in the theory of *actual* causality [13].

© The Author(s), under exclusive license to Springer Nature Switzerland AG 2023
A. Ciortea et al. (Eds.): EMAS 2023, LNAI 14378, pp. 95–112, 2023.
https://doi.org/10.1007/978-3-031-48539-8_7

There exist two different types of causality. The first one is so-called *type causality*, and is critical in machine learning and for prediction purposes. This kind of causality concerns general statements such as 'smoking causes lung cancer', and can be used to predict, e.g., the probability that someone who smokes gets lung cancer. The second one is termed *actual causality*, and is essential in tracing and explaining the cause of a specific outcome, which in turn is essential for assigning responsibility for the outcome to a specific component of an AI system. The theory of actual causality was developed in [11–14, 21].

We assume that the decision-making mechanism of each agent is specified as a part of a causal model, more specifically, as a function that determines the agent's decision based on the current context, the decisions of the agents that she depends on, and the state of the environment. Simply speaking, given an actual context (e.g., a mortgage application is submitted), the decisions of all agents can be determined through the causal model (e.g., the decision of a loan officer is determined by the submitted mortgage application, its decision-making function that specifies an accept/reject decision based on the decisions of her managers, and perhaps the previous mortgage applications of the same applicant stored in the administration database). In this paper, we investigate how agents can change the causal dependency of their decisions, and thereby the structure of their organization. This allows us to reason about causal structures of organisations and their dynamics. So, the proposed causal modelling approach allows us to reason about causal dependencies between agents and possible interventions of agents to modify their dependencies.

From a technical perspective, we employ MAS models to represent and reason about different causal settings. In such causal settings, the agents' behaviour (decisions) is determined by the structure of a causal model and an assignment of exogenous variables called context. At the same time, each agent has a choice to modify her part of the model, which results in an updated causal model. In a new causal setting for updated model and fixed context, the decisions of agents may be different, as well as the state of the environment. We consider the set of all causal settings to be a set of states in a Concurrent Game Structure (CGS). The updates (called interventions) generate the set of possible actions (choices) for the agents. Then the transitions between states of such CGS can be interpreted as strategic abilities of the agents to enforce the corresponding dependency over their decisions and the environment. In this sense, our approach goes along with other works on CGS semantics for different logics. In particular, CGS semantics for logics of "sees to it that" (STIT) was proposed in [3]. Although STIT-style approach and causal reasoning use different formalisms, both [3] and our work aim to study the connection between the original logics with existing logics for MAS, such as coalition logic, alternating-time temporal logic and strategy logic. Our work is also close to [16], where the framework for reasoning about agents' knowledge about actual causes is proposed. The main difference with our approach is that [16] uses different formalization, namely situation calculus (SC), while we stick to original Structural Equations Models (SEM) approach and straightforwardly unfold such SEM into CGS. Our approach allows us to employ well-known MAS machinery for reasoning about transformations of causal models interpreted as the choices of multi-agent organizational structures.

The remainder of this paper is structured as follows. In Sect. 2 we introduce formal definitions related to causal models. In Sect. 3 we discuss Concurrent Game Structures and demonstrate how to represent possible interventions in a causal model in terms of CGS models. In Sect. 4 we propose the generalized notion of interventions for causal models that allow us to reason about more complicated behavior of the agents. Finally, in Sect. 5 we discuss how to model uncertainty in our settings, then we define the notion of strategic responsibility and demonstrate that the proposed generalized interventions can be more suitable for reasoning about agents' responsibility. For simplicity, in this definition we consider only one-step interactions and leave ATL-style machinery for future work.

2 Preliminaries: Causal Models

We start with the general definition of a causal model as used in [13,14,21].

Definition 1 (Causal Model). *A signature is a tuple* $S = (\mathcal{U}, \mathcal{V}, \mathcal{R})$, *where* $\mathcal{U}$ *is a finite set of exogenous variables,* $\mathcal{V}$ *is a finite set of endogenous variables, and* $\mathcal{R}$ *associates with every variable* $Y \in \mathcal{U} \cup \mathcal{V}$ *a finite nonempty set* $\mathcal{R}(Y)$ *of possible values for* Y, *also called range of* Y. *A causal model over a signature* S *is a tuple* $\mathcal{M} = (S, \mathcal{F})$, *where* $\mathcal{F}$ *associates with every endogenous variable* $X \in \mathcal{V}$ *a function* $\mathcal{F}_X$ *such that* $\mathcal{F}_X$ *maps* $\times_{Z \in (\mathcal{U} \cup \mathcal{V} - \{X\})} \mathcal{R}(Z)$ *to* $\mathcal{R}(X)$. *That is,* $\mathcal{F}_X$ *describes how the value of the endogenous variable* X *is determined by the values of all other variables in* $\mathcal{U} \cup \mathcal{V}$. *The values of exogenous variables* $\mathcal{U}$ *are determined outside of the model and usually referred to as a context* $\vec{u}$.

To illustrate this definition, consider Example 1, originating in [17] and extensively analysed in the theory of actual causality [13].

Example 1 (Rock-throwing). Suzy and Billy both pick up rocks and throw them at a bottle (encoded as ST = 1 and BT = 1 respectively). Suzy's rock gets there first, shattering the bottle. We denote the fact that Suzy's rock hits the bottle as SH = 1. Similarly, BH = 0 denotes the fact that Billy's rock does not hit the bottle. Finally, BS = 1 means 'the bottle shatters'. We also know that because both throws are perfectly accurate, Billy's would have shattered the bottle had it not been preempted by Suzy's throw.[1]

---

[1] Although we use this example due to its simplicity and its extensive analysis in the literature, we can also use new interpretation of this example to illustrate the dependencies of agents' decisions in multi-agent organisations. Let Suzy and Billy be two loan officers working in a bank, who decide to accept or reject a mortgage application. Then $ST = 1$ (and $BT = 1$) can indicate that Suzy (and Billy respectively) rejects an application. Then $SH = 1$ (and $BH = 1$) mean that Suzy's (and Billy's) rejection is registered in the administration database. We also assume that Suzy has a priority, so Billy's rejection is registered ($BH = 1$) only if Suzy's is not ($SH = 0$). Then, the mortgage is rejected ($BS = 1$) if $SH = 1$ or $BH = 1$.

So, our endogenous variables $\mathcal{V}$ are $\{ST, BT, SH, BH, BS\}$. Our exogenous variables $\mathcal{U} = \{U_{ST}, U_{BT}\}$ determine the values of ST and BT variables respectively. For all $Y \in (\mathcal{U} \cup \mathcal{V})$, $\mathcal{R}(Y) = \{0, 1\}$. $\mathcal{F}$ in this example can be defined as follows. Let $\vec{z}$ be an assignment of all variables $(\mathcal{U} \cup \mathcal{V}) \backslash \{X\}$ for corresponding $\mathcal{F}_X$.

$$\mathcal{F}_{SH}(\vec{z}) = \begin{cases} 1 & \text{if } (ST = 1) \in \vec{z}, \\ 0 & \text{if } (ST = 0) \in \vec{z}; \end{cases} \quad \mathcal{F}_{BH}(\vec{z}) = \begin{cases} 1 & \text{if } (ST = 0, BT = 1) \in \vec{z}, \\ 0 & \text{otherwise}; \end{cases}$$

$$\mathcal{F}_{BS}(\vec{z}) = \begin{cases} 1 & \text{if } (SH = 1) \in \vec{z} \text{ or } (BH = 1) \in \vec{z}, \\ 0 & \text{otherwise}; \end{cases}$$

Intuitively, $\mathcal{F}_X$ describes some structural equation that specifies how the value of the endogenous variable X is determined by (and depends on) the values of all other variables in $(\mathcal{U} \cup \mathcal{V}) - \{X\}$. For example, in a causal model with three variables X, Y and Z, the function $\mathcal{F}_X(Y, Z) = Y + Z$ defines the structural equation $X = Y + Z$, while $\mathcal{F}_Y(X, Z) = Z$ defines the structural equation $Y = Z$, etc. The later equation demonstrates that Y does not depend on X. For example, given three variables X, Y and Z, the structural equation for X can be defined as X = Y + Z, X = max(Y, Z), X = Y, or any other complex functional specifications. The later equation demonstrates that X does not depend on Z. Additionally, these equations can be written with an 'iff' notation, for example $X = 1$ iff min(Y, Z) = 0, and $X = 0$ iff min(Y, Z) ≠ 0. For the case of binary variables it is often more convenient to define structural equations using boolean connectives, e.g. $X = \neg(Y \vee X)$. So, by structural equation for any endogenous variable X we understand the way of specifying how the value of X is determined by the values of other variables[2].

Causal models can be represented as a dependency graph. The nodes of such graph represent variables $\mathcal{U} \cup \mathcal{V}$ (we usually omit exogenous variables from the figures), and edges represent the dependencies between the variables. The dependency graph for Example 1 is presented in Fig. 1.

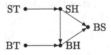

Fig. 1. A dependency graph for the Rock-throwing example.

Now, we need to discuss some restrictions on $\mathcal{F}$ and highlight the difference between recursive and non-recursive models. Following [13], we say that variable Y is independent of X in $(\mathcal{M}, \vec{u})$ if, for all settings $\vec{z}$ of the endogenous variables other than X and Y, and all values x and x' of X, $\mathcal{F}_Y(x, \vec{z}, \vec{u}) = \mathcal{F}_Y(x', \vec{z}, \vec{u})$. A

---

[2] The detailed overview can be found in [13].

model $\mathcal{M}$ is then considered as *recursive* if, for each context $\vec{u}$, there is a partial order $\leq_{\vec{u}}$ of the endogenous variables such that unless $X \leq_{\vec{u}} Y$, Y is independent of X in $(\mathcal{M}, \vec{u})$. It guarantees that no cycles can occur in the dependency graph of such model, and then structural equations $\mathcal{F}$ have a unique solution for any $\vec{u}$ [13]. Let $Sol(\vec{u})$ denote a set of all $(X = x)$, where $X \in \mathcal{V}, x \in \mathcal{R}(X)$, such that X has a value x in the unique solution of equations in $\mathcal{M}$ for a context $\vec{u}$.

Causal models allow us to reason not only about an actual context, but also about counterfactual scenarios. These counterfactual scenarios can be described by interventions of the form $[\vec{Y} \leftarrow \vec{y}](Z = z)$, where $\vec{Y} \leftarrow \vec{y}$ abbreviates $(Y_1 \leftarrow y_1, \ldots, Y_k \leftarrow Y_k)$ for $Y_1, \ldots, Y_k \in \mathcal{V}$. We read these formulas as "if $\vec{Y}$ were set to $\vec{y}$, then Z would have a value z". The intervention $\vec{Y} \leftarrow \vec{y}$ in a model $\mathcal{M}$ results in an updated model $\mathcal{M}^{\vec{Y} \leftarrow \vec{y}} = (\mathcal{S}, \mathcal{F}^{\vec{Y} \leftarrow \vec{y}})$.

Definition 2 (Updated Model). *Given a model $\mathcal{M} = (\mathcal{S}, \mathcal{F})$ and intervention $\vec{Y} \leftarrow \vec{y}$, an updated model $\mathcal{M}^{\vec{Y} \leftarrow \vec{y}} = (\mathcal{S}, \mathcal{F}^{\vec{Y} \leftarrow \vec{y}})$ is such that for all $(Y = y) \in \vec{Y} \leftarrow \vec{y}$ and for any assignment $\vec{Z} = \vec{z}$ of all variables other than $Y, \mathcal{F}_Y^{\vec{Y} \leftarrow \vec{y}}(\vec{z}) = y$. So, $\mathcal{F}_Y^{\vec{Y} \leftarrow \vec{y}}$ is a constant function returning y for any input and all $\mathcal{F}_X^{\vec{Y} \leftarrow \vec{y}}$ for $X \notin \vec{Y}$ remain unchanged.*

Next we can define the basic causal language $\mathcal{L}(\mathsf{C})^3$ [13].

Definition 3 ($\mathcal{L}(\mathsf{C})$ Syntax). *Given a signature $\mathcal{S} = (\mathcal{U}, \mathcal{V}, \mathcal{R})$, a primitive event is a formula of the form $X = x$, for $X \in \mathcal{V}$ and $x \in \mathcal{R}(X)$. A causal formula (over $\mathcal{S}$) is one of the form $[Y_1 \leftarrow y_1, \ldots, Y_k \leftarrow y_k]\varphi$, where φ is a Boolean combination of primitive events, $\{Y_1, \ldots, Y_k\} \subseteq \mathcal{V}$, $y_i \in \mathcal{R}(Y_i)$.*

Language $\mathcal{L}(\mathsf{C}(\mathcal{S}))$ for $\mathcal{S} = (\mathcal{U}, \mathcal{V}, \mathcal{R})$ consists of all Boolean combinations of causal formulas, where the variables in the formulas are taken from $\mathcal{V}$ and the sets of possible values of these variables are determined by $\mathcal{R}$.

Causal formulas from $\mathcal{L}(\mathsf{C})$ can be evaluated on a causal settings $(\mathcal{M}, \vec{u})$ as follows:

Definition 4 (Semantics). *Given a causal settings $(\mathcal{M}, \vec{u})$, and $\mathcal{L}(\mathsf{C})$ formula φ we define $\vDash_{HP}$ relation inductively as follows:*
$(\mathcal{M}, \vec{u}) \vDash_{HP} (X = x)$ *iff* $(X = x) \in Sol(\vec{u})$,
$(\mathcal{M}, \vec{u}) \vDash_{HP} \neg\varphi$ *iff* $(\mathcal{M}, \vec{u}) \nvDash_{HP} \varphi$,
$(\mathcal{M}, \vec{u}) \vDash_{HP} (\varphi \wedge \psi)$ *iff* $(\mathcal{M}, \vec{u}) \vDash_{HP} \varphi$ *and* $(\mathcal{M}, \vec{u}) \vDash_{HP} \psi$,
$(\mathcal{M}, \vec{u}) \vDash_{HP} [\vec{Y} \leftarrow \vec{y}]\varphi$ *iff* $(\mathcal{M}^{\vec{Y} \leftarrow \vec{y}}, \vec{u}) \vDash_{HP} \varphi$.

As you can see, the nesting of $[\vec{Y} \leftarrow \vec{y}]$ operators is not allowed in $\mathcal{L}(\mathsf{C})$. But if we interpret it as an update operator as Definition 2 suggests, then we can define the result of multiple updates $[\vec{X} \leftarrow \vec{x}][\vec{Y} \leftarrow \vec{y}]$ as a model $(\mathcal{M}^{\vec{X} \leftarrow \vec{x}})^{\vec{Y} \leftarrow \vec{y}}$ updated twice. So, we could reason about the series of model transformations by consecutive interventions $[\vec{X} \leftarrow \vec{x}] \ldots [\vec{Y} \leftarrow \vec{y}]$ (of some agents) on the variables $\mathcal{V}' \subseteq \mathcal{V}$. For example $(\mathcal{M}, \vec{u}) \vDash_{HP} [\vec{X} \leftarrow \vec{x}][\vec{Y} \leftarrow \vec{y}]\varphi$ iff $(\mathcal{M}^{\vec{X} \leftarrow \vec{x}}, \vec{u}) \vDash_{HP} [\vec{Y} \leftarrow \vec{y}]\varphi$ iff $((\mathcal{M}^{\vec{X} \leftarrow \vec{x}})^{\vec{Y} \leftarrow \vec{y}}, \vec{u}) \vDash_{HP} \varphi$.

---

^{3} Please note that for notational convenience we use $\mathcal{L}(\mathsf{C})$ instead of $\mathcal{L}(\mathsf{C}(\mathcal{S}))$.

3 Concurrent Game Structures

We use Concurrent Game Structures semantics for reasoning about causal models' transformations, through which agents' decision-making dependencies (and thereby organisational structure) may change, and strategic abilities of the agents controlling such transformations. In order to do this, we need to distinguish agents from environment in causal models. As we have seen in Example 1, in causal models variables V can represent both facts about the agents and the environment. So, in our example, ST and BT can be seen as agents' variables for Suzy and Billy respectively, while SH, BH and BS express some facts about the environment. In these models decisions of agents (understood as the values of agents' variables V_a) determine the values of (some) environmental variables (V_e). But the decisions of these agents can also depend on environmental variables and the decisions of other agents. So, it would be interesting to study what agents can enforce by the right choice of the interventions on their variables. At the same time we do not want to consider how environmental variables could be modified, since we treat the causal dependencies of environmental variables as fixed.

In order to study these series of causal models' transformations, first of all we want to generate a Concurrent Game Structure (CGS) for a given causal model. Concurrent Game Structures are usually defined as follows.

Definition 5 (CGS, pointed). *A concurrent game structure (CGS) is a tuple* $\Gamma = (\mathbb{AG}, Q, \Pi, \pi, Act, d, o)$, *comprising a nonempty finite set of all agents* $\mathbb{AG} = \{1, \ldots, k\}$, *a nonempty finite set of states* Q, *a nonempty finite set of atomic propositions* Π *and their valuation* $\pi : Q \longrightarrow \mathcal{P}(\Pi)$, *and a nonempty finite set of (atomic) actions* Act. *Function* $d : \mathbb{AG} \times Q \longrightarrow \mathcal{P}(Act) \backslash \{\varnothing\}$ *defines nonempty sets of actions available to agents at each state, and* o *is a (deterministic) transition function that assigns the outcome state* $q' = o(q, (\alpha_1, \ldots, \alpha_k))$ *to a state* q *and a tuple of actions* $(\alpha_1, \ldots, \alpha_k)$ *with* $\alpha_i \in d(i, q)$ *and* $1 \leq i \leq k$, *that can be executed by* $\mathbb{AG}$ *in* q. *A pointed CGS is given by* (Γ, q), *where* Γ *is a CGS and* q *is a state in it.*

Let q' be a successor of q if there exists a complete action profile α, such that $q' = o(q, \alpha)$. Given a CGS Γ, a *play* λ in Γ is an infinite sequence $\lambda = q_0, q_1, \ldots$ of states in Q such that, for all $i \geq 0$, the state q_{i+1} is a successor of the state q_i. For a play λ and positions $i, j \geq 0$, we use $\lambda[i], \lambda[j, i]$ and $\lambda[j, \infty)$ to denote the i'th state of λ, the finite segment $q_j, q_{j+1}, \ldots, q_i$, and the suffix $q_j, q_{j+1}, \ldots$ of λ, respectively. A positional (memoryless) *strategy* for an agent $a \in \mathbb{AG}$ or a-strategy, is a function $str_a : Q \longrightarrow d(a, Q)$. Positional strategy of a coalition G is a tuple str_G of positional strategies, one for each player in G.

We assume $V = V_a \cup V_e$, where V_a is the set of agent variables and V_e is the disjoint set of environment variables. Now we demonstrate how to generate a CSG $\Gamma_{\mathcal{M}}$ for a casual model $\mathcal{M}$. A causal model $\mathcal{M} = (\mathcal{S}, \mathcal{F})$, given a context $\vec{u}$, is translated to a CGS $\Gamma_{\mathcal{M}} = (\mathbb{AG}, Q, \Pi, \pi, Act, d, o)$, as follows

- $\mathbb{AG} = \mathcal{V}_a$;[4]
- $Q = \{\mathcal{M}^{\vec{X} \leftarrow \vec{x}} \mid \vec{X} \subseteq \mathcal{V}_a \ \& \ \vec{x} \in \times \mathcal{R}(\vec{X})\}$;
- $\Pi = \{Y = y \mid Y \in \mathcal{V} \ \& \ y \in \mathcal{R}(Y)\}$;
- π is defined as $(Y = y) \in \pi(\mathcal{M}')$ iff $(\mathcal{M}', \vec{u}) \vDash_{HP} (Y = y)$ for any $\mathcal{M}' \in Q$;
- $Act = \{X \leftarrow x \mid X \in \mathcal{V}_a \ \& \ x \in \mathcal{R}(X)\} \cup \{\top_X \mid X \in \mathcal{V}_a\}$, where $\top_X$ denotes 'no intervention on X';
- $d : \mathcal{V}_a \times Q \longrightarrow \mathcal{R}(Act)$ is defined as $d(X, \mathcal{M}') \subseteq \{X \leftarrow x \mid x \in \mathcal{R}(X)\}$ for any $X \in \mathcal{V}_a$ and $\mathcal{M}' \in Q$;
- $o : Q \times (Act_{X_1} \times \cdots \times Act_{X_k}) \longrightarrow Q$ for $Act_{X_i} = \{X_i \leftarrow x \mid x \in \mathcal{R}(X_i)\}$ and $\{X_1, \ldots, X_k\} = \mathcal{V}_a$ is such that for any $\mathcal{M}_1, \mathcal{M}_2 \in Q$, $\mathcal{M}_2 \in o(\mathcal{M}_1, Act_{\vec{X}})$ iff $\mathcal{M}_1^{Act_{\vec{X}}} = \mathcal{M}_2$.

So, our states Q are all possible results of $[\vec{X} \leftarrow \vec{x}]$ updates of $\mathcal{M}$ where $\vec{X} \subseteq \mathcal{V}_a$. In other words any $\mathcal{M}' \in Q$ is a result of replacing some $\mathcal{F}_X$'s with constant functions.[5] The set of atomic propositions Π consists of all pairs $(Y = y)$. The valuation function π agrees with $\vDash_{HP}$ relation. Every agent i in any state has a set of available actions $[X_i \leftarrow x]$ for $x \in \mathcal{R}(X_i)$ together with an 'empty' action $\top_{X_i}$ meaning 'do nothing'. So, every agent i may choose to replace her $\mathcal{F}_{X_i}$ with a constant function $\mathcal{F}_{X_i} = x$ for any $x \in \mathcal{R}(X_i)$ or not to change $\mathcal{F}_{X_i}$. The choice $(Act_{X_1} \times \cdots \times Act_{X_k})$ of all agents in any state $q \in Q$ determines its (unique) successor state q' according to o. It guarantees that $\mathcal{M}_2$ is a successor of $\mathcal{M}_1$ by a complete action profile $(\vec{X}_{\mathbb{AG}} \leftarrow \vec{x})$ in the proposed semantics if and only if $\mathcal{M}_2$ is the result of $\mathcal{M}_1^{\vec{X}_{\mathbb{AG}} \leftarrow \vec{x}}$ update.

Consider how to obtain a CGS for the causal model from Example 1. Our agents Suzy (s) and Billy (b) control variables ST and BT respectively. So, $\mathcal{V}_a = \{ST, BT\}$. Each agent has 3 options: to replace his/her function $\mathcal{F}_i$ with a constant function returning 1, to replace his/her function $\mathcal{F}_i$ with a constant function returning 0 or not to modify $\mathcal{F}_i$. So, initial state has 9 possible transitions. For example if both agent decide not to change their functions, then $o(\mathcal{M}, (\top_{ST}, \top_{BT})) = \mathcal{M}$, i.e. the agents will stay in the initial state. For other 8 action profiles there is a special state reachable from $\mathcal{M}$ in our CGS. This CGS is illustrated in Fig. 2.

Here each state is reachable from the initial one, but interestingly, not any state is reachable from the second one. Other simple properties of this CGS are

- $\mathcal{M}^{BT \leftarrow 0}$ is not reachable from $\mathcal{M}^{ST \leftarrow 0}$ in Fig. 2. Because in $\mathcal{M}^{ST \leftarrow 0}$ function $\mathcal{F}_{BT}$ is not modified: it returns 0 if $U_{BT=0}$ and 1 otherwise. While in $\mathcal{M}^{BT \leftarrow 0}$, $\mathcal{F}_{BT}^{BT \leftarrow 0}$ is a constant function, which cannot be restored to its initial configuration $\mathcal{F}_{BT}$ by any available action for agent b in $\mathcal{M}^{BT \leftarrow 0}$.

---

[4] Here we assume for simplicity that each agent in $\mathbb{AG}$ controls only one variable in $\mathcal{V}_a$, so $|\mathbb{AG}| = |\mathcal{V}_a|$. But without loss of generality one can assume that $\mathcal{V}_a$ is partitioned into disjoint subsets controlled by agents in $\mathbb{AG}$. In this case $|\mathbb{AG}| \leq |\mathcal{V}_a|$.

[5] We note that such an intervention (updates) make the agents in $\vec{X}$ independent of other agents as their decision-making functional specifications are now reduced to a constant function. Later in Sect. 4 we will introduce more general interventions (updates) that can create arbitrary dependencies between agents.

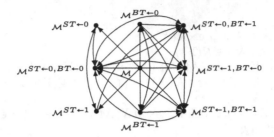

Fig. 2. CGS for the Rock-throwing example. Note that reflexive transitions are omitted from the picture and every transition must be marked with a single or multiple action profiles, which does not fit in the picture.

- There is no requirement that any action profile leads to a different state. Thus, both action profiles $(BT \leftarrow 0, \top_{ST})$ and $(\top_{BT}, \top_{ST})$ in $\mathcal{M}^{BT \leftarrow 0}$ results in a reflexive transition to the same state. But, for example, $(BT \leftarrow 1, \top_{ST})$ will result in the transition to $\mathcal{M}^{BT \leftarrow 1}$ and $(\top_{BT}, ST \leftarrow 0)$ results in the transition to $\mathcal{M}^{BT \leftarrow 0, ST \leftarrow 0}$.
- Different states of such CGS may agree on the valuation on all variables. For example, given a context $\vec{u}$, $(\mathcal{M}, \vec{u})$ and $(\mathcal{M}^{ST \leftarrow 1, BT \leftarrow 1}, \vec{u})$ agree on all $(Y = y)$. But we still treat them as separate states, since these models have different $\mathcal{F}$'s.

Now we can extend $\mathcal{L}(\mathsf{C})$ and allow the nesting of $[\vec{Y} \leftarrow \vec{y}]$ operators.

Definition 6 ($\mathcal{L}(\mathsf{C}_e)$ syntax).

$$\varphi ::= (X = x) \mid \neg\varphi \mid \varphi \wedge \varphi \mid [\vec{Y} \leftarrow \vec{y}]\varphi,$$

where X ranges over $\mathcal{V}$, $\vec{Y}$ over $2^{\mathcal{V}}$, x over $\mathcal{R}(X)$ and each y in $\vec{y}$ over $\mathcal{R}(Y)$. We use standard abbreviations for $\top, \bot, \vee$ and $\rightarrow$.

So, now we assume that agents may perform series of updates $[\vec{X} \leftarrow \vec{x}], \ldots, [\vec{Y} \leftarrow \vec{y}]$ in the extended language $\mathcal{L}(\mathsf{C}_e(\mathcal{S}))$. $\mathcal{L}(\mathsf{C}_e(\mathcal{S}))$ formulas can be evaluated by $\vDash_{HP}$ satisfiability relation defined in the same way as in Definition 4.

Proposition 1. *Any $[\vec{X} \leftarrow \vec{x}] \ldots [\vec{Y} \leftarrow \vec{y}]\varphi \in \mathcal{L}(\mathsf{C}_e(\mathcal{S}))$ is equivalent to some $[\vec{X}' \leftarrow \vec{x}', \ldots, \vec{Y}' \leftarrow \vec{y}']\varphi \in \mathcal{L}(\mathsf{C}(\mathcal{S}))$.*

Proof. $[\vec{X} \leftarrow \vec{x}] \ldots [\vec{Y} \leftarrow \vec{y}]$ generates a model $\mathcal{M}^{\vec{X} \leftarrow \vec{x} \cdots \vec{Y} \leftarrow \vec{y}}$ updated multiple times. Our goal is to prove that there exists a model $\mathcal{M}^{\vec{W} \leftarrow \vec{w}}$, such that $\vec{W}$ is a set of variables that occur in $\vec{X}, \ldots, \vec{Y}$ and $\vec{w}$ are the values that occur in $\vec{x}, \ldots, \vec{y}$, such that $\mathcal{M}^{\vec{W} \leftarrow \vec{w}} = \mathcal{M}^{\vec{X} \leftarrow \vec{x} \cdots \vec{Y} \leftarrow \vec{y}}$.

So, let $\vec{W}$ be a set of all variables that occur in $\vec{X}, \ldots, \vec{Y}$. Let $\vec{Z}$ denote a vector $(\vec{X} = \vec{x}, \ldots, \vec{Y} = \vec{y})$. To determine that value of every $W_i \in \vec{W}$ we need to find the right-most $W_i = w_i$ in $\vec{Z}$. So, there is $k \leq |\vec{Z}|$, such that $\vec{Z}[k] = (W_i = w_i)$ (here $\vec{Z}[k]$ denotes the k's element of $\vec{Z}$ of the form $X = x$) and for any $n > k$ and any $w' \in \mathcal{R}(W_i)$ it holds that $\vec{Z}[n] \neq (W_i = w')$. By doing this we enforce that in our model $\mathcal{M}^{\vec{W} \leftarrow \vec{w}}$ all functions $\mathcal{F}_X \in \vec{W}$ are set to constant functions in the exactly same way as they are set in $\mathcal{M}^{\vec{X} \leftarrow \vec{x} \cdots^{\vec{Y} \leftarrow \vec{y}}}$. It guarantees that $(\mathcal{M}, \vec{u}) \vDash_{HP} [\vec{X} \leftarrow \vec{x}] \ldots [\vec{Y} \leftarrow \vec{y}]\varphi$ iff $(\mathcal{M}, \vec{u}) \vDash_{HP} [\vec{W} \leftarrow \vec{w}]\varphi$.

But since it is also clear that every $\varphi \in \mathcal{L}(\mathsf{C})$ is a $\mathcal{L}(\mathsf{C}_e)$ formula, $\mathcal{L}(\mathsf{C})$ and $\mathcal{L}(\mathsf{C}_e)$ are equally expressive. The same result can be seen on CGS's also. For any CGS $\Gamma_{\mathcal{M}}$ obtained from $\mathcal{M}$, it holds that if some state $q' \in \Gamma_{\mathcal{M}}$ is reachable from initial state q_0, then it is reachable in 1 step.

4 Arbitrary Updates

In this section we demonstrate how the proposed framework can be generalized to allow creating arbitrary dependencies between agents. This is done by allowing interventions that change the functional specifications $\mathcal{F}_X$ to an arbitrary $\mathcal{F}'_X$ for any agent X. It is clear that interventions $[\vec{X} \leftarrow \vec{x}]$ are not the only possible operations modifying $\mathcal{F}$. In other words, there are more ways to update $\mathcal{F}$ instead of replacing some $\mathcal{F}_X$'s with a constant functions. For example, we can allow agents to modify the value of $\mathcal{F}_X(\vec{z})$ on a specific input $\vec{z}$. We denote it as $X(\vec{z}) \leftarrow x$, where $X \in \mathcal{V}, x \in \mathcal{R}(X)$ and $\vec{z}$ is the assignment of all variables in $\mathcal{V}$ except X.

To illustrate it, assume that in the Rock-throwing example we allow Suzy to make an additional action (act^*): to update $\mathcal{F}_{ST}$ in such a way that $\mathcal{F}_{ST}^{act^*}(\vec{z}) = 1$ on all inputs $\vec{z}$ containing $(U_{ST} = 1)$. Now we can generate a new CGS Γ' which contains more possible transitions. The updated CGS is presented in Fig. 3.

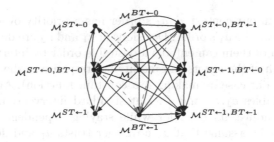

Fig. 3. Extended CGS Γ' for the Rock-throwing example. Dashed blue arrows indicate new transitions. (Color figure online)

We see that after intervention $ST \leftarrow 0$ Suzy can always 'return' $\mathcal{F}_{ST}$ to the initial behavior by act^*. So, the blue transitions are the new options. Now, from $\mathcal{M}^{ST \leftarrow 0}$ Billy and Suzy can return to $\mathcal{M}$ if their action profile is $(act^*, \top_{BT})$.

Note also that no new states were generated in the extended example. Because additional action act_1^* for Suzy cannot produce new configuration of $\mathcal{F}_{ST}$ which is different from $\mathcal{F}_{ST}, \mathcal{F}_{ST}^{ST \leftarrow 1}$ or $\mathcal{F}_{ST}^{ST \leftarrow 0}$. But assume that we add another possible action act_2^* which can be expressed as $ST(\mathcal{U}_{ST}=1) \leftarrow 0$, meaning that $\mathcal{F}_{ST}^{act_2^*}(\vec{z})=0$ if $(\mathcal{U}_{ST}=1) \in \vec{z}$. How should we generate a CGS Γ' now? In this case there will be a possible Suzy's strategy to make $ST \leftarrow 1$ intervention first and then act_2^*. Then, whatever Billy does, $ST = 1$ if $\mathcal{U}_{ST} = 0$ and $ST = 0$ if $\mathcal{U}_{ST} = 1$. But such model cannot be reached by any strategy if only possible actions for Suzy are interventions $ST \leftarrow 1$ and $ST \leftarrow 0$. To better illustrate the problem, consider another example.

Example 2. Suppose that there are two agents a_1 and a_2 who can give an order to the third agent a_3. There are three alternative decisions a_1 and a_2 may choose: order '1', order '−1' and not to give an order '0'. The only environmental variable P determines the priority of a_1's or a_2's order. Finally, a_3 must choose one of three possible actions: 1, −1 or 0 (to 'wait').

More formally, our variables are $\mathcal{V}_a = \{a_1, a_2, a_3\}, \mathcal{V}_e = \{P\}$. Their ranges are $\mathcal{R}(a_1) = \mathcal{R}(a_2) = \mathcal{R}(a_3) = \{-1, 0, 1\}, \mathcal{R}(P) = \{1, 2\}$. The values of a_1, a_2 and P depend on the context $\vec{u}$, while a_3 depends on all of them. The values for a_3 are determined as follows $\mathcal{F}_{a_3}(\vec{z}) = 1$ if $((P = 1) \in \vec{z}$ and $(a_1 = 1) \in \vec{z})$ or $((P = 2) \in \vec{z}$ and $(a_2 = 1) \in \vec{z})$, $\mathcal{F}_{a_3}(\vec{z}) = 0$ if $((P = 1) \in \vec{z}$ and $(a_1 = 0) \in \vec{z})$ or $((P = 2)$ and $(a_2 = 0))$, $\mathcal{F}_{a_3}(\vec{z}) = -1$ if $((P = 1) \in \vec{z}$ and $(a_1 = -1) \in \vec{z})$ or $((P = 2) \in \vec{z}$ and $(a_2 = -1) \in \vec{z})$. So, agent a_3 checks who has a priority and follows the order (Fig. 4).

Fig. 4. Dependency graph for Example 2.

Assume that in our context $\vec{u}$, a_1's order has a priority over a_2's according to $\mathcal{F}_P$, so a_3 follows the a_1's order. Decisions of a_1 and a_2 are determined by the context, but each of them can enforce a desirable order by intervention on their variables. So, each of the agents can modify her response to the environment by updating $\mathcal{F}_{a_i}$ (in our case by making it a constant function). Agent a_3 depends on all other variables a_1, a_2 and P. But standard interventions $[X \leftarrow x]$ does not allow a_3 to adjust its behavior while staying dependent on a_1's or a_2's orders. For example, assume that a_3 no longer trusts a_1 and decides to ignore him completely and always follow the a_2's order. This situation is clearly not expressible by standard interventions. But if we extend possible actions of a_3 with any combination of $a_3(\vec{z}) \leftarrow x$, where $x \in \mathcal{R}(a_3)$ and $\vec{z}$ is the assignment of all variables expect a_3, then we can encode much more complex behavior. In particular, let trust_{a_2} be an action encoded as

$$\bigcup_{\vec{z}, s.t.(a_2=1)\in\vec{z}} (a_3(\vec{z}) \leftarrow 1) \cup \bigcup_{\vec{z}', s.t.(a_2=0)\in\vec{z}'} (a_3(\vec{z}') \leftarrow 0) \cup \bigcup_{\vec{z}'', s.t.(a_2=-1)\in\vec{z}''} (a_3(\vec{z}'') \leftarrow -1)$$

This action allows a_3 to modify $\mathcal{F}_{a_3}$ and obtain $\mathcal{F}_{a_3}^{\text{trust}_{a_2}}$. According to this function, agent a_3 always follows the order of a_2 and ignores a_1. We can also imagine that order 1 is very risky for a_3 and in case this agent receives this order from the prioritized agent, he wants to check if second agent also gives this order independently of P's value. This behavior can also be encoded with basic general interventions of the form $X(\vec{z}) \leftarrow x$. Let a_3's action doublecheck be defined as follows

$$\bigcup_{\vec{z}',s.t.(P=1,a_1=1,a_2\neq1)\in\vec{z}'} (a_3(\vec{z}') \leftarrow 0) \cup \bigcup_{\vec{z}'',s.t.(P=2,a_2=1,a_1\neq1)\in\vec{z}''} (a_3(\vec{z}'') \leftarrow 0)$$

In this settings, if a_3 receives an order 1 from the prioritized agent, but the order of second agent is not 1, then a_3 decides to wait ($a_3 = 0$) according to $\mathcal{F}_{a_3}^{\text{doublecheck}}$. So, this action will result in one of the updated models $\{\mathcal{M}_1', \ldots, \mathcal{M}_l'\}$, depending on the actions of other agents. But we know that for any such model $\mathcal{M}_i'$ it holds that $(\mathcal{M}_i', \vec{u}) \vDash ((a_1 \neq 1) \vee (a_2 \neq 1)) \rightarrow (a_3 \neq 1)$.

We can formalize these generalized interventions as follows.

Definition 7 (Generally updated model). *For any $X \in V_a$, any assignment $\vec{z}$ of all variables other than X and any $x \in \mathcal{R}(X)$, let $X(\vec{z}) \leftarrow x$ be a generalized intervention that results in the update $\mathcal{F}_X^{X(\vec{z})\leftarrow x}$ of function $\mathcal{F}_X$, such that*

$$\mathcal{F}_X^{X(\vec{z})\leftarrow x}(z') = \begin{cases} x & \text{if } \vec{z}' = \vec{z}, \\ \mathcal{F}_X(\vec{z}') & \text{otherwise;} \end{cases}$$

Let $\vec{X}(\vec{z})\leftarrow\vec{x}$ denote $X_1(\vec{z})\leftarrow x_1, \ldots, X_k(\vec{z}')\leftarrow x_k$, where same variable from V_a can occur multiple times in $X_1, \ldots, X_k$. For any general intervention $\vec{X}(\vec{z}) \leftarrow \vec{x}$, an updated model is a pair $\mathcal{M}^{\vec{X}(\vec{z})\leftarrow\vec{x}} = (\mathcal{S}, \mathcal{F}^{\vec{X}(\vec{z})\leftarrow\vec{x}})$.

The intervention $[X \leftarrow x]$ can be encoded as a set of generalized interventions: $X \leftarrow x \equiv \cup_{\vec{z}} X(\vec{z}) \leftarrow x$. Since $X \leftarrow x$ replaces the value of $\mathcal{F}_X$ for each input $\vec{z}$.

Now we can extend our generalized syntax $\mathcal{L}(C_g)$ with a new operator:

Definition 8 ($\mathcal{L}(C_g)$ syntax).

$$\varphi ::= (X = x) \mid \neg\varphi \mid \varphi \wedge \varphi \mid [\vec{Y}(\vec{z}) \leftarrow \vec{y}]\varphi,$$

Note that since any variable Y may occur multiple times in $[\vec{Y}(\vec{z}) \leftarrow \vec{y}]$, every agent $i \in \mathbb{AG}$ can modify $\mathcal{F}_i$ in an arbitrary way in $\mathcal{L}(C_g)$. The satisfiability relation $\vDash_g$ is identical to Definition 4 in all items other than $[\vec{Y}(\vec{z}) \leftarrow \vec{y}]\varphi$, for which it is defined as

$$(\mathcal{M}, \vec{u}) \vDash_g [\vec{Y}(\vec{z}) \leftarrow \vec{y}]\varphi \text{ iff } (\mathcal{M}^{\vec{Y}(\vec{z})\leftarrow\vec{y}}, \vec{u}) \vDash \varphi.$$

Now we can generate a CGS for the extended set of operations on models. Note that the set $\{X(\vec{z}) \leftarrow x \mid X \in V_a \ \& \ \vec{z} \in \times_{Z\in(U\cup V)\setminus\{X\}}\mathcal{R}(Z) \ \& \ x \in \mathcal{R}(X)\}$ will generate a larger set of actions Act^* for Γ^*. The set of states Q^* in Γ^* will also contain more elements, because now we have more choices to construct updated causal model $\mathcal{M}^{\vec{X}(\vec{z})\leftarrow\vec{x}}$ for any $\vec{X}(\vec{z})\leftarrow\vec{x}$. In fact, we need to be sure that we will generate every $\mathcal{M}^{\vec{X}(\vec{z})\leftarrow\vec{x}\cdots\vec{Y}(\vec{z'})\leftarrow\vec{y}}$. This is possible because there are only finitely many such models: there only finitely many possible functions $\mathcal{F}_X$ mapping $\times_{Z\in(\mathcal{U}\cup\mathcal{V}-\{X\})}\mathcal{R}(Z)$ to $\mathcal{R}(X)$. So, we want the set of states $Q^*\in\Gamma^*$ to contain a model $\mathcal{M}'$ for any possible updated functions $\mathcal{F}'_{X_1},\ldots,\mathcal{F}'_{X_k}$ for $\mathcal{V}_a=\{X_1,\ldots,X_k\}$. But as we show in Proposition 2, the set of all $\mathcal{M}^{\vec{X}(\vec{z})\leftarrow\vec{x}}$'s is equal to the set of all $\mathcal{M}^{\vec{X}(\vec{z})\leftarrow\vec{x}\cdots\vec{Y}(\vec{z'})\leftarrow\vec{y}}$'s. Next, Π^*, π^* and d^* are defined as before. We say that $o(\mathcal{M}',\vec{X}(\vec{z})\leftarrow\vec{x})=\mathcal{M}''$ iff $\mathcal{M}''=(\mathcal{M}')^{\vec{X}(\vec{z})\leftarrow\vec{x}}$. Thus, given a causal model $\mathcal{M}=(\mathcal{S},\mathcal{F})$ and a context $\vec{u}$ we can generate a general CGS $\Gamma^*_{\mathcal{M}}$ as follows

- $\mathbb{AG}=\mathcal{V}_a$;
- $Q^*=\{\mathcal{M}^{\vec{X}(\vec{z})\leftarrow\vec{x}}\mid\vec{X}\subseteq\mathcal{V}_a\ \&\ \vec{x}\in\times\mathcal{R}(\vec{X})\ \&\ \vec{z}\in\times_{Y\in\mathcal{U}\cup\mathcal{V}}\mathcal{R}(Y)\}$;
- $\Pi^*=\{Y=y\mid Y\in\mathcal{V}\ \&\ y\in\mathcal{R}(Y)\}$;
- π^* is defined as $(Y=y)\in\pi(\mathcal{M}')$ iff $(\mathcal{M}',\vec{u})\vDash'(Y=y)$ for any $\mathcal{M}'\in Q$;
- $Act^*=\{X(\vec{z})\leftarrow x\mid X\in\mathcal{V}_a\ \&\ \vec{z}\in\times_{Z\in(\mathcal{U}\cup\mathcal{V})\setminus\{X\}}\mathcal{R}(Z)\ \&\ x\in\mathcal{R}(X)\}\cup\{\top_X\mid X\in\mathcal{V}_a\}$, where $\top_X$ denotes 'no intervention on X';
- $d^*(X,\mathcal{M}')\subseteq\{X(\vec{z})\leftarrow x\mid x\in\mathcal{R}(X),\vec{z}\in\times_{Z\in(\mathcal{U}\cup\mathcal{V})\setminus\{X\}}\mathcal{R}(Z)\}$ for any $X\in\mathcal{V}_a$ and $\mathcal{M}'\in Q$;
- $o^*(\mathcal{M}',\vec{X}(\vec{z})\leftarrow\vec{x})=\mathcal{M}''$ iff $\mathcal{M}''=\mathcal{M}'^{\vec{X}(\vec{z})\leftarrow\vec{x}}$ for any $\mathcal{M}',\mathcal{M}''\in Q^*$;

This general CGS differs from our previous construction, because the set of general interventions $X(\vec{z})\leftarrow x$ generates a different set of actions Act^* and a set of possible states Q^* comparing to standard interventions $X\leftarrow x$. Now we can establish the result similar to Proposition 1.

Proposition 2. *For any $\mathcal{L}(\mathsf{C}_g)$ formula of the form $[\vec{X}(\vec{z})\leftarrow\vec{x}]\ldots[\vec{Y}(\vec{z'})\leftarrow\vec{y}]\varphi$ there exists an equivalent formula of the form $[X'(\vec{z_i})\leftarrow x',\ldots,Y'(\vec{z_j})\leftarrow y']\varphi$.*

Proof. Let $\vec{Z}$ be a vector $(\vec{X}(\vec{z})\leftarrow\vec{x},\ldots,\vec{Y}(\vec{z'})\leftarrow\vec{y})$. So, each element of $\vec{Z}$ is a basic intervention of the form $Y(\vec{z})\leftarrow y$. We denote k's element of $\vec{Z}$ as $\vec{Z}[k]$. Let W be a set of all pairs $(Y,\vec{z})$ for which $Y(\vec{z})\leftarrow y$ occurs in $\vec{Z}$. So, there is $k\leq|\vec{Z}|$, such that $\vec{Z}[k]=(Y(\vec{z})\leftarrow y)$ and for any $n>k$ and any $y'\neq y$ it holds that $\vec{Z}[n]\neq(Y(\vec{z})\leftarrow y')$. Let $\vec{w}$ be vector of such values for all elements of $\vec{W}$. Then, the resulting models $\mathcal{M}^{(\vec{X}(\vec{z})\leftarrow\vec{x}\cdots\vec{Y}(\vec{z'})\leftarrow\vec{y}}$ and $\mathcal{M}^{\vec{W}\leftarrow\vec{w}}$ are equivalent. So, it holds that $(\mathcal{M}^{(\vec{X}(\vec{z})\leftarrow\vec{x}\cdots\vec{Y}(\vec{z'})\leftarrow\vec{y}},\vec{u})\vDash_g\varphi$ iff $(\mathcal{M}^{\vec{W}\leftarrow\vec{w}},\vec{u})\vDash_g\varphi$.

This proposition in particularly implies, that for any two states $q,q'\in Q^*$, if q' is reachable from q by some series of updates $[\vec{X}(\vec{z})\leftarrow\vec{x}]\ldots[\vec{Y}(\vec{z})\leftarrow\vec{y}]$, then q' is reachable from q' in one step by some update $[X'(\vec{z})\leftarrow x,\ldots,Y'(\vec{z})\leftarrow y']$.

There are of course different ways to introduce additional restrictions on the set of available actions d^*. And there may be different motivation for these restrictions. Firstly, it seems reasonable to require that if some variable $X\in\mathcal{V}_a$ is independent of some other variable $Y\in\mathcal{V}$ in the initial model, then it must remain so for any updated model. Note that the contrary does not hold: if X depends on Y it may become independent of it even after standard intervention $X \leftarrow x$ since $\mathcal{F}_X^{X \leftarrow x}$ becomes a constant function. But this restriction does not look universal: it is easy to imagine that in some situations agent may decide to take into account some information he previously ignored. Secondly, it seems important to allow agents to rewrite the changes in their $\mathcal{F}_i$'s back. Formally, assume that in some state q, the i's function is defined as $\mathcal{F}_i^1$ and i has a strategy str_i, such that for any $\lambda \in plays(q, str_i)$ it holds that in all states $q' = \lambda[1]$ i's function is defined as $\mathcal{F}_i^2$. Then, agent must have a strategy str_i^*, such that for any $\lambda \in plays(q', str_i^*)$ it holds that the $\mathcal{F}_i$ in $\lambda[1]$ is defined as $\mathcal{F}_i^1$. So, i can return $\mathcal{F}_i$ to its initial configuration after any change. This restriction sounds reasonable for multi-agent systems, yet it does not generally hold if the possible actions for agents are standard interventions $[\vec{X}_{AG} \leftarrow \vec{x}]$ described in Sect. 3. Finally, some actions (updates) can turn a recursive model into a non-recursive one. So, the choice of adequate restrictions remains an important issue.

Even though we introduced $\mathcal{L}(C_e)$ and $\mathcal{L}(C_g)$ to reason about sequences of updates performed by agents as their strategies, essentially we worked with one-shot games, because everything was reachable in one step in the corresponding CGS as shown in Propositions 1 and 2. But this may not be the case depending on the additional restrictions on the set of available actions (interventions) $d \in \Gamma$. But these restrictions go beyond the scope of this paper.

5 Uncertainty and Responsibility

Reasoning about strategic abilities often includes reasoning about agents' uncertainty [8]. For example, an agent may be unaware of other agents' choices or about some fact of the world.

Note that previously we generated a CGS for a fixed context $\vec{u}$. But now we assume that the actual context may be unknown to the agent. So, we want to model uncertainty over the pairs $(\mathcal{M}, \vec{u})$, which is a standard assumption for modelling uncertainty in causal models [5,10]. Basically, we want to generate a state for any possible pair $(\mathcal{M}^*, \vec{u'})$. Formally, given a causal model $\mathcal{M}$ we want to generate a CGS $\Gamma_{(\mathcal{M}, \vec{u})}$ for every context $\vec{u}$. Then, let Γ be a disjoint union of all $\Gamma_{(\mathcal{M}, \vec{u})}$. In other words, $Q^{\Gamma} = \{(\mathcal{M}^{\vec{X}(\vec{z}) \leftarrow \vec{x}}, \vec{u}) \mid \vec{X} \subseteq \mathcal{V}_a \ \& \ \vec{x} \in \times \mathcal{R}(\vec{X}) \ \& \ \vec{z} \in \times_{Y \in \mathcal{U} \cup \mathcal{V}} \mathcal{R}(Y) \ \& \ \vec{u} \in \times_{U \in \mathcal{U}} \mathcal{R}(U)\}$.

We say that an *Epistemic* CGS (ECGS) $\Gamma = (\mathbb{AG}, Q, \{\sim_i\}_{i \in \mathbb{AG}}, \Pi, \pi, Act, d, o)$ is a CGS extended with an epistemic relations $\sim_i \subseteq Q \times Q$ for each $i \in \mathbb{AG}$, such that all $\sim_i$'s are equivalence relations. To obtain ECGS Γ^*, we need to extend Γ with these epistemic relations $\sim_i$. We assume that they are already given.

To illustrate the role of knowledge and uncertainty, return to Example 2 again. We want to model a situation when a_3 observes only his own actions and does not know what actions other agents make. Assume also that a_3 does not know the context $\vec{u}$, i.e. the assignment of exogenous variables $\mathcal{U}$ which determine the values of a_1, a_2, P. Figure 5 represents this epistemic state for a_3.

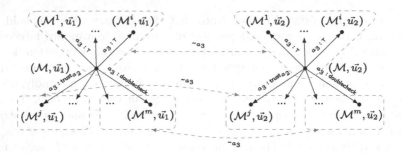

Fig. 5. Epistemic scenario with a_3's uncertainty for Example 2. Note that only two contexts $\vec{u_1}, \vec{u_2}$ are included in the picture, but in general case there can be any possible context $\vec{u'}$. The labels on the transitions demonstrates a_3's action, while other agents' decisions are omitted.

Here a_3 can choose three available actions: not to modify $\mathcal{F}_{a_3}$ (denoted as ⊤), to follow a_2's decision (trust$_{a_2}$) or to double-check order '1' (doublecheck). If a_3 decides not to modify $\mathcal{F}_{a_3}$, then he knows that he is in one of the states form $(\mathcal{M}, \vec{u_1}), (\mathcal{M}^1, \vec{u_1}), \ldots (\mathcal{M}^i, \vec{u_1})$ or $(\mathcal{M}, \vec{u_2}), (\mathcal{M}^1, \vec{u_2}), \ldots (\mathcal{M}^i, \vec{u_2})$. So, in this epistemic state the agent does not know what the actual context is as well as what the decisions of a_1 and a_2 are, i.e. how they react to the context $\vec{u}$. But a_3 still knows that $(P=1 \wedge a_1 = 0) \rightarrow (a_3 = 0)$, $(P=2 \wedge a_2 = 1) \rightarrow (a_3 = 1)$, etc. In other words, even though a_3 does not know what configuration of the environment is (will be) and how other agents (will) react on it, he still knows his own response to any possible situation (because the choice is up to him).

Syntactically, we can extend any of the previously mentioned languages with knowledge operators K_i, where the formula $K_i\varphi$ reads as 'agent i knows φ'. The standard semantics of this operator is defined as

$$(\Gamma, q) \vDash K_i\varphi \text{ iff } \forall q' \in Q, q \sim_i q' \Rightarrow (\Gamma, q') \vDash \varphi$$

Being able to model agents' strategic abilities and uncertainty, we can define such notions as strategic responsibility (or blameworthiness) in the proposed framework.

5.1   Expressing Strategic Responsibility

There are a number of approaches dealing with notions of responsibility and blameworthiness proposed in a literature on causal models [2,5,10,13] as well as for CGS semantics [4,19,22]. The various definitions differ in details, but the main idea is that the group of agents G is responsible for some outcome φ if G could prevent φ independently of their epistemic state. For blameworthiness it is usually required that G had a knowledge *how to* (and hence *could*) prevent φ. Though this distinction is useful in many settings, in this section we discuss the notion of strategic responsibility, which takes into account both strategic ability and epistemic state.

Another important criteria for the definition of responsibility is a minimality condition. We want to claim that the group G is responsible for φ only if G is the minimal coalition that could prevent φ. Without this condition, responsibility would always be distributed to super-groups, so the grand coalition $\mathbb{AG}$ would be responsible for φ whenever a sub-group $G \subset \mathbb{AG}$ is. Note that there can be multiple minimal coalitions responsible for the same φ.

Finally, some approaches (e.g. [2,5,10,13]) deal with a notion of a *degree* of responsibility (or blameworthiness). In these settings, if the group G is responsible (blameworthy) for some outcome φ, then this responsibility (blameworthiness) can be shared and distributed over individual members of G. In this paper we do not discuss the degree of responsibility and assume that the group responsibility is not distributed to the individual members of the group. But, of course, additional procedure for such distribution of responsibility can be defined as an extension. So, in our framework it is the case that if a group G is responsible for φ, then for all $i \in G$ it holds that i is not responsible for φ. If it does not hold and some $i \in G$ is responsible for φ, then G does not satisfy the minimality condition, which contradicts our initial assumption. This property may look counterintuitive, but it guarantees that agents are not considered responsible for φ until they have no strategic power to prevent it (given their uncertainty).

Before we provide a formal definition, we need to introduce the notion of a uniform strategy. Formally, a strategy str_a for agent $a \in \mathbb{AG}$ is called *uniform* if for any states $q, q' \in Q$, such that $q \sim_a q'$, it holds that $str_a(q) = str_a(q')$. A coalition strategy str_G is uniform if it is uniform for every $a \in G$. As we said before any $q \in Q$ is reachable from q_0 in one step. So, it is sufficient to check the strategic ability of agents in the initial state q_0. Let φ be a Boolean combination of basic formulas of the form $Y = y$ for $Y \in \mathcal{V}, y \in \mathcal{R}(Y)$.

Definition 9 (Strategic Responsibility). *A group G is strategically responsible for φ in (Γ, q) if the following three conditions hold:*

1. $\Gamma, q \vDash \varphi$;
2. *There is a uniform strategy str_G for G, such that for all q', s.t. $q_0 \sim_G q'$ and for all $\lambda \in plays(q', str_G)$ it holds that $\Gamma, \lambda[1] \vDash \neg\varphi$;*
3. *No proper subset of G satisfies (2),*

Using this definition we can better illustrate the role of general interventions proposed in Sect. 4.

Example 3. Imagine a simple model with two agents i and j. Let j depend on i's decision, so $\mathcal{F}_j(\vec{z}) = x$ iff $(i = x) \in \vec{z}$. Variable O (outcome) depends on both i and j as follows: $O = 1$ if $i \neq j$ and $O = 0$ otherwise. All variables are binary: $\mathcal{R}(i) = \mathcal{R}(j) = \mathcal{R}(O) = \{0, 1\}$. Assume also that j is uncertain about the actual context as well as about i's actions.

Clearly, agent i cannot prevent $O = 0$ in this settings, so, i is not responsible for $O = 0$. But for agent j the situation is more complicated. If the set of available actions for j is defined by the interventions $[\vec{X} \leftarrow \vec{x}]$ from $\mathcal{L}(\mathsf{C})$ language, then j

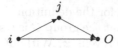

Fig. 6. Dependency graph for Example 3.

has an option to guess i's decision and make an intervention $j \leftarrow x$, where $x = \mathcal{F}_i(\vec{u})$. But until we assume that j is unaware of i's decision and/or the context $\vec{u}$, then Definition 9 does not identify j being responsible for $O = 0$. According to our definition the group $\{i, j\}$ is the minimal coalition that can prevent $O = 0$ given the uncertainty (by choosing either $(i \leftarrow 1, j \leftarrow 0)$ or $(i \leftarrow 0, j \leftarrow 1)$). But if we allow the generalized interventions $[\vec{X}(\vec{z}) \leftarrow \vec{x}]$ from $\mathcal{L}(\mathsf{C}_g)$ to form the set of available actions Act, then $\{i, j\}$ is no longer the minimal coalition that can enforce $O = 1$. Now agent j has available action

$$\mathsf{not}_i := \bigcup_{(i=0) \in \vec{z}} (j(\vec{z}) \leftarrow 1) \cup \bigcup_{(i=1) \in \vec{z}} (j(\vec{z}) \leftarrow 0)$$

Now j can enforce the fact that his decision is opposed to that of i in any context. Thus, action not_i for j can prevent $O = 0$ in his epistemic state and hence j is strategically responsible according to Definition 9. So, the distinction between standard $\vec{X} \leftarrow \vec{x}$ and proposed $\vec{X}(\vec{z}) \leftarrow \vec{x}$ interventions is important for reasoning about responsibility (Fig. 6).

6   Discussion

In this paper we demonstrate how causal models can be used for modeling multi-agent interaction in organizational structures, where decisions of agents may depend on other agents as well as the environment. Such causal models provide us a tool for specification of the behaviour of the agents and the changes of the environment. Moreover, these models contain additional counterfactual information. So, they describe the behaviour of agents and the environment not only for the actual context, but also for any counterfactual scenario. Then we demonstrate how to reason about updates (interventions) of such models in terms of concurrent game structures. In such CGS, agents can choose to modify their reaction on the environment and other agents' decisions by updating their part of a causal model. Then we discuss how the notion of intervention on a causal model can be generalized for reasoning about more complex behavior. Finally, we demonstrate how strategic responsibility can be defined in our settings. We believe that the proposed framework can be useful for reasoning about multi-agent systems.

However, there are still many open questions left for future work. Firstly, as we mentioned before, different restrictions of the set of available actions for agents require closer study. The choice of these restrictions affects the strategic power of the agents and thus determines what these agents can achieve, which may obviously affect responsibility statements. Secondly, we represent the transformations of a causal model in terms of standardly defined CGS, which allows us to deploy a well-known machinery developed in the field of multi-agent systems for reasoning about such structures. The obvious examples of such machinery are widely used logics dealing with strategic power, such as Coalition logic CL [20], Alternating-time temporal logic ATL [7] and Strategy logic SL [18].

References

1. Ahmady, G.A., Mehrpour, M., Nikooravesh, A.: Organizational structure. Procedia. Soc. Behav. Sci. **230**, 455–462 (2016)
2. Alechina, N., Halpern, J.Y., Logan, B.: Causality, responsibility and blame in team plans. In: Das, S., Durfee, E., Larson, K., Winikoff, M. (eds.) Proceedings of the 16th International Conference on Autonomous Agents and Multiagent Systems, AAMAS 2017 (2017)
3. Boudou, J., Lorini, E.: Concurrent game structures for temporal STIT logic. In: Proceedings of the 17th International Conference on Autonomous Agents and MultiAgent Systems, AAMAS 2018, pp. 381–389. International Foundation for Autonomous Agents and Multiagent Systems, Richland (2018)
4. Bulling, N., Dastani, M.: Coalitional responsibility in strategic settings. In: Leite, J., Son, T.C., Torroni, P., van der Torre, L., Woltran, S. (eds.) CLIMA 2013. LNCS (LNAI), vol. 8143, pp. 172–189. Springer, Heidelberg (2013). https://doi.org/10.1007/978-3-642-40624-9_11
5. Chockler, H., Halpern, J.Y.: Responsibility and blame: a structural-model approach. J. Artif. Intell. Res. **22**, 93–115 (2004)
6. Dastani, M., van der Torre, L.W.N., Yorke-Smith, N.: Commitments and interaction norms in organisations. Auton. Agents Multi Agent Syst. **31**(2), 207–249 (2017). https://doi.org/10.1007/s10458-015-9321-5
7. Demri, S., Goranko, V., Lange, M.: Temporal Logics in Computer Science: Finite-State Systems. Cambridge University Press, Cambridge (2016)
8. Fagin, R., Halpern, J.Y., Moses, Y., Vardi, M.: Reasoning About Knowledge. MIT Press, Cambridge (1995)
9. Ferber, J., Gutknecht, O., Michel, F.: From agents to organizations: an organizational view of multi-agent systems. In: Giorgini, P., Müller, J.P., Odell, J. (eds.) AOSE 2003. LNCS, vol. 2935, pp. 214–230. Springer, Heidelberg (2004). https://doi.org/10.1007/978-3-540-24620-6_15
10. Friedenberg, M., Halpern, J.Y.: Blameworthiness in multi-agent settings. In: Proceedings of the AAAI Conference on Artificial Intelligence, vol. 33, pp. 525–532 (2019)
11. Halpern, J.Y.: A modification of the Halpern-Pearl definition of causality. In: Proceedings of the 24th International Joint Conference on Artificial Intelligence (IJCAI 2015), pp. 3022–3033 (2015)
12. Halpern, J.Y.: Axiomatizing causal reasoning. J. Artif. Intell. Res. **12**, 317–337 (2000)
13. Halpern, J.Y.: Actual Causality. The MIT Press, Cambridge (2016)
14. Halpern, J.Y., Pearl, J.: Causes and explanations: a structural-model approach. Part I: causes. Br. J. Philos. Sci. **56**(4), 843–887 (2005)
15. Hübner, J.F., Boissier, O., Kitio, R., Ricci, A.: Instrumenting multi-agent organisations with organisational artifacts and agents. Auton. Agents Multi Agent Syst. **20**, 369–400 (2010). https://doi.org/10.1007/s10458-009-9084-y

16. Khan, S.M., Lespérance, Y.: Knowing why - on the dynamics of knowledge about actual causes in the situation calculus. In: Proceedings of the 20th International Conference on Autonomous Agents and MultiAgent Systems, AAMAS 2021, pp. 701–709. International Foundation for Autonomous Agents and Multiagent Systems, Richland (2021)
17. Lewis, D.: Causation as influence. J. Philos. **97**(4), 182–197 (2000)
18. Mogavero, F., Murano, A., Perelli, G., Vardi, M.Y.: Reasoning about strategies: on the model-checking problem. ACM Trans. Comput. Log. **15**(4), 1–47 (2014)
19. Naumov, P., Tao, J.: An epistemic logic of blameworthiness. Artif. Intell. **283**, 103269 (2020)
20. Pauly, M.: A modal logic for coalitional power in games. J. Log. Comput. **12**(1), 149–166 (2002)
21. Pearl, J.: Causality: Models, Reasoning, and Inference. Cambridge University Press, Cambridge (2000)
22. Yazdanpanah, V., Dastani, M., Jamroga, W., Alechina, N., Logan, B.: Strategic responsibility under imperfect information. In: Proceedings of the 18th International Conference on Autonomous Agents and MultiAgent Systems, AAMAS 2019, pp. 592–600. International Foundation for Autonomous Agents and Multiagent Systems, Richland (2019)

Multi-armed Bandit Based Tariff Generation Strategy for Multi-agent Smart Grid Systems

Sanjay Chandlekar[1]([envelope]) [ORCID], Easwar Subramanian[2] [ORCID], and Sujit Gujar[1] [ORCID]

[1] International Institute of Information Technology (IIIT) Hyderabad, Hyderabad, India
`sanjay.chandlekar@research.iiit.ac.in, sujit.gujar@iiit.ac.in`
[2] TCS Innovation Labs, Hyderabad, India
`easwar.subramanian@tcs.com`

Abstract. The emergence of smart grid technology has opened the door for wide-scale automation in decision-making. A distribution company, an integral part of a smart grid system, has to procure electricity from the wholesale market and then sell it to customers in the retail market by publishing attractive tariff contracts. It can deploy autonomous agents to make decisions on its behalf. In this work, we describe the tariff contracts generation strategy of one such autonomous agent, which is based on a Contextual Multi-armed Bandit (ConMAB) based learning technique to generate tariff contracts for various types of customers in the retail market of smart grids. We particularly utilize the Exponential-weight algorithm for Exploration and Exploitation (EXP-3) for ConMAB-based learning. We call our proposed strategy GENERATETARIFFS-EXP3. Our previous work shows that maintaining an appropriate market share in the retail market yields high net revenue. Thus, we first present a game-theoretic analysis that determines an optimal level of market share. Then we train our proposed strategy to achieve and maintain the suggested level of market share by adapting to the market situation and revising the tariff contracts periodically. We validate our proposed strategy in PowerTAC, a close-to real-world smart grid simulator, and showcase that it is able to maintain the suggested market share.

Keywords: Contextual Multi-armed Bandit (ConMAB) · EXP3 · Smart Grids · Tariff Generation in Multi-agent Environment · PowerTAC

1 Introduction

Recent years have seen rapid growth in smart grid technology. Some developed nations have already adopted smart grid technology to replace the conventional grid system. Fundamentally, just like a conventional grid, a *smart grid* is also an electricity network that supplies electricity to customers; however smart grid enables two-way digital communication where customers can also communicate with electricity providers. It also allows for monitoring, analysis, control and communication between participants to improve the efficiency, transparency, and reliability of the system [14].

The smart grid system comprises the wholesale and retail markets, transmission lines, and distribution company (DC) as the prominent players. The DCs play a significant role in smart grid operations and are responsible for the efficient functioning of the system. The major tasks of DC are to buy electricity from the wholesale market, sell electricity to retail customers by generating lucrative yet profitable tariff contracts, and manage the supply-demand balance in the smart grid system. The transmission lines are responsible for electricity transmission from GenCos to retail customers.

The retail market of a smart grid, which is the focus of this work, incorporates various types of customers like households, office spaces, villages, producers (customers having solar panels or wind turbines), electric vehicles, battery storage, and a few others. Some of these customers have the capability to change their electricity usage pattern based on the signals from the DC, commonly in the form of tariff contracts. To cater to the variety of customers, tariff contracts too can be of multiple types. For example, (i) Fixed Price Tariff (FPT) having the same rate values for all hours in a day/week, (ii) Time of Use (ToU) tariff having different rate values for different hours in a day/week, (iii) Tier tariffs having different rate values corresponding to different usage slots, (iv) variable tariffs where rate values can change dynamically, or (v) combination of any of the above tariff types. DCs decide the appropriate tariff types and tariff rate values for the customers in its portfolio.

The smart grid system is quite complex in nature, and it is practically impossible to test or validate the new strategies on the real-world smart grid system. Thus, in order to aid in smart grid research, Power Trading Agent Competition (PowerTAC) designed a close-to-real-world smart grid simulator [4]. PowerTAC simulates all the crucial elements of a smart grid system mentioned above. In PowerTAC, DC are commonly known as *electricity broker* or *broker* or *agent*. PowerTAC embodies a variety of customer models to represent the wide variety of customers as seen in the real world. It supports all kinds of tariff contracts mentioned earlier. Furthermore, PowerTAC introduces a balancing market that handles the real-time balancing of supply and demand. It penalizes agents in case of an imbalance in their portfolio.

The smart grid technology enables the use of adaptive autonomous agents to make crucial decisions on behalf of DC, and a simulator like PowerTAC helps analyze the effectiveness of such agents. To this end, PowerTAC organizes an annual tournament where participating teams design an autonomous agent that acts as DC and makes all the decisions in the simulated smart grid environment. The agents are required to design suitable strategies for the wholesale, retail and balancing markets. In this work, we specifically focus on the *tariff contract generation* problem in the retail market of the smart grid. To generate a new tariff contract, an agent needs to decide the tariff contract type and the tariff contract's rate values. The tariff contracts are public information; any agent and a customer in the simulation can see all the active tariffs in the retail market.

Thus, if an agent does not adapt to the changing market situation and does not update its tariff contracts periodically, any opponent agent can offer better tariff contracts and take away all the customers. Thus, it is paramount to update tariff contracts periodically, which can be done using either heuristic-based approaches or learning-based approaches.

In the PowerTAC literature, authors have proposed gradient-based MDP-based strategies [2], optimization strategies [15], and genetic algorithm-based approaches [16] to publish tariff contracts in the retail market. The experimental evidence suggests that the seemingly optimal class of strategies of capturing all the market share may suffer from high grid balancing penalties as all the customers are subscribed to one agent, and that agent alone has to bear the total penalty for the grid imbalance. To remedy this, agent TUC_TAC proposed a strategy aimed at acquiring only half the retail market share [10]. However, all the above strategies except TUC_TAC sought to maximize the revenue/profit without explicitly controlling the agent's market share. Furthermore, the majority of the above retail strategies, including TUC_TAC, have been generic and are not effectively specialized for different player configurations and therefore fail to maintain performance across different player configurations.

To overcome the above problems, we, team *VidyutVanika*, designed an autonomous agent that emerged as the champion of the PowerTAC tournament in the year 2021 and 2022 [1]. The tariff strategy of our agent is inspired by the game theory literature that decides the optimal market share for various player configurations and uses heuristic-based techniques to achieve and maintain that market share during the simulation. In this work, we replace our heuristics-based strategy with a learning-based strategy to achieve similar performance. For that, we design a tariff strategy that learns to achieve and maintain the optimal market share. We model this problem by utilizing techniques derived from *Contextual Multi-armed Bandit (ConMAB)* and solve using the *Exponential-weight algorithm for Exploration and Exploitation (EXP-3)*. Our novelty lies in the formulation of the learning framework; as opposed to previous strategies that aim to maximize profit, we aim to maintain the optimal market share via a learning-based strategy which in turn reduces other costs and makes our agent profitable. We use ConMAB as its problem setting resembles the tariff generation problem in hand, where given a context, an agent has to pick an appropriate tariff (an optimal arm of ConMAB) that enables it to maintain the appropriate market share and, in turn, delivers higher returns. In summary, our contributions are as follows:

- We present game theoretical analysis to determine an optimal market share for various player configurations by modeling the PowerTAC games as two-player zero-sum games and calculate their mixed strategy Nash equilibrium.
- We propose a novel Contextual Multi-armed Bandit-based tariff contract generation strategy GENERATETARIFFS-EXP3, that learns to achieve and maintain the market share suggested by game theoretical analysis.
- We showcase the policies learned by the proposed strategy and its efficacy in maintaining the suggested market share during the PowerTAC games.

2   Related Work

Many approaches in the literature have been suggested to tackle the tariff generation problem, and a few have been implemented in PowerTAC as well. In the retail market of smart grids, techniques such as demand response, peak demand pricing, and learning-based approaches have been proposed to design competitive tariffs. Many multi-armed bandit-based strategies have been proposed to publish tariffs in the smart grid domain. Most of this work focuses on demand response in a smart grid where customers are incentivized via tariffs to curtail their usages in response to electricity supplier's signals [3,5–7,9,13].

In the past PowerTAC tournaments, Markov Decision Process (MDP) based strategies were most popular in the retail market. The past brokers like COLD Energy and VidyutVanika18, as well as Reddy & Veloso, modeled the decision process in the retail market as an MDP to generate tariff contracts [2,11,12]. In fact, both COLD Energy and VidyutVanika18's tariff strategies were motivated by Reddy & Veloso. In these approaches, the state space is constituted by market parameters such as market rationality, agent's portfolio status etc. and action space was designed with actions to increase or decrease the rate value of tariffs by a certain amount. The reward function was profit in the market. TacTex'13 employed a gradient-based optimization method for tariff generation, and AgentUDE17 utilized a genetic algorithm-based tariff strategy [15,16]. However, all the above strategies incur high grid imbalance costs as they do not focus on the market share of customers in their portfolio. Agent TUC_TAC proposed a strategy to acquire only half the retail market share [10] for each type of game configuration. Motivated by TUC_TAC's idea, we designed a heuristic-based tariff strategy backed by game theoretical analysis to determine the optimal market for various game configurations [1]. Furthermore, instead of focusing on revenue/profit, we aimed to maintain the appropriate market share, which helped us earn high returns. However, none of the previous works present an equilibrium-based strategy that can be learned online in the retail market. The novelty of this work lies in designing a game-theory-inspired ConMAB-based retail strategy that *learns* to achieve and maintain equilibrium market share in the retail market.

3   PowerTAC Simulator: An Overview

PowerTAC is a simulation platform that mimics essential components of a smart-grid ecosystem comprising retail, wholesale, balancing markets, and distribution companies (DCs). The wholesale market consists of GenCo, which sells electricity via auctions; the balancing market manages the real-time balance of supply and demand. The retail market consists of state-of-the-art customer models that simulate real-world smart grid users, including consumers, producers, and storage users such as households, offices, villages, hospitals, and renewable energy producers. Storage customers use electric vehicles or batteries to store electricity and supply it to the grid on demand. PowerTAC allows deploying an autonomous

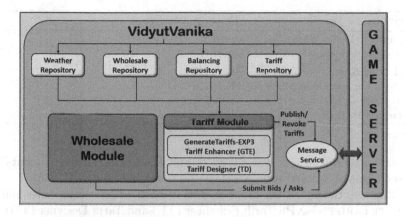

Fig. 1. System Architecture of VidyutVanika

agent to automate a DC's operations in retail, wholesale, and balancing markets to earn profits. PowerTAC also organizes an annual tournament in which numerous teams deploy autonomous brokers to compete in all three markets. The tournament consists of multiple games organized between agents in different player configurations and varying weather conditions, with each game lasting around 60 simulation days. During the game, an agent aims to develop a subscriber base in the retail market by offering competitive tariffs, such as FPT, tiered, variable or ToU, to sell energy bought in the wholesale market. Agents can also manage grid imbalances through subscriptions to storage customers. Agents update their tariffs periodically based on other available tariffs in the market, market and weather conditions, and customers' responses to previous tariffs. In the simulation environment, agents are provided with information that helps them make decisions. All agents in the retail market can see new and revoked tariffs and weather information. The final cash position of all brokers across games is aggregated to determine the tournament winner. A comprehensive simulator description is available in the 2020 PowerTAC specifications by Ketter et al. [4].

4 VidyutVanika (VV): Retail Module

In this section, we show the generic system architecture of our agent *Vidyut-Vanika*, which emerged as the champion in the last two editions of the PowerTAC tournaments, namely PowerTAC'21 and PowerTAC'22. As shown in Fig. 1, VidyutVanika incorporates a wholesale module and a retail (tariff) module. It also has various repositories to store the important information received from the server. These repositories contain information about the weather, wholesale market procurement cost, all available tariffs in the market and customers' electricity usage patterns. In the current work, we only focus on the retail module; thus, we take our wholesale module as a black box that places bids in the wholesale market auction and procures the required energy. We replaced the heuristic-based

---

Algorithm 1. TariffDesigner(avgPrice, powerType)

1: pattern ← DefineWeeklyTariffPattern().
2: $s[]$ ← DefineSurplusMultipliers(pattern)
3: find $normRate : \frac{\sum_{i=1}^{168} s_i * normRate}{168} = avgPrice$
4: rate[i] ← $s_i * normRate, for\ i \in \{1, 2, ..., 168\}$
5: ToUTariff ← CreateTariff(rate, powerType)
6: **return** ToUTariff

---

retail strategy used in the PowerTAC'21 and PowerTAC'22 tournaments with proposed ConMAB-based retail strategy, GENERATETARIFFS-EXP3.

As shown in the figure, the retail module consists of two submodules, namely, GENERATETARIFFS-EXP3 Tariff Enhancer (TE) and Tariff Designer (TD). The TE submodule comprises the proposed ConMAB-based tariff contract generation strategy, which is solved using the EXP-3 algorithm. This submodule observes the optimal market share for the ongoing game's player configuration by contacting the game theory module, then based on the ConMAB-based learning till that point, it picks the suitable action to enhance the current tariff. This TE sub-module calculates mean tariff rates that would maintain the appropriate market share. The TD sub-module designs weekly ToU tariffs by taking the mean rates suggested by TE as input. Below, we describe the details of the TD sub-module, while the details of the TE sub-module are deferred to the following sections.

Tariff Designer (TD): Algorithm 1 outlines TD, which is responsible for designing a weekly ToU tariff based on the average input price (*avgPrice*) received from TE. TD first generates a binary weekly tariff pattern using the *DefineWeeklyTariffPattern()* method, which identifies peak and non-peak hours by analyzing historical net market demand values retrieved from past PowerTAC tournaments. Peak hours are determined to be times of high demand, such as morning and evening hours. TD then uses the *DefineSurplusMultipliers()* method to set surplus multipliers s_i for each of the 168 hours in a week. These multipliers are greater than 1 for peak hours and 1 for non-peak hours. s_i depends on the peak magnitude observed from market demand data for peak hours. Thereafter, we calculate the *normRate*, which, after getting multiplied with s_i values of the week, results in *avgPrice* on an average. These *normRate* values with surplus s_i values are the rate values of the newly generated ToU tariff.

5   Game Theory to Determine Optimal Market-Share

This section presents the game-theoretical analysis to decide an optimal market share for various player configurations of PowerTAC games, which is then used in the TE submodule to design suitable ToU tariffs. We show the analysis for three different player configurations of PowerTAC games, namely, 2-Player, 3-Player, and 5-Player games. We construct a utility matrix for each player configuration by modeling the PowerTAC games as *two-player zero-sum games*, solving which results in an equilibrium market share. To assist the reader, we introduce a few definitions before proceeding further.

The below analysis is first presented in our previous work [1], where we presented the analysis briefly. Here, we include more details and present the complete analysis for all three player configurations under consideration, along with respective utility matrices. Furthermore, we utilized the below analysis to design a heuristics-based tariff strategy for our broker VidyutVanika during the PowerTAC'21 and PowerTAC'22 tournaments. The tariff strategy aimed to maintain the market share suggested by the game theory analysis using intelligent heuristics. In this work, too, we aim to maintain the suggested market share, albeit by following a more methodological way, that is, by incorporating the game theoretical analysis in the tariff strategy and framing the tariff contracts generation problem as a learning problem; and learning to improve tariffs *online* by looking at the market situation with the help of ConMAB-based techniques. A detailed description of the tariff strategy framework is included in Sect. 6.

Definition 1 (Mixed Strategy). *For player i, its mixed strategy σ_i is a probability distribution over the strategy set S_i, i.e., $\sigma_i(s_i), s_i \in S_i$ indicates the probability with which player i plays s_i.*

Definition 2 (Mixed Strategy Nash Equilibrium (MSNE)). *Given a N player game $\Gamma = <N, (S_i), (u_i)>$, a mixed strategy profile $(\sigma_1^*, ..., \sigma_n^*)$ is called a mixed strategy Nash equilibrium if, $\forall i \in N$, $u_i(\sigma_i^*, \sigma_{-i}^*) \geq u_i(\sigma_i, \sigma_{-i}^*), \forall \sigma_i \in \Delta(S_i)$. σ_{-i}^* denotes mixed strategies of all players except i.*

The utility of the row player is defined in Eq. 1, which is the difference between the average final cash positions of the row and column players. This way of modeling the utility matrix helps us to maximize the difference between VidyutVanika's average cash position and the opponent's average cash position, thereby helping VidyutVanika generate higher profits than opponents. As we formulate this as a zero-sum game, the column player gets negative of the utility calculated in Eq. 1.

$$u_1(s_i, s_{-i}) = \frac{1}{T} \sum_{i=1}^{T} x_i - \frac{1}{n} \sum_{k=1}^{n} (\frac{1}{T} \sum_{i=1}^{T} y_{ik}) \tag{1}$$

In Eq. 1, x_i denotes the final cash balance of VidyutVanika in the game i, while y_{ik} denotes the final cash balance of opponent agent k in the game i and n denotes the number of opponent agents in the game. For our analysis, the average values are taken over $T = 5$ games.

In our modeling, we select VidyutVanika as the row player, and a subset of opponents, depending on the player configuration, act as a sole column player. The row player's (VidyutVanika's) strategy set is given by $S_1 = \{0\%, 15\%, 30\%, 45\%, 60\%, 75\%, 100\%\}$, where each element in the set $S1$ specifies the target market share that VidyutVanika has to maintain during the simulated

VV / Opp	(TT, VV18)	(TT, C)	(TT, VV20)	(TT, A)	(VV18, C)	(VV18, VV20)	(VV18, A)	(C, A)	(VV20, C)	(VV20, A)
0%	0.1103	-0.6891	-1.2093	-0.1409	-0.8984	-0.1235	0.3564	0.7303	-0.9107	0.608
15%	0.2327	-0.8492	-1.478	0.1224	-0.3161	0.8468	1.0907	0.6508	-0.4521	0.6338
30%	0.0913	-0.168	-0.4011	-0.208	-0.1865	0.9829	1.235	0.8528	-0.0197	0.8661
45%	0.8468	0.1589	0.1358	0.155	0.1415	1.8847	1.3087	0.8597	0.2026	0.8561
60%	1.069	0.0414	0.1811	0.2057	0.5651	1.3724	1.0288	0.8264	-0.2484	0.8409
75%	0.9615	-0.1678	-0.5645	0.1384	-0.0956	1.3274	1.0251	0.1766	-0.1712	0.3298
100%	0.7881	-0.5495	-1.0114	-0.5146	-0.6076	0.4744	-0.0569	-0.069	-1.3863	0.0263

Fig. 2. 3-Player Games Analysis (Utility Values in Millions) (Color figure online)

games. We have five agents from past PowerTAC tournaments to act as opponents in our analysis, namely, TUC_TAC (TT) [10], VidyutVanika18 ($VV18$) [2], VidyutVanika20 ($VV20$), CrocodileAgent (C) and AgentUDE (A) [16]. The column player strategy set $S2$ depends on the player configuration. For example, in a 2-Player game configuration, we need only one opponent against VidyutVanika; thus, $S2 = \{TT, VV18, VV20, C, A\}$. Similarly, in a 3-Player game configuration, we need two opponents against VidyutVanika, which is to be selected from the available set of five agents; thus, total $5c2$ elements is the set $S2$ as shown in Fig. 2.

VV / Opp	(TT, VV18, VV20,C)	(TT, VV18, VV20,A)	(TT, VV18, A,C)	(TT, A, VV20,C)	(A, VV18, VV20,C)
0%	-0.893	-0.298	-0.169	-0.156	1.737
15%	-0.199	-0.017	-0.205	-0.146	1.581
30%	0.112	-0.049	0.106	0.044	1.898
45%	-0.083	0.041	0.159	0.143	1.808
60%	-0.312	0.027	-0.288	-0.102	1.741
75%	-0.493	-0.228	-0.373	-0.409	1.025
100%	-0.498	-0.561	-0.188	-0.188	0.996

VV / Opp	TT	VV18	VV20	C	A
0%	-1.115	-0.7268	-1.4139	-0.7265	-0.6337
15%	-2.9234	-1.7458	-2.028	0.3205	-1.6095
30%	-1.9241	-0.8775	-1.1025	0.3325	-0.3431
45%	-0.5181	-0.1804	0.0142	0.7307	0.2069
60%	-0.0596	0.5893	0.461	0.4369	1.3764
75%	-0.1405	1.3299	0.0818	-0.9286	1.8755
100%	-0.267	0.9995	-0.3381	-0.8462	0.7812

(a) 5-Player Games Analysis   (b) 2-Player Games Analysis

Fig. 3. Games Analysis (Utility Values in Millions) (Color figure online)

Equilibrium Calculation: Figures 3b, 2 and 3a show the utility matrices for 2-Player, 3-Player, and 5-Player configurations, respectively. Each cell describes the utility value, a cash difference in millions calculated by playing a set of T games. The same process is repeated for all the combinations of VidyutVanika's strategies ($S1$) and opponents' strategies ($S2$) to create the full utility matrix. Thereafter, we use Gambit [8] to solve the game and output the Nash Equilibrium. We found that each of the above three player configurations exhibits Mixed Strategy Nash Equilibrium (MSNE).

- **For 2-Player Configurations:** Based on Fig. 3b, the utility matrix leads to Pure Strategy Nash Equilibrium of 60% market shares.
- **For 3-Player Configurations:** Based on Fig. 2, the utility matrix leads to MSNE of randomizing between 45% and 60% market shares with probabilities 0.8 and 0.2, respectively, which results in equilibrium market share of 48% ($0.8 * 45 + 0.2 * 60$).
- **For 5-Player Configurations:** Based on Fig. 3a, the utilitys matrix leads to MSNE of randomizing between 30% and 45% market shares with probabilities 0.43 and 0.57, respectively, which translates to equilibrium market share of 38.55% ($0.43 * 30 + 0.57 * 45$).

The same results can be seen visually as well; the green-shaded regions in the figures show the strategies having the higher utilities $u_1(\sigma_1^*, \sigma_{-1}^*)$ than the remaining strategies $u_1(\sigma_1, \sigma_{-1}^*)$ for row-player VidyutVanika, which leads to above-calculated MSNEs.

Adopting Equilibrium in PowerTAC Games: The above analysis suggests how we should randomize to achieve equilibrium market share. However, due to the stochasticity of the PowerTAC simulation and customer models, it is not easy to maintain one particular market share across different games. Hence, we aim to maintain market share within specific bounds ([*middle, high*]). Thus, in our experiments, we treat the above-calculated equilibrium market shares as the higher bounds (*high*) on the desired market share. We further define the middle bounds (*middle*), which is $0.7 * high$. We aim to maintain the market share between *middle* and *high*, and thus, to train GENERATETARIFFS-EXP3, we give $0.85 * high$ $((1 + 0.7)/2 = 0.85)$ as the target optimal market share. So, for 2-Player, 3-Player, and 5-Player configurations, target optimal market shares for GENERATETARIFFS-EXP3 are 51%, 40.8%, and 32.3%, respectively.

6   Tariff Strategy: A Contextual MAB Approach

In the previous section, we showcase how we determine the optimal market for various player configurations. Based on our previous work, we also stated that maintaining a market share close to the optimal market share is sufficient to achieve effective profits in the market. Motivated by this, in this section, we showcase the formulation of the proposed GENERATETARIFFS-EXP3. The proposed strategy is modeled as a Markov Decision Process (MDP) consisting of a tuple $<S, A, P, R>$. S represents the state space of the MDP, A denotes the action space and R denotes the rewards of the MDP. P represents the transition probabilities of the MDP, that is, the probability with which MDP transitions to the next state by taking action in the current state. However, the model does not know the transition probabilities. To learn the optimal action in each state (called a policy) in the absence of transition probabilities, we use ConMAB techniques along with the EXP-3 algorithm. Below we describe how the MDP is formulated and optimal policies are learned.

6.1   State Space

Here, we define the state space of the GENERATETARIFFS-EXP3 We construct state space depending on the difference between the current market share (CMS) of the GENERATETARIFFS-EXP3 and the optimal market share (OMS) suggested by the game theory module in Sect. 5. Let us denote the difference between both the market shares by Δ, so

$$\Delta = (OMS - CMS).$$

We categorize Δ into seven buckets, as shown below.

- State 0: $|\Delta| \leq OMS * 0.1$
- State 1: $\Delta > OMS * 0.1$ and $\Delta \leq OMS * 0.4$
- State 2: $\Delta > OMS * 0.4$ and $\Delta \leq OMS * 0.7$
- State 3: $\Delta > OMS * 0.7$
- State 4: $-\Delta > OMS * 0.1$ and $-\Delta \leq OMS * 0.4$
- State 5: $-\Delta > OMS * 0.4$ and $-\Delta \leq OMS * 0.7$
- State 6: $-\Delta > OMS * 0.7$

The above state space is designed in such a way that it gives the reflection of the GENERATETARIFFS-EXP3's current situation in the tariff market. These numbers that get multiplied with OMS are chosen heuristically based on rigorous experimental analysis. For example, suppose the OMS for a game configuration is 50%, then the State 0 occurs when the broker's CMS is within ±5% difference of the OMS (i.e., between 45% to 55%). Similarly, State 1 happens when the broker's CMS is lower than the OMS, and the difference between OMS and CMS ($OMS - CMS$) is more than 5%, but less than 20% (between 30% to 45%). The states 1, 2 and 3 represent the situation when the broker's CMS is lower than the OMS. Replicating the similar logic for the other side as well, states 4, 5, and 6 represent the situation when the broker's CMS is higher than the OMS. The State 4 results in when the difference between CMS and OMS ($-OMS + CMS$) is more than 5%, but less than 20% (between 55% to 70%). The above seven states cover all possible differences between the broker's CMS and the OMS.

6.2   Action Space

The action space of the GENERATETARIFFS-EXP3 generates a new tariff contract in the tariff market. As discussed in Sect. 3, a broker needs to come up with rate values to design a new tariff contract. GENERATETARIFFS-EXP3's action space modifies the currently active tariff or suggests keeping the sane tariff active. Below is the action space,

- Action 0: $step = 0.0$ [$Maintain$]
- Action 1: $step = -0.02$ [$Lower1$]
- Action 2: $step = -0.04$ [$Lower2$]
- Action 3: $step = 0.02$ [$Higher1$]
- Action 4: $step = 0.04$ [$Higher2$]

As shown in the action space, GENERATETARIFFS-EXP3 can choose one of the five actions at any instance. The action selection problem is modeled as a MAB problem, which is solved using EXP-3 algorithm in Sect. 6.4. At any instance, GENERATETARIFFS-EXP3 can choose to maintain or modify the current tariff. If it chooses to modify the current tariff, it can either decrease the rate value of the currently active tariff or increase the rate value. The above action space provides two options for both scenarios; $Lower1$ or $Lower2$ to decrease the rate value and $Higher1$ or $Higher2$ to increase the rate value.

After selecting an action, we decide the rate value of the new tariff by adding the *step* value of the selected action to the currently active tariff's average rate value. The step sizes are chosen based on the PowerTAC customers' reactions to tariffs. Thus generated new rate value is given to the TD sub-module that designs and publishes the new ToU tariff in the market. Note that, in PowerTAC sign convention, consumption tariffs are negatively valued as customers need to *pay* that amount; thus, actions such as *Lower1* and *Lower2* would make tariffs more negative (less attractive for customers), and actions such as *Higher1* and *Higher2* would make tariff less negative (more attractive for customers).

6.3   Reward

The reward function is defined in line with the state space, as shown below.

- reward = 1.00, if $|\Delta| \leq 5\%$
- reward = 0.50, if $|\Delta| \leq 20\%$
- reward = 0.25, if $|\Delta| \leq 35\%$
- reward = 0.00, otherwise

The above reward function awards the GENERATETARIFFS-EXP3 based on its ability to achieve market share close to the OMS. It gets the highest reward of 1 when the absolute difference between the broker's CMS and the OMS is less than 5%. Similarly, it gets a slightly worse reward when the difference is more than 5% (but less than 20%). The worst case happens when the market share achieved by GENERATETARIFFS-EXP3 is far away from the OMS (the difference is more than 35%); in that case, GENERATETARIFFS-EXP3 receives a zero reward. The numbers 5%, 20% and 35% are translated from the state space, that multiplies OMS with 10%, 40% and 70% to wrap OMS from both the sides (less than OMS and greater than OMS). While giving rewards, we are considering the difference between CMS and OMS from any one side, thus, the state space numbers are divided by 2 to get the reward function.

6.4   EXP-3 Algorithm

The above contextual MAB-based tariff generation problem is solved using the *Exponential-weight algorithm for Exploration and Exploitation (EXP-3 algorithm)*. Generally, EXP-3 is used for non-contextual MAB problems but can also be extended for contextual MAB problems. For each state in the state space, It maintains a list of weights for each action in the action space. Using these weights, it stochastically decides which action to take next, and based on the reward received, it increases or decreases the relevant weights. Thus generated table resembles with Q-Table in Reinforcement Learning (RL). In RL Q-Table, the values of the state-action pairs denote how good it is to take that action in the given state in the long run, whereas, in ConMAB, the state-action pairs have the same interpretation albeit for an immediate future. Due to the similarity,

---

Algorithm 2. Contextual EXP-3(state s)

1: Initialize/Load table$[|S|][|A|]$

2: $prob(s,i,t) = (1-\gamma)\frac{table(s,i,t)}{\sum_{a=1}^{|A|} table(s,a,t)} + \frac{\gamma}{|A|}, \forall i \in \{1,2,...,|A|\}$

3: Sample next action act stochastically from $[prob(s,1,t), prob(s,2,t), ..., prob(s,|A|,t)]$

4: Observe reward $r(s,act,t)$ for taking action act in state s at t

5: Update the reward:

   $\hat{r}(s,a,t) = r(s,a,t)/prob(s,a,t)$, if $a = act_t$

   $\hat{r}(s,a,t) = 0$, otherwise

6: $table(s,i,t+1) = table(s,i,t) * e^{\gamma*\hat{r}(s,i,t)/|A|}, \forall i \in \{1,2,...,|A|\}$

---

we call the table generated by ConMAB as Q-Table. We introduce an egalitarianism factor $\gamma \in [0,1]$, tuning the desire to randomly pick an action. That is, if $\gamma = 1$, the weights do not affect the choices at any step. Algorithm 2 shows the modified EXP-3 algorithm for contextual MAB:

Algorithm 2 takes the current state s as the input. If the *table* is empty (at the start of the training), then initialize it with suitable values; otherwise, load the previously created *table* into memory. As described earlier, the dimensions of this table are $|S| * |A|$ (the size of state space S * the size of action space A). In the next step, we weigh the actions based on the corresponding values stored in the *table*. The probability of selecting an action i in state s at time t ($prob(s,i,t)$) is directly proportional to the corresponding state-action pair at time ($table(s,i,t)$). Here, an egalitarianism factor $\gamma \in [0,1]$ also plays a role in action selection; $\gamma = 0$ would calculate probabilities purely based on *table* values, while $\gamma = 1$ would assign the same probability to each of the actions. After calculating the probabilities for each action i in state s, in step 3, the algorithm stochastically picks one action based on the calculated probabilities. In step 4, the algorithm observes the reward $r(s,a,t)$ for taking action a in state s at time t. After that, in step 5, the algorithm updates the reward based on whether the action was selected or not; the new reward function $\hat{r}(s,a,t)$ is inversely proportional to the probability $prob(s,a,t)$. If the action was not selected, then the $\hat{r}(s,a,t)$ is set to zero, as expected. Finally, in step 6, the algorithm updates the *table*; only the state-action pair that got selected at time t gets updated, while other values in *table* remain unchanged. These updates are exponential in nature and proportional to the new reward $\hat{r}(s,a,t)$.

The EXP-3 algorithm deals with the explore-exploit dilemma by stochastically selecting an action based on the calculated probabilities in step 3. This step ensures picking the best-known action till now with higher probability while also occasionally selecting 'not so good' actions. After selecting any action and getting the corresponding reward in that state, it weighs the reward with respect to the probability. A reward for low-probability actions gets enhanced even further, allowing the algorithm to revisit those actions. Thus, the EXP-3 algorithm visits all the state-action pairs a sufficient number of times. In the next section, we show how GENERATETARIFFS-EXP3 learns the policies to maintain the optimal market shares in each player configuration.

7   PowerTAC: Experiments and Results

In this section, we describe how the strategy described in Sect. 6 is deployed to the PowerTAC games. We further demonstrate how the learning process for EXP-3 is carried out in PowerTAC environment. We start by detailing the experimental setup, followed by the results and discussions.

7.1   Experimental Set-Up

Q-Table Training: As the broker needs to adapt to various player configurations in PowerTAC, we deploy separate tariff MDP and EXP-3 algorithms in each configuration. In this experiment, we train three different models for three-player configurations, namely, 2-Player, 3-Player, and 5-Player. We chose these three configurations as the last PowerTAC tournament (PowerTAC22) had the same configurations. In each player configuration, we played 50 PowerTAC games, where each game simulates the smart grid operations for two months. At the start of the training, we initialize the Q-Table with appropriate values and publish an initial tariff in the market. We keep the same tariff active for a day (24 hours) and then update the tariff at the start of the next day. While updating the tariff, we note the CMS and decide the reward to update the Q-Table as shown in Algorithm 2. This constitutes one epoch of training. After that, based on the CMS, we calculate the current state and choose an action following the EXP-3 algorithm, and publish a new ToU tariff in the market by using the TD sub-module. We continue this process and record the Q-Table after every checkpoint (typically after every 100 epoch) as well as at the end of the game. While starting a new game, we read and update the previously stored Q-Table while training. We train GENERATETARIFFS-EXP3 for around 3000 epochs for each configuration and store the final Q-Tables.

Performance Testing: We conduct performance testing to verify whether GENERATETARIFFS-EXP3 is able to maintain the desired market share during the games after getting trained. As mentioned previously, we store intermediate Q-Tables after every checkpoint and test the effectiveness of GENERATETARIFFS-EXP3 at various stages of the training. For this, we take Q-Tables from seven different checkpoints, play 10 games with each Q-Table, and record the average market shares during the games. At the end of 10 games, we record the average and standard deviation of market shares after 10 games; we do this for all seven Q-Tables. In this paper, we present the performance testing for the 3-Player configuration. The following section showcases the results of this experiment.

7.2   Results and Discussion

In this section, we present the results of the Q-Table training for the above-mentioned 2-Player, 3-Player, and 5-Player configurations. Furthermore, we also show the efficacy of the GENERATETARIFFS-EXP3 in maintaining the suggested market share during the games.

Q-Table Training: Figure 4, 5, and 6 are the final Q-Tables after training GENERATETARIFFS-EXP3 for 50 games (around 3000 epochs) for each player configuration. In Q-Tables, the higher the value (green-shaded region) for any state-action pair, the higher the probability of that action getting selected in the given state.

First, focus on the 2-Player Q-Table in Fig. 4. GENERATETARIFFS-EXP3 learns to maintain the currently active tariff if the current state is State 0, which is the best thing to do as the market share is already in the desired range. In State 1 as well, it chooses to continue with the current tariff. When the CMS is lower than OMS in State 2 and 3, it learns to select *Higher2* action to make tariff cheaper and very much attractive for customers to increase the CMS and go closer to OMS (*Higher2* would add a high positive step value in the negatively valued tariff, which makes tariff cheaper from customers' perspective). The same explanation is valid for the other side of the state space when the CMS is higher than OMS. It chooses to *Maintain* in State 4 and go for *Lower2* for remaining states State 5 and 6 in order to make tariff less attractive for customers and decrease the CMS and reach closer to OMS.

Action State	Maintain	Lower1	Lower2	Higher1	Higher2
0	33.64	16.99	10.35	28.90	14.85
1	361.41	30.35	11.11	18.30	167.86
2	18.07	4.04	3.59	22.95	32.24
3	2.02	1.74	1.32	3.66	7.94
4	40.02	27.96	19.82	20.95	10.69
5	4.33	7.35	15.81	4.31	2.36
6	1.17	2.46	4.47	1.13	1.32

Fig. 4. Q-Table for 2-Player Configuration [After 50 Games] (Color figure online)

The other two player configurations too converge to similar Q-Tables; however, the values are very different from each other. For example, in State 2, 3-Player Q-Table would select the *Higher2* with high probability, while 5-Player Q-Table would pick *Higher1* or *Higher2* with almost equal probability. In summary, GENERATETARIFFS-EXP3 learns to decide the suitable action in each state for all three player configurations, which empirically looks like the correct action to pick given the state. To prove that the above Q-Tables actually learn the best actions in each state to achieve the goal of maintaining the desired market, we carried out a performance testing for the 3-Player configuration and report the results below.

Action State	Maintain	Lower1	Lower2	Higher1	Higher2
0	31.88	31.01	12.77	31.08	16.02
1	56.31	31.82	9.31	46.91	60.29
2	11.92	5.25	3.81	10.75	35.35
3	4.11	1.20	1.30	4.82	24.37
4	26.51	46.61	49.11	23.80	11.94
5	2.91	6.58	4.56	2.74	1.43
6	1.45	2.68	8.40	1.96	1.32

Fig. 5. Q-Table for 3-Player Configuration [After 50 Games] (Color figure online)

Action State	Maintain	Lower1	Lower2	Higher1	Higher2
0	2.30	1.54	1.41	2.00	1.36
1	4.83	2.00	1.47	4.23	2.19
2	2.90	1.45	1.07	6.24	6.40
3	1.72	1.00	1.04	5.85	33.89
4	2.14	5.61	1.78	1.62	1.51
5	1.66	3.60	1.81	1.22	1.10
6	1.36	12.27	10.62	1.44	1.69

Fig. 6. Q-Table for 5-Player Configuration [After 50 Games] (Color figure online)

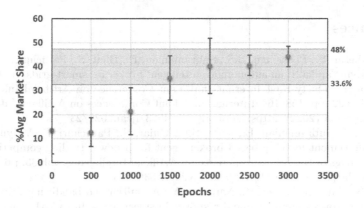

Fig. 7. Market Share Maintained by GENERATETARIFFS-EXP3 w.r.t Number of Epochs of Training for 3-Player Configuration (Color figure online)

Performance Testing: Figure 7 shows the market share maintained by Q-Tables stored at various checkpoints (at the 0th epoch, 500th epoch etc.) for a 3-Player configuration. The light blue color strip in the graph shows the desired market share range for the 3-Player configuration. As seen from the graph, for the 0th epoch Q-Table which has an equal probability for each section getting selected, the market share maintained by GENERATETARIFFS-EXP3 is very far from the desired range. After 500 and 1000 epochs, too, it is not able to maintain market share in the desired range. However, after getting trained for 1500 epochs, it reaches closer to the desired range. After that, for the higher number of epochs, it maintains the market share within the desired range. The variance (shown as the bars around the dot) is also low after 2500 epochs of training. A similar result is achieved for the 2-Player and 5-Player configurations as well. This shows the efficacy of GENERATETARIFFS-EXP3 that learns to update tariffs online and maintains the desired market share during the games.

8   Conclusion

Using the Contextual Multi-armed Bandit-based technique, we described the design of an adaptive tariff contract generation strategy, GENERATETARIFFS-EXP3, to sell electricity in the retail market. In particular, we demonstrated how tariff contracts could be adapted in real-time based on the market situation using the EXP-3 algorithm that efficiently managed the explore-exploit dilemma and visited all the states a sufficient number of times. In our strategy, we first determined the optimal market share and trained GENERATETARIFFS-EXP3 to achieve and maintain that market share during the game. We showcased that after training for an adequate number of games, GENERATETARIFFS-EXP3 learns the optimal action for a given state and learns to maintain the appropriate market share during the PowerTAC games.

References

1. Chandlekar, S., Pedasingu, B.S., Subramanian, E., Bhat, S., Paruchuri, P., Gujar, S.: VidyutVanika21: an autonomous intelligent broker for smart-grids. In: Proceedings of the Thirty-First International Joint Conference on Artificial Intelligence, IJCAI-2022, pp. 158–164. International Joint Conferences on Artificial Intelligence Organization (2022). https://doi.org/10.24963/ijcai.2022/23
2. Ghosh, S., Subramanian, E., Bhat, S.P., Gujar, S., Paruchuri, P.: VidyutVanika: a reinforcement learning based broker agent for a power trading competition. In: Proceedings of the AAAI Conference on Artificial Intelligence, vol. 33, pp. 914–921 (2019). https://doi.org/10.1609/aaai.v33i01.3301914
3. Jain, S., Narayanaswamy, B., Narahari, Y.: A multiarmed bandit incentive mechanism for crowdsourcing demand response in smart grids. In: AAAI Conference on Artificial Intelligence, Canada (2014)
4. Ketter, W., Collins, J., de Weerdt, M.: The 2020 power trading agent competition. ERIM report series reference no. 2020-002 (2020). https://doi.org/10.2139/ssrn.3564107
5. Li, Y., Hu, Q., Li, N.: Learning and selecting the right customers for reliability: a multi-armed bandit approach. In: 2018 IEEE Conference on Decision and Control (CDC), pp. 4869–4874 (2018). https://doi.org/10.1109/CDC.2018.8619481

6. Ma, H., Parkes, D.C., Robu, V.: Generalizing demand response through reward bidding. In: Proceedings of the 16th Conference on Autonomous Agents and MultiAgent Systems, AAMAS 2017, Brazil, pp. 60–68. (2017). http://dl.acm.org/citation.cfm?id=3091125.3091140

7. Ma, H., Robu, V., Li, N.L., Parkes, D.C.: Incentivizing reliability in demand-side response. In: The Proceedings of the 25th International Joint Conference on Artificial Intelligence (IJCAI 2016), pp. 352–358 (2016). http://www.ijcai.org/Abstract/16/057

8. McKelveya, R.D., McLennan, A.M., Turocy, T.L.: Gambit: software tools for game theory, version 16.0.1 (2014). http://www.gambit-project.org. Accessed 27 Dec 2021

9. Methenitis, G., Kaisers, M., La Poutré, H.: Forecast-based mechanisms for demand response. In: Proceedings of the 18th International Conference on Autonomous Agents and MultiAgent Systems, pp. 1600–1608 (2019)

10. Orfanoudakis, S., Kontos, S., Akasiadis, C., Chalkiadakis, G.: Aiming for half gets you to the top: winning PowerTAC 2020. In: Rosenfeld, A., Talmon, N. (eds.) EUMAS 2021. LNCS (LNAI), vol. 12802, pp. 144–159. Springer, Cham (2021). https://doi.org/10.1007/978-3-030-82254-5_9

11. Reddy, P.P., Veloso, M.M.: Strategy learning for autonomous agents in smart grid markets. In: Proceedings of the Twenty-Second International Joint Conference on Artificial Intelligence, IJCAI 2011, vol. 2, pp. 1446–1451. AAAI Press (2011)

12. Serrano Cuevas, J., Rodriguez-Gonzalez, A.Y., Munoz de Cote, E.: Fixed-price tariff generation using reinforcement learning. In: Fujita, K., et al. (eds.) Modern Approaches to Agent-based Complex Automated Negotiation. SCI, vol. 674, pp. 121–136. Springer, Cham (2017). https://doi.org/10.1007/978-3-319-51563-2_8

13. Shweta, J., Sujit, G.: A multiarmed bandit based incentive mechanism for a subset selection of customers for demand response in smart grids. In: Proceedings of the AAAI Conference on Artificial Intelligence, vol. 34, pp. 2046–2053 (2020)

14. Techopedia.com: Smart Grid (2021). https://www.techopedia.com/definition/692/smart-grid. Accessed 19 Jan 2023

15. Urieli, D., Stone, P.: Autonomous electricity trading using time-of-use tariffs in a competitive market. In: Proceedings of the Thirtieth AAAI Conference on Artificial Intelligence (AAAI-2016). Association for the Advancement of Artificial Intelligence (2016)

16. Özdemir, S., Unland, R.: AgentUDE17: a genetic algorithm to optimize the parameters of an electricity tariff in a smart grid environment. In: Demazeau, Y., An, B., Bajo, J., Fernández-Caballero, A. (eds.) PAAMS 2018. LNCS (LNAI), vol. 10978, pp. 224–236. Springer, Cham (2018). https://doi.org/10.1007/978-3-319-94580-4_18

Load Balancing in Distributed Multi-Agent Path Finder (DMAPF)

Poom Pianpak[1(✉)], Jiaoyang Li[2], and Tran Cao Son[1]

[1] New Mexico State University, Las Cruces, NM, USA
{ppianpak,stran}@nmsu.edu
[2] Carnegie Mellon University, Pittsburgh, PA, USA
jiaoyangli@cmu.edu

Abstract. The Multi-Agent Path Finding (MAPF) is a problem of finding a plan for agents to reach their desired locations without collisions. Distributed Multi-Agent Path Finder (DMAPF) solves the MAPF problem by decomposing a given MAPF problem instance into smaller subproblems and solve them in parallel. DMAPF works in rounds. Between two consecutive rounds, agents may migrate between two adjacent subproblems following their abstract plans, which are pre-computed, until all of them reach the areas that contain their desired locations. Previous works on DMAPF compute an abstract plan for each agent without the knowledge of other agents' abstract plans, resulting in high congestion in some areas, especially those that act as corridors. The congestion negatively impacts the runtime of DMAPF and prevents it from being able to solve dense MAPF problems.

In this paper, we (*i*) investigate the use of Uniform-Cost Search to mitigate the congestion. Additionally, we explore the use of several other techniques including (*ii*) using timeout estimation to preemptively stop solving and relax a subproblem when it is likely to get stuck; (*iii*) allowing a solving process to manage multiple subproblems – aimed to increase concurrency; and (*iv*) integrating with MAPF solvers from the Conflict-Based Search family. Experimental results show that our new system is several times faster than the previous ones; can solve larger and denser problems that were unsolvable before; and has better runtime than PBS and EECBS, which are state-of-the-art centralized suboptimal MAPF solvers, in problems with a large number of agents.

Keywords: Multi-Agent Path Finding (MAPF) · Distributed Multi-Agent Path Finder (DMAPF) · Load Balancing · Distributed Computing

1 Introduction

Multi-Agent Path Finding (MAPF) is a problem of finding collision-free paths for agents to move to their desired locations. It has important applications in

Tran Cao Son was partially supported by NSF awards #1757207, #1914635, and #1812628.

automated warehouse [8,13], traffic management [7], and video games [15], etc. The problem is known to be NP-hard to solve optimally [31]; therefore, a sacrifice on solution quality is usually made to make MAPF solvers practical.

Two main approaches for solving the MAPF problem are (*i*) search-based [5] and (*ii*) compilation-based [28]. Search-based MAPF solvers focus on developing search algorithms for MAPF problems. Prominent search-based algorithms include conflict-based search [24], where conflicts between single-agent plans are detected by a high-level search on a constraint tree and resolved by a low-level search; and prioritized planning [14,26], where agents with lower priority need to avoid conflicts with agents with higher priority. Compilation-based MAPF solvers translate the MAPF problem into another well-established formulation such as Answer Set Programming (ASP) [17,18], Boolean Satisfiability (SAT) [2], and Constraint Satisfaction (CSP) [4], for which efficient solvers exist.

Distributed Multi-Agent Path Finder (DMAPF) [20–22] is our framework that solves the MAPF problem by applying the divide-and-conquer idea. It decomposes a given MAPF problem instance into smaller subproblems; assigns the subproblems to solving processes – which can run on a single or multiple machines; then uses an existing MAPF solver, in any approach mentioned, to solve the smaller MAPF problem instances. The partial solutions from every solving process are combined at the end to provide a solution to the original problem.

In this paper, we introduce several mechanisms to scale up DMAPF and improve its efficiency. More specifically,

1. Improved Abstract Planning – We investigate the use of Uniform-Cost Search to make abstract plans in an attempt to mitigate congestion at a high level. An *abstract plan* of an agent is a sequence of subproblems that the agent needs to traverse to reach the area that contains its desired location. This enables DMAPF to take on denser maps as it decreases the chance of being in a situation where no agent is able to progress to the next subproblem in its abstract plan because the next subproblem of every agent is overcrowded. It also reduces the runtime because the MAPF problem instances to solve tend to be less dense. See Subsect. 3.1 for details.
2. Timeout Mechanism – We introduce a timeout estimation mechanism to allow DMAPF to preempt its underlying MAPF solver from solving subproblem instances that are likely to take a prohibitively long time to solve. Any subproblem instance that is stopped will be relaxed by having some of its agents' targets temporarily removed. Then, it will be solved again until either a plan is found or it cannot be relaxed further. This helps to prevent DMAPF from getting stuck on subproblem instances that would be unsolvable without the relaxation, thus, improving the success rate. In many cases, it also improves the overall runtime as it tends to be faster to avoid solving difficult subproblem instances. See Subsect. 3.2 for details.
3. Multiple Subproblems Assignment – We extend our previous work on DMAPF in [21] by allowing each solving process to manage multiple subproblems instead of one. This enables DMAPF to handle MAPF problem

instances of any size as it would not be restricted by the number of subproblems, which corresponds one-to-one to the number of solving processes in the old design. This improvement has a significant impact on the applicability of DMAPF, but is purely engineering. It involved heavy re-organization of the code base; therefore, we omit the details here. Instead, its implications can be seen from the experimental results in Subsect. 4.1.

4. Integration with CBS-based MAPF Solvers – In addition to ASP, we explore the use of CBSH2-RTC [11], EECBS [12], and PBS [14], as an underlying MAPF solver for DMAPF. The requirements for integrating a MAPF solver with DMAPF and modifications to the CBS-based MAPF solvers are explained in Subsect. 3.3.

2   Background

2.1   Multi-agent Path Finding

The MAPF problem can be defined as $P = (G, A, I, T)$, where $G = (V, E)$ is a graph such that V is a set of vertices corresponding to locations in the graph; $E \subseteq V \times V$ denotes pairs of locations where agents can traverse in some direction; A is a set of agents; and $I, T \subseteq A \times V$ denote start and goal locations of the agents, respectively. An agent at location v_1 can either *move* from v_1 to v_2 in one time step if $(v_1, v_2) \in E$ or *stay* at v_1. The most common restrictions are that (i) each location can be occupied by at most one agent at a time; and (ii) two agents cannot swap locations in a single time step. Violating any of these restrictions is said to cause a *conflict*. A solution to a MAPF problem instance is a set of movement plans (i.e., a sequence of vertices) for every agent that allows them to go to their goal locations without causing the conflict. The quality of a solution is usually measured in terms of (i) *makespan* – the longest length of the movement plans in the solution; and (ii) *sum-of-cost* – the sum of lengths of the movement plans in the solution.

There are several variants of the MAPF problem [27]. DMAPF follows the mentioned restrictions and assumes that every agent has unique start and goal locations; and they need to stay at their goals at the end of the solution.

2.2   Distributed Multi-Agent Path Finder

Distributed Multi-Agent Path Finder (DMAPF) applies the divide-and-conquer idea to solve the MAPF problem. Given a MAPF problem instance P, DMAPF partitions P into a set of smaller subproblems $S = \{S_1, \ldots, S_n\}$. A subproblem S_i is defined as $((V_i, E_i), A_i, I_i, T_i)$ where $V_i \subseteq V$, $E_i \subseteq E$, $A_i \subseteq A$, $I_i \subseteq I$, and $T_i \subseteq T$. Pairs of locations in E_i are only between vertices in V_i; agents in A_i are only those that have their start location in V_i; and start and goal locations respectively in I_i and T_i are only for agents in A_i. In our previous works, each solving process is only assigned one different subproblem in S. In this work, we extend the system to allow assigning multiple subproblems to each solving process, provided that every subproblem is only assigned to one solving process.

Solving processes work together in parallel. Every solving process has full knowledge of adjacency between all the subproblems. Subproblems S_1 and S_2 are adjacent and are called *neighbors* iff there exists vertices $v_1 \in S_1$ and $v_2 \in S_2$ such that v_1 and v_2 are adjacent (i.e., $(v_1, v_2) \in E$). In addition, each solving process knows every vertex in its assigned subproblems that is adjacent to a neighboring subproblem. DMAPF allows subproblems to contain sets of disconnected vertices called *areas* and operates on them, but for simplicity, we will use the term subproblem throughout the paper unless a clear distinction is required.

Every solving process starts by creating an abstract plan for each agent residing in any of its assigned subproblems. Figure 1 shows an example of a MAPF problem instance decomposed into 4 subproblems: S_1, S_2, S_3, and S_4. Suppose that subproblem S_1 is assigned to a solving process s, then s has the responsibility to create abstract plans for agents a_1 and a_2 to reach subproblem S_4 that contains their goal locations g_1 and g_2, respectively. Possible abstract plans for agents a_1 and a_2 are $\langle S_1, S_2, S_4 \rangle$, and $\langle S_1, S_3, S_4 \rangle$.

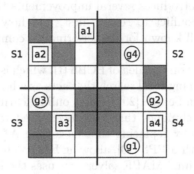

Fig. 1. An example of how a MAPF problem instance is decomposed into 4 subproblems: S_1, S_2, S_3, and S_4. Start and goal locations of agents are denoted by small squares and circles with corresponding numbers, respectively.

After an abstract plan has been created for each agent, solving processes work together round-by-round, following the protocol described in [20, 21]. Let a set N contains pairs of solving processes that have adjacent subproblems (i.e., they are called *neighbors*). The protocol consists of 3 phases: (*i*) *negotiation* – every pair in N decides which agents to *migrate* (i.e., progress to the next subproblem in the abstract plan) and to which border locations. Priority is given to agents with the longest remaining steps in the abstract plan and border locations are chosen such that the aggregate distance between agents and their assigned border locations is minimized; (*ii*) *rejection* – every pair in N detects which previously-agreed migrations will result in collision and rejects them. This ensures a collision-free migration agreement across all subproblems; and (*iii*) *confirmation* – every pair in N confirms agents that can successfully move to their assigned border locations. The agreed adjacent border locations, which are in their next subproblems, will be used as their start locations in the next round. The protocol allows solving processes to either solve or relax (see Subsect. 3.2) their own subproblem instances **in parallel** between the *rejection* and the *confirmation* phases.

The algorithm terminates when either (*i*) a plan is found where at the end every agent stays at its goal location – the solution is then reported; or (*ii*) there is a subproblem instance that cannot be solved nor relaxed further – the system then reports that it cannot find a solution.

2.3 The CBS Family

CBSH2-RTC [11] is a state-of-the-art version of Conflict-Based Search (CBS) [24]. CBS is an optimal search-based MAPF solver where a path for each agent is individually planned from its start to goal location using a space-time A* search [26] at a low level. Conflicts between agent plans are detected in a high-level search on a constraint tree. They are resolved in a low-level search by making new plans for a subset of conflicting agents that avoid the imposed constraints. CBSH2-RTC introduces several improvements that make CBS smarter in determining which conflict to resolve first, and how, using various heuristics. CBSH2-RTC is well known for its performance compared to other optimal MAPF solvers.

EECBS [12] improves on the idea of ECBS [1], which is a bounded-suboptimal variant of CBS, by replacing focal search that acts as a high-level search in ECBS with Explicit Estimation Search [29]. It uses online learning to guide the search and employs various techniques that have been used to improve CBS. It has recently been improved by replacing the space-time A* that is used as a low-level search in ECBS with SIPPS [10], allowing EECBS to be even more efficient.

PBS [14] is a suboptimal MAPF solver that uses the idea of prioritized planning [26] where agents are given different priorities and those with lower priority need to avoid higher-priority agents. Instead of planning based on some fixed priority ordering, PBS is able to (lazily) explore all total priority orderings. PBS is not complete, but very efficient, and able to find solutions for many MAPF instances where standard prioritized MAPF algorithms cannot.

3 Methodology

3.1 Abstract Planning Methods

In addition to the ASP encoding used for creating abstract plans in our previous works, we introduce 4 new abstract planning methods to DMAPF using (*i*) Breadth-First Search (BFS); (*ii*) Random Search (RAND); (*iii*) Uniform-Cost Search (UCS); and (*iv*) Centralized Uniform-Cost Search (UCSC).

Let F be a frontier containing sequences of areas that have not yet been explored. To find an abstract plan for an agent a, an initial plan containing only the area where agent a starts from is added to F. Then, one of the plans in F is removed and checked whether the last area in the plan contains the goal location of agent a. If not, new plans are created and added to F by extending the plan with every one of the adjacent areas that have not been explored. This process repeats until either an abstract plan is found or F is exhausted.

In BFS, F acts as a queue, so plans are selected in the order when they were added to F, resulting in the shortest abstract plan. RAND only differs from BFS in that F acts as a set instead of a queue, so a plan is randomly selected in each iteration, resulting in an abstract plan that may not be the shortest.

In UCS and UCSC, F acts as a priority queue where the ordering (lowest-first) is based on the congestion within each area in a plan. We define *congestion* within an area a at an abstract step t as n/v, where n is the number of agents in a at abstract step t; and v is the number of vertices in a. The overall congestion is tracked using a *congestion matrix* which contains congestion within every area at every abstract step. In UCS, every solving process makes an abstract plan for each agent in its assigned subproblems and uses the plan to update its congestion matrix locally in each iteration. In UCSC, only one solving process is designated to make an abstract plan for each agent in the original problem P and use the plan to update a single congestion matrix in each iteration. At the end, the plans are distributed to each responsible solving process. Resulting abstract plans from UCSC create less overall congestion than UCS since only a single congestion matrix is consulted and updated.

An example of how a congestion matrix is updated in each iteration by UCSC is shown in Fig. 2 where it takes the problem from Fig. 1 and sequentially updates it with abstract plans of agents $a1$, $a2$, $a3$, and $a4$, which are $\langle S1, S2, S4 \rangle$, $\langle S1, S3, S4 \rangle$, $\langle S3 \rangle$, and $\langle S4, S2 \rangle$, respectively.

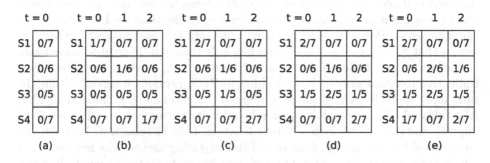

Fig. 2. An illustration on how a congestion matrix is updated over time by UCSC. (a) initial. (b) with $\langle S1, S2, S4 \rangle$. (c) with $\langle S1, S3, S4 \rangle$. (d) with $\langle S3 \rangle$. (e) with $\langle S4, S2 \rangle$. Updated values are highlighted in red. (Color figure online)

3.2 Timeout Mechanism

For a MAPF subproblem instance S_i to be processed, there must exist some agent with a *target*, either its original goal or an assigned border location in S_i. If there is some agent with an assigned border location in S_i, then the other agents without an assigned border location will be considered as having no goal

---

Algorithm 1. Solving a MAPF problem instance with timeout

Input: S_i – MAPF subproblem instance; n – #agents in S_i
Parameter: t_a – Approximate timeout per agent
f – Timeout penalty factor; ϵ – Timeout tolerance factor
Output: sol – Solution of S_i

1: **while true do**
2:    **if** S_i is solved within $n \cdot t_a \cdot \epsilon$ **then**
3:       **if** Some agent in S_i has a goal or border location assigned **then**
4:          $t_a \leftarrow t_s/n$ where t_s is the time used to solve S_i
5:       **else**
6:          $t_a \leftarrow f \cdot t_a$
7:       **return** sol
8:    **else**
9:       Stop solving S_i
10:      **if** Some agent in S_i has a border location assigned **then**
11:         Remove an assigned border location from one agent in S_i
12:      **else**
13:         **terminate**

(in the current round) to create the least constraint for the agents with assigned border locations to reach their targets.

Algorithm 1 shows the timeout estimation mechanism added to the subproblem solving procedure. Line 2 tries to solve S_i within the time limit of $n \cdot t_a \cdot \epsilon$, where n, t_a, and ϵ are the number of agents, an approximate timeout per agent, and a timeout tolerance factor, respectively. The value of ϵ is a multiplicative constant that accommodates errors from the approximation. If S_i is solved where some agent has a target, then t_a is re-estimated to the time used to solve S_i per agent (Line 4). However, if S_i is solved but there is no agent with a target, it means that S_i is has been relaxed too much. It then will be tried to solve again in the next round with a higher timeout limit of $f \cdot t_a$ where f is another multiplicative constant greater than 1 (Line 6). If S_i cannot be solved within the time limit, then the MAPF solver is stopped (Line 9) and S_i is checked whether it is relaxable (Line 10). S_i can be relaxed if it has some agent that needs to migrate and is assigned with a border location. Line 11 relaxes S_i by removing an assigned border location from one of the migrating agents. The heuristic is to select an agent with the least number of steps left in its abstract plan. Otherwise, DMAPF terminates at Line 13 and reports that it cannot find a solution.

3.3 Integration with CBS-Based MAPF Solvers

To integrate a MAPF solver with DMAPF, it needs to satisfy the requirements that: (i) agents without a goal location are allowed in the problem; and (ii) agents need to be able to avoid being in a set of certain vertices V_P at the end of the plan unless they need to go to a location in V_P. The second condition accommodates the design of DMAPF that improves its success rate by making sure there are unoccupied vertices for migrating agents to move in.

CBSH2-RTC, EECBS, PBS all use an A*-style algorithm (i.e., space-time A* [26], SIPP [19], or SIPPS [10]) to plan paths for individual agents. We modify the heuristic function and the goal test function for agents without goals as follows. For the heuristic function, the h-value of a node at a vertex that is in the prohibited set V_P is 1, and the h-value of a node at a vertex that is not in V_P is 0. For the goal test function, we claim a node at vertex v at time step t as a goal node iff vertex v is not in V_P and there are no vertex constraints that prohibit this agent from being at vertex v at any time step after t.

In addition, CBSH2-RTC and EECBS use some speedup techniques that rely on the assumption that the agents have unique goal locations. We therefore turn off those techniques when the involved agents do not have goals. Specifically, they both build MDDs [25], i.e., a direct acyclic graph that consists of all shortest paths from the start vertex to the goal vertex of an agent, for individual agents, which are used for finding cardinal conflicts [3] and rectangle conflicts [11]. We do not build MDDs for agents without goals. Thus, if such agents are involved in a conflict, we classify this conflict as semi-cardinal or non-cardinal (depending on how the MDD of the other agents involved in the conflict looks like), and do not perform rectangle reasoning for it. Moreover, target reasoning [11] happens when an agent runs into another agent that has already reached its goal location and sat there, so we perform target reasoning only if the second agent has been assigned a goal vertex.

4   Experiments

We conduct experiments in Subsects. 4.1–4.4 sequentially to determine the best parameters for DMAPF. Subsection 4.1 determines the optimal number of solving processes to be executed in parallel. Subsection 4.2 determines the optimal size of subproblems that gives the best tradeoff between performance and success rate. Subsection 4.3 determines the optimal sensitivity of timeout that allows DMAPF to appropriately stop its underlying MAPF solver. Subsection 4.4 determines the abstract planning method that computes abstract plans with the least overall congestion. Finally, Subsect. 4.5 uses the best parameters obtained from the previous subsections to compare variations of DMAPF with CBSH2-RTC [11], EECBS [12], and PBS [14].

The experiments are performed on a Dell Precision 3630 Tower with an Intel Core i9-9900K @3.60 GHz and 64 GB of RAM. The software used includes Ubuntu 20.04.5 LTS, ROS Noetic Ninjemys [23], and Clingo 5.6.2 [6]. We use maps and random scenarios from the MAPF benchmark[1] [27]. Each scenario has at most 1000 agent and each agent has unique start and goal locations. We use the following maps in our experiments: *den312d*, *random-64-64-20*, *maze-128-128-2*, *lak303d*, and *warehouse-20-40-10-2-2*, which will be referred to as den, rand, maze, lak, and ware, respectively. Unless stated otherwise, we use 20 solving processes, subproblems that contain roughly 40 vertices, timeout penalty fac-

---

[1] https://movingai.com/benchmarks/mapf/index.html.

tor (f) of 2, timeout tolerance factor (ϵ) of 10, centralized Uniform-Cost-Search to make abstract plans, and ASP as an underlying MAPF solver in DMAPF.

We use our problem divider [21] to decompose a MAPF problem into $|S|$ subproblems of roughly the same size. The divider applies the balanced k-means algorithm [16] where $|S|$ vertices are first randomly selected as centroids; then, nearby vertices (calculated by real distance) are grouped to form clusters (i.e., subproblems) around the centroids while keeping the numbers of vertices in each cluster roughly the same. The centroids are re-initialized to the center of their clusters and the process repeats until there is no change to the centroids.

For the reproducibility of our results, the experiments in the following subsections also state seed values used by the problem divider. Because the performance of DMAPF greatly depends on how the input map is decomposed, the seed values used to decompose the maps in Subsects. 4.2–4.5 are chosen from 101 to 110 for the one that gives the best runtime in the first scenario. Then, the maps decomposed with the chosen seed values will be used throughout the whole experiments. The reported values come from an average of running each random scenario from 1–10 once in the same (decomposed) map, under the time limit of 5 min, for the total of 10 times.

4.1 The Numbers of Solving Processes

Table 1 attempts to determine the optimal number of solving processes by comparing runtimes of DMAPF when using 4, 8, 12, ..., 32 solving processes on the lak map with 200, 400 and 600 agents from the first random scenario. The map is decomposed into 240 subproblems using the seed value of 2. Each solving process is randomly assigned a set of subproblems. When $p = 20$, for example, each solving process needs to manage $240/20 = 12$ subproblems. Every reported runtime is an average from solving the scenario 10 times.

Table 1. Comparing runtimes of DMAPF when using p solving processes on the lak map with n agents.

n	Runtime (s)							
	$p = 4$	$p = 8$	$p = 12$	$p = 16$	$p = 20$	$p = 24$	$p = 28$	$p = 32$
200	32.1	25.1	21.8	20.0	19.4	**18.9**	20.5	19.6
400	97.0	75.1	63.1	66.2	**52.8**	56.2	53.8	63.5
600	214.2	158.7	129.3	127.5	**110.7**	113.3	116.0	120.0

On our machine that is equipped with a CPU that has 8 cores and 16 hardware threads, the results suggest that using 20–24 solving processes, or 125%–150% of the number of hardware threads provides the best runtime. Using too few solving processes underutilizes the computational resources and using too many solving processes introduces too much competition for the resources, which are both detrimental to the performance.

4.2   The Size of Subproblems

Table 2. Comparing runtimes, makespan, sum-of-cost, and success rates of DMAPF on the **rand** map, decomposed into subproblems that contain roughly v vertices, with 1000 agents.

v	Runtime (s)	Makespan	SoC ($\times 1k$)	Success Rate
30	**39.9**	**864**	**558.4**	0.4
40	46.6	906	598.5	**1.0**
50	88.2	1041	627.9	0.8
60	80.0	1107	676.6	**1.0**
70	86.8	1070	633.6	**1.0**

Table 2 attempts to determine the optimal size of subproblems by comparing runtimes, makespan, sum-of-cost, and success rate of DMAPF on the **rand** map that has been decomposed into subproblems of different sizes: 30, 40, 50, 60, and 70 vertices, using the seed values of 107, 105, 101, 109, and 105, respectively. DMAPF with ASP as an underlying MAPF solver is optimized for makespan; therefore, makespan is a better indicator of solution quality than sum-of-cost.

The results show that, with small subproblems, DMAPF tends to run faster and give better solution quality, but have a lower success rate. DMAPF runs faster in small subproblems because ASP, which its runtime is known to be very sensitive to the number of vertices, is less affected by the sizes of the subproblems since they are small. It also gives better solution quality because as the subproblems become more fine-grained, it results in less agents waiting to move between consecutive rounds. However, the success rate is now lower because there is more chance that some subproblem instance becomes unsolvable as the ratio b/v, where b is the number of border vertices (i.e., vertices that are adjacent to vertices in another subproblem) and v is the number of vertices in the subproblem, increases. In DMAPF, agents follow their abstract plans to move into the next subproblems between two consecutive rounds. The greater the ratio b/v is, the more agents can enter (or leave) subproblems while the subproblems may contain only a few vertices, making it difficult (or impossible) to find a movement plan. Our results are consistent with the original work on DMAPF [22] that suggests that the size of subproblems around 40–60 vertices provide the best performance and solution quality.

4.3   Timeout Sensitivity

Table 3 attempts to determine the optimal value of the timeout tolerance factor ϵ by comparing runtimes, makespan, sum-of-cost, and the number of times that DMAPF preemptively stops its underlying MAPF solver because it exceeds the estimated timeout limit, under different values of ϵ. The greater the value of ϵ is, the longer DMAPF allows each subproblem instance to be solved. We decompose the **rand** map using the seed value of 105 for this experiment.

Table 3. Comparing runtimes, makespan, sum-of-cost, and the number of times DMAPF stops its an underlying MAPF solver under different timeout tolerance factors ϵ, on the **rand** map with 1000 agents.

ϵ	Runtime (s)	Makespan	SoC ($\times 1k$)	#Stops
4	51.9	906	611.9	25
6	49.2	906	600.1	13
8	48.6	**903**	607.3	7
10	46.6	906	**598.5**	3
12	**46.3**	906	603.2	1
14	49.1	908	606.8	2

The results show that setting the value of ϵ too small (i.e., $\epsilon < 10$ in Table 3) causes DMAPF to be too sensitive and stops its MAPF solver too early, resulted in worse performance. However, when the value of ϵ is too big such as when $\epsilon = 14$, DMAPF waits too long to stop its MAPF solver from solving problem instances that are likely to be too difficult, which also resulted in worse performance. The number of times that DMAPF stops its MAPF solver increases when the value of ϵ increases from 12 to 14. This shows that in practice there is a chance, especially in dense maps, that DMAPF will have to face a few difficult subproblem instances. Without the timeout mechanism (i.e., $\epsilon = +\infty$) like in our previous works, DMAPF would likely get stuck or take a very long time to solve those subproblem instances. In these situations, it would be more efficient to stop the MAPF solver early, relax the subproblem instance, and retry, which the timeout mechanism allows DMAPF to do. The results also suggest the optimal value of ϵ to be around 10–12, and there is no significant deviation of solution qualities between the different values of ϵ overall.

4.4 Congestion

Figure 3 compares congestion resulting from abstract plans created by different methods: ASP, BFS, RAND, UCS, and UCSC, on the **rand** map with 600, 800, and 1000 agents. The map is decomposed using the seed value of 105. The charts depict the trend of the congestion (min and max) in each abstract step. We are mainly concerned with the max congestion as that is usually when some subproblem instance becomes too difficult or unsolvable. The max congestion is the highest congestion across all areas at particular abstract steps. The opposite is true for the min congestion.

In Fig. 3, both ASP and BFS produce the shortest abstract plans among all the plans from all the methods; however, their plans also create the highest congestion. In the case of 800 and 1000 agents, their plans result in the value of congestion greater than 1 at abstract step 3. This means that if every agent is able to follow its abstract plan until abstract step 2, there must be at least

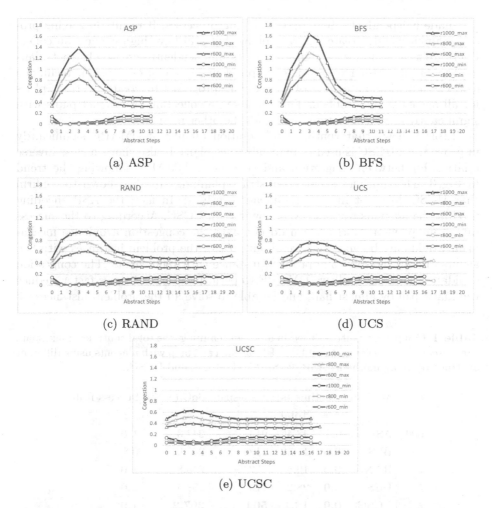

Fig. 3. Comparing the trend of congestion from abstract plans created by using Answer Set Programming (ASP), Breadth-First Search (BFS), Random Search (RAND), Uniform-Cost Search (UCS), and Centralized Uniform-Cost Search (UCSC). Each chart depicts the min and max congestion from a particular method on the **rand** map with 600, 800, and 1000 agents.

one area at abstract step 3 where the number of agents who want to be there is greater than the number of vertices in the area!

Abstract plans from both RAND and UCS show significantly lower congestion compared to those from ASP and BFS; however, the length of abstract plans from RAND is quite random (but would still be less than the total number of areas) as it selects nodes to expand randomly; and the plans from UCS, which uses the knowledge of congestion, are only slightly better than the plans from RAND. This is because the knowledge is incomplete when abstract plans are made independently by different solving processes. It results in solving processes unknowingly create abstract plans that still have high congestion collectively. Instead of having solving processes independently create abstract plans for agents within their responsible subproblems, UCSC uses the same technique as UCS, but designates one of the solving processes to create abstract plans for all agents in the problem. This results in a collection of abstract plans with significantly lower congestion among all the other methods.

Table 4 shows that runtime and solution quality of DMAPF significantly improve when UCSC is used to make abstract plans. It also shows a close inverse relationship between congestion and runtime in DMAPF, following the trend in Fig. 3. The runtimes spent on abstract planning are also shown to confirm that UCSC does not incur a significant overhead. In fact, the ASP encoding used in the previous works is even slower than UCSC. According to the success rates, our previous works which do not have the congestion avoidance mechanism would only be able to solve about 60% of the problem instances with 800 agents and unable solve any problem instance with 1000 agents. The congestion avoidance mechanism allows DMAPF to perform at least 3 times faster, reduce the makespan by almost half, and be able to solve all the problem instances.

Table 4. Comparing runtimes used in abstract planning, the total runtimes, makespan, sum-of-cost, and success rates of DMAPF on the **rand** map with n agents using different abstract planning methods: ASP, BFS, RAND, UCS, and UCSC.

n	Method	Runtime (s)		Makespan	SoC ($\times 1k$)	Success Rate
		Abs.	Total			
600	ASP	0.3	48.4	914	247.3	**1.0**
	BFS	**0.0**	110.2	1185	265.6	0.8
	RAND	**0.0**	19.8	673	236.8	**1.0**
	UCS	**0.0**	28.2	779	258.4	**1.0**
	UCSC	**0.0**	**16.1**	**564**	**207.2**	**1.0**
800	ASP	0.4	106.6	1241	511.7	0.6
	BFS	**0.0**	162.1	1367	525.3	0.1
	RAND	**0.0**	74.2	893	424.8	0.8
	UCS	**0.0**	56.1	934	451.0	0.4
	UCSC	**0.0**	**26.1**	**757**	**379.1**	**1.0**
1000	ASP	0.5	-	-	-	0.0
	BFS	**0.0**	-	-	-	0.0
	RAND	**0.0**	204.6	1058	703.9	0.1
	UCS	**0.0**	103.8	1109	740.2	0.1
	UCSC	**0.0**	**46.6**	**906**	**598.5**	**1.0**

4.5 Comparison Between MAPF Solvers

Table 5. Comparing runtimes, makespan, sum-of-cost, and success rate between MAPF solvers: (*i*) DMAPF w/ASP (*DMAPF-A*), (*ii*) DMAPF w/CBSH2-RTC (*DMAPF-C*), (*iii*) DMAPF w/EECBS (*DMAPF-E*), (*iv*) DMAPF w/PBS (*DMAPF-P*), (*v*) EECBS, and (*vi*) PBS, on the den, random, maze, lak, and ware maps, with different number of agents shown under the names of the maps. The number of vertices in each map is shown in the parentheses on the right hand side of its name.

Solver	— Runtime (seconds) —														
	den (2445)			*rand* (3270)			*maze* (10858)			*lak* (14784)			*ware* (38756)		
	200	300	400	600	800	1000	100	200	300	200	400	600	600	800	1000
DMAPF-A	6.9	18.4	39.3	16.1	26.0	46.6	20.7	40.7	-	15.6	37.9	75.9	32.5	42.4	52.3
DMAPF-C	-	-	-	-	-	-	8.5	-	-	35.7	-	-	14.2	19.8	35.2
DMAPF-E	170.6	-	-	-	-	-	9.8	-	-	10.7	-	-	14.8	20.4	62.9
DMAPF-P	3.1	-	-	-	-	-	8.1	-	-	7.5	44.2	-	13.1	17.0	20.8
EECBS	0.4	1.4	6.4	2.5	21.4	141.7	2.6	135.8	279.6	1.2	6.5	42.6	5.8	13.1	22.0
PBS	15.1	217.5	-	-	-	-	50.5	-	-	17.2	266.9	-	9.4	26.1	57.2
	— Makespan —														
DMAPF-A	475	722	980	564	757	906	3075	3704	-	1014	1794	2774	748	774	795
DMAPF-C	-	-	-	-	-	-	3091	-	-	1017	-	-	753	781	804
DMAPF-E	643	-	-	-	-	-	3072	-	-	1033	-	-	780	828	893
DMAPF-P	477	-	-	-	-	-	3069	-	-	1016	1690	-	761	779	803
EECBS	180	288	377	145	218	302	1474	1571	1702	483	511	583	451	455	457
PBS	132	158	-	-	-	-	1475	-	-	482	479	-	451	455	457
	— Sum-of-Cost (×1000) —														
DMAPF-A	51.8	117.3	248.9	207.2	379.1	598.5	181.4	511.8	-	112.9	362.2	794.9	233.1	331.3	448.3
DMAPF-C	-	-	-	-	-	-	187.2	-	-	110.7	-	-	230.7	335.8	443.2
DMAPF-E	56.4	-	-	-	-	-	175.4	-	-	110.4	-	-	236.7	356.6	498.8
DMAPF-P	54.1	-	-	-	-	-	176.2	-	-	111.8	358.7	-	231.8	334.8	449.1
EECBS	13.8	28.0	46.9	34.8	60.6	101.6	56.1	119.7	191.4	38.2	78.6	131.1	109.6	146.4	181.1
PBS	11.6	19.1	-	-	-	-	56.4	-	-	37.9	74.1	-	109.5	146.2	180.9
	—Success Rate—														
DMAPF-A	1.0	1.0	0.7	1.0	1.0	1.0	1.0	0.8	0.0	1.0	1.0	0.6	1.0	1.0	1.0
DMAPF-C	0.0	0.0	0.0	0.0	0.0	0.0	0.8	0.0	0.0	1.0	0.0	0.0	1.0	1.0	0.7
DMAPF-E	0.4	0.0	0.0	0.0	0.0	0.0	0.9	0.0	0.0	1.0	0.0	0.0	1.0	0.9	0.6
DMAPF-P	0.6	0.0	0.0	0.0	0.0	0.0	0.9	0.0	0.0	1.0	0.4	0.0	0.6	0.5	0.3
EECBS	1.0	1.0	1.0	1.0	0.9	1.0	0.9	0.9	0.1	1.0	1.0	1.0	1.0	1.0	1.0
PBS	1.0	0.8	0.0	0.0	0.0	0.0	1.0	0.0	0.0	1.0	0.3	0.0	1.0	1.0	1.0

Table 5 compares runtimes, solution quality (indicated by makespan and sum-of-cost), and success rate of DMAPF that has been integrated with 4 different MAPF solvers : (*i*) ASP; (*ii*) CBSH2-RTC[2]; (*iii*) EECBS[3]; (*iv*) PBS[4], denoted as *DMAPF-A*, *DMAPF-C*, *DMAPF-E*, and *DMAPF-P*, respectively; and EECBS and PBS, representing state-of-the-art bounded-suboptimal and optimal MAPF solvers, respectively. We enable SIPPS in EECBS and PBS (including the ones

---

[2] https://github.com/Jiaoyang-Li/CBSH2-RTC.
[3] https://github.com/Jiaoyang-Li/EECBS.
[4] https://github.com/Jiaoyang-Li/PBS.

integrated with DMAPF) and set the suboptimality factor of EECBS to 5 to ensure it gives the best runtime without caring for optimality guarantee [10]. We also compared with CBSH2-RTC, but it was not able to solve any problem instance, so we omit the results from the table. The maps: den, rand, maze, lak, and ware are used in the comparison and have been decomposed using the seed values of 107, 105, 110, 102, and 108, respectively.

In terms of runtime, EECBS typically outperforms the other solvers, but its speed deteriorates much quicker than DMAPF as the number of agents increases. This is shown when DMAPF-A is able to outperform EECBS in the random map with 1000 agents and in the maze map with 200 agents. DMAPF-P also outperforms EECBS in the warehouse map with 1000 agents.

In terms of solution quality, DMAPF returns solutions with makespan and sum-of-cost about 2–6 times higher than those returned by EECBS and PBS. However, they are comparable in the number of movements agents need to make to reach the goals – the results are omitted due to space limitation. This suggests that agents planned by DMAPF spend about the same number of movements as those planned by EECBS and PBS, but they waste a lot of time in waiting to move from one subproblem to the next between subsequent rounds.

DMAPF-C, DMAPF-E, and DMAPF-P are about twice as fast as DMAPF-A in sparse maps (i.e., maps where the number of agents is low compared to the number of vertices) such as in the warehouse map. However, they are only able to solve a few problem instances in dense maps, especially after the original map has been decomposed into smaller subproblems which introduces more conflicts. On the other hand, DMAPF-A is less affected by the number of conflicts, allowing it to solve significantly more problems instances.

The issue that hinders DMAPF-A is not the conflicts, but rather about how the problem is decomposed. Figure 4 shows subproblem instances that can easily prevent DMAPF from finding the solutions. Figure 4a typically happens in maps with narrow corridors such as the maze map – agent $a1$ needs to go to location $g1$ but is blocked by agent $a2$ that does not need to go anywhere. Figure 4b depicts a similar problem, but it is caused by a mixture of congestion and bad problem decomposition, so an improvement in either area should help to prevent this scenario.

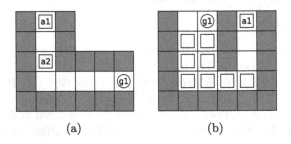

(a)   (b)

Fig. 4. Issues from bad problem decomposition. Start and goal locations of agents are denoted by small squares and circles with corresponding numbers, respectively.

5   Related Work

There are very few works on MAPF that share the idea of spatially decomposing the problem. To our knowledge, other works with a similar idea includes (*i*) Spatially Distributed Multiagent Planner (SDP) [30] separates a given MAPF problem into low-contention and high-contention areas. Special searching rules are enforced in high-contention areas to speed up the search and agents are not allowed to have a goal location in those areas; (*ii*) Hierarchical Multi-Agent Path Planner (HMAPP) [32] shares a very similar approach with DMAPF. The main difference is that it limits the direction of border vertices between adjacent subproblems, whereas DMAPF does not; and (*iii*) the shard system [9] designates special areas, connecting subproblems, to be used as buffers to improve the solution quality. In the current implementation, agents are not allowed to have a goal location in the buffer areas.

The only recent related works are HMAPP and the shard system. Their source codes are not readily available, so in our experiment we decided to compare DMAPF with EECBS and PBS instead. This design choice serves two purposes: (*i*) our results can be indirectly compared with the two systems – HMAPP has been compared with ECBS [1], the baseline of EECBS, and the shard system has been compared with EECBS; and (*ii*) it shows the behavior of DMAPF when EECBS and PBS are used as its underlying MAPF solver compared to their standalone versions.

6   Summary

We introduce several techniques to improve DMAPF, including (*i*) allowing each solving process to manage multiple subproblems; (*ii*) timeout estimation mechanism; (*iii*) congestion avoidance in abstract plans; and (*iv*) integration with other MAPF solvers. Allowing each solving process to manage multiple subproblems enables DMAPF to work with maps of any size – not limited by the number of subproblems like in our previous works. The combination of timeout estimation mechanism and congestion avoidance in abstract plans enables DMAPF to solve dense maps more efficiently and also increases the success rate. The integration with MAPF solvers from the CBS family provides an insight on the kinds of MAPF solvers that will be suitable with DMAPF for different situations. Even though the improvements we introduce are simple, they improve DMAPF significantly (as shown in Table 4) and can serve as a baseline for future improvements.

From the experiments, we found that the performance of DMAPF is very sensitive to how the problem is decomposed. Having a tool [21] that automatically decomposes a given MAPF problem is convenient, but it still does not guarantee good results. We believe that, with future improvement on problem decomposition technique and solution quality, DMAPF can be applied in real-world large-scale MAPF problems since its strength lies in scalability. Of course, environments in the real-world can be unpredictable; however, having a high-level plan for agents to coordinate is necessary.

References

1. Barer, M., Sharon, G., Stern, R., Felner, A.: Suboptimal variants of the conflict-based search algorithm for the multi-agent pathfinding problem. In: Seventh Annual Symposium on Combinatorial Search (2014)
2. Biere, A., Heule, M., van Maaren, H.: Handbook of Satisfiability, vol. 185. IOS press, Amsterdam (2009)
3. Boyarski, E., et al.: Icbs: improved conflict-based search algorithm for multi-agent pathfinding. In: Twenty-Fourth International Joint Conference on Artificial Intelligence (2015)
4. Dechter, R., Cohen, D., et al.: Constraint Processing. Morgan Kaufmann, Massachusetts (2003)
5. Felner, A., et al.: Search-based optimal solvers for the multi-agent pathfinding problem: summary and challenges. In: International Symposium on Combinatorial Search, vol. 8 (2017)
6. Gebser, M., Kaminski, R., Kaufmann, B., Ostrowski, M., Schaub, T., Wanko, P.: Theory solving made easy with clingo 5. In: Technical Communications of the 32nd International Conference on Logic Programming (ICLP 2016). Schloss Dagstuhl-Leibniz-Zentrum fuer Informatik (2016)
7. Ho, F., et al.: Decentralized multi-agent path finding for UAV traffic management. IEEE Trans. Intell. Transp. Syst. (2020)
8. Hönig, W., Kiesel, S., Tinka, A., Durham, J.W., Ayanian, N.: Persistent and robust execution of MAPF schedules in warehouses. IEEE Rob. Autom. Lett. 4(2), 1125–1131 (2019)
9. Leet, C., Li, J., Koenig, S.: Shard systems: scalable, robust and persistent multi-agent path finding with performance guarantees. In: Proceedings of the AAAI Conference on Artificial Intelligence, vol. 36, pp. 9386–9395 (2022)
10. Li, J., Chen, Z., Harabor, D., Stuckey, P.J., Koenig, S.: MAPF-LNS2: fast repairing for multi-agent path finding via large neighborhood search. In: Proceedings of the AAAI Conference on Artificial Intelligence (2022)
11. Li, J., Harabor, D., Stuckey, P.J., Ma, H., Gange, G., Koenig, S.: Pairwise symmetry reasoning for multi-agent path finding search. Artif. Intell. 301, 103574 (2021)
12. Li, J., Ruml, W., Koenig, S.: EECBS: a bounded-suboptimal search for multi-agent path finding. In: Proceedings of the AAAI Conference on Artificial Intelligence, vol. 35, pp. 12353–12362 (2021). https://doi.org/10.1609/aaai.v35i14.17466
13. Li, J., Tinka, A., Kiesel, S., Durham, J.W., Kumar, T.S., Koenig, S.: Lifelong multi-agent path finding in large-scale warehouses. In: Proceedings of the AAAI Conference on Artificial Intelligence, vol. 35, pp. 11272–11281 (2021)
14. Ma, H., Harabor, D., Stuckey, P.J., Li, J., Koenig, S.: Searching with consistent prioritization for multi-agent path finding. In: Proceedings of the AAAI Conference on Artificial Intelligence, vol. 33, pp. 7643–7650 (2019). https://doi.org/10.1609/aaai.v33i01.33017643
15. Ma, H., Yang, J., Cohen, L., Kumar, T.S., Koenig, S.: Feasibility study: moving non-homogeneous teams in congested video game environments. In: Thirteenth Artificial Intelligence and Interactive Digital Entertainment Conference (2017)
16. Malinen, M.I., Fränti, P.: Balanced K-means for clustering. In: Fränti, P., Brown, G., Loog, M., Escolano, F., Pelillo, M. (eds.) S+SSPR 2014. LNCS, vol. 8621, pp. 32–41. Springer, Heidelberg (2014). https://doi.org/10.1007/978-3-662-44415-3_4
17. Marek, V.W., Truszczyński, M.: Stable models and an alternative logic programming paradigm. In: Apt, K.R., Marek, V.W., Truszczynski, M., Warren, D.S. (eds.)

The Logic Programming Paradigm, pp. 375–398. Springer, Cham (1999). https://doi.org/10.1007/978-3-642-60085-2_17

18. Niemelä, I.: Logic programs with stable model semantics as a constraint programming paradigm. Ann. Math. Artif. Intell. **25**(3), 241–273 (1999)

19. Phillips, M., Likhachev, M.: Sipp: safe interval path planning for dynamic environments. In: 2011 IEEE International Conference on Robotics and Automation, pp. 5628–5635. IEEE (2011)

20. Pianpak, P., Son, T.C.: DMAPF: a decentralized and distributed solver for multi-agent path finding problem with obstacles. Electr. Proc. Theor. Comput. Sci. (EPTCS) **345**, 99–112 (2021). https://doi.org/10.4204/eptcs.345.24

21. Pianpak, P., Son, T.C.: Improving problem decomposition and regulation in distributed multi-agent path finder (DMAPF). In: PRIMA 2022: Principles and Practice of Multi-Agent Systems, pp. 156–172 (2023). https://doi.org/10.1007/978-3-031-21203-1_10

22. Pianpak, P., Son, T.C., Toups, Z.O., Yeoh, W.: A distributed solver for multi-agent path finding problems. In: Proceedings of the First International Conference on Distributed Artificial Intelligence (DAI), pp. 1–7 (2019). https://doi.org/10.1145/3356464.3357702

23. Quigley, M., et al.: Ros: an open-source robot operating system. In: ICRA Workshop on Open Source Software, Kobe, Japan, vol. 3, p. 5 (2009)

24. Sharon, G., Stern, R., Felner, A., Sturtevant, N.R.: Conflict-based search for optimal multi-agent pathfinding. Artif. Intell. **219**, 40–66 (2015)

25. Sharon, G., Stern, R., Goldenberg, M., Felner, A.: The increasing cost tree search for optimal multi-agent pathfinding. Artif. Intell. **195**, 470–495 (2013)

26. Silver, D.: Cooperative pathfinding. In: Proceedings of the AAAI Conference on Artificial Intelligence and Interactive Digital Entertainment, vol. 1, pp. 117–122 (2005)

27. Stern, R., et al.: Multi-agent pathfinding: definitions, variants, and benchmarks. In: Symposium on Combinatorial Search (SoCS), pp. 151–158 (2019)

28. Surynek, P.: Compilation-based solvers for multi-agent path finding: a survey, discussion, and future opportunities. arXiv preprint arXiv:2104.11809 (2021)

29. Thayer, J.T., Ruml, W.: Bounded suboptimal search: a direct approach using inadmissible estimates. In: Twenty-Second International Joint Conference on Artificial Intelligence (2011)

30. Wilt, C., Botea, A.: Spatially distributed multiagent path planning. In: Proceedings of the International Conference on Automated Planning and Scheduling, vol. 24, pp. 332–340 (2014)

31. Yu, J., LaValle, S.M.: Structure and intractability of optimal multi-robot path planning on graphs. In: Twenty-Seventh AAAI Conference on Artificial Intelligence (2013)

32. Zhang, H., et al.: A hierarchical approach to multi-agent path finding. In: Proceedings of the International Symposium on Combinatorial Search, vol. 12, pp. 209–211 (2021)

Engineering Domains and Applications

A Multi-agent Approach for Decentralized Voltage Regulation in Micro Grids by Considering Distributed Generators

Fenghui Ren[✉] and Jun Yan

School of Computing and Information Technology, University of Wollongong,
Wollongong, Australia
{fren,jyan}@uow.edu.au

Abstract. Distributed generators (DGs) are considered as significant components to modern micro grids because they can provide instant and renewable electric power to consumers without using transmission networks. However, the use of DGs may affect the use of voltage regulators in a micro grid because the DGs are usually privately owned and cannot be centrally managed. In this paper, an innovative multi-agent approach is proposed to perform automatic and decentralized control of distributed electric components in micro grids for the voltage regulation purpose. Autonomous software agents are employed to make local optimal decisions on voltage regulation by considering multiple objectives and local information; and agent-based communication and collaboration are employed toward a global voltage regulation through dynamic task allocation. The proposed approach contains three layers for representing the physical micro grid, the multi-agent system and the human-computer interface, and is implemented by using three Java-based packages, i.e. InterPSS, JADE and JUNG respectively.

Keywords: Distributed generators · voltage regulation · micro grid · multiagent system

1 Introduction

Maintaining consistent and stable voltage levels in a micro grid (MG) is very important because under-voltage can cause overheating of induction motors, and over-voltage can cause equipment damage Farag *et al.* (2012); Ufa *et al.* (2022). Voltage regulation is a procedure to keep voltages within normal limits, which is usually ±5% of the rated voltage Trip *et al.* (2018). Usually, through collecting sensor readings from predefined measurement points, a Load Tap Changer (LTC) or a Voltage Regulator (VR) can estimate the status of a grid, and perform corresponding operations to regulate voltages Deshmukh *et al.* (2012); Li et al. (2010). However, such regulation mechanisms are no longer suitable after the connection of distributed generators (DGs) to the grid.

In recent years, DGs emerge as alternative power resources and are considered as one of the most significant technologies in power grid systems Basak *et al.*

A. Ciortea et al. (Eds.): EMAS 2023, LNAI 14378, pp. 151–166, 2023.
https://doi.org/10.1007/978-3-031-48539-8_10

(2012) León *et al.* (2022); Ufa *et al.* (2022). In general, by comparison with conventional bulk generations, DGs are smaller scale and located closer to loads. However, the usage of DGs bring both benefits and trouble to existing MGs. On one hand, DGs can supply power to consumers in a MG without needing a transmission network, so as to significantly decrease power loss, voltage drop and cost Basak *et al.* (2012). Some DGs use renewable energy and contribute to the carbon emission deduction as well. On the other hand, most DGs can only provide intermittent power to a MG due to the intermittent nature of energy resources such as wind and sun Ramchurn *et al.* (2011); Wang *et al.* (2022). Also, most DGs are privately owned and a utility can not centrally control all DGs in a MG. Therefore, with an increasing level of DGs penetrations, a MG may behave quite differently from conventional operations. For example, a DG located in downstream will mislead the reading of a LTC or VR because of the LTC and the VR does not know of the existence of the DG, then the LTC or VR will definitely perform incorrect operations Basak *et al.* (2012); Farag *et al.* (2012) and the voltage level of the MG will be impacted. Also, because the power output from a DG using renewable energy to a MG can suddenly have a significant change due to weather or the DG owners' reasons, the voltage level on a DG and its affected area may also change a lot in a short time. However, because LTC or VR can not provide fast enough voltage regulation, DGs may not able to ride through emergency conditions due to voltage drops and automatically be disconnected from the MG Wang *et al.* (2022). Due to the sudden loss of a DG's power, consequential voltage instability may result more disconnects of other DGs, and such a chain reaction may eventually catastrophic power outage in a MG Wang *et al.* (2022).

Several approaches were proposed to address the above challenge in recent years. In Shaheen and El-Sehiemy (2020), an enhanced grey wolf algorithm (EGWA) is proposed to solve the optimal allocation of capacitor banks, the distributed generations, and the voltage regulators, which can increase the efficiency to detect and resume the issues caused by the voltage drop. However, as the DGs may change the behaviour of a MG, the predefined optimal allocation may not work effectively after the connection/disconnection of DGs. In Deshmukh *et al.* (2012), voltage regulation problem was formulated as an optimization problem on reactive power dispatching by considering DGs, and was solved through a large amount of calculation. Although technologies, such as distributed computing Yu *et al.* (2012), adaptive computing Li *et al.* (2010) and fuzzy control Spatti *et al.* (2010) were employed to increase the efficiency of voltage regulation, the lack of interactions between electrical components still limits dispatching efficiency by considering the dynamics of a MG and the uncertainties of DGs. In Wang *et al.* (2019), a two-layer co-planning method was used to optimize the placement of DG and battery energy storage towards the voltage regulation. However, the construction and running costs of battery energy storage are too high which stops to apply the solutions in the real-world MGs. In Farag *et al.* (2012), a Multi-Agent System (MAS) for voltage regulation and reactive power dispatching are introduced. However, the MAS employed a central controller to manage the regulation by using global information. Therefore, such centralized mechanisms can not handle the voltage regulation in a MG when private DGs are connected Rogers *et al.* (2012). Even through some decentralized MASs were also proposed to overcome such a limitation Fakham *et al.* (2011), practical issues such as how to minimize the regulation cost and time, how to effectively organise regulation through communication, and how to properly design and implement such as MAS were not properly discussed. The network self-organization approach was also combined with the MAS to handle the distributed voltage regulation issue for a large distribution network Al Faiya *et al.* (2021), issues such as asynchronous agent communication and incidences handling are still not resolved properly. The multi-agent reinforcement learning approaches Wang *et al.* (2020; 2021) were also proposed to perform the active voltage control to relieve power congestion and improve voltage quality. However, issues such as lack of training data and the uncertainties of real-world scenarios limit the usage of the solutions in real-world applications.

Theoretically, voltage levels are impacted by power delivered through it. If power injected to a MG can be quickly modified, then voltages will be adjusted in a short period accordingly. Conventional bulk generations are impractical due to their large scales, but such a problem does not exist for DGs. Therefore, adjusting DGs power outputs is considered as a matter for a fast voltage regulation. Furthermore, in order to perform more efficient regulation, DGs need to collaborate with other devices. Because of private ownership of DGs, the conventional centralised-based approaches can not efficiently coordinate all the electrical devices due to their limitations of flexibility, communication, cooperation, and decision making Razavi *et al.* (2019). Therefore, in this paper, an innovative decentralised coordinated voltage regulation approach is proposed by considering the connection of DGs in a MG. Autonomous agents are proposed to automatically and adaptive control all electrical devices in a MG, and each agent can make local optimal regulation through using local information and devices. Furthermore, the proposed coordination approach will enable the dynamic collaboration of agents in voltage regulation, which will approximate the voltage regulation of the whole MG to its optimization. Multiple objectives and constraints such as regulation time and cost are considered. A detail introduction of the MAS design and implementation is also given in this paper.

The organization of this paper is as follows. Section 2 introduces the principle and the objectives of voltage regulation by considering DGs, and Sect. 3 introduces our multi-agent approach to this decentralized voltage regulation. Section 4 demonstrates the performance of the proposed approach through a case study. Finally, the conclusion and future work are given in Sect. 5.

2 Voltage Regulation Considering DGs

2.1 Principle

Traditionally, all DGs are required to work in a power factor control model Wang *et al.* (2020), where the power factor ($PF = P/Q$) indicates the ratio between active power output (P) and reactive power output (Q).

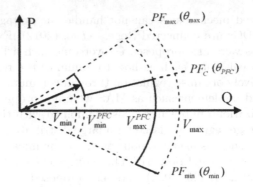

Fig. 1. Vector diagram of a DG's voltage.

As shown in Fig. 1, when DGs work in a power factor control model, a constant PF is maintained. However, if a DG's voltage approaches statutory limits, i.e. V_{min} or V_{max}, the DG can deactivate the power factor control model and regulate its voltage through adjusting its power output. Basically, in order to keep P at a requested level, a DG will increase Q when its voltage drops to the lower threshold V_{min}^{PFC}, so as to increase its voltage. On the other hand, if its voltage reaches its upper threshold V_{max}^{PFC}, the DG will decrease Q, which leads to a decrement of its voltage. Therefore, based on the Jacobian matrix of the Newton power flow Yu et al. (2012), the linear relationship between a DG's changes on its power output and voltage is displayed in Formula (4):

$$\Delta V = \Lambda_{VQ} \cdot \Delta Q + \Lambda_{VP} \cdot \Delta P. \tag{1}$$

where ΔP and ΔQ are a DG's changes on active and reactive power, ΔV is DG's corresponding voltage change, and Λ_{VP} and Λ_{VQ} are the correlations between changes of voltage, active and reactive power, respectively.

The correlation between changes of P and Q is shown as the Jacobian matrix of the Newton power flow in Formula (2) Yu *et al.* (2012).

$$\begin{pmatrix} \Delta\theta \\ \Delta V \end{pmatrix} = \begin{pmatrix} \Lambda_{\theta P} & \Lambda_{\theta Q} \\ \Lambda_{VP} & \lambda_{VQ} \end{pmatrix} \begin{pmatrix} \Delta P \\ \Delta Q \end{pmatrix} \tag{2}$$

with

$$\Lambda = \begin{pmatrix} \Lambda_{\theta P} & \Lambda_{\theta Q} \\ \Lambda_{VP} & \lambda_{VQ} \end{pmatrix}, \tag{3}$$

where ΔP and ΔQ are a DG's changes on active and reactive power, $\Delta\theta$ and ΔV are the DG's corresponding changes on PF ($PF = th(\theta)$) and voltage, respectively. Then a linear relationship between a DG's changes on its power output and voltage is displayed in Formula (4):

$$\Delta V = \Lambda_{VQ} \cdot \Delta Q + \Lambda_{VP} \cdot \Delta P. \tag{4}$$

Usually, in order to minimize impacts to a MG, active power output will not be changed, i.e. $\Delta P = 0$, and a DG will only adjust its reactive power output during a voltage regulation.

2.2   Objectives and Constraints

In this paper, three objectives for a voltage regulation are set by considering DGs, which are the time objective, the cost objective, and the population objective.

Time Objective: In order to get a fast regulation on voltage to protect DGs in emergency situations, total time spent on the regulation should be minimized, i.e.

$$\min \sum_i t(\Delta v_i), \tag{5}$$

where $t(\Delta v_i)$ is the time spent on regulating i's voltage, and Δv_i is the minimum voltage change for node i getting back to normal.

Cost Objective: A MG may connect multiple DGs, and costs of the DGs on voltage regulations will also be different by considering their motor types, resources and locations. We also want to minimize the total cost, i.e.

$$\min \sum_i \Delta Q_i \cdot c_i, \tag{6}$$

where c_i is DG i's cost of adjusting a unit reactive power, and ΔQ_i is the amount of reactive power modified.

Population Objective: In case multiple voltage fluctuations occur, voltage regulations should recover problem nodes as much as possible to their normal limits, i.e.

$$\max_i \{0.85 \ (p.u.) \le v_i \le 1.05 \ (p.u.)\}, \tag{7}$$

where v_i is the voltage of the ith problem node.

The fulfillment of the objectives should not lead to violation of operating other components; hence, several constraints are reinforced.

Current Limit: For each electrical component i, current through it should be not greater than its limit, i.e.

$$\forall i, |I_i| \le |I_i^{max}|. \tag{8}$$

where I_i is current on component i, and I_i^{max} is component i's limit on current.

Voltage Limit: The voltage regulation should not cause any new voltage fluctuation to other components, i.e.

$$\forall i, 0.95 \ (p.u.) \le v_i \le 1.05 \ (p.u.). \tag{9}$$

Reactive Power Output Limit: An DG's reactive power output should not exceed its surplus capability, i.e.

$$\forall i, |Q_i| \le |Q_i^{max}|. \tag{10}$$

where Q_i is DG i's reactive power output, and Q_i^{max} is DG i's limit on reactive power output.

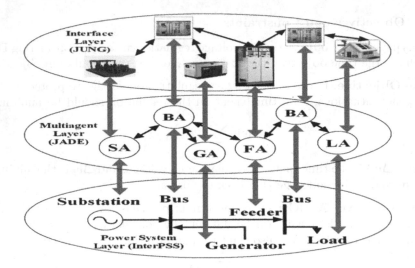

Fig. 2. A three-layer view of the proposed approach.

3   A Multi-agent Based Voltage Regulation

3.1   Principle

In order to fulfill the above objectives by considering all requested constraints, a multi-agent approach is introduced in this section. As shown in Fig. 2, the proposed approach contains three layers, i.e. a power system layer, a multi-agent layer and a interface layer. First, the power system layer locates in the bottom and presents a MG. In this paper, we consider five key electrical components for voltage regulation purposes, i.e. *substation* (controlling LTC), *feeder* (controlling VR), *busbar*, *load* and *DG*. Second, the multi-agent layer locates in the middle and presents a MAS to dominate communications, decision-makings, and collaborations between the electrical components. Five types of agents are proposed in this layer to control the five identified electrical components correspondingly, i.e. *substation agent*, *feeder agent*, *bus agent*, *load agent* and *DG agent*. Third, the interface layer locates on the top and visualizes the whole system.

By comparison with conventional centralized voltage regulations, the proposed approach has the following advantages. (i) A *decentralized management* is employed by the proposed MAS, which means that there is no central controller, and agents work automatically based on information they receive from corresponding electrical components and neighboring agents. No agent will preset the global information. (ii) Agents are represented as nodes in a peer-to-peer network, and can communicate with their neighboring agents. Non-adjacent agents can communicate and share information through in-between agents. And (iii) there is no dependency relationship between agents, and the MAS size is scalable. Agents act as a "plug and operate" component. In the following subsections, characteristics of proposed agents will be introduced firstly, then three mechanisms will be introduced to dynamically control the agents in distributed voltage regulation. Finally, implementation of the proposed MAS will be also briefly introduced.

3.2 Agent Design

We propose five agents as follows. Characteristics of the proposed five agents are introduced below.

Substation Agent (*SA*): A *SA* represents a secondary substation, and monitors current, voltage and power output of the substation. During a normal operation, the *SA* continuously exchanges information with neighboring agents, and operates a LTC under requests to perform a conventional voltage regulation. The response time and cost of a *SA* are two crucial factors for its neighboring agents to decide whether the *SA* should be requested to involve in a regulation process.

Feeder Agent (*FA*): A *FA* represents a physical feeder which delivers power to downstream components, and monitors current and voltage drop on the feeder through communicating with upstream and downstream agents. A *FA* checks cables transmission abilities to decide whether required power can be delivered. In case a *FA* is requested to join in a voltage regulation process, it will operate corresponding VRs to fulfill the request. Usually, a *FA* can provide a faster regulation than a *SA*, but a slower regulation than a GA. A *FA*'s regulation cost is impacted by the distance between its VRs and problem nodes.

Bus Agent (*BA*): A *BA* represents a physical bus-bar that conducts power between electrical components. A *BA* records information on connected electrical components, such as current and voltage. During a voltage regulation, a *BA* can make its local decisions on a local regulation plan in order to reach its local objectives. Usually, once a *BA* receives a regulation request from a neighboring agent, the *BA* will firstly search for a local solution by using only local resources. If the local resources cannot fulfil the regulation request, the *BA* and then will request help from its upstream agents. For a secondary *BA*, it will contact a *SA* to perform conventional regulation through operating a LTC.

Generator Agent (*GA*): A *GA* represents a DG. During normal operations, a *GA* monitors current, voltage and power output of a DG, and maintains the DG's power factor. During a voltage regulation process, a *GA* deactivates the DG's power factor control model and provides voltage supports to a MG through adjusting the DG's reactive power output. Also, a *GA* should ensure that the DG's reactive power output does not exceed its limit. Usually, a DG is ranked by considering its response time, cost and effect on a voltage regulation, and a *GA* also makes individual decisions on how to respond to neighboring agents regulation requests by considering the DG's capacity.

Load Agent (LA): A *LA* represents a load in a MG. A *LA* monitors current and voltage level of the load, and reports to its upstream *BA* once a voltage fluctuation is detected. Each LA is assigned a priority to indicate the significance of the load. Usually, a LA with a high priority is handled earlier than a LA with a low priority during voltage regulation. Once a regulation plan is determined, a LA will confirm with its upstream agent for execution.

3.3 Mechanism Design

In order to efficiently manage electrical components to perform distributed voltage regulations by considering the existence of DGs, three novel mechanisms are proposed to control agents and to regulate voltage during three typical operations on electrical components, i.e. the connection, the disconnection, and the voltage fluctuation. All mechanisms employ decentralized designs, and are independent on a MG or agent types.

Connection Mechanism. When a new electrical component i needs to be connected to a MG, a corresponding agent a_i will be firstly generated to represent the new component. Let a_i be represented by a seven-tuple $a_i = <AID_i, I_i^{max}, T_i^{max}, Q_i^{max}, V_i^t, C_i^t, P_i^t>$ (where AID_i is a_i's ID, $I_i^{max}, T_i^{max}, Q_i^{max}, V_i^t, C_i^t, P_i^t$ indicates a_i's max current, max regulation time, max reactive power, voltage, regulation cost and priority, respectively), and the nine-tuple $n_{i,j} = <AID_j, I_{i,j}^{max}, Q_{i,j}^{max}, T_{i,j}^{max}, I_{i,j}^t, Q_{i,j}^t, C_{i,j}^t, \Lambda_{i,j}^t, P_i^t>$ be a_i's record on its neighboring agent a_j. Then the connection process is as follows:

Step 1: a_i is created to represent the electrical component i, and is initialized according to component i's features.

Step 2: a_i sends a connection request with information $<AID_i, I_i^{max}, Q_i^{max}, T_i^{max}, C_i^t, P_i^t>$ to a_j, and waits for a_j's response. If component i cannot provide reactive power, then $Q_i^{max} = 0$, $T_i^{max} = +\inf$, and $C_i^t = +\inf$.

Step 3: a_j receives a_i's connection request. If the connection is not allowed, a_j denies the request, and the procedure goes to Step (v). Otherwise, the procedure goes to Step (iv).

Step 4: Firstly, a_j creates a new neighboring agent record according to information sent by a_i, i.e. $n_{j,i} = <AID_i, \min(I_i^{max}, I_j^{max}), Q_i^{max}, T_i^{max}, 0, 0, (C_i^t + L_{j,i}), 0, P_i^t>$ (where $L_{j,i}$ indicates a cost of power loss on a cable between components i and j), and adds $n_{j,i}$ to its neighboring agents set, i.e., $\mathbf{N_j} \leftarrow \{n_{j,i}\} \cap \mathbf{N_j}$. Secondly, a_j informs other existing neighboring agents about its update on reactive power supply, cost and priority by sending $(Q_i^{max}, T_i^{max}, (C_i^t + L_{j,i}), P_i^t)$. Thirdly, a_j's neighboring agents update their records on a_j, i.e., $Q_{k,j}^{max} \leftarrow (Q_{k,j}^{max} + Q_i^{max})$, $T_{k,j}^{max} \leftarrow \min(T_{k,j}^{max}, T_i^{max})$, $C_{k,j}^t \leftarrow \min(C_{k,j}^t, (C_i^t + L_{j,i} + L_{k,j}))$, and $P_{k,j}^t \leftarrow \max(P_{k,j}^t, P_i^t)$. Lastly, a_j's neighboring agents inform their updates to their neighboring agents, and concurrently, a_j replies a_i with an agreement.

Step 5: If a_i receives an agreement from a_j, a_i creates a new neighboring agent record according to information sent by a_j, i.e. $n_{i,j} = <AID_j, \min(I_i^{max}, I_j^{max}), \sum_k Q_{j,k}^{max}, \min(\min_k\{T_{j,k}^{max}\}, T_j^{max}), 0, 0, (\min(\min_k\{C_{j,k}^t\}, C_j^t)$

$+L_{i,j}$), 0, $\max(\max_k\{P_{j,k}^t\}, P_j^t)>$, and adds $n_{i,j}$ to its neighboring agents set, i.e. $\mathbf{N_i} \leftarrow \{n_{i,j}\} \cap \mathbf{N_i}$. After that, a_i connects to the MG. Otherwise, if a disagreement is received, the procedure is terminated.

Disconnection Mechanism. An existing electrical component may also need to be disconnected from a MG. Suppose that agent a_i wants to disconnect from a MG, and agent a_j is its upstream component, then the disconnection process is given as follows:

Step 1: a_i sends a disconnection request to a_j, and waits for a_j's response.
Step 2: a_j receives the request, and then activates the *voltage regulation mechanism* to re-dispatch reactive power without considering a_i. If a_j fails to re-allocate reactive power, then the disconnection is not allowed and the procedure goes to **Step 4**. Otherwise, the procedure goes to **Step 3**.
Step 3: Firstly, a_j deletes the record of a_i from its neighboring agents set, i.e. $\mathbf{N_j} \leftarrow \mathbf{N_j}/n_{j,i}$. Secondly, a_j informs other existing neighboring agents about its update on reactive power supply, cost and priority by sending (Q_i^{max}, $\min(\min_k\{T_{j,k}^{max}\}, T_j^{max})$, $\min(\min_k\{C_{j,k}^t\}, C_j^t)$, $\max(\max_k\{P_{j,k}^t\}, P_j^t)$) (where $k \in \mathbf{N_j}, k \neq i$). Thirdly, a_j's neighboring agents update their records on a_j, i.e., $Q_{k,j}^{max} \leftarrow (Q_{k,j}^{max} - Q_i^{max})$, $T_{k,j}^{max} \leftarrow \min(\min_k\{T_{j,k}^{max}\}, T_j^{max})$, $C_{k,j}^t \leftarrow \min(\min_k\{C_{j,k}^t\}, C_j^t)$, and $P_{k,j}^t \leftarrow \max(\max_k\{P_{j,k}^t\}, P_j^t)$. Lastly, a_j's neighboring agents inform their updates to their neighboring agents, and concurrently, a_j replies a_i with an agreement on disconnection.
Step 4: If a_i receives an agreement from a_j, a_i will delete the record of a_j from its neighboring agents set, i.e. $\mathbf{N_i} \leftarrow \mathbf{N_i}/n_{i,j}$, and then a_i disconnects from components j. Otherwise, a_i should keep the connection with a_j, and seeks for another disconnection from the MG in future.

Distributed Voltage Regulation Mechanism. If any voltage fluctuation happens on any electrical component, this mechanism will be activated automatically to regulate voltages by considering all the objectives and constraints mentioned in Subsect. 3.1. Basically, a decentralized design is employed in this mechanism. Agents make local reasoning and decision making on their regulation plans based on their local information, which includes the calculation of regulation solutions, reactive power resource selections, and reactive power dispatching. A recursive strategy is employed during the regulation when multiple agents are involved. The regulation process is introduced as follows.

Step 1: Let a_k be the agent which firstly notices a voltage fluctuation, i.e. its voltage is beyond its limit $\pm 5\%$ (p.u.), and V_k^t be the voltage value. Then a_k firstly calculates the difference between its existing voltage and its target voltage using Formula (11). In this paper, the target voltage is set to 0.85 (p.u.) for any existing voltage lower than 0.85 (p.u.), and is set to 1.05 (p.u.) for any existing voltage higher than 1.05 (p.u.).

$$\Delta V_k^t = \begin{cases} 0.85 - V_k^t, & \text{if } V_k^t < 0.85, \\ 1.05 - V_k^t, & \text{if } V_k^t > 1.05. \end{cases} \tag{11}$$

Step 2: In order to choose a right adjustment for a voltage regulation, a_k makes a combined consideration on different factors, i.e. regulation speed, cost and effectiveness. Let a_i be a_k's *ith* neighboring agent, and a_k firstly evaluates a_i by using Formula (12).

$$E(a_k, a_i) = \frac{1/T_{k,i}^{max}}{\sum_j 1/T_{k,j}^{max}} \cdot W_k^s + \frac{1/C_{k,i}^t}{\sum_j 1/C_{k,j}^t} \cdot W_k^c + \frac{\Lambda_{k,i}^t}{\sum_j \Lambda_{k,j}^t} \cdot W_k^e, \quad (12)$$

where W_k^s, W_k^c, and W_k^e are a_k's preferences on the speed, cost and effectiveness of the regulation respectively, and $W_k^s + W_k^c + W_k^e = 1$.

Then, a_k ranks all neighboring agents as $\mathbf{N_k^r}$, i.e. $\forall a_i, a_j \in \mathbf{N_k^r}, a_i \geq a_j \Rightarrow E(a_k, a_i) \geq E(a_k, a_j)$. Let a_i be a next agent in $\mathbf{N_k^r}$, then a_k calculates a voltage change that a_i should provide by considering a line's loss as $\Delta V_{k,i}^t = \Delta V_k^t + L_{k,i}$. Also, a_k calculates a possible change on a_i's reactive power output in order to cover $\Delta V_{k,i}^t$ according to Formula (4) under an assumption that $\Delta P = 0$, i.e. $\Delta Q_{k,i}^t = \Delta V_{k,i}^t / \Lambda_{k,i}^t$. If a_k believes that a_i can afford such a modification, i.e. $\Delta Q_{k,i}^t + Q_{k,i}^t \leq Q_{k,i}^{max}$, a_k will send the voltage change request $req_{k,i}^t = \Delta V_{k,i}^t$ to a_i. Otherwise, the voltage change request will be updated by considering a_i's maximum reactive power output as $req_{k,i}^t = \Delta V_{k,i}^{u,t} = \Lambda_{k,i}^t \cdot (Q_{k,i}^{max} - Q_{k,i}^t)$, and leave the remaining voltage change, i.e. $\Delta V_{k,i}^{r,t} = \Delta V_{k,i}^t - \Delta V_{k,i}^{u,t}$, to a next neighboring agent in $\mathbf{N_k^r}$.

Step 3: Once a_i receives a_k's regulation request, the request will be inserted into a_i's request queue, i.e. $\mathbf{req_i}$, by considering a_k's priority and time when the request was received. Let $req_{k,i}^t$ and $req_{j,i}^t$ be two requests in $\mathbf{req_i}$, then $req_{k,i}^t$ is in front of $req_{j,i}^t$ iff $R(i, req_{k,i}^t) > R(i, req_{j,i})$, where $R(i, req_{k,i})$ is defined in Formula (13).

$$R(i, req_{k,i}) = \frac{1/(t_k - t_1)}{\sum_k 1/(t_k - t_1)} \cdot W_i^t + \frac{P_{i,k}^t}{\sum_k P_{i,k}^t} \cdot W_i^p, \quad (13)$$

where t_k is time when the request $req_{k,i}^t$ was received, and $P_{i,k}^t$ is a_i's record on a_k's priority. W^t and W^p are a_i's weighting on time and priority, respectively. Each time when a_k receives a new request, queue $\mathbf{req_i}$ will be updated.

Let us assume that a_i already completes all requests in front of $req_{k,i}^t$, and starts to process request $req_{k,i}^t$. If a_i represents an electrical component which can adjust reactive power directly (i.e. a DG, a feeder or a substation), then a_i can make a decision on the request $req_{k,i}^t$ without contacting other agents. In order to do that, a_i firstly calculates its remaining supply ability to a_k as $Q_{i,k}^{r,t} = Q_i^{max} - \sum_k Q_{i,k}^t$, and replies to a_k to indicate the actual amount that a_i can supply, i.e. $rsp_{i,k} = \min(Q_{i,k}^{r,t}, |req_{k,i}^t|)$. However, if a_i cannot adjust reactive power directly, a_i needs to contact its neighboring agents for a_k's request. To do that, a_i needs to employ *voltage regulation mechanism* again by seeking $req_{k,i}^t$ change on its voltage. Obviously, such a recursive procedure will be repeated until an electrical component, which can adjust reactive power directly, is reached.

Step 4: Suppose that a_i receives a response from a neighboring agent a_j, i.e. $rsp_{j,i}^t$. If a_i's request can be fully satisfied by a_j, i.e. $rsp_{j,i}^t = req_{i,j}^t$, then a_i will respond $rsp_{i,k}^t \leftarrow rep_{j,i}^t$ to a_k directly. Otherwise, a_i will seek for the remaining voltage $\Delta V_{i,m}^{r,t} \leftarrow (\Delta V_{k,i}^t - rsp_{j,i}^t \cdot \Lambda_{i,j}^t)$ from its next neighboring agent by sending a request $req_{i,m}^t = \Delta V_{i,m}^{r,t}/\Lambda_{i,m}^t$. Such a procedure will be repeated until a_i's request is fully satisfied by its neighboring agents or no more neighboring agent can be contacted. Finally, a_i responds to a_k by combing all the responses from neighboring agents, i.e. $rsp_{i,k}^t = \sum_j rsp_{j,i}^t$. Then a_i is ready for executing operations and waits for a_k's confirmation. However, if a_i receives a cancellation request from a_k before operations can be executed, a_i will cancel the regulation and forward the cancellation to related neighboring agents.

Step 5: Once a_k receives a_i's response, a_k will reply to a_i with a confirmation for executing. If a_k's request can be fully satisfied by a_i, i.e. $rsp_{i,k}^t = req_{k,i}^t$, then the regulation is complete. Otherwise, a_k will seek for the remaining voltage change $\Delta V_{k,m}^{r,t} \leftarrow (\Delta V_{k,i}^t - rsp_{i,k}^t \cdot \Lambda_{k,i}^t)$ from its next neighboring agent by sending a request $req_{k,m}^t = \Delta V_{k,m}^{r,t}/\Lambda_{k,m}^t$. Then the steps **(ii)–(iv)** will be repeated until a_k's original request is fully satisfied by its neighboring agents cumulatively. Because conventional LTC and VR are involved in the procedure and represented by SAs or FAs, we assume that a_i's original request on voltage change can be satisfied eventually.

Step 6: a_i receives a_k's confirmation, and forwards the confirmation to related neighboring agents. The agents, which receive the confirmation, start to adjust their reactive power as promised.

3.4   System Development

As shown in Fig. 2, our MAS solution contains three layers and we employ three well-known Java-based packages, i.e. InterPSS (Internet technology based Power System Simulator), JADE (Java Agent Development Framework), and JUNG (Java Universal Network/Graph Framework), for the development of each layer, respectively. InterPSS is an open-source Java-based development project to enhance power system design, analysis, diagnosis and operation Zhou *et al.* (2019). We employ InterPSS for the development of the power system layer. JADE is a free agent development framework, and the communication among agents in JADE is carried out according to FIPA-specified Agent Communication Language (ACL) KS (2019). We employ JADE on top of InterPSS to develop the middle layer to monitor and control electrical components. JUNG (Java Universal Network/Graph Framework) is a free software library that provides a common and extendable language for modeling, analysis, and visualization of data that can be represented as a graph or network Team (2016). We employ JUNG on the top of InterPSS and JADE to visualize the whole system.

4   Simulation

In this section, we demonstrate the performance of the proposed MAS through a case study. In Fig. 3, a MG is firstly output by using InterPSS. The MG contains

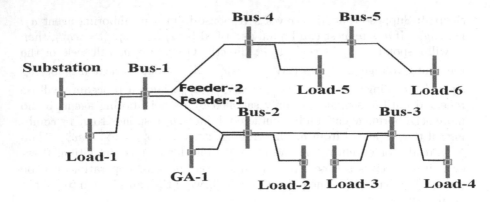

Fig. 3. An InterPSS output showing a power micro grid.

one substation, two feeders, five buses, six loads, and one generator. The limits of reactive power flow for the substation, buses and feeders are set to 500 MVar. The maximum reactive power supply for the substation is set to 300 MVar, and the MG is also connected to a 100 MVar DG. It is also assumed that the DG's response time on a voltage regulation is much shorter than a LTC or VR, and we set those two response times to 0.1 p.u./s and 0.02 p.u./s, respectively. The cost of voltage regulations is depended on the type of control devices, and the distance between a problem node and a control device.

We set the cost for adjusting 1 MVar as \$20 through a LTC and VR, and as \$10 through a DG. The delivery of 1 MVar through 1 km is assumed to be \$1, and the distance between any two electrical components is assumed to be 1 km. In Fig. 4, the multi-agent simulation of the MG using JADE and JUNG is illustrated. The graph illustrates reactive power dispatching in the MG at a certain moment. Information about reactive power such as direction, amount and price are displayed in the simulation.

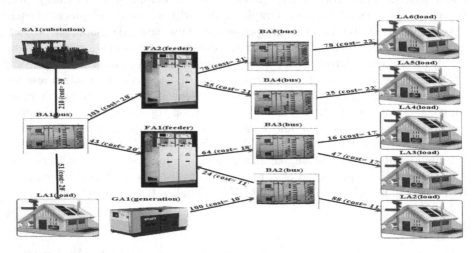

Fig. 4. A multi-agent simulation of a micro grid.

In order to show continuous adjustments on reactive power, Agent $BA1$'s historical records on reactive power adjusting through neighboring agents are displayed in Fig. 5. The negative power indicates the power input from the upper-stream Agent $SA1$, and the positive power values indicate the power outputs to the downstream Agents $LA1$, $FA1$, and $FA2$. All agents will apply the mechanisms introduced in Sect. 3.3 to automatically balance the power inputs and outputs dynamically by considering the three objectives. Through the communication and collaboration of all agents, the voltage level of the MG can be regulated automatically through adjusting the reactive power of each associated agent accordingly. Due to the page limit, the historical records of other agents are not presented in this paper.

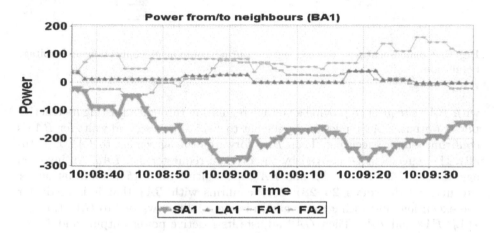

Fig. 5. The historical records of $BA1$.

In order to test the proposed mechanisms, another generator, i.e. DG2 (rated at 50 MVar), is proposed to connect the MG through $BA5$. In Fig. 6, communications between agents during DG2's connection, and a voltage regulation through $GA2$ are displayed. Explanations are given below.

(**Messages 1–2**): $GA2$ sends a request to $BA5$ for connection, and $BA5$ agrees with the connection. (**Messages 3–16**): $BA5$ informs its updates (i.e., limit, cost and sensitivity) to its neighboring agents, i.e. $FA2$ and $LA6$. Then $FA2$ further informs its neighboring agents, i.e. $BA1$ and $BA4$, about its update. Such a procedure is executed by other agents recursively, and eventually all agents receive update notices from their neighboring agents. (**Messages 17–20**): $LA5$ sends a voltage regulation request to $BA4$, and $BA4$ forwards such a request to $FA2$. Because $BA5$ already informed $FA2$ that a faster, cheaper, and more efficient voltage regulation service can be provide after $GA2$'s connection, through comparison with the voltage regulation service provided by $BA1$ (i.e. provided by $SA1$ through adjusting LTC actually), $FA2$ decides to contact $BA5$ firstly, and then $BA5$ forwards the request to $GA2$. (**Messages 21–24**): $GA2$ agrees

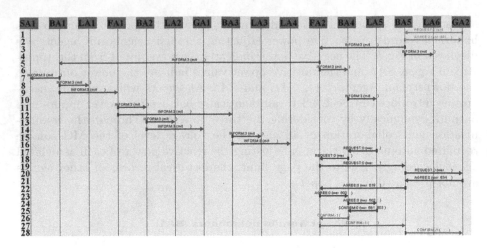

Fig. 6. Communications between agents during component connection and voltage regulation

with *BA5*'s request to provide a voltage regulation through adjusting its reactive power output. *GA2* replies an agreement to *BA5*'s request, and waits for *BA5*'s confirmation for executing. Then *BA5* forwards the agreement to *FA2*. Eventually, the agreement is received by the original requester, i.e. *LA5*. All involved agents, i.e. *GA2*, *BA5*, *FA2*, and *BA4*, are waiting for *LA5*'s confirmation for executing. (**Messages 25–28**): *LA5* confirms with *BA4* that it is ready for the execution, and such a confirmation is eventually forwarded to *GA2* through *BA4*, *FA2* and *BA5*. Then *GA2* adjusts its reactive power output, and *LA5*'s voltage is regulated.

The above case study shows that the proposed MAS solution can effectively manage a MG with DGs in a simulation environment, and perform distributed voltage regulations by using of local information and agent communication. The proposed agents can make decentralized decisions to control corresponding electrical components and perform self-adaptive voltage regulation services. The procedures, i.e. selecting reactive power resources by considering their limits, costs and sensitivities, planing reactive power dispatching by considering the dynamics of neighboring agents, and executing of voltage regulation plans, show the good performance of the proposed agents.

5   Conclusion and Future Work

The DG is considered to be a significant technologies in power grids, and provides supplemental electric energy to modern MGs without using transmission networks. However, the uncertainty and dynamics of DGs can make conventional voltage regulations become deactivated. In this paper, a decentralized multi-agent approach for dynamic and distributed voltage regulation by considering the DGs was proposed. The proposed approach not only provides sufficient autonomy for an individual agent to make local optimal decisions on local voltage regulation by using local information, but also supports dynamic agent collaborations for searching a global voltage regulation solution by using agent communication, dynamic task allocation and team forming. Multiple objectives and constraints are considered by the proposed agents during their distributed voltage regulations, and agents can dynamically adjust their regulation plans according to environmental changes. Development of the proposed approach by using InterPSS, JADE and JUNG was introduced, and the good performance of the proposed approach on voltage regulation in a simulated MG was also demonstrated.

Future work of this research will focus on comprehensive systemic testing and evaluation through using large scale MGs and numerous DGs with different energy resources and supply capabilities.

References

Al Faiya, B., et al.: A self-organizing multi-agent system for distributed voltage regulation. IEEE Trans. Smart Grid **12**(5), 4102–4112 (2021)

Basak, P., Chowdhury, S., Halder nee Dey, S., Chowdhury, S.P.: A literature review on integration of distributed energy resources in the perspective of control, protection and stability of microgrid. Renew. Sustain. Energy Rev. **16**(8), 5545–5556 (2012)

Deshmukh, S., Natarajan, B., Pahwa, A.: Voltage/VAR control in distribution networks via reactive power injection through distributed generators. IEEE Trans. Smart Grid **3**(3), 1226–1234 (2012)

Fakham, H., Colas, F., Guillaud, X.: Real-time simulation of multi-agent system for decentralized voltage regulation in distribution network. In: IEEE Power and Energy Society General Meeting, pp. 1–7 (2011)

Farag, H.E.Z., El-Saadany, E.F., Seethapathy, R.: A two ways communication-based distributed control for voltage regulation in smart distribution feeders. IEEE Trans. Smart Grid **3**(1), 271–281 (2012)

Gayathri Devi, K.S.: Hybrid genetic algorithm and particle swarm optimization algorithm for optimal power flow in power system. J. Comput. Mech. Power Syst. Control **2**, 31–37 (2019)

León, L.F., Martinez, M., Ontiveros, L.J., Mercado, P.E.: Devices and control strategies for voltage regulation under influence of photovoltaic distributed generation. A review. IEEE Latin Am. Trans. **20**(5), 731–745 (2022)

Li, H., Li, F., Xu, Y., Rizy, D.T., Kueck, J.D.: Adaptive voltage control with distributed energy resources: algorithm, theoretical analysis, simulation, and field test verification. IEEE Trans. Power Systems **25**(3), 1638–1647 (2010)

Ramchurn, S.D., Vytelingum, P., Rogers, A., Jennings, N.R.: Agent-based homeostatic control for green energy in the smart grid. ACM Trans. Intell. Syst. Technol. **2**(4), 35 (2011)

Razavi, S.-E., et al.: Impact of distributed generation on protection and voltage regulation of distribution systems: a review. Renew. Sustain. Energy Rev. **105**, 157–167 (2019)

Rogers, A., Ramchurn, S.D., Jennings, N.R.: Delivering the smart grid: challenges for autonomous agents and multi-agent systems research. In: Proceedings of the 26th AAAI Conference on Artificial Intelligence, pp. 2166–2172 (2012)

Shaheen, A.M., El-Sehiemy, R.A.: Optimal coordinated allocation of distributed generation units/capacitor banks/voltage regulators by EGWA. IEEE Syst. J. **15**(1), 257–264 (2020)

Spatti, D.H., da Silva, I.N., Usida, W.F., Flauzino, R.A.: Real-time voltage regulation in power distribution system using fuzzy control. IEEE Trans. Power Deliv. **25**(2), 1112–1123 (2010)

JUNG Development Team. Java universal network/graph framework (2016)

Trip, S., Cucuzzella, M., Cheng, X., Scherpen, J.: Distributed averaging control for voltage regulation and current sharing in DC microgrids. IEEE Control Syst. Lett. **3**(1), 174–179 (2018)

Ufa, R.A., Malkova, Y.Y., Rudnik, V.E., Andreev, M.V., Borisov, V.A.: A review on distributed generation impacts on electric power system. Int. J. Hydrogen Energy **47**(47), 20347–20361 (2022)

Wang, L., Yan, R., Saha, T.K.: Voltage regulation challenges with unbalanced PV integration in low voltage distribution systems and the corresponding solution. Appl. Energy **256**, 113927 (2019)

Wang, S., et al.: A data-driven multi-agent autonomous voltage control framework using deep reinforcement learning. IEEE Trans. Power Syst. **35**(6), 4644–4654 (2020)

Wang, J., Xu, W., Gu, Y., Song, W., Green, T.C.: Multi-agent reinforcement learning for active voltage control on power distribution networks. In: Advances in Neural Information Processing Systems, vol. 34, pp. 3271–3284 (2021)

Wang, R., Ma, D., Li, M.-J., Sun, Q., Zhang, H., Wang, P.: Accurate current sharing and voltage regulation in hybrid wind/solar systems: an adaptive dynamic programming approach. IEEE Trans. Consum. Electron. **68**(3), 261–272 (2022)

Yu, L., Czarkowski, D., de León, F.: Optimal distributed voltage regulation for secondary networks with DGs. IEEE Trans. Smart Grid **3**(2), 959–967 (2012)

Zhou, M., Yan, J., Feng, D.: Digital twin framework and its application to power grid online analysis. CSEE J. Power Energy Syst. **5**(3), 391–398 (2019)

Synthesizing Multi-agent System Organization from Engineering Descriptions

Ganesh Ramanathan[1,2](✉) [iD]

[1] Siemens AG, Zürich, Switzerland
ganesh.ramanathan@siemens.com
[2] University of St. Gallen, St. Gallen, Switzerland

Abstract. Automation of electro-mechanical systems, such as the ones deployed in a building or a factory, is engineered based on the *design-time knowledge* of requirements, system configuration, physical processes, and control and coordination strategies. However, any change in these aspects during the system's operation requires manually adapting the affected automation programs. Multi-agent systems (MAS) offer the potential to tackle dynamic changes in the system by letting the software agents autonomously reason about the means of achieving their goals at runtime while collaborating socially and being aware of the environment in which they operate. Nevertheless, designing a MAS-based solution for engineering applications is challenging because decomposing engineering system descriptions into MAS abstractions is a manual process and requires knowledge of the design and programming paradigm. This paper shows that the MAS organization dimension, which serves as the top-down specification of agent behavior, can be automatically decomposed from engineering system descriptions. The system descriptions, which are fragmented, are interlinked using an integration ontology developed for the purpose. Evaluation of the approach in a real-life deployment of a building automation system showed reduced engineering effort to deploy the MAS, and the resulting runtime was adaptive to changes.

Keywords: Multi-agent Systems · Automation Systems · Engineering

1 Introduction

Electro-mechanical systems, such as the ones in a building or a factory, are complex compositions of subsystems and components that carry out the desired transformation of states of substances through physical processes such as thermal, electrical, or chemical reactions. Since such processes invariably involve some form of controlled energy or mass transfer (e.g., exchange of thermal energy from hot water to air when it comes to heating), automation systems regulate the physical processes and establish the coordinated operation of the interdependent subsystems.

System Descriptions (SDs) is a broad term used in factory, process, and building automation (BA) to describe knowledge that is contained in engineering

© The Author(s), under exclusive license to Springer Nature Switzerland AG 2023
A. Ciortea et al. (Eds.): EMAS 2023, LNAI 14378, pp. 167–177, 2023.
https://doi.org/10.1007/978-3-031-48539-8_11

artifacts, such as the documentation of the requirements, the description of the subsystems and their physical processes, and the regulations and norms that govern their operation. Automation system implementation is generally based on the SDs available at design time. Consequently, they face the challenge that changes in requirements, system capabilities, or regulations and norms during the lifetime of the system require manual (and, often costly) re-engineering of the control and coordination programs [29,38].

To support use cases such as automated fault detection [27], SDs are becoming increasingly available in machine-readable and machine-understandable forms [25,28,29,31]. Though such machine-understandable SDs could also help us tackle the challenge of adaptivity, it is yet to be seen in the practice in the automation industry because it also requires an architectural paradigm that supports *knowledge-driven run time behavior*. Current approaches in automation only address methods to use system knowledge to design procedures for control and coordination as purely reactive programs.

Rational agents in Multi-agent systems (MAS) are conceptually grounded to use system knowledge at run time to proactively deliberate about local behavior and social collaboration in their pursuit of fulfilling the requirements. The benefit of using MAS to tackle dynamic environments has been demonstrated in domains such as collaborative robotics [6], power engineering [19], and in some particular cases, in factory automation [8], and BA [40].

Although the architectural properties of MAS are well suited to building adaptive systems, the widespread adoption of MAS in engineering applications is yet to be seen [7,13,17,23,24]. In my study on the feasibility of implementing a MAS-based building automation system, the primary challenge lies in deriving the design from SDs in an *automated* manner. Automated design is vital because relying on a developer to manually carry out the design and maintain it during the system's lifetime is cumbersome (and costly) for real-life applications. Also, a MAS developer cannot be expected to possess the domain expertise of an automation engineer to understand the SDs (and vice-versa, an automation engineer is not likely to be well-versed in the principles of MAS design).

The challenge of automatically synthesizing MAS design from SDs raises the question of the relevant design abstractions. In my approach, I show that the dimension of MAS design that most *naturally* captures automation system design is the notion of the agent organization. The organization is a top-down design specification that mandates the agents to jointly consider (in a global manner) the structural contexts in which they operate (i.e., the parts of the system and the physical processes involved) and thereby adopt appropriate local control and coordination functions.

Though there are existing approaches to express individual aspects of the SDs in a machine-understandable form, an *integrated view* with semantic relationships between the aspects is missing. Such a cohesive SD is essential for the automated synthesis of MAS organization specifications. For this purpose, I have developed an *integrating* ontology that links concepts in the existing engineering ontologies, allowing us to express a *unified* SD.

Therefore, the twofold contributions of this paper are to show that MAS organization specification is an essential top-down design abstraction that is valid for automation systems, and its automated synthesis can be enabled by integrating the hitherto fragmented SDs.

I tested my approach on a real-life setup of automation for heating, ventilation, and lighting systems in a room. This scenario is representative of a complex composition of engineering subsystems and their interdependencies. The evaluation demonstrated that the organization specification, which could be automatically synthesized from the *unified* SD, was adequate for the automation agents to know about their local control goals and global coordination tasks. Changes in the SD were reflected in the organization specification, causing the agents to adapt their behavior.

2   Related Work

2.1   MAS Organization and Its Relevance to Engineering Systems

MAS-based solutions for large systems require *social organization* to direct the local autonomy of the agents towards global goals [16]. Organization specification in the form of structures, roles, and functions also reflects the top-down system design [10]. Organization as means of *orchestrated autonomy* led to research on conceptual models of MAS organization along with its formalization (see [9], and [1] for details). The model of an organization depends on the desired runtime characteristics and formation methods. Horling and Lesser have described paradigms such as hierarchies, holarchies, teams, etc. [14] and their relevance to different systems. In this regard, most automation systems can be viewed as hierarchies of software agents based on a *physical decomposition* [33] of the system. Other paradigms like holarchies, coalitions, teams and markets are also seen in applications like distributed sensing [35]. A model of the organization with hierarchies of groups with one or more functional roles [11] matches well with the design approach in the automation system. MOISE+ [15] goes beyond the focus on structures by adding the abstractions of functional schemes and norms that bind roles to the goals. As we shall see later, the abstraction of functional schemes in MOISE+ supports the modeling of automation strategies, which is also a hierarchical composition of functions.

My investigation of design methodologies in engineering domains showed that top-down physical decomposition involving structural abstractions (systems, subsystems, aggregates, and components) and its co-relation to functional abstractions (composition of process functions) is well known and is practiced in process engineering [21].

Similarly, a study of design practices prevalent in automation engineering [20, 26] revealed that the deployment and behavior of the automation programs are decided based on the structure of the electro-mechanical systems and the process functions which they expected to fulfill. Figure 1 summarizes the parts of the SD and the role they play in the design of the automation system. Juxtaposed to top-down approaches, automation in domains like power engineering [19] (e.g.,

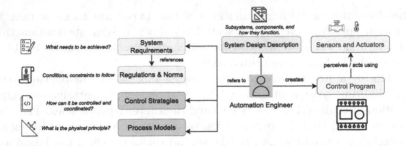

Fig. 1. Aspects of the SDs which are used for automation engineering.

smart grids) and collaborative robotics (e.g., autonomous ground vehicles) deal with an environment that cannot be determined or designed upfront [6]. In such cases, the autonomous agents primarily rely on self-organization while using predefined rules regarding forming groups and adopting roles [18,30]. While agent-centric architecture can cater to highly dynamic environments, industrial systems lay greater emphasis on having a clear definition and an understanding of the responsibilities of the agents for the sake of operational overview, explainability, and establishing rules for conflict avoidance – and this is the principal argument for an organization-centered design.

2.2   The Challenge of Synthesising MAS Organisation

Though there is a conceptual match between the engineering design of systems and the model of MAS organization, to the best of my knowledge, an automated synthesis of MAS organization specification from SDs is yet to be explored. Bastos and Castro have hinted at the possibility [3], and Freitas [12] has shown the potential of using ontology-based design.

The key aspects in SDs that are essential for decomposing the organization specification of a MAS are the description of the requirements, system design, model of the physical processes, and automation strategies. Engineering ontologies based on Semantic Web technologies have enabled machine-understandable descriptions of these aspects. Methods such as goal-oriented requirements engineering [37], which advocate the formulation of requirements in such a manner that software programs can use them to reason about the goals [4] are being used in practice [34]. Similarly methods to express machine-understandable system design [5] (for e.g., BRICK [2]), physical processes (for e.g., OntoCape [22]), and automation functions [32] are also available being put to use.

However, understanding the construction and functioning of a system, which is the basis for automation system design, requires an *integrated view* of the SDs. A major shortcoming in the current state of machine-understandable SDs is that the concepts in the individual descriptions are not interlinked. For example, a method to co-relate requirements, elements in the system design, physical processes, and automation functions is missing.

Therefore, to address the challenge of automated synthesis of organization specification of MAS, we need to identify the relevant entities and relationships in the SDs and enable its expression by integrating the fragmented knowledge.

3 Approach

3.1 Finding Organization Abstractions in System Descriptions

Amongst the abstractions in the MAS organization specification, the hierarchical group structure can be obtained rather directly from the hierarchies of subsystems and their technical equipment. In the next step, we need to define roles and assign them to groups in the structural hierarchy. For example, given that the heating system in a room needs to be automated, the question that comes up when deciding the deployment of agent(s) is *what* (in broad sense) is expected of the agent(s)? However, the notion of a role is not directly expressed in SDs, and the closest that appears as a role is the abstract conception of tasks that an automation program needs to carry out. For example, if the program for the heating system automation needs to measure air temperature and modulate a heating valve based on some control logic, we can envision its *automation role* as being the *temperature controller*. To understand how such *automation roles* are determined during the design of the (traditional) automation systems, consider the following deliberations that occur:

1. Co-relation of requirements to states in the physical processes.
2. Identifying the system parts which play a role in the physical process and the available means of sensing and actuation.
3. Programming (or choosing) an appropriate control strategy for automating the physical process using the identified system parts.
4. Identifying inter-dependent system parts and determining the coordination strategy.

Therefore, if requirements can be linked to respective subsystems and states of the physical processes, we first can infer the *physical effect* that the automation agent needs to achieve using the designated system components. For example, in the case of a heating system, the requirement of maintaining thermal comfort in the room is expected to be achieved through controlling the heat-exchange process conducted by the radiator. This indicates the *automation role* the agent plays (i.e., *temperature controller* using a radiator that conducts heat exchange).

Similarly, dependencies between the system parts, or dependencies between physical processes, should result in the linking of the respective automation roles. For example, if the room's heating system depends on the central boiler's functioning, then roles in the respective groups should also be linked. The semantics of the relationship between the roles captures the coordination foreseen in the system design.

Once we have the definition of a role (in terms of what it is meant to achieve), we need to describe *how* this role can be fulfilled. In other words, the control and coordination tasks that must be carried out by an agent adopting the role.

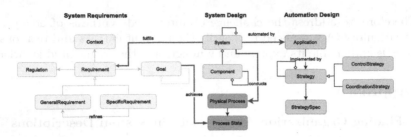

Fig. 2. The integration of engineering ontologies is achieved by establishing relationships (shown as bold red lines) between the aspects (Color figure online)

Regarding agents adopting roles, there are two *agentification* scenarios to consider. The automation system could contain *idle* agents that are looking to adopt roles, or a *management program* recognizes unfulfilled roles and deploys agents to take up those roles. In either case, the implication of adopting a role, i.e., the control and coordination tasks, must be considered to verify whether an agent can execute those functions. For example, a control function may require access to sensors, actuators, or specific computational resources.

In domains such as BA and factory automation, SDs include descriptions of *automation applications* (for e.g., see [39]). At an abstract level, an *automation application* represents a collection of control and coordination strategies suitable for a subsystem-process combination. At design-time, a role is linked to the *automation application*, and at run time the agents need to adopt concrete control and coordination strategies depending upon the state of the system and the processes. Therefore, the abstract *application* can have one or more *functional schemes* containing the control and control strategies that an agent can follow. Since MOISE+ supports this concept by decomposing goals and plans, I have used it to model the automation applications.

3.2   Integrating the System Descriptions

Having identified the entities and relationships that need to be visible (and linked) in the SDs, the challenge was then to bridge the concepts in the existing engineering ontologies such that the structural and functional abstractions of the organization can be synthesized from it. The existing ontologies are based on Resource Description Framework (RDF), which is a W3C standard as a part of the Semantic Web Technologies for expressing knowledge as interlinked resources. The ontologies use the Ontology Web Language (OWL), which is grounded in Description Logics, to model concepts as classes and relationships formally. I developed a bridging or *integrating* ontology[1] which allows linking of requirement goals to system components and process goals. System components that need to be automated are linked to abstract *automation application*, which

---

[1] Can be accessed here: https://github.com/codepasta/autonomous-buildings.git.

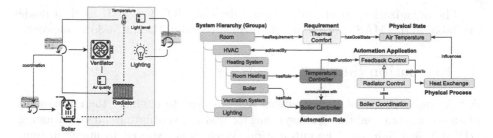

Fig. 3. The scenario for room automation (left) showing the subsystems, the process relationships (in dotted lines), and the roles designed for the automation devices. On the right we see how automation roles are recognized and correlated to functions.

captures the high-level intent of the required automation. A high-level overview of the required integration of the concepts is shown in Fig. 2.

3.3   Automated Synthesis of Organisation Specification

The concepts and relationships in an *unified* SD^2 facilitate the automated synthesis of the organization specification. The SD and the ontologies are stored in a Knowledge Graph (KG), which can be queried using SPARQL[3] statements. The automated synthesis of the specification as MOISE+ model (serialized as XML) is done by a software program that interfaces with the KG. Obtaining the structural abstraction is relatively straightforward as it queries for the subsystem hicrarchy and the inter-subsystem relationships, if any.

On the other hand, roles need to be identified based on the kind of physical process, the desired goal state, and the subsystem that can be used for the purpose. For example, the process *HeatExchange* conducted by a *Radiator* to maintain *Temperature* is construed as a role definition. For each such role, we need to tell (the role-playing agent) what functions are expected to be carried out – in other words, the *norms* that required to be respected. It is important to note that such functions are seen from system-level perspective, and not meant to tell *exactly* what the agent program should be doing. For example, in the role of a TemperatureController, the agent is expected to execute a suitable control logic for maintaining temperature (about which it autonomously deliberates) while coordinating with the central energy supplier (which it is constrained to do).

Roles are linked to each other if either the system components or the process functions are interdependent. If the semantics of the link requires the agents to communicate, then the link is annotated with reference to a coordination strategy (in form of a protocol) which the agents need to use to interact with each other.

---

[2] System Description as a singular is used here to emphasise that it now appears as cohesive knowledge.

[3] https://www.w3.org/TR/rdf-sparql-query/.

The organization specification synthesized as MOISE+ XML is then made available to the MAS runtime was implemented using the JaCaMo framework.

4   Evaluation Setup

A BA engineering tool from Siemens AG was used to engineer the automation of an office room containing subsystems for heating, ventilation, air-conditioning (HVAC), and lighting. The automation system was required to maintain temperature, humidity, air quality, and light level in an energy-efficient manner. The engineering tool exports the KG containing the SD, which is then stored in a graph database.

The JaCaMo framework was used to implement the MAS. The agents, each dedicated for the individual subsystems, were deployed in three automation hardware nodes on the network. A bootstrapping code accesses the knowledge graph containing the SD to create the organization specification as MOISE XML, along with the organizational entities representing the groups (i.e., the subsystems) and corresponding automation roles. Figure 3 shows a simplified representation of the room's heating system for which the role of the *temperature controller* has been inferred. Similarly, roles for the *ventilation controller*, *boiler controller*, and *lighting controller* are created and assigned to the respective subsystem groups. On initialization, the BDI agents in the controllers accessed the organization definition and evaluated their ability to play one or more automation roles. After adopting a role, they initialized the required control program, and if the role was linked to another role, then a suitable coordination program was also initialized.

5   Results and Discussions

A manual verification of the organization specification by an automation engineer confirmed that it contained the required subsystems and that the automation roles assigned to them were correct. Similarly, the choice of control and coordination programs made by the agents at runtime was confirmed to be correct. In addition, functional tests of the system functions confirmed that the specified requirements were met. Changes in the SD resulted in an update of the organization specification and the agents adapting their plans - this was tested for some sample cases involving changes in requirements and system components.

Though the current state of my evaluation shows encouraging results about the possibility of synthesizing organization specification from SD in the case of BA, this needs to be validated against design descriptions in more diverse domains. Similarly, aspects such as defining the semantic relationships between the roles (to recognize coordination), modeling regulations and norms and ensuring their compliance at runtime, and agents discovering features in the system [36] that may not be explicitly captured in the system design are planned to be researched in future steps.

Acknowledgements. I am grateful to Simon Mayer, Andrei Ciortea, and Danai Vachtsevanou, for the many discussions and inputs which has helped shape my approach to the problem. I also thank my employers Siemens AG, Smart Infrastructure Division, who have actively supported my research and provided the opportunity to conduct evaluations in real-life setups.

References

1. Abbas, H.A., Shaheen, S.I., Amin, M.H.: Organization of multi-agent systems: an overview. J. Intell. Inform. Syst. **4**(3) (2015)
2. Balaji, B., et al.: Brick: towards a unified metadata schema for buildings. In: Proceedings of the 3rd ACM International Conference on Systems for Energy-Efficient Built Environments, pp. 41–50 (2016)
3. Bastos, L.R., Castro, J.F.: From requirements to multi-agent architecture using organisational concepts. In: Proceedings of the Fourth International Workshop on Software Engineering for Large-Scale Multi-agent Systems, pp. 1–7 (2005)
4. Bencomo, N., Whittle, J., Sawyer, P., Finkelstein, A., Letier, E.: Requirements reflection: requirements as runtime entities. In: Proceedings of the 32nd ACM/IEEE International Conference on Software Engineering, vol. 2, pp. 199–202 (2010)
5. Butzin, B., Golatowski, F., Timmermann, D.: A survey on information modeling and ontologies in building automation. In: 43rd Annual Conference of the IEEE Industrial Electronics Society, pp. 8615–8621. IEEE (2017)
6. Cena, C.G., Cardenas, P.F., Pazmino, R.S., Puglisi, L., Santonja, R.A.: A cooperative multi-agent robotics system: design and modelling. Expert Syst. Appl. **40**(12), 4737–4748 (2013)
7. Ciortea, A., Mayer, S., Gandon, F., Boissier, O., Ricci, A., Zimmermann, A.: A decade in hindsight: the missing bridge between multi-agent systems and the world wide web. In: Proceedings of the International Conference on Autonomous Agents and Multiagent Systems (2019)
8. Ciortea, A., Mayer, S., Michahelles, F.: Repurposing manufacturing lines on the fly with multi-agent systems for the web of things. In: Proceedings of the 17th International Conference on Autonomous Agents and Multiagent Systems, pp. 813–822 (2018)
9. Dorri, A., Kanhere, S.S., Jurdak, R.: Multi-agent systems: a survey. IEEE Access **6**, 28573–28593 (2018)
10. Ferber, J., Gutknecht, O., Michel, F.: From agents to organizations: an organizational view of multi-agent systems. In: Giorgini, P., Müller, J.P., Odell, J. (eds.) AOSE 2003. LNCS, vol. 2935, pp. 214–230. Springer, Heidelberg (2004). https://doi.org/10.1007/978-3-540-24620-6_15
11. Ferber, J., Michel, F., Baez, J.: AGRE: integrating environments with organizations. In: Weyns, D., Van Dyke Parunak, H., Michel, F. (eds.) E4MAS 2004. LNCS (LNAI), vol. 3374, pp. 48–56. Springer, Heidelberg (2005). https://doi.org/10.1007/978-3-540-32259-7_2
12. Freitas, A., Bordini, R.H., Vieira, R.: Designing multi-agent systems from ontology models. In: Weyns, D., Mascardi, V., Ricci, A. (eds.) EMAS 2018. LNCS (LNAI), vol. 11375, pp. 76–95. Springer, Cham (2019). https://doi.org/10.1007/978-3-030-25693-7_5
13. Hendler, J.: Where are all the intelligent agents? IEEE Intell. Syst. **22**(03), 2–3 (2007)

14. Horling, B., Lesser, V.: A survey of multi-agent organizational paradigms. Knowl. Eng. Rev. **19**(4), 281–316 (2004)
15. Hübner, J.F., Sichman, J.S., Boissier, O.: MOISE+ towards a structural, functional, and deontic model for mas organization. In: Proceedings of the First International Joint Conference on Autonomous Agents and Multiagent Systems: Part 1, pp. 501–502 (2002)
16. Jennings, N.R.: On agent-based software engineering. Artif. Intell. **117**(2), 277–296 (2000)
17. Mascardi, V., Weyns, D., Ricci, A., Earle, C.B., Casals, A., Challenger, M., Chopra, A., Ciortea, A., Dennis, L.A., Díaz, Á.F., et al.: Engineering multi-agent systems: state of affairs and the road ahead. ACM SIGSOFT Softw. Eng. Notes **44**(1), 18–28 (2019)
18. Mathieu, P., Routier, J.C., Secq, Y.: Dynamic organization of multi-agent systems. In: Proceedings of the First International Joint Conference on Autonomous Agents and Multiagent Systems: Part 1, pp. 451–452 (2002)
19. McArthur, S.D., et al.: Multi-agent systems for power engineering applications-part I: concepts, approaches, and technical challenges. IEEE Trans. Power Syst. **22**(4), 1743–1752 (2007)
20. Mitzutani, I., Ramanathan, G., Mayer, S.: Semantic data integration with DevOps to support engineering process of intelligent building automation systems. In: Proceedings of the 8th ACM International Conference on Systems for Energy-Efficient Buildings, Cities, and Transportation, pp. 294–297 (2021)
21. Moran, S.: An Applied Guide to Process and Plant Design. Elsevier, Amsterdam (2019)
22. Morbach, J., Wiesner, A., Marquardt, W.: OntoCape-a (re) usable ontology for computer-aided process engineering. Comput. Chem. Eng. **33**(10), 1546–1556 (2009)
23. Müller, J.P., Fischer, K.: Application impact of multi-agent systems and technologies: a survey. In: Shehory, O., Sturm, A. (eds.) Agent-Oriented Software Engineering, pp. 27–53. Springer, Heidelberg (2014). https://doi.org/10.1007/978-3-642-54432-3_3
24. Pechoucek, M., et al.: Agents in industry: the best from the AAMAS 2005 industry track. IEEE Intell. Syst. **21**(2), 86–95 (2006)
25. Ploennigs, J., Hensel, B., Dibowski, H., Kabitzsch, K.: BASont-a modular, adaptive building automation system ontology. In: IECON 2012–38th Annual Conference on IEEE Industrial Electronics Society, pp. 4827–4833. IEEE (2012)
26. Ramanathan, G., Husmann, M.: Semantic description of equipment and its controls in building automation systems. In: Groth, P., et al. (eds.) ESWC 2022. LNCS, vol. 13384, pp. 307–310. Springer, Cham (2022). https://doi.org/10.1007/978-3-031-11609-4_47
27. Ramanathan, G., Husmann, M., Niedermeier, C., Vicari, N., Garcia, K., Mayer, S.: Assisting automated fault detection and diagnostics in building automation through semantic description of functions and process data. In: Proceedings of the 8th ACM International Conference on Systems for Energy-Efficient Buildings, Cities, and Transportation, pp. 228–229 (2021)
28. Runde, S., Dibowski, H., Fay, A., Kabitzsch, K.: Integrated automated design approach for building automation systems. In: IEEE International Conference on Emerging Technologies and Factory Automation, pp. 1488–1495 (2008)
29. Runde, S., Heidemann, A., Fay, A., Schmidt, P.: Engineering of building automation systems-state-of-the-art, deficits, approaches. In: IEEE 15th Conference on Emerging Technologies & Factory Automation (ETFA 2010), pp. 1–8. IEEE (2010)

30. Ruta, M., Scioscia, F., Loseto, G., Di Sciascio, E.: Semantic-based resource discovery and orchestration in home and building automation: a multi-agent approach. IEEE Trans. Industr. Inf. **10**(1), 730–741 (2013)
31. Schneider, F., Berenbach, B.: A literature survey on international standards for systems requirements engineering. Procedia Comput. Sci. **16**, 796–805 (2013)
32. Schneider, G.F., Pauwels, P., Steiger, S.: Ontology-based modeling of control logic in building automation systems. IEEE Trans. Industr. Inf. **13**(6), 3350–3360 (2017)
33. Shen, W., Hao, Q., Yoon, H.J., Norrie, D.H.: Applications of agent-based systems in intelligent manufacturing: an updated review. Adv. Eng. Inform. **20**(4), 415–431 (2006)
34. Siegemund, K., Thomas, E.J., Zhao, Y., Pan, J., Assmann, U.: Towards ontology-driven requirements engineering. In: Workshop Semantic Web Enabled Software Engineering at 10th International Semantic Web Conference (ISWC) (2011)
35. Sims, M., Corkill, D., Lesser, V.: Automated organization design for multi-agent systems. Auton. Agent. Multi-Agent Syst. **16**, 151–185 (2008)
36. Vachtsevanou, D., Ciortea, A., Mayer, S., Lemée, J.: Signifiers as a first-class abstraction in hypermedia multi-agent systems (2023). https://doi.org/10.48550/ARXIV.2302.06970, https://arxiv.org/abs/2302.06970
37. Van Lamsweerde, A.: Goal-oriented requirements engineering: a guided tour. In: Proceedings fifth IEEE International Symposium on Requirements Engineering, pp. 249–262. IEEE (2001)
38. Vogel-Heuser, B., et al.: Challenges for software engineering in automation. J. Softw. Eng. Appl. (2014)
39. Wetter, M., Grahovac, M., Hu, J.: Control description language. In: Proceedings of the American Modelica Conference 2018, pp. 17–26. Linköping University Electronic Press (2019)
40. Zia, T., Lang, R., Boley, H., Bruckner, D., Zucker, G.: An autonomous adaptive multiagent model for building automation. IFAC Proc. Vol. **42**(3), 250–254 (2009)

Towards Developing Digital Twin Enabled Multi-Agent Systems

Stefano Mariani[1]([⊠])(iD), Marco Picone[1](iD), and Alessandro Ricci[2](iD)

[1] Department of Sciences and Methods of Engineering, University of Modena and Reggio Emilia, Reggio Emilia, Italy
{stefano.mariani,marco.picone}@unimore.it
[2] Department of Computer Science and Engineering, University of Bologna, Cesena, Italy
a.ricci@unibo.it

Abstract. The Multi-Agent Systems (MASs) literature provides abstractions, techniques, and development platforms to design and implement the *virtual environment* within which agents operate. However, coupling such an environment with a *physical* counterpart is still cumbersome, as existing approaches deal with the issue in an ad-hoc way, without general purpose abstractions and methods. Recently, a new paradigm could complement the agent-oriented one to deal with digitalisation of physical environments in a more principled and interoperable way: the Digital Twin (DT). In this paper, we propose a first principled integration between MAS and DTs for MAS environment engineering.

Keywords: Digital Twin · Multi-agent System · WDLT · JaCaMo

1 Introduction

Multi-Agent Systems (MAS) are the premiere source of abstractions and methods (and programming and execution platforms as well) to model and engineer *complex* systems [7]. Examples include Cyber-Physical Systems (CPS) [5], e.g. the monitoring and control software of a manufacturing factory, where agents collect measurements from machinery and equipment (i.e. their digital representations) to support human supervision and decision making; Web of Things deployments [2], e.g. the software controlling energy consumption of smart appliances in a smart building like an hotel, where different agents are in charge of negotiating the best settings to find the optimal trade-off against competing interests (e.g. management's cost saving policies and guests' comfort).

The MAS literature provides plenty of agent models and development (and execution) platforms, ranging from simple *reactive* agents mostly used for simulation [15,25], to pro-active *cognitive* agent architectures meant to autonomously carry out sophisticated reasoning [8,21]. There are also models and methods to engineer the environment that agents must interact with to carry out their duties,

Work partially supported by Italian PRIN "Fluidware" (N. 2017KRC7KT).

such as the A&A meta-model [17] providing *artefacts* as the first-class abstraction meant to digitally represent both physical resources and legacy software (e.g. databases or external services). However, the nuts and bolts of connecting a digital representation to its physical counterpart (e.g. an individual sensor, a manufacturing equipment, or even a whole production line), and the implementation of the process that keeps the two *aligned* at all times are not well engineered. Indeed, often the focus is on the *interface* between the agent and the artefact (or whatever other abstraction is provided), not between the artefact and the physical *thing*. This forces programmers to "re-invent the wheel" for every new development, or hides potentially reusable designs in each team or organisation own implementations, leading to fragmentation.

A solution could come from *Digital Twins* (DTs) [14], that is, digital representations of an (physical) entity of interest (e.g. object, location, person, process) *continuously reflecting* its state and behaviour in a software object, meant to provide services to other software entities (e.g. business applications) [22]. Amongst the many applications of the concept [27], that of exposing a *uniform and interoperable* digital layer to applications and services, tightly coupled with the physical world but hiding to such applications the heterogeneity and complexity of managing resources and processes, is relevant for MAS engineering.

Accordingly, in this paper we propose DTs as a *complement* to existing models and methods for MAS environment engineering, with the goals of (i) achieving a principled way to couple digital representations of entities to their physical counterparts, and (ii) decouple MAS environment engineering methods from the intricacies and peculiarities of accessing to and interacting with physical devices. We argue, in fact, that it is conceptually wrong, and technically inconvenient, to model a DT, or a CPS component, as an agent. For the former, modelling DTs as agents would clash with the definitions we adopt (see Sect. 3.1); for the latter, DTs are better candidates to model them. MAS designers would gain tangible benefits in terms of (i) *separation of concerns*, as they can engineer their solution in terms of MAS abstractions without "polluting" them with devices or protocol-specific technicalities, and (ii) *independent evolution*, as once the DTs interface to the MAS is established, developers of the MAS functionalities and those managing the physical layer can evolve their implementations separately.

2 State of the Art

The vision we aim to realise with this paper is aligned with the view fostered in [12], where agents and DTs are seen as complementary abstractions whose principled integration can bring benefits to two tasks, mostly: (i) engineering the MAS environment, and (ii) orchestrating and coordinating (e.g. dynamically compose) agents and DTs' offered services. In particular, we exploit the kind of *separation of concerns* therein defined, where DTs are meant to operate (i.e. perceive, act) within the boundaries set by the *local* context of their associated physical twin, whereas agents are meant to pursue the application goals in the *global* context of all the resources and services available to the whole MAS. Figure 1 in Sect. 3 depicts our envisioned architecture aligned with this view.

There are a few works in the literature about exploiting agents and DTs synergistically in the perspective described above, that is, where DTs take care of interacting with the environment on behalf of agents, and agents use and orchestrate DTs for achieving their goals. For instance, in [3] DTs model environment resources so as to support the agents' decision making, while agents gather knowledge from multiple DTs to achieve their goals. In [16] a specific instance of the concept of DT, called "Asset Administration Shell" (AAS), enables agents' operations on a physical production system, by mediating access to all the different physical devices. In [10] DTs are used in a manufacturing CPS to better manage communication of data from the physical devices to the MAS monitoring and controlling the system, for instance by performing protocol translation, buffering, etc. Even if restricted to communication issues, DTs actually encapsulate the resources in the MAS environment (the manufacturing CPS). Finally, in [28] a distributed simulation platform is shaped around DTs: each DT simulates a specific asset or set of assets, and agents orchestrate such DTs to dynamically compose them in a single coherent simulation. In a sense, also here DTs encapsulate a portion of the environment, although in this case such environment is purely simulated.

However, in all the aforementioned works, either agents directly interact with DTs [10,16,28], or the concept of DT is directly implemented with the abstractions (and techniques) made available by the MAS—in the case of [3], as a CArtAgO artefact [24]. In next section, we propose an integration architecture complementing, not replacing, MAS environment abstractions with DTs.

Besides these research works, there are others that do not explicitly mention DTs but nevertheless aim at controlling CPSs with a MAS, while pursuing a kind of separation of concerns similar to ours. For instance, authors of [26] recognise that the agent is responsible for the high-level control functions, while the physical asset's "controller" ensures the execution of the agent's high-level decision. Furthermore, they advocate the added value brought by the concept of AAS [16] as a way to provide a standardized description of the asset information. In turn, this helps creating the agent's local knowledge in a standard way and thus ensures interoperability. However, such AAS is mostly a data repository, and the physical controller is not further abstracted away. In [4], *resource access* is identified as a common functionality provided by MAS when applied to CPS. In fact, the RAMI reference architecture adopted in the paper deploys agents mostly everywhere, there included the "asset" level. In this paper, we advocate that (and motivate why) DTs should be adopted instead. In [19] there is only Java as the abstraction layer towards the physical system. In [9] "agentification" is heavily used, that is, wrapping of services and resources within an agent, and no further abstraction is provided at the border with the physical layer.

Finally, Multi-Agent Robot Systems (MARS) could be considered as a special case of CPSs, hence efforts to integrate MAS control in multi-robot systems should be taken into account. In MARS architectures, intelligence, proactivity, and social aspects are usually located within agents at the application layer, whereas handling of all the hardware robotic devices and providing functionality for robotics algorithms is responsibility of the lower layers. However, in [6], authors argue for a different separation of concerns, where agents are also used in lower layers as they provide better abstractions for the intelligence required to perform some functional tasks. At the same time, yet, they recognise that there are still components for which the agent abstraction is "just too much", but fail to provide an alternative abstraction besides Robot Operating Systems (ROS) nodes. In this paper, we argue and motivate why DTs could be better candidates for this. In [13] a MARS architecture is proposed where cognitive and operative layers implement separation of concerns between agents and robotic hardware, but where between the agent runtime (JADE) and ROS there is pure Java, and no further abstraction layer. The same happens in [11].

3   Integration Architecture

First, we propose a *conceptual* architecture not tied to any particular implementation platform, but only to a MAS meta-model (i.e. A&A [17]), in Sect. 3.1. Then, we follow-up with a *technical* instantiation of such a conceptual architecture with specific technologies (i.e. JaCaMo [1] and the WLDT library [20]), in Sect. 3.2. The former shows how the different abstractions provided by DTs and MAS fit together in a coherent paradigm for MAS environment engineering— and, engineering of any CPS. The latter clarifies how such a conceptual framework can be realised with current technologies. JaCaMo is a cognitive MAS development and execution framework, relying on the Belief-Desire-Intention (BD) architecture for agent inner reasoning. WLDT is a Java framework providing highly modular and re-usable code to create and maintain DTs of physical world entities (https://github.com/wldt).

3.1   Conceptual

Our conceptual integration architecture is depicted in Fig. 1. The definition of terms "agent" and "artefact" that we adopt in this paper is taken from the A&A meta-model [17]. The definition of DT is mostly taken from [14], that tries to sort out the many different definitions already existing for DTs in a coherent one. However, we also adopt the systemic view fostered in [22] about the modelling of an ecosystem of DTs semantically interlinked.

The lowest layer is the physical world, where all the objects, resources, devices, people, processes, and every other entity of interest in a given CPS, that is not conceptually suitable to be modeled as an agent, resides. This is a highly heterogeneous world, where virtually every entity has its own access protocol, measurable properties, functionalities, behaviours, etc. With the purpose of making such substrate more homogeneous (e.g. in terms of network access protocols) a DT layer is placed on top, shielding applications from the technical intricacies of the CPS. DTs are, in fact, perfectly suited to encapsulate physical resources and make them accessible to applications. This two layers compose the CPS layer, as the part of the system strictly intertwined with the physical world.

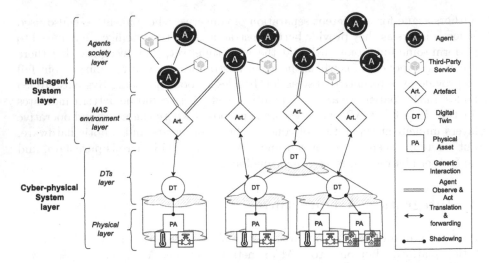

Fig. 1. Conceptual integration architecture. DTs complement artefacts in mediating agents' access to physical resources, by shielding artefacts (and agents in turn) from the heterogeneity of communication protocols, data exchange formats, etc., while providing additional services (e.g. fault tolerance, simulation, prediction, etc.).

Above them, the MAS layer begins, composed by two sub-layers. The lower one, closer to DTs, is the MAS environment layer, where everything that is not an agent is represented. In this paper, non-agent entities are represented as *artefacts* according to the A&A meta-model [17], that is the most principled solution to date [23]. An artefact represents any environmental resource (physical or virtual, such as a database or external service) in terms of admissible actions and available perceptions, perfectly matching most of agent models from reactive to cognitive ones—where an agent is usually defined as an autonomous entity situated in an environment that it can perceive through sensors and act upon through actuators [25]. However, any other environment engineering abstraction would be fine to adopt, as long as it brings the level of abstraction and the programming paradigm closer to the agent-oriented one.

Now, it should be already clear why we crossed the line between CPS and MAS here, at the frontier between DTs and artefacts: the former still promote a development paradigm centred around the physical twin properties and functions – closer to devices –, whereas the latter abstracts them away into perceptions and actions—closer to the agents. In other words, here is where most of the separation of concerns happen.

The highest layer of our conceptual architecture is thus the agents one, where multiple agents cooperate towards the system goals. Such agents actually form a (more or less structured) *society*, that is, a population of agents with roles and missions to accomplish, competing or collaborating within the rules (or "laws") set by the system designer or enforced by some institutional entity that oversees the society as a whole. For instance, in a MAS deployed to control automation of a manufacturing factory, multiple agents can be deployed with different responsibilities, but is likely that they need to interact in a well structured way to achieve complex system goals (e.g. automate assembly, pick up, and packaging of a product). Structuring the inter-dependencies between these responsibilities can be done via the abstraction of a society, where each agent has a certain role (e.g. the assembler, the collector) and commits to meet others' expectations regarding a specific task or deliverable (e.g. assemble the product correctly, pick up the right parts). Here, agents exploit artefacts as extensions or augmentations of their innate capabilities, or as the mediators of interaction with the resources in their environment—while still reasoning in terms of actions and perceptions. At this level, agents may be completely unaware that artefacts are actually encapsulating DTs, in the same way as DTs may be unaware that their services are being exposed as actions and perceptions to agents. This is the whole point of the principle of separation of concerns and independent evolution brought forward in this paper: they don't need to, and probably don't want to. Agents (as well as their developers) want to think in terms of actions and perceptions on artefacts, whereas DTs (and their developers) need to deal with the physical world technicalities, and do not want to be casted into any specific development framework or mindset dictated by higher layers of the architecture.

However, at the interface between artefacts and DTs, there needs to be a way to "connect" an artefact to a DT and viceversa, while still maintaining loose coupling. How this can be achieved in practice is detailed in next section.

3.2   Technical

Figure 2 depicts the technical integration architecture we propose in this paper, as a practical design of the conceptual one described in previous section. As such, it is a zoom-in of the frontier between the MAS environment layer and the DTs layer of Fig. 1. The main components of the integration layer are: the DTDescriptor and WLDTDiscoveryService, that are included in the WLDT library; the DTWorkspace and DTDiscoveryArtefact, that are newly introduced as part of our technical integration design.

The DTDescriptor is a complete description of a given DT provided by the WLDT library: (i) the list of *properties* available for inspection (name-datatype pairs), (ii) the list of *actions* than can be requested to the DT (name, input and output parameters as name-datatype pairs), (iii) the list of *behaviours* that the DT can carry out (name, input parameters, stop condition), (iv) the list of *relationships* the DT has with other DTs (kind, target DT unique identifier), (v) as well as all the metadata needed to interact with the DT—such as an address where to push actions and pull data, the supported protocol(s) (e.g. websocket vs. plain REST CRUD operations), the supported representation format(s) (e.g. JSON, YAML), and any other information needed by external components to directly interact with the DT. Such a descriptor is published by the WLDTDiscoveryService to a well known address as soon as a DT is created and bound to its physical twin by the WLDT platform. External components can query it for a list of available DTs, and get the descriptor of any of them.

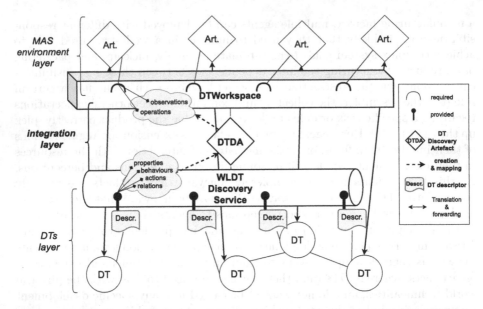

Fig. 2. Technical integration architecture. The `DTDiscoveryArtefact` (i) reads the `DTDescriptors` advertised by the WLDT platform on known endpoints, (ii) dynamically instantiates the corresponding CArtAgO artefacts by mapping entities in descriptors to CArtAgO artefacts' *observable properties* and *operations*, and (iii) sets up a persistent bi-directional connection to keep synchronised the artefact and the DT.

Thanks to this service, and to JaCaMo artefacts programmatic APIs, our `DTDiscoveryArtefact` can automatically create the artefacts corresponding to the available DTs by simply retrieving their descriptors and mapping elements therein to the appropriate CArtAgO abstraction: DT properties to artefacts *observable properties*, DT actions to artefacts *operations*, DT behaviours to both (each behaviour is an operation with additional life-cycle related observable properties), and DT relationships to *links* with other artefacts [18]. Metadata regarding the interaction protocol(s) are used to dynamically create a dedicated bi-directional communication "channel" between the artefact and the corresponding DT (e.g. a websocket or a sequence of REST request-response calls), so that the `DTDiscoveryArtefact` won't be a bottleneck by having to handle (collect and forward) all the interactions between all the DTs and all the artefacts. Such a link is meant to improve the scaling capabilities by decentralising the execution of communication actions, without imposing a *tight coupling* between components. First, such a coupling only happens at run-time and fully automatically, without requiring design-time knowledge. Second, whenever such a bi-directional link fails (e.g. due to disconnections, components crashing, etc.), both the artefact and the DT may fall back to the mediation of the `DTDiscoveryArtefact` for the time needed to recover (e.g. restoring the communication link, replacing the faulty DT, etc.).

Each artefact dynamically created by the `DTDiscoveryArtefact` is added to the ad-hoc JaCaMo workspace `DTWorkspace` so that any agent in the MAS can discover and exploit them. The focal point of the whole integration just described is the `DTDiscoveryArtefact`, as it is the component that synergistically exploits existing JaCaMo and WLDT services (e.g. dynamic artefacts creation, in-workspace discovery, DT descriptors and their publication) to make totally transparent to the MAS developers the existence and utilisation of DTs. In fact, MAS developers need only to (i) configure the `DTDiscoveryArtefact` we designed with the well known address of `WLDTDiscoveryService`, and (ii) start the automatic "creation & mapping" process described above, by launching the dedicated operation provided by this library artefact. If the DTs layer is already up & running, the MAS environment will be automatically shaped accordingly. Moreover, as the `DTDiscoveryArtefact` is subscribed to changes in the `WLDTDiscoveryService`, newly created DTs will be promptly discovered and mapped to JaCaMo at run-time. Even agents with no prior knowledge (e.g. because some DTs are later added to the CPS) can discover what the environment has to offer by exploiting Jason reasoning capabilities and CArtAgO inspection services (e.g. get a list of available artefacts, get observable properties of an artefact, get its operations, etc.).

This openness and dynamism gives benefits in terms of separation of concerns and independent evolution, as MAS developers and DTs engineers can deal with their own part of the system using their preferred abstractions: MAS designers can think at the application as agents cooperating towards a given goal while interacting with available artefacts – regardless of how artefacts interact with physical entities –, whereas CPS engineers model physical resources and devices as DTs, and make their services (e.g. observing properties and requesting operations) available in a standard way (e.g. with web ready protocols and data formats).

4   Conclusion

In this paper, we outlined an integration architecture between MASs and DTs, to improve the way *environment engineering* is carried out in agent-oriented development practice, by exploiting the notion of DTs and their natural coupling with physical entities. In particular, we described such integration from both the conceptual and technical design perspective, relying on the A&A meta-model for the former, and on JaCaMo and WLDT development platforms for the latter.

With our proposal, greater separation of concerns both at run-time (between software components) and during design (between developers) is enabled, and system engineers can develop their own part of the system, the MAS and the CPS, independently. Implementation of the proposed design is already ongoing, as both JaCaMo and WLDT already offer most of the needed mechanisms. The `DTDiscoveryArtefact` will be release as a sort of "library artefact" ready to be used in any JaCaMo deployment.

References

1. Boissier, O., Bordini, R.H., Hübner, J.F., Ricci, A., Santi, A.: Multi-agent oriented programming with JaCaMo. Sci. Comput. Program. **78**(6), 747–761 (2013)
2. Ciortea, A., Boissier, O., Ricci, A.: Engineering world-wide multi-agent systems with hypermedia. In: Weyns, D., Mascardi, V., Ricci, A. (eds.) EMAS 2018. LNCS (LNAI), vol. 11375, pp. 285–301. Springer, Cham (2019). https://doi.org/10.1007/978-3-030-25693-7_15
3. Croatti, A., Gabellini, M., Montagna, S., Ricci, A.: On the integration of agents and digital twins in healthcare. J. Med. Syst. **44**(9), 161 (2020). https://doi.org/10.1007/s10916-020-01623-5
4. Cruz Salazar, L.A., Ryashentseva, D., Lüder, A., Vogel-Heuser, B.: Cyber-physical production systems architecture based on multi-agent's design pattern–comparison of selected approaches mapping four agent patterns. Int. J. Adv. Manuf. Technol. **105**(9), 4005–4034 (2019). https://doi.org/10.1007/s00170-019-03800-4
5. Gorodetsky, V.I., Kozhevnikov, S.S., Novichkov, D., Skobelev, P.O.: The framework for designing autonomous cyber-physical multi-agent systems for adaptive resource management. In: Mařík, V., et al. (eds.) HoloMAS 2019. LNCS (LNAI), vol. 11710, pp. 52–64. Springer, Cham (2019). https://doi.org/10.1007/978-3-030-27878-6_5
6. Iñigo-Blasco, P., Díaz-del-Río, F., Romero-Ternero, M.C., Cagigas-Muñiz, D., Diaz, S.V.: Robotics software frameworks for multi-agent robotic systems development. Robot. Auton. Syst. **60**(6), 803–821 (2012). https://doi.org/10.1016/j.robot.2012.02.004
7. Jennings, N.R.: An agent-based approach for building complex software systems. Commun. ACM **44**(4), 35–41 (2001). https://doi.org/10.1145/367211.367250
8. Laird, J.E.: The SOAR cognitive architecture (2012)
9. Latsou, C., Farsi, M., Erkoyuncu, J.A.: Digital twin-enabled automated anomaly detection and bottleneck identification in complex manufacturing systems using a multi-agent approach. J. Manuf. Syst. **67**, 242–264 (2023). https://doi.org/10.1016/j.jmsy.2023.02.008, https://www.sciencedirect.com/science/article/pii/S0278612523000328
10. Latsou, C., Farsi, M., Erkoyuncu, J.A., Morris, G.: Digital twin integration in multi-agent cyber physical manufacturing systems, vol. 54, pp. 811–816 (2021). https://doi.org/10.1016/j.ifacol.2021.08.096
11. Liu, Z., Mao, X., Yang, S.: AutoRobot: a multi-agent software framework for autonomous robots. IEICE Trans. Inf. Syst. **101-D**(7), 1880–1893 (2018). https://doi.org/10.1587/transinf.2017EDP7382
12. Mariani, S., Picone, M., Ricci, A.: About digital twins, agents, and multiagent systems: a cross-fertilisation journey. In: Melo, F.S., Fang, F. (eds.) Autonomous Agents and Multiagent Systems. Best and Visionary Papers. AAMAS 2022. LNCS, vol. 13441, pp. 114–129. Springer, Cham (2022). https://doi.org/10.1007/978-3-031-20179-0_8
13. Martin, J., Casquero, O., Fortes, B., Marcos, M.: A generic multi-layer architecture based on ROS-JADE integration for autonomous transport vehicles. Sensors **19**(1), 69 (2019). https://doi.org/10.3390/s19010069
14. Minerva, R., Crespi, N.: Digital twins: properties, software frameworks, and application scenarios. IT Prof. **23**(1), 51–55 (2021). https://doi.org/10.1109/MITP.2020.2982896

15. North, M.J., et al.: Complex adaptive systems modeling with Repast Simphony. Complex Adapt. Syst. Model. **1**, 3 (2013). https://doi.org/10.1186/2194-3206-1-3
16. Ocker, F., Urban, C., Vogel-Heuser, B., Diedrich, C.: Leveraging the asset administration shell for agent-based production systems, vol. 54, pp. 837–844 (2021). https://doi.org/10.1016/j.ifacol.2021.08.186
17. Omicini, A., Ricci, A., Viroli, M.: Artifacts in the A&A meta-model for multi-agent systems. Auton. Agents Multi Agent Syst. **17**(3), 432–456 (2008). https://doi.org/10.1007/s10458-008-9053-x
18. Omicini, A., Ricci, A., Zaghini, N.: Distributed workflow upon linkable coordination artifacts. In: Ciancarini, P., Wiklicky, H. (eds.) COORDINATION 2006. LNCS, vol. 4038, pp. 228–246. Springer, Heidelberg (2006). https://doi.org/10.1007/11767954_15
19. Pedersen, S., Foss, B., Schjølberg, I., Tjønnås, J.: MAS for manufacturing control: a layered case study. In: van der Hoek, W., Padgham, L., Conitzer, V., Winikoff, M. (eds.) International Conference on Autonomous Agents and Multiagent Systems, AAMAS 2012, Valencia, Spain, 4–8 June 2012 (3 Volumes), pp. 1169–1170. IFAAMAS (2012). http://dl.acm.org/citation.cfm?id=2343903
20. Picone, M., Mamei, M., Zambonelli, F.: WLDT: a general purpose library to build IoT digital twins. SoftwareX **13**, 100661 (2021). https://doi.org/10.1016/j.softx.2021.100661
21. Rao, A.S., Georgeff, M.P.: BDI agents: from theory to practice. In: Lesser, V.R., Gasser, L. (eds.) Proceedings of the First International Conference on Multiagent Systems, 12–14 June 1995, San Francisco, California, USA, pp. 312–319. The MIT Press (1995)
22. Ricci, A., Croatti, A., Mariani, S., Montagna, S., Picone, M.: Web of digital twins. ACM Trans. Internet Technol. **22**(4) (2022). https://doi.org/10.1145/3507909
23. Ricci, A., Omicini, A., Denti, E.: Activity theory as a framework for MAS coordination. In: Petta, P., Tolksdorf, R., Zambonelli, F. (eds.) ESAW 2002. LNCS (LNAI), vol. 2577, pp. 96–110. Springer, Heidelberg (2003). https://doi.org/10.1007/3-540-39173-8_8
24. Ricci, A., Piunti, M., Viroli, M., Omicini, A.: Environment programming in CArtAgO. In: El Fallah Seghrouchni, A., Dix, J., Dastani, M., Bordini, R.H. (eds.) Multi-Agent Programming, pp. 259–288. Springer, Boston, MA (2009). https://doi.org/10.1007/978-0-387-89299-3_8
25. Russell, S.J., Norvig, P.: Artificial Intelligence - A Modern Approach: The Intelligent Agent Book. Prentice Hall series in artificial intelligence, Prentice Hall, Hoboken (1995). https://www.worldcat.org/oclc/31288015
26. Sakurada, L., Leitão, P., de la Prieta, F.: Engineering a multi-agent systems approach for realizing collaborative asset administration shells. In: IEEE International Conference on Industrial Technology, ICIT 2022, Shanghai, China, 22–25 August 2022, pp. 1–6. IEEE (2022). https://doi.org/10.1109/ICIT48603.2022.10002770
27. Tao, F., Zhang, H., Liu, A., Nee, A.Y.C.: Digital twin in industry: state-of-the-art. IEEE Trans. Ind. Inform. **15**(4), 2405–2415 (2019). https://doi.org/10.1109/TII.2018.2873186
28. Zekri, S., Jabeur, N., Gharrad, H.: Smart water management using intelligent digital twins. Comput. Inform. **41**(1), 135–153 (2022). https://doi.org/10.31577/cai_2022_1_135

Agents in Hypermedia Environments

Towards Context-Based Authorizations for Interactions in Hypermedia-Driven Agent Environments - The CASHMERE Framework

Alexandru Sorici[(✉)][iD] and Adina Magda Florea[iD]

National University of Science and Technology POLITEHNICA Bucharest, Splaiul
Independentei 313, Bucharest, Romania
{alexandru.sorici,adina.florea}@upb.ro

Abstract. Agent-oriented software engineering has recently seen a sustained effort towards the definition of a new class of Multi-Agent System design, called Hypermedia MAS, which promotes an alignment between MAS engineering and the Web architecture to enable development of large, open, dynamic and long-lived interaction systems. A major challenge in these envisioned MAS environments is enabling agents to *discover* the resources whose affordances they require. Hypermedia MAS design principles push for discovery and use of resources by exploiting the link structure of web resources, but little focus has been placed thus far in ensuring *authorized* access to the resources of a large MAS environment. To address this, we propose a framework for *context-based* authorizations for access and discovery of resources in a Hypermedia MAS, inspired by work on Attributed-Based Access Control and RDF Stream Reasoning. We detail the design of the framework functionality and the proposed integration with current Hypermedia MAS platforms, highlighting advantages, challenges and current limitations of the approach.

Keywords: Hypermedia MAS · Web-of-Things · Context · RDF Stream Processing · Context-Based Access Control

1 Introduction

In recent years agent-oriented software engineering has seen a sustained contribution effort towards a vision that enables the deployment of world-wide hybrid communities of people and artificial agents, making use of the Web. A new class of multi-agent system (MAS) design is being defined, referred to as *Hypermedia MAS* [12], which posits that MAS engineering should be aligned with the web architecture so as to enable large, open, dynamic and long-lived interaction systems. The cornerstone of the approach is the use of semantic hypermedia to enable the interaction among heterogeneous entities in MAS, such as software agents, sensors, devices, services and people.

A. Ciortea et al. (Eds.): EMAS 2023, LNAI 14378, pp. 191–207, 2023.
https://doi.org/10.1007/978-3-031-48539-8_13

One leading engineering model within Hypermedia MAS [14] proposes an alignment between the Agent & Artifacts MAS development meta-model [26] and the Web-of-Things (WoT) W3C Thing Description (TD) specification [7]. The Agents & Artifacts model introduces an explicit dimension for programming of the environment of a MAS, which happens in terms of *Artifacts* and their deployment into various *Workspaces*. Artifacts encapsulate the functionality of digital services, sensors or actuators and expose their working in terms of observable properties and events, as well as actions that can be invoked on them. On the other hand, the W3C WoT TD specification describes a formal information model and a common representation for the Web-of-Things, where Things (e.g. web-enabled services, devices, sensors) are characterized by their property, event and action affordances which clients can use by means of RESTful interactions following the HATEOAS principles (Hypermedia As The Engine Of Application State). It is easy to see the similarity of the A&A and TD models which is why Hypermedia MAS platforms such as Yggdrasil [14] build on their integration, creating MAS environments which have an explicit web-resource based representation of the artifacts they contain.

A major challenge in developing application over large, open and dynamic hypermedia MAS environments is enabling agents to *discover* the resources whose affordances they require. While the design principles of Hypermedia MAS promote discovery by navigating the link structure constructed between WoT Things, there currently is no indication on how to search and use Web Things in an *authorized* manner, which would respect the access policies that heterogeneous designers wish to set in place for the Things they deploy in a large hypermedia MAS environment. Furthermore, there is no indication of a *process* by which authorization would be granted or revoked, which is suited to a large, open and dynamic environment.

Running Scenario. To give an example of the mentioned challenges, we introduce a simple scenario that is a straightforward adaptation from the use case introduced in [14] where a digital assistant (modeled as a BDI agent) has to notify a person every time a relevant event occurs. The BDI agent is situatated in a hypermedia environment and is able to discover an artifact controlling a smart light bulb. The agent uses the light bulb to implement a blinking pattern that visually notifies the user of new events. Changing the color of the light helps distinguish between positive and negative notifications. Our adaptation of this scenario relies on adding more details to the situation, which quickly give rise to the need for authorized access. The visual notification service is desired by a university which implements a hypermedia MAS environment at the level of the whole campus. The university encourages each lab to be individually responsible for the smart devices it installs in their room, as long as they are made available in the hypermedia environment. However, the university considers that *discovery* of the artifacts wrapping over any smart device is only allowed for employed personnel who are physically present in the rooms where the devices reside, to prevent BDI agents of university visitors from interacting with the devices, as well as any kind of remote control.

Context. The running scenario defines a situation where the *context* of a user (e.g. employment status, physical location) has to directly inform the interactions that the BDI agent of the user can execute in the hypermedia MAS environment. We interpret the notion of *context information* according to a general, application-specific definition given in the framework of Ambient Intelligence (AmI): "Context is any information that can be used to characterize the situation of an entity. An entity is a person, place, or object that is considered relevant to the interaction between a user and an application, including the user and applications themselves" [18].

We also argue that the *operational perspective* [32] of logically partitioning context information along dimensions of engagement (e.g. individual, space, time, activity, relational) can be usefully exploited to inform a mechanism for *context-based* authorization of interactions within a hypermedia MAS. This view is further strengthened by the AmI perspective that specific enough *shared context* between two entities acts as a permission and even obligation for information exchange between the entities [22].

In light of the above, our contributions in this work are:

- Describe the need for and the design of a framework for Context-Aware Search and Discovery in Hypermedia MAS Environments (CASHMERE). The center focus of the approach is providing a method for *context-based authorization*.
- Present a development and integration road map, detailing how the CASHMERE framework can be integrated into the working of a Hypermedia MAS Environment. We present advantages, challenges and limitations of the envisioned approach.

The remainder of the article is structured as follows. Section 2 provides background on the Hypermedia MAS environments, frameworks to establish authorization policies in dynamic systems, as well as the use of RDF streaming technologies to implement context-based policy rules. Section 3 details the core functionality of the CASHMERE framework explaining the means for context representation and shared context identification. The design of the integration between CASHMERE and a Hypermedia MAS environment is presented in Sect. 4, while the challenges and current limitations of the approach are discussed in Sect. 5. We conclude the paper with the outline of upcoming development work in Sect. 6.

2   Background

We start by analysing the motivation behind and technologies that support our proposed framework. We submit that: (i) current principles underlying design of Hypermedia MAS Environments are incomplete with respect to authorized access to the resources they enable exploring, (ii) authorization in large scale, dynamic MAS environments must employ an equally dynamic access control mechanism, (iii) events and actions, collectively called *context information*, which are shared by agents and resources in an environment can *count-as* justification for authorizing agent access to a resource, and (iv) modeling the events and actions as RDF information streams is a natural and flexible means to reason about the conditions that count-as *sharing context*.

2.1 Hypermedia Driven Agent Environments

Ciortea et al. introduce three main principles for the design of Hypermedia Multi-Agent Systems [14]. The first principle promotes a uniform representation (e.g. in the form of an RDF graph) of resources and the relations between them in a hypermedia environment. One intended consequence of the uniform representation of relations between entities (e.g. agents, tools, organizations) is the improved ability to crawl and discover entities *of interest*. However, the text in [14] does not make clear how *interest* is defined and no distinction is made between *discoverability* (e.g. through a search engine) and then *use* of a resource by invoking the affordances it provides.

Crawling entities based on their uniform representation to build a *directory* of resources is seen as an effective means to exploit the distributed nature of hypermedia, while also enabling agents to go beyond *locality*. The latter concept seems to be interpreted as a limitation of FIPA-based MAS to only gain access to resources and service that are advertised by the agents themselves in a local network. However, another interpretation of *locality*, not addressed in [14], relates again to the *interest* of the interaction, to the conditions under which a resource or service is accessed. From this perspective of context management, it is desirable to keep information consumption and interactions *localized*, meaning that both provider and consumer of the affordances exposed by a resource engage with each other under an *authorization* granted by the existence of a *common context* (e.g. related to a shared space, a joint activity, a membership in an organizational structure).

Principles 2 and 3 from [14] advocate for the use of a single-entry point into an Hypermedia MAS environment, as well as the *observability* of resources. Taken together, these guidelines affirm that any resource in a Hypermedia MAS that is of potential *interest* to agents should make itself actively observable through its explicit representation and notification of changes to its state or affordances. Furthermore, once an entry-point in the resource representation of a MAS environment has been gained, link relations between entities in the environment should enable the exploration of other resources in the environment. These principles are required to design evolvable and long-lived hypermedia MAS, but they are also in need of additional considerations with respect to the deployment of hypermedia MAS. Uniform representation and observability can enable a machine readable description of security schemes (e.g. token based, OAuth2 based - see also Security Schema of WoT Thing Description [7]), but it does not define the *conditions* under which such a secured access to changes in states and affordances of a resource are obtained.

We claim that *observability* should be amended to consider a *common context* driven *authorization* mechanism that can narrow down what different resource developers consider should be of *interest* to different agents in the hypermedia MAS.

2.2 Dynamic Access Control

The WoT Thing Description [7] specification provides a vocabulary to set *schemes* in place (e.g. API key, Bearer, OAuth2) which *secure the access* to a resource. However, with the exception of OAuth2, no other modeled security scheme defines *authorizations* for the different resource affordances. Furthermore, even in the case of OAuth2, there is no model of a mechanism by which to decide which authorizations to include within the OAuth2 token depending on the *situation* (e.g. the capabilities and intention of the agent, the state of the environment).

The idea of an authorized exploration and use of resources in a hypermedia MAS is partially acknowledged in [15], where the challenges to *autonomy* in the WoT list the notion of *regulation as a first-class abstraction*, citing common practices of ensuring fair resource access, such as the Robots Exclusion Protocol, rate limiting or licensing policies. The authors bring forth normative MAS research [9,20,23] to mention that regulative norms and prescriptions can be used to specify and enforce how agents can interact with each other and their environment, enforced either through social means or a top-down authority manner. However, no concrete mechanism of integrating an authorization method into the workings of existing hypermedia MAS platforms (e.g. Yggdrasil [14]) is advanced.

The core of the dynamic access control problem in the context of hypermedia MAS poses the following question: how can resources signify to an agent the *set of conditions* and the *process of reasoning* about them which determines the granting or revocation of a permission to exploit an affordance of the resource? CASHMERE starts from the premise that application specific agent and environment *context* can *count as* the catalyst by which normative dimensions such as *permission/prohibition* are expressed and implemented at the level of a hypermedia MAS. This view is further supported by work in the domain of Access Control for the Internet-of-Things. The survey of Qiu et al. [24] highlights that in *dynamic* and *open* computing environments traditional access control models such as Role-Based Access Control (RBAC) are not adapted to fit application dynamics. For such cases an alternative model is gaining popularity[1][2], namely Attribute-Based Access Control (ABAC) [13] which proposes that subject requests to perform operations on a resource are granted or denied based on *attributes* of the subjects, resources or the environment and policies that relate to these attributes [27]. Extensions of the ABAC model which use an ontology to define roles and attributes and SWRL rules to infer additional attributes have

---

[1] NextLabs ABAC solution for business-critical data control: https://www.nextlabs.com/products/technology/abac/.

[2] Styra - authorization as a service at scale: https://www.styra.com/blog/dynamic-authorization-with-policy-based-access-management/.

also been proposed [19]. These include other external context sources for a richer attribute space and cases of multiple agents interacting with the same resource have been proposed.

The thought and motivation behind the CASHMERE proposal for context-based authorization is also founded on work in *situated artificial institutions* [16] which defines a framework for expressing and reasoning about *count-as* situations with respect to norms in agent organizations. Specifically, the SAI framework is concerned with relating normative regulation to some *interpretation* of the environment that *counts as* the constitution of role assuming, obligations, permissions or prohibitions.

While SAI is explicit in formalizing constitutive specifications in terms of rules for agent-, environment/event- and state-status functions, the CASHMERE framework is more pragmatic in its use of the *count-as* principle. In a manner to be detailed in Sect. 3.1, CASHMERE proposes a rule-based mechanism to identify the agent and thing related context information and the conditions under which these *count-as* a *shared context*. The shared context acts as a constitutive function that creates a *permission* of interaction between agents and the resource affordances they seek to use.

2.3 Modeling Context Information with CONSERT

CASHMERE proposes having an explicit model of *context* (agent abilities, environment state, organizational situation) and its *dynamics* (how context changes in time) as the underpinning for the mechanism by which authorized discovery of resources is implemented. To accomplish this, a model for *context representation* is required.

Context information representation relies on the CONSERT meta-model [29] which introduces the *work horse* representations of *ContextAssertions* and *ContextAnnotations*. *ContextAssertions* use the predicate in a subject-predicate-object triple as the main model entity. A statement such as `locatedAt(agent_alex, lab308)` is modeled as a binary *ContextAssertion*, whereby the central element is the fact of being `LocatedAt` and the subject and object entities are `agent_alex` and `lab308`. This form of reification has the advantage that it can naturally support the addition of supplementary information (*ContextAnnotations*) such as timestamp of assertion, temporal validity or provenance of the information. ContextAssertions are also characterized by a *mode of acquisition* which defines an operational attribute signaling how *dynamic* the assertion is. The CONSERT Model distinguishes between *static* (assertions which hold true indefinitely - e.g. the spatial containment of a room in a building), *profiled* (ContextAssertion who have a long-term, but still limited temporal validity - e.g. the employment status of a researcher), *sensed* (event-like ContextAssertions, who are assumed to change frequently in a system - e.g. the physical location of a person in a building) and *derived* (produced by some inference method whose input consists of other ContextAssertions) acquisition modes.

The ability to model annotations and to distinguish between sources/flows of context information is beneficial because it provides a clearer way to identify different sources of context, as well as to reason over its validity in time in a environment that captures dynamic events and actions of agents (see example in Listing 1.1 and Sect. 3.2.

2.4 RDF Stream Reasoning

The context-aware ABAC model introduced in [19] makes use of ontologies to express attributes and SWRL rules to define policies that implement access control. However, many WoT application scenarios involve conditions that are dynamic in nature (e.g. relate to mobility of agents, are tied to a cycle of activity) which require an interpretation of context information as it changes *in time*. As detailed further in Sect. 3, CASHMERE expresses rules to identify conditions for *shared context* using RDF Stream Processing [17] techniques (RSP). RDF Stream Processing has emerged in recent years as a collection of approaches (e.g. C-SPARQL [10], CQELS [21]) involving extensions to RDF representation and the SPARQL query language which are meant to address the *continuous processing* requirement of *semantic data streams*. This collection has been later unified under a single query model, RSP-QL [17], which can be interpreted in a prototype engine (Yasper [31]) and for which an API specification (RSP4J [30]) has been defined, that enables the construction of RDF Stream generators, consumers, as well as custom operators and interpretation engines.

RSP-QL defines the semantics of interpreting *time-varying* RDF graphs, it describes means to define the duration and trigger conditions for *evaluation windows* and it defines the functionality of relational-to-relational (equivalent to SPARQL 1.1 operational semantics), relational-to-stream (from solution mappings to RDF streams), stream-to-relational (from a stream to a single graph coalesced from the union of all RDF graphs within ane evaluation window) and stream-to-stream operators. The latter operators distinguish between modes of operation that allow for (i) generating a stream of solution mappings (RSTREAM) and (ii) determining which solution mappings have been newly added (ISTREAM) or removed (DSTREAM) with respect to those obtained from the previous evaluation window.

Since hypermedia MAS environments promote the explicit semantic representation of entities as web resources using RDF, the use of RSP within CASHMERE to reason about the attributes and context of the MAS environment and its actors is an obvious advantage. A further benefit is the ability to factor in reasoning over the temporal dimension of the context streams and extract streams of authorization grants and revocations, as will be detailed in Sect. 3.2.

3 Shared Context Identification

The core of the CASHMERE vision lies in the idea that the *context of the interaction* between agents and the resources in their environment is a *conditioning space* which can be expressed in sufficiently rich detail that it can leveraged to grant authorization for discovery and use of artifact affordances in a hypermedia-driven agent environment. The extremes of this context-based access range from having no condition whatsoever on the interaction (i.e. public access) to requiring a role that is specifically conditioned to be played by a single entity. For anything in between, it becomes highly relevant to design a method that is both flexible and comprehensive enough to include static and dynamic environment and agent-generated events into conditions that *count as* context *shared* by an agent and a resource. The shared context then warrants the *authorization* of the interaction.

In what follows, we describe our means of identifying *shared context* in terms of (i) how we can partition context information into *domains of interest* and (ii) how we express rules that determine whether two entities share the same *context domain*.

3.1   ContextDomains: Partitioning Context Information

The CONSERT context management deployment specifications [28] introduce two concepts that enable a system to logically partition the context information that it has to provision to consumers. *ContextDimensions* are *ContextAssertions* (from among the ones that a system handles) that define a *privileged* direction (e.g. spatial, activity related, relational) of context provisioning. Along each *ContextDimension* a set of *ContextDomain* (potentially hierarchically aranged) can be defined. In our running example an obvious spatial *ContextDimension* is given by the `locatedAt(Agent, UniversitySpace)` *ContextAssertion*, which gives rise to *ContextDomains* that refer to indoor locations of the university (such as `lab308`). Because indoor locations have a natural spatial inclusion relation (which can be captured by a *static ContextAssertion*, such as `containedIn(UniversitySpace, UniversitySpace)`, a hierarchy of *ContextDomains* becomes possible.

We can now posit that resources (e.g. devices, services) and consumers who are part of the information provisioning setup of the same *ContextDomain* (e.g. agents and devices in `lab308`) are inherently *sharing context*. Therefore, our method of shared context identification can resolve to verifying if two entities are *members* of the same *ContextDomain*. The next section defines the reasoning mechanism which interprets the conditions under which *ContextDomain* membership is granted or revoked.

3.2   Stream Processing for Shared Context Identification

In Sect. 2.4 we discussed RSP as an approach suited to implement the rules by which one or more entities are considered to share a context. The main advantage of this approach lies in the ability to process streams of RDF information which can encompass the *ContextAssertions* that are considered *sufficient* to denote *membership* in the same *ContextDomain*.

In the simplest case, the sufficiency criterion can limit itself to the observance of a *sensed ContextAssertion* that defines the *ContextDimension* and the instance of the *ContextDomain* which partition the context information. In our running example, the sensed *ContextAssertion* `locatedAt(agent_alex, lab308)` could *count as* sufficient to establish `agent_alex` as a member of the *ContextDomain* associated with Lab 308. However, in some cases (like in our running scenario) it is desirable to have conditions of *ContextDomain* membership which are more restrictive, considering that shared context is used to authorize access to artifacts whose affordances are ascribed to the same *ContextDomain*. In our example, the ability to discover the existence of the smart light bulb from Lab 308 and to control it is limited to agents that represent people who are employees of the university and are physically present in the room.

```
1   PREFIX consert: <http://pervasive.semanticweb.org/ont/2017/07/consert/core/>
2   PREFIX ann: <http://pervasive.semanticweb.org/ont/2017/07/consert/annotation/>
3   PREFIX foaf: <http://xmlns.com/foaf/0.1/>
4   PREFIX vcard: <http://www.w3.org/2006/vcard/ns#>
5   PREFIX precis: <http://aimas.cs.pub.ro/consert/ontologies/precis#>
6
7   REGISTER STREAM <SharedLab308Context> AS
8   CONSTRUCT ISTREAM {
9       precis:lab308group vcard:member ?agent .
10  }
11  FROM NAMED :staticAssertions
12  FROM NAMED :profiledAssertions
13  FROM NAMED WINDOW :pLoc [RANGE PT10S STEP PT10S] ON STREAM :PersonLocated
14  WHERE
15  {
16      GRAPH :staticAssertions { ?agent rdf:type foaf:Person . }
17      GRAPH :profiledAssertions {
18          ?worksAssertion a precis:WorksAt ;
19              consert:assertionSubject ?agent ;
20              consert:assertionObject precis:upb ;
21              ann:hasAnnotation ?validAnn .
22          ?validAnn a ann:TemporalValidityAnnotation ;
23              ann:startTime ?employmentStart ;
24              ann:endTime ?employmentEnd .
25      }
26      WINDOW :pLoc {
27          ?persLocAssertion a precis:LocatedAt;
28              consert:assertionSubject ?agent ;
29              consert:assertionObject precis:lab308 .
30      }
31      BIND (xsd:dateTime(NOW()) AS ?date)
32      FILTER (?date > ?employmentStart && ?date < ?employmentEnd)
33  }
```

Listing 1.1. Demonstrator scenario shared context identification query

Listing 1.1 shows the SPARQL CONSTRUCT query that acts as a typical rule by which membership in a *ContextDomain* is determined. In line 9, the rule conditions already assume the existence of resource (`precis:lab308group`) denoting a *ContextDomain Group* modeled as an instance of vcard[3] organization to adhere to Web Access Control specifications [6] (see also Sect. 4). The CONSTRUCT statement is accompanied by an ISTREAM keyword (an example of a stream-to-stream operator) which signifies that the result of the query is an RDF Stream itself which will trigger with a new event only when the query produces a different output compared to previous time instances (cf. [17] for more detail on RDF stream operators). The body of the query distinguishes three

---

[3] https://www.w3.org/TR/vcard-rdf/.

context information input sources (different SPARQL graphs), depending on the *mode* of acquisition: static assertions (which identify the agent - line 16), profiled assertions (the employment status of the agent - lines 17–25) and a *named window* defining the stream of *sensed* `PersonLocated` *ContextAssertion* instances (lines 26–30). RDF stream windows are defined using range (window duration) and step (the temporal slide from one window content evaluation timestamp to the next) parameters (line 13). The value of these parameters is dependent on the application use case and is required to be set in tune with the frequency of `PersonLocated` instances that arrive on the stream. Notice that, since the `precis:WorksAt` *ContextAssertion* instance is a *profiled* one, it is interrogated for its `TemporalValidityAnnotation` (lines 22–24), which is then used to check validity of the employment status (line 32).

In Listing 1.1 we see an example of the `ISTREAM` stream-to-stream operator, which streams new events only if they differ from the previous window evaluation. In a HyperAgent environment deployment, the *ContextDomainGroup* Artifact that manages the *ContextDomain* membership would also have a query registered that has an equivalent body, but a `DSTREAM` operator in the CONSTRUCT head. The `DStream` operator triggers with the events that existed in the previous window evaluation, but not the current one. This effectively enables a *ContextDomainGroup* Artifact to manage both new memberships (`ISTREAM`), as well as expiring ones (`DSTREAM`).

4 Integration in Hypermedia-Driven Agent Environments

As mentioned in Sect. 2.1, we consider hypermedia-driven agent environments (of which Yggdrasil [14] is an exponent) as a main type of platform benefiting from the CASHMERE framework. The general overview of the information and interaction flow that realizes the integration of CASHMERE into a hypermedia MAS platform is presented in Fig. 1. Steps (1) and (2) summarize the functionality described in Sect. 3. Steps (3) and (4) highlight the fact that the context-aware

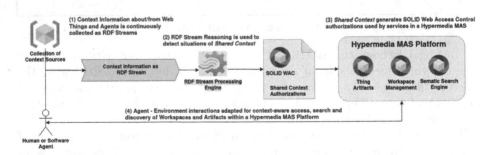

Fig. 1. General overview of the information and interaction flow that integrates the CASHMERE context-aware access functionality into a hypermedia-driven multi-agent platform.

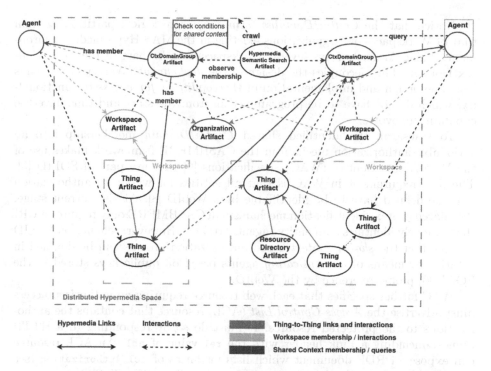

Fig. 2. Diagram showing the integration of ContextDomain Group Artifacts into a typical Agents and Artifacts hypermedia environment deployment

authorization functionality can be exploited at different levels within a Hypermedia MAS - from adapting the interaction with each individual Thing Artifact to enhancing the functionality of a semantic hypermedia search engine.

Step (3) is further detailed integration-wise in the block diagram of Fig. 2, which is designed as a reinterpretation of the conceptual overview of hypermedia MAS environments presented in works such as [11,14,25]. The diagram shows the envisioned composition of an Agents & Artifacts Container. Notice the addition of the artifacts managing *ContextDomain Groups*, which expose observable properties that signal the *membership* in the same *ContextDomain*. Things, Workspaces, ResourceDirectories, Organization Artifacts and Semantic Hypermedia Search Engines can subscribe to such observations and justify authorizing the access of an agent to all their affordances based on *sharing the same context*. This means that the effects of context-aware authorized access can reflect at several levels of granularity. For example, Thing and Workspace artifacts may refuse a *focus* request from agents that do not share any context. A Hypermedia Search Engine can omit sending notifications (e.g. through WebSub) about answers to queries of agents who do not share the same *ContextDomain* as the Things that are a response to their queries.

Notice that the *ContextDomains* form a separate logical partitioning than that of Workspaces or Organizations existing in the MAS Hypermedia Environment. Thing Artifacts from several Workspaces can be part of the same ContextDomain. This decouples the design of the *deployment* (Workspaces) means from the design and implementation of the *conditions for access* to functionality, which do not have to be programmed in from the start and thus have the capability to evolve.

To transform the identified shared *ContextDomain* membership into an actionable authorization mechanism the CASHMERE framework makes use of the Web Access Control (WAC) specifications [6] that are part of SOLID [5]. The first requirement in WAC is that all entities for whom an authorization is to be defined have to be identifiable by a WebID [8]. At the current stage, the shared context identification mechanism in CASHMERE only requires a URI that uniquely identifies a an entity (agent, artifact). However, reliance on WebID ensures that the *shared context* based authorization process can be doubled in security by means of *authenticating* agents based on public keys stored in the FOAF [3] profile reference by the WebID.

WAC further specifies that each web resource requiring an authorized access must advertise the *Access Control List* (ACL) resource that contains the authorizations to the protected resource. It must do so by responding to a HTTP request including a Link header with the `rel` value of `acl`. An ACL resource can expose an RDF document which lists instances of `acl:Authorization` (see the ACL Ontology [2]). An `acl:Authorization` will specify: (i) the resource for which it provides an authorization (`acl:accessTo`), (ii) the access mode (e.g. `acl:Read`, `acl:Write`, `acl:Control`) and (iii) whom the authorization applies to (e.g. `acl:agent`, `acl:agentClass`, `acl:agentGroup`). The `acl:agentGroup` mode of identifying authorization subject is particularly suitable for the CASHMERE setup, because it allows identifying an instance of a `vcard:Group` which can contain individual FOAF profiles as members. This maps directly to the *ContextDomain* membership CONSTRUCT outputs that have been presented in Sect. 3.2.

An ACL resource representation also includes an `acl:default` predicate which specifies the container resource in a hierarchy of containment, whose Authorization can be applied by default when no custom Authorization is defined for an individual protected resource. In a Hypermedia MAS as defined in [14,25], the *Workspace* hierarchy governing the deployment of Thing Artifacts can be used to manage an Authorization hierarchy. In our running scenario, the Authorization resource which enables access to smart light in Lab 308 to university employees physically present in the room can be attached to the *Workspace* containing the smart light Thing (and, possibly, other Things) instead of the Thing itself.

Figure 3 summarizes the way in which the representation and functionality of entities in a Hypermedia MAS environment have to be complemented to make use of the WAC-based authorized access proposed in CASHMERE. Each artifact that implements the functionality of a Thing or Workspace is additionally tasked with exposing a representation for the ACL resource that contains the authorizations defined for the artifact, which include access permissions granted by the observed memberships in different *ContextDomain* Groups (Lab308 in our

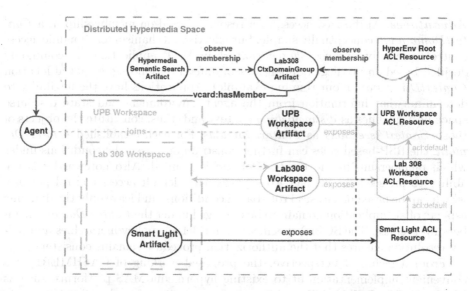

Fig. 3. Summarized view of WAC usage based on shared *ContextDomain* for typical artifact instances - Thing, Workspace, Semantic Search Engine - encountered in a Hypermedia MAS Environment.

running example). The artifacts that want to enable context-aware authorized access need to also implement the *authorization match* procedure as indicated by WAC specifications [6], which involves running a SPARQL ASK query over the RDF graphs containing `acl:Authorization` instances. In particular, for checking memberships produced by the *ContextDomain* membership streaming procedure detailed in Sect. 3.2, artifacts have two options: (i) use a *federated* SPARQL query for the group membership verification, running it against the RDF graph stored by the *ContextDomainGroup* artifact, (ii) use the stream output of the *ContextDomainGroup* artifact to keep local caches of *ContextDomain* memberships and run the query against the latter. Notice that Workspace hierarchy can be exploited to address default authorizations, where the root most ACL resource is defined at the level of the Hypermedia MAS environment itself.

Semantic Search Engines service, like the one introduced in [11], are meant to enable discovery of Thing Artifacts by *type* or *functionality descriptions*. When observing *ContextDomain* memberships, the functionality of the search engines can be adapted such that the result bindings that are answers to subscribed queries are filtered to contain only Artifact instances that share the same context as the agent making the subscription.

5 Discussion

The described functioning of CASHMERE and its integration into a Hypermedia MAS environment has certain advantages, but it is not without its challenges and limitations, which we discuss in the following.

Advantages. Authorized access to a resource based on membership in a *ContextDomain* is a conceptually simple, but effective mechanism for dynamic access control, precisely because *shared context* in WoT applications is commonly decided based on privileged dimensions of differentiation (e.g. a spatial location *ContextDimension* in our running example). Applications have the flexibility to determine what information from the agent, environment and state discourse space best qualifies as *distinguishing* context and, thus, constitute the objects of those *ContextAssertions* as *ContextDomains*. For each established *ContextDomain*, the RSP-based rules can further constrain or loosen the conditions under which membership in the *ContextDomain* is granted. Also noteworthy is the ability to pre-seed the artifact workspaces with default access control policies, which can be based on classical role-based conditions, and leave only the dynamic aspects of an application domain to be managed under the *ContextDomain* membership premise. The SOLID specification for default policy hierarchies and policy resolution ensures that the authorization procedure remains consistent.

From a technical perspective, the proposed working of CASHMERE is a convenient implementation fit to existing hypermedia MAS platforms, such as Yggdrasil. The RSP4J API enables extending artifact functionality to operate as both generators (to feed the context information streams) and consumers (to make use of the stream of *ContextDomain* membership granting or revocations) of RDF streams.

Challenges. For the development roadmap, several design and implementation challenges stand before. An initial observation to be made is that we made no assumption about the sources of the context information streams. In particular, we currently place no restriction on whether the source of context information is found only within the artifacts deployed in a hypermedia MAS environment, or whether they can also be external to the environment (but capture information *about* events in the environment). For within environment sources, the main technical challenge lies in developing the interface through which existing artifacts can turn their observable properties and events into RDF streams. For external sources, either direct usage of the RDF4J API or platforms such as OntopStream [4] (which performs streaming semantic data access from heterogeneous sources such as Kafka, Kinesis or JDBC databases), could be used.

An additional implementation challenge relates to the artifact functionality extensions required to evaluate access policies, as well as to perform policy conflict resolution. To address these, the CASHMERE framework proposes following the SOLID Access Control Policies specifications [1].

A design issue currently still under investigation is how different entities of a hypermedia MAS environment react upon authorization revocations. Should an access denial imply that the artifact be not discoverable (in a manner similar to the no-crawl policies used for websites), or should the artifact remain observable (and describable) in the workspace, but unfocusable by an agent? The former option is simpler to manage and safer conceptually. However, it contradicts the *Observability* principle mentioned in [14] and could burden development of use cases where agents wish to use *planning* methods to compose a future functionality, even though the *current* context denies them access to the artifacts required in the plan result. The latter option implies that artifact affordances remain discoverable at all time but that their *use* is conditioned by shared context. In this case, a method for *explaining* denied use is required, such that any planning methods can understand what *context* the agent needs to be a part of to gain access to the artifact functionality. The reified form of *ContextAssertions* and parsable SPARQL syntax of membership rules already makes it feasible to identify the list of conditions and find references to agents (using the `assertionSubject` predicate) that are bound by them. However, further research is required to develop an appropriate method to offer easily consumable access approval or denial explanations to agents.

Limitations. One point that is relevant in MAS interactions, but currently not addressed by CASHMERE is making the distinction between an agent and a *client* (e.g. another artifact) acting on behalf of the agent. *ContextDomain* membership is determined with respect to the agent requesting access and the artifacts which it can potentially use. Potential support in this issue is switching from use of the SOLID ACL [2] ontology to the more comprehensive ACP ontology [1] which makes the distinction clear, but the underlying issue of having a means to determine whether an agent intention is behind a *linked* artifact operation invocation remains an open problem, requiring artifacts to explicitly advertise the issuer of their original operation invocation.

On the technical side, the CASHMERE framework currently makes no indication on the way in which to perform periodic evaluation of the RSP queries for *ContextDomain* verification. The default is to use the *step* parameter indications for window definitions. However, depending on the application, an evaluation triggered by the arrival of a new *ContextAssertion* might be more computationally appropriate than periodic re-evaluations. Instrumenting application specific guidelines and configuration options for membership rule trigger conditions remains an aspect of future work.

6   Conclusion

In this paper we presented the current state of design principles for hypermedia multi-agent system platforms which give rise to current instances, such as Yggdrasil. We highlighted that, while these principles encourage development of large-scale and long-lived agent interaction spaces, they do not cover the relevant aspect of managing an authorized access to the resources exposed in hypermedia environments. Building on work and ideas from domains such as Context Management in Ambient Intelligence (Sects. 2.3 and 3.1), Dynamic Access Control and Situated Artificial Institutions (Sect. 2.2), as well as RDF Stream Processing (Sects. 2.4 and 3.2) we presented the CASHMERE framework, whose purpose it is to provide a solution for authorized resource access in a hypermedia MAS environments based on the premise of *shared context*. We further presented the design of the integration of CASHMERE into existing hypermedia MAS solutions which adopt the Agents & Artifacts paradigm as their core abstraction (Sect. 4).

In future work we plan to first focus on the development roadmap of the CASHMERE functionality laid out in Sect. 3 by leveraging the RSP4J API [30] and the Yasper [31] engine to build an artifact implementing shared *ContextDomain* identification rules. A subsequent development effort targets implementation of the SOLID ACP policy evaluation functionality, which must be available at the level of several key components of a hypermedia MAS environment (e.g. individual artifact, workspace and semantic search engine). In longer term research we plan to provide point wise guidelines and solutions to the identified challenges and limitations of the CASHMERE framework.

Acknowledgement. This work has been supported by funding under grant agreement PN-III-P1-1.1-PD-2021-0756 from the Romanian National Research, Development and Innovation Plan.

References

1. Access control policy specification. https://solid.github.io/authorization-panel/acp-specification. Accessed 15 Feb 2023
2. Acl ontology. http://www.w3.org/ns/auth/acl. Accessed 15 Feb 2023
3. Foaf vocabulary specification. http://xmlns.com/foaf/0.1/. Accessed 15 Feb 2023
4. Ontopstream development repository: streaming semantical data access of relational data streams. https://github.com/chimera-suite/OntopStream. Accessed 17 Feb 2023
5. Solid project. https://solidproject.org/. Accessed 15 Feb 2023
6. Web access control specification. https://solid.github.io/web-access-control-spec. Accessed 15 Feb 2023
7. Web of things (wot) thing description 1.1, w3c candidate recommendation. https://www.w3.org/TR/wot-thing-description/. Accessed 15 Feb 2023
8. Webid specifications. https://www.w3.org/2005/Incubator/webid/spec/. Accessed 15 Feb 2023
9. Balke, T., et al.: Norms in mas: definitions and related concepts. In: Dagstuhl Follow-Ups, vol. 4. Schloss Dagstuhl-Leibniz-Zentrum fuer Informatik (2013)
10. Barbieri, D.F., Braga, D., Ceri, S., Valle, E.D., Grossniklaus, M.: C-SPARQL: a continuous query language for RDF data streams. Int. J. Semant. Comput. 4(01), 3–25 (2010)
11. Bienz, S., Ciortea, A., Mayer, S., Gandon, F., Corby, O.: Escaping the streetlight effect: semantic hypermedia search enhances autonomous behavior in the web of things. In: Proceedings of the 9th International Conference on the Internet of Things, pp. 1–8 (2019)
12. Boissier, O., Ciortea, A., Harth, A., Ricci, A.: Autonomous agents on the web. In: Dagstuhl-Seminar 21072: Autonomous Agents on the Web, p. 100p (2021)
13. Bonatti, P.A., Samarati, P.: A uniform framework for regulating service access and information release on the web. J. Comput. Secur. 10(3), 241–271 (2002)
14. Ciortea, A., Boissier, O., Ricci, A.: Engineering world-wide multi-agent systems with hypermedia. In: Weyns, D., Mascardi, V., Ricci, A. (eds.) EMAS 2018. LNCS (LNAI), vol. 11375, pp. 285–301. Springer, Cham (2019). https://doi.org/10.1007/978-3-030-25693-7_15
15. Ciortea, A., Mayer, S., Boissier, O., Gandon, F.: Exploiting interaction affordances: on engineering autonomous systems for the web of things (2019)

16. De Brito, M., Hübner, J.F., Boissier, O.: Situated artificial institutions: stability, consistency, and flexibility in the regulation of agent societies. Auton. Agents Multi-Agent Syst. **32**, 219–251 (2018)
17. Dell'Aglio, D., Della Valle, E., Calbimonte, J.P., Corcho, O.: RSP-QL semantics: a unifying query model to explain heterogeneity of RDF stream processing systems. Int. J. Semant. Web Inf. Syst. (IJSWIS) **10**(4), 17–44 (2014)
18. Dey, A.K.: Understanding and using context. Pers. Ubiquit. Comput. **5**, 4–7 (2001)
19. Dong, Y., Wan, K., Huang, X., Yue, Y.: Contexts-states-aware access control for internet of things. In: 2018 IEEE 22nd International Conference on Computer Supported Cooperative Work in Design ((CSCWD)), pp. 666–671. IEEE (2018)
20. Hübner, J.F., Boissier, O., Kitio, R., Ricci, A.: Instrumenting multi-agent organisations with organisational artifacts and agents: giving the organisational power back to the agents. Auton. Agents Multi-Agent Syst. **20**, 369–400 (2010)
21. Le-Phuoc, D., Dao-Tran, M., Xavier Parreira, J., Hauswirth, M.: A native and adaptive approach for unified processing of linked streams and linked data. In: Aroyo, L., et al. (eds.) ISWC 2011. LNCS, vol. 7031, pp. 370–388. Springer, Heidelberg (2011). https://doi.org/10.1007/978-3-642-25073-6_24
22. Olaru, A., Florea, A.M., El Fallah Seghrouchni, A.: A context-aware multi-agent system as a middleware for ambient intelligence. Mob. Netw. Appl. **18**(3), 429–443 (2013)
23. Ossowski, S.: Agreement Technologies, vol. 8. Springer Science & Business Media, Dordrecht (2012). https://doi.org/10.1007/978-94-007-5583-3
24. Qiu, J., Tian, Z., Du, C., Zuo, Q., Su, S., Fang, B.: A survey on access control in the age of internet of things. IEEE Internet Things J. **7**(6), 4682–4696 (2020)
25. Ricci, A., Ciortea, A., Mayer, S., Boissier, O., Bordini, R.H., Hübner, J.F.: Engineering scalable distributed environments and organizations for mas. In: Proceedings of the 18th International Conference on Autonomous Agents and MultiAgent Systems (AAMAS), 2019, Canadá (2019)
26. Ricci, A., Piunti, M., Viroli, M.: Environment programming in multi-agent systems: an artifact-based perspective. Auton. Agents Multi-Agent Syst. **23**, 158–192 (2011)
27. Servos, D., Osborn, S.L.: Current research and open problems in attribute-based access control. ACM Comput. Surv. (CSUR) **49**(4), 1–45 (2017)
28. Sorici, A., Picard, G., Boissier, O., Florea, A.: Multi-agent based flexible deployment of context management in ambient intelligence applications. In: Demazeau, Y., Decker, K.S., Bajo Pérez, J., de la Prieta, F. (eds.) PAAMS 2015. LNCS (LNAI), vol. 9086, pp. 225–239. Springer, Cham (2015). https://doi.org/10.1007/978-3-319-18944-4_19
29. Sorici, A., Picard, G., Boissier, O., Zimmermann, A., Florea, A.: CONSERT: applying semantic web technologies to context modeling in ambient intelligence. Comput. Electr. Eng. **44**, 280–306 (2015)
30. Tommasini, R., Bonte, P., Ongenae, F., Della Valle, E.: RSP4J: an API for RDF stream processing. In: Verborgh, R., et al. (eds.) ESWC 2021. LNCS, vol. 12731, pp. 565–581. Springer, Cham (2021). https://doi.org/10.1007/978-3-030-77385-4_34
31. Tommasini, R., Della Valle, E.: Yasper 1.0: towards an RSP-QL engine. In: ISWC (Posters, Demos & Industry Tracks) (2017)
32. Zimmermann, A., Lorenz, A., Oppermann, R.: An operational definition of context. In: Kokinov, B., Richardson, D.C., Roth-Berghofer, T.R., Vieu, L. (eds.) CONTEXT 2007. LNCS (LNAI), vol. 4635, pp. 558–571. Springer, Heidelberg (2007). https://doi.org/10.1007/978-3-540-74255-5_42

Towards Framing the Agents & Artifacts Conceptual Model at the Knowledge Level: First Ideas and Experiments

Samuele Burattini[1]([✉]), Andrei Ciortea[2], Meshua Galassi[1],
and Alessandro Ricci[1]

[1] Dipartimento di Informatica - Scienza e Ingegneria, Alma Mater Studiorum,
Università di Bologna, Cesena Campus, Bologna, Italy
{samuele.burattini,a.ricci}@unibo.it, meshua.galassi@studio.unibo.it
[2] School of Computer Science, University of St.Gallen, St. Gallen, Switzerland
andrei.ciortea@unisg.ch

Abstract. In this contribution, we propose an extension of the Knowledge Level as introduced by Newell in the A.I. context and refined by Jennings in agent-based software engineering to include also the agent environment as a first-class analysis/design dimension. We revisit and refine the Agents & Artifacts (A&A) conceptual model to be at the Knowledge Level by explicitly introducing a semantic layer based on Knowledge Graphs, and we discuss the benefits with some practical examples.

Keywords: Knowledge Level · Agent-Oriented Software Engineering · Agents & Artifacts · Knowledge Graphs · Semantic Web · CArtAgO

1 Introduction

Four decades ago, Allen Newell introduced the *knowledge level* analysis to characterise intelligent agents as knowledge-based systems, abstracting from application-specific details and implementations [14,16]. According to this characterisation, a computational system can be viewed across multiple levels of abstraction — a hierarchy of computer system descriptions[1]. The Knowledge Level is just another level within that same hierarchy: a way to describe the behaviour of (intelligent) systems with wide-ranging capabilities, where capability is defined in terms of having "knowledge" and behaving in light of it. The key feature of the Knowledge Level from a software engineering viewpoint is that it abstracts completely from the internal processing and the internal representation: all that is left is the content of the representation and the goals towards which that content will be used.

The concept has become a keystone in agent-oriented software engineering [10], along with the very similar characterisation introduced, in the same period, by Dennett with the *intentional stance* [6] — effectively setting the level

---

[1] Appendix A reports the levels as depicted by Newell in [15].

A. Ciortea et al. (Eds.): EMAS 2023, LNAI 14378, pp. 208–219, 2023.
https://doi.org/10.1007/978-3-031-48539-8_14

of abstraction that we expect when modelling and designing a software component as an intelligent agent. Two decades ago, the concept was further extended by Jennings in the context of agent-oriented software engineering to also include the social/organisational dimensions [10][2].

After two decades, we further extend this important conceptual framework with a missing element that proved to be, both in the case of humans and in Agent-Oriented Software Engineering (AOSE), an important dimension for analysing and designing systems: the agent environment. This extension aims at providing a uniform level of abstraction to describe both the goal-oriented behaviour of software agents and the environment they can exploit to achieve such goals by discovering, manipulating and creating resources and services.

Accordingly, the first contribution of this paper is about framing and discussing the role of the agent/MAS environment as a first-class design abstraction at the Knowledge Level. To achieve that, we look at ways in which knowledge about the real world is currently being represented and shared in other kinds of systems, following the evolution of the digital transformation of different domains using the Semantic Web — for instance, in the Web of Things[3]. In Sect. 2, we discuss this point, using the Agents & Artifacts (A&A) conceptual modelling [17], which was implicitly conceived to be at the Knowledge Level.

The A&A meta-model was conceived informally, without identifying a clear connection at the knowledge level with domains. Accordingly, as a second core contribution of this paper, in Sect. 3 we discuss a refinement and extension of the A&A meta-model to be fully effective for supporting the Knowledge Level, and in Sect. 4 we briefly describe a first extension of the CArtAgO framework [19] implementing it. We conclude the paper with a brief road-map for future work in Sect. 5.

2 Enriching the Knowledge Level with Artifact-Based Environments

As remarked in AOSE literature [21–23], the environment can be used as a first-class abstraction when designing and programming agent-based systems. In particular, it can be used for encapsulating and providing functionalities to agents at different levels [22]: a *basic level*, to enable direct access to the deployment context; an *abstraction level*, providing agents with an abstraction level that shields low-level details of the deployment context — as well as other resources in the system; an *interaction-mediation level*, providing agents an interaction-mediation level to support mediated interaction in the environment; a *reflective level*, providing a reflective interface to the functionality supported by the environment, enabling agents to modify the functional behavior of the environment [18].

---

[2] Appendix B reports a description of the knowledge level and the social level as depicted by Jennings in [10].
[3] See the W3C Web of Things: https://www.w3.org/TR/wot-architecture/.

At the Knowledge Level, this accounts for enriching Newell's and Jennings's conceptual framework to include the environment at the same level of abstraction with agents and agent organisations, modelling the open of resources and tools as first-class *artifacts* — as introduced by A&A [17] — that agents and organisations may build, use, and share in order to accomplish their individual and social goals. The concept of artifact and the overall A&A conceptual model were mainly inspired by Activity Theory [18,20] and Distributed Cognition [9], which are prominent conceptual frameworks and theories that investigated the role the environment for supporting human activities at large (cognition, reasoning, learning, etc.).

From an engineering point of view, artifacts model those parts of the system that are not effectively described as goal-oriented knowledge-based systems, acting to attain goals, but more as *function-oriented* or *service-oriented* components used by the goal-oriented ones. Like artifacts designed for humans, a key feature of artifacts designed for agents is given by the affordances that they provide to enable their (effective) use by agents, defining the underlying interaction model at the proper level of abstraction. In the A&A model, these affordances are based on observable properties, operations (actions, from the agents' viewpoint), and observable events [19]. Another concept is the artifact *manual*, i.e. a document describing what are the functionalities of an artifact and how to interact with it.

Nevertheless, in order to be exploited by intelligent agents at the Knowledge Level, artifacts should be designed and conceived at the same level. In the next section, as a core contribution of this paper, we discuss how the A&A conceptual model can be further refined and extended for this purpose.

3   Artifact-Based Environments at the Knowledge Level

Using A&A at the Knowledge Level means that the artifact-based environment is meant to be used by intelligent agents to perceive and act upon domain entities — possibly representing assets in the real world — as well as to create and exploit resources and tools that are instrumental for attaining their goals. For this purpose, we envision a further refinement or characterisation of the A&A model in which:

– Artifacts should be *semantically ground to domain entities at the Knowledge Level*: their affordances and their manuals should be described at that same level of abstraction;
– *Relationships among entities* at the domain level should be explicitly represented and reified at the artifact level so that agents can reason about them;
– *Workspaces* – another main concept in A&A - can be used to define boundaries for agent activities, i.e. contexts where one or multiple agents can create and share one or multiple artifacts, as well as logical contexts that share the same domain vocabulary to describe the entities within them.

To support this refinement, we introduce an explicit semantic layer for A&A, not bound to any specific domain but expressive enough to support the design of

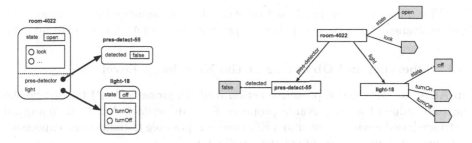

Fig. 1. Smart room scenario. On the left: the three artifacts, representing a room, a presence sensor, and a light. On the right: the corresponding Knowledge Graph.

artifact-based environments eventually involving multiple domains and ontologies. The semantic layer is based on the concept of *knowledge graph* [8]. A Knowledge Graph (KG) is *"a graph of data intended to accumulate and convey knowledge of the real world, whose nodes represent entities of interest and whose edges represent relationships between these entities"* [8]. An artifact-based environment can then be mapped into a KG where each artifact has a corresponding node in the graph — representing an entity of interest at the domain level. Following the A&A meta-model, artifacts feature observable properties, actions, and observable events. These are represented in the KG by (dynamic) data properties of the corresponding entity, i.e. as a relationship between the entity and a typed value. To capture relations among entities (edges between nodes) we extend the artifact meta-model with the concept of (observable) relationship.

As an example, let's consider a toy smart room scenario in an Internet of Things (IoT) context (see Fig. 1). The scenario includes a room, a presence detector, and a light as domain entities. The figure shows the three artifacts modelling this environment (on the left), and the corresponding KG (on the right). Let's consider a very simple intelligent agent, situated in this environment, designed to accomplish an energy-saving goal by turning off the light when no one is in the room, and turning it on if someone enters (and the light is off). In order to accomplish its goal — defined at the Knowledge Level — the agent can exploit the artifact-based environment, whose semantics are defined by the corresponding KG. In particular, the agent may continuously observe the presence detector and turn on/off the light by acting on the lamp. For this purpose, the agent may start observing the presence detector by doing a *focus* on the corresponding artifact. In A&A, by issuing a focus on some artifact Ar, an agent starts perceiving the observable state of Ar and the observable events generated by Ar, including those related to changes about observable properties. Then, as soon as it perceives that someone has been detected, e.g. by perceiving an observable event generated by the artifact representing the presence detector, the agent may turn on the light by acting on the corresponding artifact — if the light was not already on (this state can be perceived by the agent by observing the lamp as well).

The semantic extension based on KG allows to substantially empower the expressiveness of the basic capabilities provided by artifact-based environments.

3.1 Querying and Observing at the Knowledge Level

In A&A, an agent has a primitive action read-obs-property(Ar,P) to retrieve the current value of an observable property P of an artifact Ar. By mapping an artifact-based environment into a KG view it is possible to make more expressive queries, involving graphs of entities (artifacts).

In this paper, we consider RDF[4] as a standardised data model for representing KGs. A KG can be represented as an RDF graph, that is a set of triples (subject, predicate, object) where each triple represents a property or relationship of the subject entity. For instance, in our case, the subject could be an artifact identified by a uniform identifier (e.g., a URI[5] or an IRI[6]). The predicate could describe a data property – as triples where the identifier of the property is used as predicate – or a relationship to another artifact – as triples where the identifier of the relationship is used as predicate and the object is the identifier of another artifact. Given an RDF representation of a KG, the graph can then be queried using SPARQL[7].

Accordingly, any artifact-based environment extended at the Knowledge Level can then be described in RDF and queried by agents using SPARQL. For example, in the toy scenario suppose that the room may have multiple lights referred to by the light relationship. An agent can query the environment to find out which lights in the room are on:

```
SELECT ?light
WHERE { "room-4022" :light ?light .
        ?light :state "on" .}
```

Besides querying, continuous observation can also be empowered. In particular, we can introduce and exploit a variant focus-all of the focus primitive action so that by issuing a focus-all on an artifact Ar, an agent may perceive the observable state and future observable events not only of the specific artifact but of all artifacts linked to that artifact, according to the relationships in place. In the toy scenario, for instance, a focus-all on room-4022 would imply to start observing the room, as well as the presence detector and the light.

3.2 Semantic-Driven Creation of Artifacts in Workspaces

Framing an artifact-based environment at the Knowledge Level implies that the dynamic construction and extension of the environment should be characterised at that level as well. In particular, the dynamic creation of an artifact, possibly

---

[4] https://www.w3.org/TR/rdf11-concepts/.
[5] https://www.rfc-editor.org/rfc/rfc3986.
[6] https://www.rfc-editor.org/rfc/rfc3987.
[7] https://www.w3.org/TR/sparql11-query/.

linked to or linked by some other artifacts, should be a possibility provided by the environment — grounded at the domain/semantic level.

For instance, extending the smart room example introduced above, a personal assistant agent could detect that its user has entered a room. Accordingly, it might want to make some data about the user available to other agents (e.g. a room manager agent) by creating a UserProfile artifact in the smart room workspace, linked by the room artifact by means of a user relationship, to expose data about his desired light level.

In basic A&A, a primitive action make-artifact is provided for instantiating a new artifact by specifying the template and construction parameters [19]. The action corresponds to an operation provided by a pre-defined *workspace artifact* available in each workspace, providing basic capabilities to work inside that workspace (to create and dispose of artifacts, to focus on artifacts, etc.).

Raising A&A at the Knowledge Level implies to revise this mechanism in order to allow for *driving and constraining artifact creation at the domain/semantic level*. Accordingly, each workspace, as a context of semantically-driven agents' activities, may be initially configured — at workspace creation time — with an artifact representing from the agent point of view the *single entry point* of the context, providing the initial set of actions to extend/develop it, according to the possibility defined for that context at the semantic level. In the smart room scenario, the SmartRoom artifact would function as an entry point, providing a notifyNewUser operation, creating a new UserProfile artifact and the relationship user linking to it.

4   Bringing CArtAgO at the Knowledge Level

To start exploring in practice the vision brought by this paper, we developed a semantic layer on top of the existing CArtAgO framework, which is the main reference implementation for the A&A meta-model and part of the JaCaMo [1] platform. For this first integration, we focused on generating a semantic description of the artifacts so that agents could exploit the resulting Knowledge Graph to query the environment. We considered examples with just one workspace with a centralised KG associated to it to start with.

The KG is empty at the beginning of the application. When instantiating new artifacts, they automatically add their own semantic description and generate an ontology based on the artifact class implementation. The implementation uses Apache Jena[8] framework and RDF triplestore wrapped in a SemanticEnvironment interface. The class SemanticArtifact extends the CArtAgO Artifact base class, adding to the base behaviour the automatic insertion and update of RDF triples to the KG when needed (e.g. when initialising the artifact, when updating observable properties, etc.).

Listing 1.1 shows how an artifact can be defined with the new API. The lightswitch artifact has a pressed observable property and a controls relationship with the light artifact it is controlling.

---

[8] https://jena.apache.org/.

```
1  public class LightSwitchArtifact extends SemanticArtifact {
2
3    void init(boolean isPressed, String idConnection){
4      super.init(this, this.getId().getName());
5      defineObsProperty("pressed", "boolean", isPressed);
6      defineRelationship("controls", idConnection);
7    }
8    @OPERATION void press() { setPress(true); }
9    @OPERATION void release(){ setPress(false); }
10
11   private void setPress(boolean p){
12     updateValue(pressProperty, this.press);
13   }
14 }
```

Listing 1.1. An example of how to use the `SemanticArtifact` API to define an artifact.

The corresponding Knowledge Graph will have the definition of the ontology, and of the instances of the artifacts in the environment. In Listing 1.2, an RDF serialisation of the knowledge graph with the instances of two artifacts is shown using Turtle syntax.

```
1  @prefix : <http://example.org/> .
2  @prefix owl: <http://www.w3.org/2002/07/owl#> .
3
4  :lamp_0      a owl:NamedIndividual, :Lamp ;
5               :stateOn false .
6
7  :lightSwitch_0 a owl:NamedIndividual, :LightSwitch ;
8               :controls :lamp_0 ;
9               :pressed false .
```

Listing 1.2. Knowledge Graph serialisation with a Lamp and a LightSwitch

Agents can then query the generated Knowledge Graph containing all the data about the environment exploiting the semantic layer to discover information about the available artifacts. (Listing 1.3).

```
1  +!findSwitch
2  <- query("SELECT ?l WHERE {?l rdf:type :Lamp}", R1);
3    getValue(0, "l", R1, LampId);
4    .concat("SELECT ?d WHERE { ?d :controls :",LampId,".}",Q)
       ;
5    query(Q, R2);
6    getValue(0, "d", R2, SwitchId);
7    .println(SwitchId, " controls ", LampId).
```

Listing 1.3. A Jason agent plan performing SPARQL queries on the environment to find a Lamp and then the Switch connected to it.

5   The Road Ahead

In this paper we started crunching a vision extending A&A at the Knowledge Level, doing some first experiments using CArtAgO. The idea has been strongly influenced by existing work in literature about Hypermedia MAS [4,5], in which A&A and artifact-based environments have been taken as a conceptual model to characterise agents situated on the Web, in a wide perspective including also Semantic Web and Web of Things. Besides Hypermedia MAS, related works include the wide literature in MAS and AOSE about integrating ontologies and Semantic Web technologies in agent/MAS languages and platforms [3,7,11–13].

This vision introduces challenges and open issues at different levels, to be tackled in future research efforts. In the following, we discuss three main ones:

Querying and observing graphs of artifacts: A main issue is about the atomicity and consistency of SPARQL queries involving dynamic graphs of artifacts, possibly evolving concurrently. Artifacts in an artifact-based environment may evolve concurrently, for instance, by means of actions performed by different agents. That is: each artifact is guaranteed to evolve atomically, but different artifacts may evolve concurrently. The question then is: what kind of consistency can an agent have by performing a SPARQL query over an evolving graph? In our first exploration, a simple solution is adopted based on workspaces, functioning as a context delimiting consistency. SPARQL queries are guaranteed to be atomic for the graph of artifacts that belong to the same workspace. Nevertheless, in the model proposed in this paper, artifacts in one workspace can link via relationships to artifacts in other workspaces — in a pure Linked Data spirit. This implies handling queries across workspaces.

Working with ontologies: An artifact-based environment at the Knowledge Level could concern entities belonging to different domains, possibly described at the semantic level using different ontologies. For this purpose, the Semantic Web provides a full stack of technologies in addition to RDF, such as RDF Schema (RDFS), the Web Ontology Language (OWL), or the Shapes Constraint Language (SHACL). A main exploration concerns then how to enrich the support for the Knowledge Level as introduced in this paper by considering the full spectrum of Semantic Web technologies. The abundant literature about integrating ontologies in agent/MAS design and programming (e.g. [3,7,11–13]) will be an important reference here.

Multi-agent Oriented Programming at the Knowledge Level: In platforms like JaCaMo [1,2], the agent, environment, and organisation dimensions are integrated into a coherent and synergistic model. A main issue then is to preserve a coherent view about the Knowledge Level across the different dimensions. In particular, in JaCaMo the A&A conceptual model – implemented by CArtAgO – is integrated with the BDI model/architecture adopted for designing and programming agents in Jason. Accordingly, the A&A/CArtAgO extension is going to impact the way in which the knowledge about the environment is represented on the agent side, in terms of beliefs about artifacts' observable state and events, as well as the actions that can be performed on artifacts. Existing work around AgentSpeak-DL [13] –s integrating Description Logics for knowledge representation in AgentSpeak(L) — and JASDL [11] — combining BDI and Jason with Semantic Web Technologies – will be an important reference to consider for tackling this point.

A   The Hierarchy of Computer Systems

(See Fig.2).

Knowledge-level systems
Medium: Knowledge   Laws: Principle of Rationality
Program-level systems
Medium: Data structures, programs   Laws: Sequential interpretation of programs
Register-transfer system
Medium: Bit vectors   Laws: Parallel logic
Logic circuits
Medium: Bits   Laws: Boolean algebra
Electric circuits
Medium: Voltage/current   Laws: Ohm's law, Kirchhoff's law
Electronic devices
Medium: Electrons   Laws: Electron physics

Fig. 2. The hierarchy of computer systems, as reported in [15] (pag. 47)

B Knowledge Level and Social Level

(See Table 1).

Table 1. Summary of the knowledge and social levels as reported in [10]

Dimension	Description	Knowledge level	Social level
System	Entity to be described	(asocial) Agent	Agent organisation
Components	The system's primitive elements	Goals, Actions	Agents, Interaction channels, Dependencies, Organisational relationships
Compositional law	How the components are assembled	Various	Roles, Organisation's rules
Behaviour law	How the system's behaviour depends upon its composition and components	Principle of rationality	Principle of organisational rationality
Medium	The elements to be processed to obtain the desired behaviour	Knowledge	Organisation and social obligations, Means of influencing others, Means of changing organisational structures

References

1. Boissier, O., Bordini, R., Hubner, J., Ricci, A.: Multi-agent Oriented Programming: Programming Multi-agent Systems Using JaCaMo. Intelligent Robotics and Autonomous Agents series, MIT Press (2020). https://books.google.it/books?id=GM_tDwAAQBAJ
2. Boissier, O., Bordini, R.H., Hübner, J.F., Ricci, A., Santi, A.: Multi-agent oriented programming with JaCaMo. Sci. Comput. Program. **78**(6), 747–761 (2013)
3. Chella, A., Lanza, F., Seidita, V.: Representing and developing knowledge using Jason, Cartago and owl. In: Workshop From Objects to Agents (2018)

4. Ciortea, A., Boissier, O., Ricci, A.: Engineering world-wide multi-agent systems with hypermedia. In: Weyns, D., Mascardi, V., Ricci, A. (eds.) EMAS 2018. LNCS (LNAI), vol. 11375, pp. 285–301. Springer, Cham (2019). https://doi.org/10.1007/978-3-030-25693-7_15

5. Ciortea, A., Mayer, S., Gandon, F., Boissier, O., Ricci, A., Zimmermann, A.: A decade in hindsight: the missing bridge between multi-agent systems and the world wide web. In: Proceedings of the International Conference on Autonomous Agents and Multiagent Systems (2019)

6. Dennett, D.C.: The Intentional Stance. MIT press, Cambridge (1987)

7. Freitas, A., Schmidt, D., Panisson, A.R., Meneguzzi, F., Vieira, R., Bordini, R.H.: Knowledge-level integration for JaCaMo. In: Fifth International Workshop on Collaborative Agents - Research & Development, CARE for Intelligent Mobile Services (CARE) (2014)

8. Hogan, A., et al.: Knowledge graphs. ACM Comput. Surv. (CSUR) 54(4), 1–37 (2021)

9. Hutchins, E.: Distributed cognition. Int. Encycl. Soc. Behav. Sci. Elsev. Sci. 138, 1–10 (2000)

10. Jennings, N.R.: On agent-based software engineering. Artif. Intell. 117(2), 277–296 (2000). https://doi.org/10.1016/S0004-3702(99)00107-1

11. Klapiscak, T., Bordini, R.H.: JASDL: a practical programming approach combining agent and semantic web technologies. In: Baldoni, M., Son, T.C., van Riemsdijk, M.B., Winikoff, M. (eds.) DALT 2008. LNCS (LNAI), vol. 5397, pp. 91–110. Springer, Heidelberg (2009). https://doi.org/10.1007/978-3-540-93920-7_7

12. Mascardi, V., Ancona, D., Barbieri, M., Bordini, R.H., Ricci, A.: Cool-AgentSpeak: Endowing AgentSpeak-DL agents with plan exchange and ontology services. Web Intell. Agent Syst. Int. J. 12(1), 83–107 (2014)

13. Moreira, Á.F., Vieira, R., Bordini, R.H., Hübner, J.F.: Agent-oriented programming with underlying ontological reasoning. In: Baldoni, M., Endriss, U., Omicini, A., Torroni, P. (eds.) DALT 2005. LNCS (LNAI), vol. 3904, pp. 155–170. Springer, Heidelberg (2006). https://doi.org/10.1007/11691792_10

14. Newell, A.: The knowledge level. Artif. Intell. 18(1), 87–127 (1982). https://doi.org/10.1016/0004-3702(82)90012-1

15. Newell, A.: Unified Theories of Cognition. Harvard University Press, USA (1990)

16. Newell, A.: Reflections on the knowledge level. Artif. Intell. 59(1–2), 31–38 (1993)

17. Omicini, A., Ricci, A., Viroli, M.: Artifacts in the A&A meta-model for multi-agent systems. Auton. Agents Multi-agent Syst. 17(3), 432–456 (2008). https://doi.org/10.1007/s10458-008-9053-x

18. Ricci, A., Omicini, A., Denti, E.: Activity theory as a framework for MAS coordination. In: Petta, P., Tolksdorf, R., Zambonelli, F. (eds.) ESAW 2002. LNCS (LNAI), vol. 2577, pp. 96–110. Springer, Heidelberg (2003). https://doi.org/10.1007/3-540-39173-8_8

19. Ricci, A., Piunti, M., Viroli, M.: Environment programming in multi-agent systems: an artifact-based perspective. Auton. Agents Multi-agent Syst. 23(2), 158–192 (2011). https://doi.org/10.1007/s10458-010-9140-7

20. Vygotsky, L.S., Cole, M.: Mind in Society: Development of Higher Psychological Processes. Harvard University Press, Cambridge (1978)

21. Weyns, D., Michel, F.: Agent environments for multi-agent systems – a research roadmap. In: Weyns, D., Michel, F. (eds.) E4MAS 2014. LNCS (LNAI), vol. 9068, pp. 3–21. Springer, Cham (2015). https://doi.org/10.1007/978-3-319-23850-0_1

22. Weyns, D., Omicini, A., Odell, J.: Environment as a first class abstraction in multiagent systems. Auton. Agents Multi-agent Syst. **14**(1), 5–30 (2007). https://doi.org/10.1007/s10458-006-0012-0

23. Weyns, D., Van Dyke Parunak, H., Michel, F., Holvoet, T., Ferber, J.: Environments for multiagent systems state-of-the-art and research challenges. In: Weyns, D., Van Dyke Parunak, H., Michel, F. (eds.) E4MAS 2004. LNCS (LNAI), vol. 3374, pp. 1–47. Springer, Heidelberg (2005). https://doi.org/10.1007/978-3-540-32259-7_1

Pody: A Solid-Based Approach to Embody Agents in Web-Based Multi-Agent-Systems

Antoine Zimmermann[1], Andrei Ciortea[2,3(✉)], Catherine Faron[3], Eoin O'Neill[4], and María Poveda-Villalón[5]

[1] Mines Saint-Étienne, Univ. Clermont Auvergne, INP Clermont Auvergne, CNRS, UMR 6158 LIMOS, Saint-Étienne, France
`antoine.zimmermann@emse.fr`
[2] University of St. Gallen, St. Gallen, Switzerland
`andrei.ciortea@unisg.ch`
[3] Université Côte d'Azur, CNRS, Inria, I3S, Sophia Antipolis, France
`faron@i3s.unice.fr`
[4] University College Dublin, Dublin, Ireland
`eoin.o-neill.3@ucdconnect.ie`
[5] Ontology Engineering Group, Universidad Politécnica de Madrid, Madrid, Spain
`mpoveda@fi.upm.es`

Abstract. In this paper we discuss the problem of situatedness for agents perceiving and acting on the Web (namely, "Web agents"). Assuming Web agents are *embodied* on the World Wide Web, then we must define what is a Web agent's *body*. We first provide an abstract definition of a Web agent's body in terms of what it should comprise. Then we propose a concrete definition of it relying on Solid, a recent Web technology for Social Linked Data: we implement a Web agent's body as a data pod. Consequently, we coin the term *pody* to refer to the Web entity that embodies an agent on the Web with Solid. This paper summarises the findings of a working group from the *Dagstuhl Seminar 23081: Agents on the Web* (February 19–24, 2023).

Keywords: MAS · Semantic Web · Solid · Embodiment · Situatedness

1 Introduction

Situatedness and *embodiment* are key notions in research on intelligent agents. The dominant view is that intelligent, rational behaviour is closely related to the environment an agent occupies and is not disembodied [17]. This view emerged in the late'80 s in close relationship with research on intelligent robots [11], which are naturally situated and embodied in a physical environment. The complexity of virtual environments, such as the Web, now rivals that of physical environments. Furthermore, with the recent standardisation of the Web of Things at the W3C and the IETF, the Web now extends to the physical world – and

A. Ciortea et al. (Eds.): EMAS 2023, LNAI 14378, pp. 220–229, 2023.
https://doi.org/10.1007/978-3-031-48539-8_15

thus becomes a uniform hypermedia fabric that interconnects virtual and physical environments. This evolution unlocks new practical use cases for intelligent agents on the Web, that need to be situated and embodied in their environment. This vision that can be traced back to the early days of the Web[1].

In this paper, we discuss how Web agents can be embodied into the Web, both at an abstract level and concretely using Web standards and technologies. In a nutshell, we envision a Web agent's body as a collection of Web resources and Web interfaces that are attached to the identity of the agent. The Web agent's body allows the agent to participate in collective work as part of a multi-agent system (MAS) on the Web: to perceive and actuate Web resources (including Web-enabled devices), to be discovered and perceived by other agents, to participate in organisations, to communicate with other agents, etc. We illustrate this vision through a concrete example of Web agents embodiement using Solid pods, the core concept and technology from Sir Tim Berners-Lee's project for **Social Linked Data** – an initiative to preserve the decentralised nature of the Web and to radically decentralise personal data. In particular, this enables to seamlessly address MAS use cases where a strong emphasis on ownership of the agents' personal data and resources is needed.

The paper is organized as follows: We first present in Sect. 2 the context in which our proposal arose. Then we present in Sect. 3 our vision of how agents should be situated and embodied on the Web, independently of the technologies used. Finally we show in Sect. 4 how this can be implemented using Solid. In the end, we discuss in Sect. 5 what other abstractions would be needed to articulate *podies* with other essential dimensions of Web-based MAS and we conclude in Sect. 6.

2   Background

In this section, we first discuss the notions of situatedness and embodiment in Artificial Intelligence – and, in particular, in MAS engineering (Sect. 2.1). Then we provide an overview of the main Semantic Web concepts, principles, and technologies on which the implementation of our proposal is relying (Sect. 2.2). Finally, we present Solid, the key technology at the center of our proposal (Sect. 2.3).

2.1   Situatedness and Embodiment in Multi-Agent Systems

In the mid-80 s, a new view emerged in the research field of intelligent agents: an agent is considered situated in its environment, in the sense that it is directly connected to its problem domain through sensors and actuators, and it can effect changes in this domain through actuators [11]. This view contrasted prior views in AI research, in which an agent would typically amount to a program to which

---

[1] See the keynote of Sir Tim Berners-Lee at the First International Conference on the World Wide Web (WWW'94): https://videos.cern.ch/record/2671957.

a formal specification of a problem is provided as input – and then the program returns a result.

The notion of *situatedness* originated from research on mobile robots, with Brooks being one of its main originators [4]. It is now generally accepted for any system that needs to autonomously fulfill its design objectives in a dynamic, unpredictable environment – be it physical or virtual [11]. Most definitions of what is an *intelligent* or *autonomous agent* are centered around this notion of *situatedness* (e.g., see [6] for a detailed discussion of various definitions).

Another notion closely related to *situatedness* is the *embodiment* of an agent. In [3], Brooks defined this notion to articulate that robots have bodies and "their actions are part of a dynamic with the world" (e.g., their actions have immediate feedback on their own perception). Close to situatedness, this notion of embodiment originally applied to mobile robots can be extended to agents in virtual environments.

Most notably, in the Agents&Artifacts (A&A) metamodel [13] for MAS engineering, agents are situated in *workspaces* where they are embodied through *body artifacts*. A body artifact holds an agent's context within a workspace: it allows the agent to perceive and act within the workspace, and it allows other agents situated in the same workspace to perceive and interact with the agent. An agent holds a body artifact in each workspace it is a part of. From an engineering viewpoint, this separation of concerns between an agent's mind and its body artifact allows heterogeneous agents (e.g., using different architectures or frameworks) to be reified within the same workspace in a uniform way.

2.2   A Web for Machines

In 2001, the Semantic Web was defined as an extension of the Web relying on new models and technologies to provide structure and meaning to the content available on the Web [2]. The Semantic Web relies on the Resource Description Framework (RDF), a graph model to structure data by expressing relations between entities, and on RDF Schema and the Ontology Web Language to represent the ontologies used in RDF graphs, thus providing semantics to them.

Early research on the Semantic Web was mostly focused on ontology engineering and knowledge representation, but in 2006 Tim Berners-Lee introduced the Linked Data principles [1], that are summarised as follows: 1) use URIs to name things; 2) use HTTP URIs so that things' names can be looked up; 3) describe things using standards (RDF) so useful information is provided for URIs; and 4) include links to other URIs in things descriptions.

Ontologies and linked data together provide the means by which an agent can reliably interpret resources described on the Web, whether they are digital resources or real-world resources. Additionally, with links, a Web resource leads to other resources, and so forth, so as to make agents aware of the environment that the Web constitutes. Some standardised ontologies also define, in their specification, conformance obligations that say how to operate with resources described using them. For instance, the W3C Thing Description standard [9] provides both an ontology to describe possible interactions with *things* on the Web, and the way those descriptions can be leveraged to operate these things.

2.3   Solid: Social Linked Data

Solid is a project launched by Tim Berners-Lee in reaction to the growing centralisation of Web platforms that collect more and more personal data. Instead, Solid aims at decentralising personal data management in such a way that Web users regain ownership and control over their data. At the core of Solid technologies, there is the Solid *pod* (personal online data store) that hosts the user's data and is implemented as a Linked Data Platform [16] with access control on top of it. Pods are mostly used to provide data to online applications, such as social platforms, that are granted access by the pod's owner. This way, not only the data are externalised from Web platforms, but also the same identity, described inside the pod, can be reused across multiple applications.

Identity is managed using a customised protocol based on WebID [14] that allows one to retrieve credentials from a URI that not only identifies the user (as an account login) but also dereferences to the owner's data pod, thus enabling applications to get appropriate data from the user.

Solid pods can host any kind of data but are designed in particular to easily manage RDF datasets with fine-grained read/write operations. Overall, the Solid Protocol [5] specifies authentication, storage, access control, and interactions that must be implemented by Solid pods and Solid platforms in order to interoperate with each others and with applications that builds on them.

3   Embodiment and Situatedness of Agents on the Web

The **situatedness** of an agent, as introduced in Sect. 2.1, refers to the relationship that exists between the agent and its environment. In order for an agent to be situated in its environment, it must have the ability to perceive and act on it. In the case of a *Web agent* addressed in this paper, the environment comprises the Web, and the interactions are the basic interaction protocols defined for the Web. The minimum requirement for a *Web agent* is the ability to interact with hypermedia resources on the Web.

The **embodiment** of an agent on the Web requires a representation of the agent to exist within the Web. We define the *embodiment* of a *Web agent* as the composite set of resources it exposes within a Web-based hypermedia environment, including any (semantic) descriptions of such resources. A defining characteristic of an agent's embodiment in the Web is that the set of resources constituting an agent's **Web body** is innately tied to the agent's identity: the agent may be acting through its Web body, and other agents observing the body would assume that the entity controlling and acting through the body is indeed the reified agent. An agent could have multiple Web bodies, each representing the agent's context in a specific hypermedia environment. This paper posits that the minimum requirement for an "embodied Web agent" is a hypermedia resource that provides the semantically defined abstraction of an **Agent Description**, which may link to any Web bodies the agent might have. This is the top-level abstraction that describes the agent's resources on the Web—and the entry point into what we are considering to be the *embodiment* of the agent.

In order to facilitate interactions within a Web-based MAS, additional abstractions may be defined to provide the necessary contextual information, such as: **Communication Interfaces**, **Preferences**, **Goals**, or **Beliefs** — which are important abstractions for supporting collaboration and coordination in MAS (e.g., see [12,15]. Such abstractions may be shared based on conditional access. The **Communication Interface** abstraction is the element of the agent's embodiment that facilitates interaction between agents and allows for an agent to become an entity directly accessible within the Web. The **Preferences** abstraction provides information such as an agent's preferred methods of interaction, but it is not limited to that. It can also be a domain-specific abstraction that defines the agent's preferred environmental state or any other preference with regard to the agent's embodiment in a particular environment.

If an agent has an explicit internal representation of its goals, the **Goals** abstraction would allow the agent to expose a set of goals. The agent may not necessarily be actively pursuing these goals but by merely exposing a set of goals publicly as a resource, the agent can have an effect on other agents within the system. This can result in benevolence between agents or agents acting in the disinterest of other agents within the system, depending on the context and implementation. Similar to the **Goals** abstraction, if an agent represents its knowledge of the world in terms of beliefs (e.g., as it is the case for BDI agents [7]), the **Beliefs** abstraction exposes a set of beliefs as Web resources, so that other agents can query the supposed beliefs of the agent. Additionally, the publicly available beliefs of the agent may or may not be beliefs that the agent maintains, but can be an attempt to influence the environment state through the actions of other agents that inhabit it.

4   Podies: Solid Pods Implementing Web Agents' Bodies

In this section, we show how Solid pods can be used to implement the abstractions introduced in Sect. 3. The Solid protocol states that "an agent is a person, social entity, or software identified by a URI; e.g., a WebID denotes an agent". We then assume that such a URI would dereference to an entry point for the data pod of the agent, where an **Agent Description** would be provided as an RDF graph, in addition to the mandatory credentials for authenticating the agent. We call the Solid pod implementing an agent's Web body a *pody*. Listing 1.1 shows an example **Agent Description** for a self-driving bus agent's pody. It identifies the self-driving bus as an instance of the `foaf:Agent`[2], class from the Friend-of-a-Friend (FOAF) vocabulary (part of the Solid protocol) and it provides basic information about the agent (e.g., a name, a relevant image) and links to other resources that are part of the agent's Web body, namely: a **Communication Interface** in the form of a mailbox that can be used to contact the agent, and the agent's **Preferences**.

---

[2] See term definition: http://xmlns.com/foaf/0.1/#term_Agent.

Listing 1.1. Example self-driving bus agent's pody: RDF representation of its **Agent Description** (in Turtle).

```
1  @prefix foaf: <http://xmlns.com/foaf/0.1/> .
2  @prefix pody: <http://someuri.ext/pody/> .
3  @prefix solid: <http://www.w3.org/ns/solid/terms#> .
4
5  <#agent-desc> a foaf:PersonalProfileDocument ;
6      foaf:primaryTopic <#webagent> .
7
8  <#webagent> a foaf:Agent ;
9      foaf:name "Self-driving Bus 101" ,
10     # Link to a communication interface (e.g., mailbox, news feed, etc.)
11     pody:contact <mbox> ;
12     # Link to preferences (entry point to different kinds of preferences)
13     pody:preferences <pref> ;
14     # Links to the OpenID Provider that will validate the authentication
15     # (part of the Solid protocol)
16     solid:oidcIssuer <https://oidc.example> ;
17     # Links to a relevant image of the bus
18     foaf:img <images/picture.jpg> .
```

Listing 1.2 shows a sample description of the bus agent's mailbox. In this example, the mailbox is, in fact, a Web service that can be used to contact the bus agent – and the service is described by a W3C WoT Thing Description. The mailbox's Thing Description allows other agents to use the service based on an abstract semantic model of the mailbox (rather than having to hardcode the specific interface of the mailbox). Other similar approaches, such as Hydra [10], could be used to describe the interface of the mailbox.

Listing 1.2. WoT description of the self-driving bus agent's mailbox (in Turtle).

```
1  @prefix td: <https://www.w3.org/2019/wot/td#> .
2  @prefix hctl: <https://www.w3.org/2019/wot/hypermedia#> .
3  @prefix pody: <http://someuri.ext/pody/> .
4  @prefix xsd: <http://www.w3.org/2001/XMLSchema#> .
5
6  <mbox> a td:Thing;
7    td:hasActionAffordance [
8      a pody:SendDirectMessage ;
9      td:name "send-mail";
10     td:hasForm [
11       hctl:hasTarget "https://domain.ext/mbox/inbox"^^xsd:anyURI
12     ]
13   ] .
```

Listing 1.3 shows a sample representation of the bus agent's **Preferences**. In this example, the preferences expose a basic access control policy using the Web Access Control[3] vocabulary (part of the Solid protocol). Other preferences could express, for instance, a prioritization of the **Communication Interfaces** exposed by the agent – similar to the preferred ordering of contact addresses in a FIPA Agent Identifier as defined by the FIPA Agent Management Ontology[4].

---

[3] https://solidproject.org/TR/wac.
[4] See the FIPA Agent Management Specification for details: http://fipa.org/specs/fipa00023/SC00023K.html.

Listing 1.3. RDF description of the self-driving bus agent's preferences (in Turtle).

```
1 @prefix acl: <http://www.w3.org/ns/auth/acl#> .
2
3 <pref> acl:accessControl [
4     acl:accessTo <mbox> ;
5     acl:agent <http://example.edu/p/Alice#Msc>,
6         . <http://example.com/people/Mary/card#me> ;
7     acl:mode acl:Read
8 ] .
```

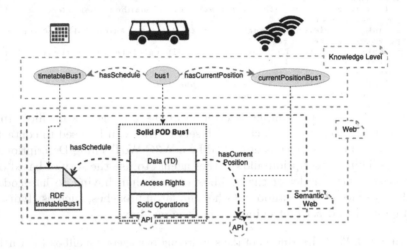

Fig. 1. Example bus agent embodied on the Web, its Solid pod implemented using Semantic Web models. The bus agent publishes on the Web its up-to-date position stored in its pody.

In addition to the resources described so far, the embodiment of the bus agent could include additional resources. A more elaborate illustration of this use case is shown in Fig. 1. The bus agent could use its Solid pod, for instance, to publish an up-to-date schedule or its current position. Because such information is published under the bus agent's pody, other agents would assume that it is indeed the bus agent communication through its pody — similar to how a Twitter user would communicate updates via their Twitter account.

5 Discussion

Our proposal gives uniformity to how agents are embodied on the Web. The notion of *pody* makes use of technologies that are mostly based on standards, as well as work that is under active development by public organisations and companies. The use of Linked Data enforces uniform identification (with URIs), a common data model (with RDF), and a way of serendipitously exploring data, especially for what concerns agents, their means of communication, and their specificities.

With agents embodied in the Web through *podies*, we can envision how they can be situated and related to other dimensions of a multi-agent system. Other abstractions would have to be introduced to describe the Web counterpart of a physical location. We can assume that agents will cooperate on the Web within abstract areas that delimit the scope of their interaction and offer the required resources to address specific missions, goals, and endeavours. For instance, agents may collaborate in Github projects, with a repository acting as a workspace where they are situated. These "abstract areas" or workspaces can themselves be described in podies that would also offer interaction facilities, links to the agents situated in them, ways of taking roles, etc.

Additionally, agents cooperating in complex organisations, possibly with a mix of human beings, software agents, or robots, should be able to obtain organisational information, such as norms, regulation, and so forth, in a form that is easily machine-processable. Interestingly, existing Web ontologies already cover parts of these abstractions, and research communities are actively working on providing shared vocabularies that enable to precisely to describe these things.

6   Conclusion

Web agents can be embodied via a Solid pod that: 1) provides a recognisable identity to the agents acting/interacting on and via the Web; 2) provides a "shape" to the agent in the form of an agent description, materialised as an RDF graph; 3) provides an interface through which other agents can communicate with the embodied agent; 4) may optionally provide supporting features such as preferences, claimed goals and beliefs, all possibly represented using standards.

This paper posits a shape, and an implementation method, that may be used to represent the intelligent agents that inhabit the Web, the same intelligent agents that Hendler was querying the existence of in [8]. We see this as a step in the direction of allowing agent technologies to be utilized in a Web context consuming semantically enriched data and interacting in an ad-hoc fashion with heterogeneous, semantically described Web services in order to provide services and pursue and achieve goals of their own. By defining a standard abstract "shape" for a *Web agent*, using Web standard technologies, we introduce the possibility of cross-organisational interaction and collaboration.

The contribution of this paper is a vision that still requires a realisation in an actual MAS. We argue that this vision already shows the benefits for engineering Web-based MAS. Future work will determine, by experimentation, the feasability, usability, ease of development, scalability, and perhaps limitations for Web-based Multi-Agent Systems engineering.

Acknowledgement. We thank Alessandro Ricci and Jomi Hübner for our fruitful discussions during the Dagstuhl Seminar 23081 that led to the ideas presented in this paper. Antoine Zimmermann and Andrei Ciortea had funding related to project HyperAgents from grants ANR-19-CE23-0030-01 and SNSF No. 189474. María Poveda-Villalón received funding from the Spanish project KnowledgeSpaces (PID2020-118274RB-I00).

References

1. Berners-Lee, T.: Linked data. Published online by the author as a Web design issue (2006). http://www.w3.org/DesignIssues/LinkedData.html
2. Berners-Lee, T., Hendler, J., Lassila, O.: The semantic web. Sci. Am. **284**(5), 34–43 (2001). https://www.scientificamerican.com/article/the-semantic-web/
3. Brooks, R.A.: Intelligence without reason. In: Mylopoulos, J., Reiter, R. (eds.) Proceedings of the 12th International Joint Conference on Artificial Intelligence. Sydney, Australia, 24–30 August 1991, pp. 569–595. Morgan Kaufmann (1991). http://ijcai.org/Proceedings/91-1/Papers/089.pdf
4. Brooks, R.A.: A robust layered control system for a mobile robot. IEEE J. Robot. Autom. **2**(1), 14–23 (1986). https://doi.org/10.1109/JRA.1986.1087032
5. Capadisli, S., Berners-Lee, T., Verborgh, R., Kjernsmo, K.: Solid protocol. W3c solid community group working draft, World Wide Web Consortium (2021). https://solidproject.org/TR/2021/protocol-20211217
6. Franklin, S., Graesser, A.: Is it an agent, or just a program?: a taxonomy for autonomous agents. In: Müller, J.P., Wooldridge, M.J., Jennings, N.R. (eds.) ATAL 1996. LNCS, vol. 1193, pp. 21–35. Springer, Heidelberg (1997). https://doi.org/10.1007/BFb0013570
7. Georgeff, M.P., Lansky, A.L.: Reactive reasoning and planning. In: Forbus, K.D., Shrobe, H.E. (eds.) Proceedings of the 6th National Conference on Artificial Intelligence. Seattle, WA, USA, July 1987, pp. 677–682. Morgan Kaufmann (1987). http://www.aaai.org/Library/AAAI/1987/aaai87-121.php
8. Hendler, J.: Where are all the intelligent agents? IEEE Intell. Syst. **22**(03), 2–3 (2007). https://doi.org/10.1109/MIS.2007.62
9. Kaebisch, S., Kamiya, T., McCool, M., Charpenay, V., Kovatsch, M.: Web of Things (WoT) Thing Description. W3C Recommendation, World Wide Web Consortium (2020). http://www.w3.org/TR/2020/REC-wot-thing-description-20200409/
10. Lanthaler, M., Gütl, C.: Hydra: a vocabulary for hypermedia-driven web APIs. In: Bizer, C., Heath, T., Berners-Lee, T., Hausenblas, M., Auer, S. (eds.) Proceedings of the WWW2013 Workshop on Linked Data on the Web, Rio de Janeiro, Brazil, May 14 2013. CEUR Workshop Proceedings, vol. 996. Sun SITE Central Europe (CEUR) (2013). http://ceur-ws.org/Vol-996/papers/ldow2013-paper-03.pdf
11. Maes, P.: Modeling adaptive autonomous agents. Artif. Life **1**(1_2), 135–162 (1993). https://doi.org/10.1162/artl.1993.1.1_2.135
12. Nwana, H.S., Lee, L., Jennings, N.R.: Co-ordination in multi-agent systems. In: Nwana, H.S., Azarmi, N. (eds.) Software Agents and Soft Computing Towards Enhancing Machine Intelligence. LNCS, vol. 1198, pp. 42–58. Springer, Heidelberg (1997). https://doi.org/10.1007/3-540-62560-7_37
13. Omicini, A., Ricci, A., Viroli, M.: Artifacts in the A&A meta-model for multi-agent systems. Auton. Agent. Multi-agent Syst. **17**(3), 432–456 (2008). https://doi.org/10.1007/s10458-008-9053-x
14. Sambra, A., Corlosquet, S.: WebID 1.0 - Web Identity and Discovery. W3C IG Editor's draft, World Wide Web Consortium (2015). https://dvcs.w3.org/hg/WebID/raw-file/tip/spec/identity-respec.html
15. Sichman, J.S.A., Conte, R., Castelfranchi, C., Demazeau, Y.: A social reasoning mechanism based on dependence networks. In: Proceedings of the 11th European Conference on Artificial Intelligence, pp. 188–192. ECAI 1994, Wiley, USA (1994)

16. Speicher, S., Arwe, J., Malhotra, A.: Linked data platform 1.0. W3C recommendation, world wide web consortium (2015). http://www.w3.org/TR/2015/REC-ldp-20150226/
17. Wooldridge, M.: Intelligent agents. In: Weiss, G. (ed.) Multiagent Systems: A Modern Approach to Distributed Artificial Intelligence, pp. 27–72. The MIT Press (2000). http://mitp-content-server.mit.edu:18180/books/content/sectbyfn?collid=books_pres_0&id=4791&fn=9780262731317_sch_0001.pdf

Frameworks, Tooling, and DevOps

Fantastic MASs and Where to Find Them: First Results and Lesson Learned

Daniela Briola[1], Angelo Ferrando[2]([✉]), and Viviana Mascardi[2]

[1] University of Milano-Bicocca, Milan, Italy
daniela.briola@unimib.it
[2] University of Genova, Genova, Italy
{angelo.ferrando,viviana.mascardi}@unige.it

Abstract. Nowadays, the Multiagent Systems research community is facing new challenges related to engineering the overall process of software development, tailoring it to the specific needs of the community, and integrating SE techniques into many studies in the MAS area. More and more frequently, researchers need already developed MASs for validating their new proposals. Often, they spend time in looking for the code of existing tools to compare with the state of the art. Unfortunately, accessing this kind of resources, which are the starting point for many SE activities, is not always easy. In this paper, we present the first outcome of the initiative "Fantastic MAS and where to find them", launched in June 2022, where we asked the agent community to contribute in the creation of a repository to facilitate the sharing of the already existing tools (agent development frameworks, libraries, add ons of already existing platforms) and MASs with their code. The "Fantastic MAS" goals are to i) improve the sharing and reusing of research results ii) support the SE activities in our research community, iii) help making a step towards the Open Science movement, which has been already widely adopted in other research communities. Besides providing an overview of the submissions we got, we discuss the open problems that emerged in these eight months of the initiative, so that to stimulate the discussion in the community.

Keywords: Agent-Oriented Software Engineering · Multiagent systems · Agent development framework

1 Introduction

In the last years, the research community related to agents and Multiagent Systems (MASs) opened more and more to software engineering problems related to all the aspects of designing and implementing MASs [39]. This is mandatory to face the growing complexity of this variegate research field: indeed, testing approaches and tools, formal methods, simulators of MASs, and design methodologies are emerging in our community, in response to the need of researchers and in line with the advances in the Software Engineering (SE) research area.

A. Ciortea et al. (Eds.): EMAS 2023, LNAI 14378, pp. 233–252, 2023.
https://doi.org/10.1007/978-3-031-48539-8_16

As a community, we are consequently facing the problems associated with this transformation toward a more "software engineering approach", which provides great benefits but also requires a change in the way the research results are presented and shared. The Software Engineering community has adopted from way back a systematic approach regarding how research results should be presented, above all in the top level scientific venues, which follows a sort of standard and a common list of requirements to assure the quality of the published products and to enhance their sharing and reusability. The underlying idea is that the value of a research result relies not only in the new proposal presented in the paper itself, but in the associated produced tool, exploited data, and whatever was used for achieving the results presented in the paper. So, the research result has a double value, the state of the art contribution and the availability of associated data and software to be reused by the community. This approach is in line with the view proposed by the Open Science movement[1], which is getting more and more attention by all the academic world. Considering the top rated SE conferences (ICSE[2], ESEC/FSE[3], ICST[4]), their call for papers clearly mention the *"Open Science Policy"*, stating that:

"the steering principle is that all research results should be accessible to the public and, if possible, empirical studies should be reproducible. In particular, we actively support the adoption of open data and open source principles and encourage all contributing authors to disclose (anonymised and curated) data to increase reproducibility and replicability. Note that sharing research data is not mandatory for submission or acceptance. However, sharing is expected to be the default, and non-sharing needs to be justified. We recognise that reproducibility or replicability is not a goal in qualitative research and that, similar to industrial studies, qualitative studies often face challenges in sharing research data".

And also *"submissions must supply all information that is needed to replicate the results, and therefore are expected to include or point to a replication package with the necessary software, data, and instructions. Reviewers may consult these packages to resolve open issues. There can be good reasons for the absence of a replication package, such as confidential code and/or data, the research being mostly qualitative, or the paper being fully self-contained. If a paper does not come with a replication package, authors should comment on its absence in the submission data".*

This strong commitment toward the sharing of software and data (the lack of this information seriously undermines the acceptance of a paper in those venues), even if complex to be accomplished, plays an important role in the improvement and simplification of the research activities, in particular:

- Results replicability: the presented results can be checked by the community, so that they are more reliable.

---

[1] https://www.unesco.org/en/open-science.

[2] http://www.icse-conferences.org/.

[3] https://www.esec-fse.org/upcoming_events.

[4] https://icst2022.vrain.upv.es/series/icst.

- Comparability: when a new technique is presented, it can be compared in a simpler way with the previous ones, since it can be tested on the same dataset/testbed the previous ones were tested on.
- Testbed availability: years after years, repository with applications, libraries, source code are created and maintained, so that they can be directly exploited to verify and validate new tools and techniques.
- Dissemination inside the community: the availability of the code of a tool, possibly with test suites and data for testing, makes those research results more known, cited and reused inside the community

On the contrary, the aforementioned points are painful for our community, even if we are moving toward them too (e.g., in the AAMAS 2023 call for paper, a reference can be found to this aspect: *"We highly encourage authors to make their source code (if any) publicly available after their papers are accepted. The link should be in their paper and will also be publicised on the AAMAS website"*). Nonetheless, it is really difficult to find the code (open source or compiled) of proposed frameworks/tools and of "real MASs" to be used to validate new runtime techniques, or to be used as testbed for new testing approaches, or to be analysed in their structure for reverse engineering activities. For example, a simple research on Gitlab through its topics shows that few projects exist under "Multiagent", but also if searching in general on the web, finding MASs that are more than a toy example, or some academic project, well documented, reusable, is quite impossible. So, we often rely on "toy examples" or "MASs developed by the same research group", that is, internal resources, to substantiate our claims. This makes the validation and verification of new tools and techniques weaker: from a SE point of view, this is a clear threat to validity. Also, when searching the state of the art for similar approaches or tools, to perform a comparison, it is often difficult to find an artefact to be used. While we can find works to compare with, rarely a thorough and real comparison can be performed that goes beyond reading the paper. This, sometimes, is determined by the fact that the code used in existing papers is not available to the community. While these aspects do not decrease the intrinsic quality of the research, they limit its visibility and make it less shareable, both inside and outside the community.

To help solving these problems, and to support the sharing of the results of the community, we promoted the "Fantastic MASs and where to find them" initiative, aimed at:

- Promoting the visibility of the results of the research, to facilitate the study of the state of the art, by offering a repository of works, organised in macro areas.
- Promoting the creation of a repository of MASs, to be used as third party testbed and so simplifying the validation and verification of new tools and approaches.
- Promoting the reproducibility of the results, and the sharing of the code of tools, algorithms and so on, so that to simplify the comparison with previous works.

– Supporting the Software Engineering activities for the community, sharing information regarding bugs, test suites and so on associated with already existing MASs and tools.

To create this repository, we decided not to perform a standard Systematic Literature Review (SLR), mainly due to two reasons:

– Some of the information of our interest are not available in papers (e.g., bugs, previous versions, and so on).
– We focus on artefacts to be shared inside the community – not mere theoretical approaches –, with a format that can be reused by others; such information is often missing in papers, or even not published.

So, the idea was to perform a sort of crowdsourcing of information; thus, bottom up (rather than top down, as in a SLR). Our goal is to help the community grow and share existent agent-based technology. This is advantageous both for those contributing to the repository who will have the opportunity to increase the visibility of their work, and for its end users who will find existent works in a simpler way. This initiative may be seen as orthogonal to other top down reviews, like for example [43] that surveyed the literature to evaluate the practical application impact of Multiagent Systems and Technologies (MAS&T), or for example to the platform AI4europe[5].

The paper is organised as follow: Sect. 2 describes the process we followed to set up the call of the initiative, Sect. 3 reports the submissions we collected till the 20th of February 2023, Sect. 4 presents some considerations and lesson learned, and Sect. 5 concludes.

2   Selection Process

Before reporting the results and discussing them, we linger on the process we followed to set up the repository. Specifically, the main categories we used to classify the contributions, and which kind of questions we asked, and to whom.

The aim of the repository is dual:

1. To offer a collection of MASs to be used as testbed for Verification and Validation (V&V) activities.
2. To offer an overview of available MAS development frameworks, libraries and tools available to the community, to support the study of the state of the art and at the same time offering a simple way to retrieve the code/source code of the identified artefacts, so that to be able to concretely use them for extension, adoption or comparison.

So, the foreseen contributions cover a large variety of types, and some classification was needed both to collect them, and to organise them in the repository. We decided to distinguish three main types of contributions: i) MASs ii) Frameworks and iii) Extensions. Contributions that are labelled as "Framework" are

---

[5] https://www.ai4europe.eu/.

completely new agent development frameworks to create MASs (something with the same aim of Jade, Jason and so on), while contributions labelled as "Extensions" are libraries/add-ons for already existing frameworks that improve the latter's capabilities, without turning it into a completely new framework. From this viewpoint, the add-ons that can be found on the Jade webpage[6] are, in our classification, "Extensions", while JACK [34] is a new "Framework".

The collected entries have been further divided into 3 different categories, that are (citing the labels offered in the submission form):

- "Agent-based simulation (you developed a MAS, or a framework/library/ add-on to simulate physical and natural phenomena)": these entries pertain to the Multiagent Based Simulations (MABS) area, so MASs where many agents have been used to **Simulate a specific situation** (like systems frequently developed for example in Netlogo), or frameworks and extensions offering support in this area.
- "Agent-oriented software engineering (you developed a MAS that is the "real" system, for example for implementing decision support systems/ solving industrial problems/implementing smart systems, or a framework/library/ add-on to develop such real MASs)": the MASs in this category are **Systems exploiting the MAS paradigm** to solve a specific task (often developed for example in Jade or JaCaMo), or frameworks and extensions offering some SE related activity in this area.
- "Other": other entries that do not specifically fall in the two previous categories (and in this case, we let the submitter to insert a description).

The category is chosen by the author creating the entry, as all the other information. However, after the first round of call, we realised that some submissions were borderline between the two macro categories or have been labelled with "Other", so we plan to add a further category (as reported below, it could be "V&V tools for MASs") and to explain better how to classify, with respect to the adopted classification, a product to be inserted in the repository.

In the following, we only report the most relevant questions asked to the submitters: for a complete understanding, readers can refer to the website containing the results of our call[7], and the form to submit a new contribution.

For each entry – which can be a MAS, a framework, or an extension – we asked where to find its repository and whether previous repositories exist: the second question is important to better track the history of the entry. Other than that, we also asked for main publications (whether available) where the entry had been firstly introduced.

Then, we asked for additional details on its development: for instance, if any software engineering approach was followed.

Last, but not least, we asked about its being tested. This aspect is important to understand the maturity of the entry. Specifically, we were interested in knowing whether some specific approach had been followed to test the entry, if

---

[6] https://jade.tilab.com/download/add-ons/.

[7] https://mas-unige.github.io/fantastic_mass/.

the test suites were available too, and if a bug/issue tracker/list was available too (and where to find them).

Moreover, only for MASs and extensions, we asked additional questions about its corresponding framework, such as where the extended framework can be found, which version has been considered, and so on.

The second aspect of interest in the selection process is to whom we asked the questions. To be as fair as possible, and at the same time, as general as possible, we submitted a call on the most influential mailing lists in the agent community (e.g., agents@cs.umbc.edu, and so on).

The outcome of our call for frameworks, MASs, and extensions is a publicly available repository: https://mas-unige.github.io/fantastic_mass/. The repository contains relevant information such as: links to the resources, links to scientific articles, and general information about the development of the resource.

3   Results

In this section, we report the results of our call. In detail, we received 33 submissions, classified as follows:

- 4 implementations (MASs),
- 21 frameworks,
- 8 existing framework extensions.

3.1   MASs

Here, we report the MASs that have been gathered in our call. In total, 4 MASs have been reported; the first two are in the AOSE area, while the others are in the MABS area.

AdaptSchedule [27] is a MAS designed to assist adolescents, particularly adolescents with disabilities, transition towards independent management of their own schedules. It allows them to set up a daily schedule with all activities that must be performed and any constraints between those activities.

MAPS-HOLO [19] proposes a Holonic Multiagent System (HMAS) to assign and manage parking spaces in a smart parking system called Holonic Multiagent Parking System (MAPS-HOLO) developed through the JaCaMo Framework described in Sect. 3.2. Besides assigning parking space, the system will be able to handle run-time agents failures in different levels: driver agent, sector agent, and manager agent failure.

Deep Q-Learning agents for traffic signal control [57] presents a Reinforcement Learning approach to traffic lights control, coupled with a microscopic agent-based simulator (Simulation of Urban MObility - SUMO) providing a synthetic but realistic environment in which the exploration of the outcome of potential regulation actions can be carried out.

The Affective Agents [6,31] project aims at modeling interactions between people considering their *affective state* (representing their attitude towards other people wearing or not a mask, if they are indoor or outdoor, considering their age and gender and their mood expressed as a mix of fear of the contagious of covid19 and "internal and external social distance"). The combination of these parameters makes the subject to adopt a different "hall space" (that is, the distance from another person that a subject consider safe for him). The data guiding these simulations implemented in Netlogo (3 different models are currently offered) have been collected in the field thanks to two experiments with human subjects.

3.2 Frameworks

We report all the frameworks that have been collected in our call. We split them into four categories: the classification we use in the sequel is not the same we used to guide the selection process. Specifically, in the selection process, we asked the community to classify each entry w.r.t. three possible keywords: "Agent-Oriented Software Engineering", "Agent-Based Simulation", and "Other". However, when reporting the obtained results, another keyword emerged, that is "Verification of MAS". Thus, in the following, we reported the collected frameworks also in terms of this additional label.

Amongst the gathered frameworks, 14 works are in the agent-based software engineering area, 3 are in the verification area, 2 in the agent-based modeling and simulation area, and 2 in another area. Furthermore, considering the supported agent architectures [17], we may find 6 contributions adopting the BDI one, while the others do not follow any specific agent architecture.

Both well-established and newly born frameworks have been reported. Some of them are based upon implemented Domain Specific Languages, DSL.

Agent-Oriented Software Engineering. AgentScript   Cross-Compiler (ASC2) [47] is a MAS framework mainly for agents created with the AgentScript agent programming language[8]. The language of ASC2 is based on Jason [15]. The novelty of this framework is in relying on the Actor model, instantiating each intentional agent as an autonomous micro-system run by actors. ASC2 works as a cross-compiler that translates the high level language of AgentScript into lower level executable languages, such as Scala. Possible interactions between the agent-based programming framework ASC2 and various testing approaches (unit/agent testing, integration/system testing, continuous integration) have been extensively evaluated in [46].

ASTRA [21, 26] stands for AgentSpeak(TR) Agents and is an Agent-Oriented Programming Language combining AgentSpeak(L) [50] and Teleo Reactive programming [44]. ASTRA is designed to be easy to learn and familiar to developers who are experienced in using mainstream Object-Oriented Programming Languages.

---

[8] https://github.com/mostafamohajeri/scriptcc-translator.

DALI [22] is a meta interpreter built on top of Sicstus Prolog[9]. DALI is an Active Logic Programming language, designed for executable specification of logical agents, without committing to any specific agent architecture. DALI allows the programmer to define one or more agents, interacting among themselves, with an external environment, or with a user.

JaCaMo [13,14] is composed of three technologies, Jason, CArtAgO [51], and Moise [35], each representing a different abstraction level. Jason is used for programming the agent level, CArtAgO is responsible for the environment level, and Moise for the organisation level. JaCaMo integrates these three technologies by defining a semantic link among concepts in different levels of abstraction (agent, environment, and organisation). The end result is the JaCaMo MAS development platform. It provides high-level first-class support for developing agents, environments, and organisations, allowing the development of more complex MASs.

Jade [8,9] is an open source platform for the development of agent based applications. Besides the agent abstraction, it also provides: task execution and composition model, peer-to-peer agent communication based on asynchronous message passing, and a yellow page service that supports the publish and subscribe discovery mechanism. JADE-based systems can be distributed across machines with different operational systems, and has been used by many languages (e.g., Jason and JaCaMo) as a distribution infrastructure.

Jadescript [10,11] is a recent AOP language designed to develop Jade agents. It provides a set of agent-oriented linguistic constructs and related abstractions, namely agents, (agent) behaviours, and (communication) ontologies. Agents written in Jadescript are executed in JADE platforms, and they interact via asynchronous messaging. Therefore, Jadescript adopts an event-driven programming style.

Python Agent DEvelopment (PADE) framework [41] is an open source platform implemented in Python language and conceived for the implementation of MASs on power systems. PADE is compliant with specifications of the Foundation for Intelligent Physical Agents (FIPA) and eases the development of solutions to power systems based on MAS.

Another framework similar to PADE is Python Intelligent Agent Framework (PIAF)[10], which has not been already published.

BSPL [52,55] stands for the Blindingly Simple Protocol Language and is an information-based protocol language. In BSPL, it is possible to describe the communication protocols as well as the corresponding agents' enactment of the latter.

Deserv [53,56] is a protocol-based programming model for decentralized applications that is suited to the cloud. Specifically, Deserv demonstrates how to leverage function-as-a-service (FaaS), a popular serverless programming model, to implement agents.

---

[9] https://sicstus.sics.se/.
[10] https://gitlab.com/ornythorinque/piaf.

Hercule [54] an approach for declaratively specifying blockchain applications in a manner that reflects business contracts. Hercule represents a contract via regulatory norms that capture the involved parties' expectations of one another. It computes the states of norms (hence, of contracts) from events in the blockchain.

JS-son [36] is a lean JavaScript library prototype for implementing reasoning-loop agents. The library focuses on core agent programming concepts and refrains from imposing further restrictions on the programming approach.

SMASTA+ [7] is a Scala implementation of the Extended Multi-agents Situated Task Allocation.

StreamB [29] is a Domain Specific Language (DSL) for processing data streams in abstract environments. With StreamB it is possible to guide the translation from low-level information (e.g. sensors) to high-level concepts (e.g. beliefs). Thanks to its declarative nature, StreamB is much more intuitive and helps the user to create abstract environments, by reducing the amount of actual code to be produced; since the mapping process is automatically synthesised by StreamB. In more detail, StreamB is built upon the notion of Stream Processing, and allows the user for a flexible yet straightforward way to map low-level environment data, to high-level agent beliefs.

Verification of MAS. EVE (Equilibrium Verification Environment) [32,33] is a formal verification tool for the automated analysis of temporal equilibrium properties of concurrent and multiagent systems represented as multi-player games. Systems are modeled using the Simple Reactive Module Language (SRML) as a collection of independent system components (players/agents in a game), which are assumed to have goals expressed using Linear Temporal Logic (LTL) formulae. In particular, EVE checks for the existence of Nash equilibria in such systems and can be used to do rational synthesis and verification automatically.

The MCAPL [23,24] (Model-checking Agent Programming Languages) framework is a suite of tools for building interpreters for agent programming languages and verifying the correctness of programs running in these interpreters using the model checking technique. It consists of the Agent Infrastructure Layer (AIL) toolkit for building interpreters for rational agent programming languages (BDI languages) and the Agent JavaPathFinder (AJPF) model checker [25].

STV [37,38] is a collection of algorithms for verifying Alternating-time Temporal Logic (ATL) properties on models with perfect (resp. imperfect) information, and exploiting imperfect recall strategies.

Agent-Based Simulation. CellNet Network [45] is an open-source Java-based software developed as a research resource to study MAS, evolutionary game theory and cellular automata simulations. CellNet works in two modes: (i) using a graphical user interface (GUI) for doing micro-simulations or (ii) using a batch mode for doing macro-simulations.

Swarm-Like Protocol in Python (SLAPP) [12,40] comes from Swarm [42]. SLAPP is only one of the possible flavors of Swarm; it is a simplified flavor, because it is written in Python.

Others. MatchU [30] is a web-based platform that offers an interactive framework to find how to form mutually-beneficial relationships, decide how to distribute resources, or resolve conflicts through a suite of matching algorithms rooted in economics and artificial intelligence.

MAPF[11] is a collection of techniques and tools to perform Multi-Agent Path Finding (MAPF). Such repository has been submitted to our call, but no specific framework has been pointed out. Thus, the analysis we perform on the other tools cannot be performed on this repository as well. Nonetheless, even though in the following we do not analyse MAPF with the rest of the tools, we recognise its importance and legitimacy in being listed with the other MAS frameworks in our repository.

3.3   Extensions

Here, we report the frameworks' extensions that have been gathered in our call. In total, 8 different extensions have been reported. Of these, 4 are extensions of JaCaMo, 1 is an extension of Cartago, 1 is an extension for Jade, 1 is an extension of SUMO, and 1 is an extension of MCAPL. Since both JaCaMo and MCAPL are based on the BDI architecture, 4 out of 5 extensions can be classified as BDI projects.

2COMM [4] is an extension of the JaCaMo framework for defining social relationships, represented as social commitments, among parties, conceived as autonomous agents.

JaCaMo+Accountability [5] proposes an extension of JaCaMo with the notion of accountability, grounded on responsibility, that supports the development of robust distributed systems.

JaCaMo+Exceptions [3] is an extension of Moise, the organizational model and infrastructure adopted in JaCaMo, that explicitly encompasses the notion of exception as a first-class element in the design of a multiagent organization.

Multi-Agent MicroServices (MAMS) [20] is an architectural style for integrating MASs into Microservices architectures. It extends Cartago and achieves this by modeling agents as entities that have hypermedia bodies that are exposed as REST APIs. This provides a standard REST API that plain-old microservices can exploit.

ROS-A [18] an interface for integrating BDI-based agents into robotic systems developed using ROS [49]. The authors use the Gwendolen language to program the BDI agents and to make use of the AJPF model checker in order to verify properties related to the decision-making in the agent programs.

---

[11] http://mapf.info.

SUMO-RL [1] provides a simple interface to instantiate Reinforcement Learning environments with SUMO¹² for Traffic Signal Control. SUMO-RL provides a simple interface to instantiate Reinforcement Learning environments with SUMO for Traffic Signal Control. Goals of this repository: (i) provide a simple interface to work with Reinforcement Learning for Traffic Signal Control using SUMO (ii); support Multiagent RL; (iii) compatibility with gym.Env and popular RL libraries such as stable-baselines3 and RLlib; (iv) easy customisation: state and reward definitions are easily modifiable.

LEARN [16] is an extension of the standard JADE platform, enhancing it with peer-to-peer (p2p) capabilities. The general idea of LEARN is offer a set of specific agents (JADE agents to be created on a standard JADE platform) able to create a logic p2p layer over a set of JADE platforms, so that to make them able to dynamically discover other platforms without knowing their IP (so in a real p2p fashion) and then invoking services over the p2p layer.

RV4JaCa [28] is an extension of JaCaMo which allows performing runtime verification of agents' messages. It represents the agent-based istantiation of RML (Runtime Monitoring Language) [2], a simple but powerful Domain Specific Language (DSL) for runtime verification.

4   Discussion and Lessons Learned

In this section, we analyse and discuss the results obtained in our call, focusing on the aspects strictly related to the software engineering area: since the collected MASs are few (which is already a reason for reflection), we limit this analysis to the framework and extension entries. With this analysis we pay attention not on the functionalities of the proposed frameworks and extensions (we will refer to them with the term "tool" in the remaining of the section), but on the aspects concerning their re-usability as subjects for future research.

Table 1 reports the results of our analysis for 27 out of 29 collected tools. In detail, each tool is analysed w.r.t. six different features:

– *Previous Versions*: This feature concerns the presence of previous versions and/or commits on the tool's repository. This aspect is important to better understand and study the tool's evolution, like for example when searching for architectural smells, as done in [48].
– *Documentation*: This feature is about the availability of some form of documentation supporting the tool. This is of paramount importance to increase the tool's usability. Furthermore, a good documentation can be exploited for example for automatic oracles extraction, or reverse engineering tasks.
– *Issue and Bug tracker*: This feature concerns the presence in the tool's repository of well-documented issues and bugs, possibly with information regarding if, and how, they were fixed. This kind of information is used in SE to validate, for example, tools for automatic bugs identification.

---

¹² https://github.com/eclipse/sumo.

Table 1. Summary of the submissions (Frameworks and Extensions), excluding MAPF and MatchU, that cannot be compared based on these features.

Subject	Ref.	Versioning	Document.	Issue-tracker	Tested	Test Suites	Linked	Source
ASC2	[47]	✓	✓	✗	✓	(✓)	✓	✓
ASTRA	[21,26]	✓	✓	✓	✓	✓	✓	✓
BSPL	[52,55]	✓	✓	✗	✓	✓	✓	✓
CellNet	[45]	✓	✓	✗	✓	✗	✓	✓
DALI	[22]	✓	✓	✓	✓	(✓)	✓	✓
Deserv	[53,56]	✓	✓	✗	✓	(✓)	✓	✓
EVE	[32,33]	✓	✓	✗	✓	✗	✓	✓
Hercule	[54]	✓	✓	✗	✓	✓	✓	✓
JaCaMo	[13,14]	✓	✓	✓	✓	✗	✓	✓
Jade	[8,9]	✓	✓	(✓)	(✓)	✓	✓	✓
Jadescript	[10,11]	✓	✓	✓	✓	✓	✗	✓
JS-son	[36]	✓	✓	(✓)	✓	✓	✓	✓
MCAPL	[23,24]	✓	✓	✗	✓	✓	✓	✓
PADE	[41]	✓	✓	✗	✗	✗	✓	✓
Piaf		✓	✓	✓	✓	✓	✗	✓
SLAPP	[12,40]	✓	✓	✓	✓	✗	✓	✓
SMASTA+	[7]	✓	✓	✗	✓	✗	✓	✓
StreamB	[29]	✓	✓	✗	✓	✗	✓	✓
STV	[37,38]	✓	✓	✗	✓	✗	✗	✓
2COMM	[4]	✓	✗	✗	✓	✗	✓	✓
JaCaMo+Acc	[5]	✓	✓	✗	✓	✗	✗	✓
JaCaMo+Exc	[3]	✓	✓	✗	✓	✗	✓	✓
LEARN	[16]	✗	✓	✗	✓	✗	✗	✓
MAMS	[20]	✓	✓	✓	✓	✗	✗	✓
ROS-A	[18]	✓	✓	✗	✓	✗	✓	✓
RV4JaCa	[28]	✓	✓	✗	✓	✗	✓	✓
SUMO-RL	[1]	✓	✓	✓	✓	✓	✗	✓
Total:	27	26 ✓ 0(✓) 1 ✗	26 ✓ 0(✓) 1 ✗	8 ✓ 2(✓) 17 ✗	25 ✓ 1(✓) 1 ✗	8 ✓ 3(✓) 16 ✗	20 ✓ 0(✓) 7 ✗	27 ✓ 0(✓) 0 ✗

- *Tested*: This feature denotes whether the tool has been tested by the developers. This step may consist in systematic, or manual, tests. Note that, as clarified in the next point, being tested does not imply the tests are available to the community (through a test suite).
- *Test Suites*: This feature is about the availability of tests, or at least information regarding inputs and expected outputs, so that tests can be re-created. Test suites that can be downloaded along with the tool can be used, for example, for regression testing, or to validate tools for automatic test generation.
- *Original Link*: In this column we report if a link to the code (source or compiled, stored on a public repository on online so that it is downloadable) was already present in the principal papers (as indicated by the author who created the entry in our repository) or not.
- *Source Code*: All the entries collected on our repository link to a downloadable version of the tool, but the availability of the source code is optional. The source code of the tool, with an open licence to reuse it, makes it simply to be reused by other researchers both for extending, both for other activities, like for example static analysis

For each feature, we report ✓ (resp., ✗) when a tool offers (resp., does not offer) such a feature. Moreover, in case the feature is partially supported, the symbol (✓) is used. For instance, considering the documentation feature, the symbol ($\checkmark$) is reported if the tool offers some documentation, but, the latter is minimal. The last row of the table reports the count of $\checkmark$, ($\checkmark$) and $\times$, so that the reader can simply have an overview of the results. Please note that 1) Table 1 is a screenshot of the state of the shared repositories at the end of June 2023 (so, information may become out of date if they are updated), and 2) that the information reported is both coming from the data directly inserted by the submitters and from a check done by the authors for what regards above all the *Test Suites*: anyway, we contacted again who participated to check this table before publishing it. It is important to clarify that the authors did not tried to install the tools, they only read the documentation and had a look inside the repositories, to better understand for example if a form of test suites existed or not, so that to provide in Table 1 an homogeneous analysis of the collected data.

Also note that, in Table 1, MatchU [30] is not reported since it is a web service: none of the previously listed features is offered. For a different reason, as mentioned previously, also MAPF is not reported in Table 1; indeed, MAPF is not a framework, but a collection of frameworks. Thus, a comparison w.r.t. the features of interest would have been unnatural.

Considering the column *Source*, clearly there is a general positive propensity to share the source code, which makes these tools usable for further extensions or analysis. Anyway, as shown in column *Linked*, the source code was not always originally shared with the paper presenting the work (even in important venues like AAMAS or international journals), but was made public in a second moment[13]. This shows that the sharing of the tool itself with the paper is not yet so widely adopted by the community. Nevertheless, the shared software is usually well documented.

An interesting result from the analysis is that quite all the shared tools (all but one) present a form of versioning, that allow users to access previous versions and commits: this may be of interest for those working with software evolution.

A clear problematic aspect is the one related to the management of bugs and issues, and the usage and sharing of test suites: only eleven tools reported some information related to the availability of a test suite or something similar, and only ten tools (interestingly, not all the same reporting information regarding test suites) refer to a bug/issue tracker (or something related to this aspect). This is anyway not surprising: the management of bugs and issues is a complex task, usually requesting the support of specific tools, some dedicated resource (tester) or at least time. If the project is not yet very large, does not have a large community interested in it and supporting it, or is primarily academic, the burden requested for managing such aspects may be not manageable. Unfortunately, not having a list of known bugs/issues, associated with a specific version of a tool, makes the SE operations like automatic test generation or self healing hard to be performed (in the sense that, if we miss the bugs history it is impossible to verify if the new technique is able to identify known bugs, which would be the ground truth), or not really effective.

---

[13] To answer the call for creating the "Fantastic MASs" repository, or simply in a different moment from the publication.

Furthermore, the reality gap between frameworks, and their possible real-world uses, can also be observed in the answers we obtained. Specifically, for each framework, we asked about existing real-world uses. By doing so, we observed that the majority of frameworks do not have (to the best of their creators' knowledge) any real-world application; indeed, the majority of the collected frameworks are mainly used in academia. Nonetheless, some frameworks reported existing real-world applications, such as Jade, ASC2 [47], that has been used by the TNO Netherlands Asser Institute[14], or DALI [22], that has been used by a company[15].

Last but not least, we only received 4 submissions (on a total of 33) regarding real MASs, which were unexpectedly few with respect to our expectations: surely it could be only a case, and maybe considering a longer time to collect submissions this proportion could change, or we could have not be effective in reaching all the community, but the initial feeling is that the community prefers sharing frameworks and extensions instead of MASs. This could be due to the fact that often a MAS itself (or a system) is seen not as a research result, but more as a way to exemplify some new tool/approach etc. Even if this thought may have some true aspects (considering the academic area and our community, where an important focus is given to new languages, models, architectures and so on, so, some more theoretic results), this mindset leads to not giving sometime the correct importance to the produced software itself (and this is related to the often missing link to the code too, discussed previously). Another motivation could be related to the "foreseen time to live" of a MAS: if a framework/extension could be ideally born after many months/years of research and would remain the subject of future research, so involving many people in a long lifespan, the development of a MAS may be a work that is self contained (it is developed when it is needed, to solve a specific problem, and then it is done), and its developers may also be no longer available in future time. For this reason, sharing it (and consequently maintaining it a little) may be itself a demanding task, not perceived providing a valuable "return of investment". Anyway, we hope that this initiative supports a change in the mindset, since as said in the introduction, the unavailability of real MASs prevent from performing unbiased activities of V&V.

5   Conclusions and Future Work

In this paper, we reported the results obtained by asking the agent community about existing frameworks for developing MASs, their extensions (libraries, add ons and similar), and MASs, with the aim of creating a public repository of them to be shared, similarly to some initiatives from the Software Engineering community (for example the "Self-Adaptive Systems Artifacts and Model Problems" repository[16]): the overall aim of our initiative is to promote the shar-

---

[14] https://www.asser.nl.

[15] SPEE Srl (https://www.spee.it).

[16] https://www.hpi.uni-potsdam.de/giese/public/selfadapt/exemplars/.

ing of research results and to support the SE activities needing MAS models, frameworks and extensions to be performed. We presented our selection process, and we briefly summarised each collected work till now. The outcome of this work is a publicly available repository, where all the collected works can be easily accessed. Other than serving as a common place for retrieving agent-based frameworks, their extensions, and MAS models, the repository serves as a milestone to keep track of relevant engineering information. This last aspect is going to be important to maintain a historical memory on agent technologies, and their engineering.

Future work includes maintaining and improving the "Fantastic MASs" repository: for example, as emerged by the analysis of the submissions, it could be better to add a new category regarding V&V. During the discussion at EMAS23[17], where these first results were presented, some other interesting suggestions to improve the collected data were: 1) to collect scenarios as well, so that to provide common complex scenarios to be implemented to show (and compare) different approaches/languages/tools, 2) to let the submitters classify their MAS models for example as "Little/Medium/Large", 3) to promote the sharing of open source code following some already existing guidelines (an example may be https://opensource.guide/). All these suggestions are interesting and could help in improving the collected data, and we will carefully evaluate how to integrate them, if possible, in our web form and website.

Also, we plan to add an interface for querying and ordering the results, to facilitate the usage of the repository.

Moreover, to keep track of new developments, and existing ones that did not yet participate in our call, we are going to let researchers propose new entries in the repository, keeping the form to submit new entries always available on the website of the repository. We also hope that sharing these first results with the community will help in getting new submissions. This will allow the repository to remain updated, and to properly resemble the current agent-based technology ecosystem.

As a final activity, the already mentioned European AI-on-demand (AIOD) platform, https://www.ai4europe.eu/, seeks to bring together the AI community and act as facilitator of knowledge transfer from research to multiple business domains. Making the results of the "Fantastic MAS" initiative available on that platform, or just linked from there, would make them more visible and more useful, also outside the Engineering MAS community.

Acknowledgements. We thank Olivier Boissier, Rafael Heitor Bordini, Jomi Fred Hübner, and Giuseppe Vizzari for the precious feedback they provided while designing the "Fantastic MAS" submission form, and all the contributors.

---

[17] https://emas.in.tu-clausthal.de/2023/.

References

1. Alegre, L.N.: SUMO-RL (2019). https://github.com/LucasAlegre/sumo-rl
2. Ancona, D., Franceschini, L., Ferrando, A., Mascardi, V.: RML: theory and practice of a domain specific language for runtime verification. Sci. Comput. Program. **205**, 102610 (2021). https://doi.org/10.1016/j.scico.2021.102610
3. Baldoni, M., Baroglio, C., Boissier, O., Micalizio, R., Tedeschi, S.: Distributing responsibilities for exception handling in JaCaMo. In: Dignum, F., Lomuscio, A., Endriss, U., Nowé, A. (eds.) AAMAS '21: 20th International Conference on Autonomous Agents and Multiagent Systems, Virtual Event, United Kingdom, 3–7 May 2021, pp. 1752–1754. ACM (2021). https://doi.org/10.5555/3463952.3464226, https://www.ifaamas.org/Proceedings/aamas2021/pdfs/p1752.pdf
4. Baldoni, M., Baroglio, C., Capuzzimati, F., Micalizio, R.: Commitment-based agent interaction in JaCaMo+. Fundam. Inform. **159**(1-2), 1–33 (2018). https://doi.org/10.3233/FI-2018-1656
5. Baldoni, M., Baroglio, C., Micalizio, R., Tedeschi, S.: Robustness based on accountability in multiagent organizations. In: Dignum, F., Lomuscio, A., Endriss, U., Nowé, A. (eds.) AAMAS '21: 20th International Conference on Autonomous Agents and Multiagent Systems, Virtual Event, United Kingdom, 3–7 May 2021, pp. 142–150. ACM (2021). https://doi.org/10.5555/3463952.3463975, https://www.ifaamas.org/Proceedings/aamas2021/pdfs/p142.pdf
6. Bandini, S., Briola, D., Dennunzio, A., Gasparini, F., Giltri, M., Vizzari, G.: Integrating the implications of distance-based affective states in cellular automata pedestrian simulation. In: Chopard, B., Bandini, S., Dennunzio, A., Arabi Haddad, M. (eds.) Cellular Automata. ACRI 2022. LNCS, vol. 13402, pp. 259–270. Springer, Cham (2022). https://doi.org/10.1007/978-3-031-14926-9_23
7. Beauprez, E., Caron, A., Morge, M., Routier, J.: A multi-agent negotiation strategy for reducing the flowtime. In: Rocha, A.P., Steels, L., van den Herik, H.J. (eds.) Proceedings of the 13th International Conference on Agents and Artificial Intelligence, ICAART 2021, vol. 1, Online Streaming, 4–6 February 2021, pp. 58–68. SCITEPRESS (2021). https://doi.org/10.5220/0010226000580068
8. Bellifemine, F., Caire, G., Poggi, A., Rimassa, G.: JADE: a software framework for developing multi-agent applications. lessons learned. Inf. Softw. Technol. **50**(1–2), 10–21 (2008). https://doi.org/10.1016/j.infsof.2007.10.008
9. Bellifemine, F., Poggi, A., Rimassa, G.: Developing multi-agent systems with a FIPA-compliant agent framework. Softw. Pract. Exp. **31**(2), 103–128 (2001). https://doi.org/10.1002/1097-024X(200102)31:2⟨103::AID-SPE358⟩3.0.CO;2-O
10. Bergenti, F., Caire, G., Monica, S., Poggi, A.: The first twenty years of agent-based software development with JADE. Auton. Agents Multi Agent Syst. **34**(2), 36 (2020). https://doi.org/10.1007/s10458-020-09460-z
11. Bergenti, F., Monica, S., Petrosino, G.: A scripting language for practical agent-oriented programming. In: Koster, J.D., Bergenti, F., Franco, J. (eds.) Proceedings of the 8th ACM SIGPLAN International Workshop on Programming Based on Actors, Agents, and Decentralized Control, AGERE!@SPLASH 2018, Boston, MA, USA, 5 November 2018, pp. 62–71. ACM (2018). https://doi.org/10.1145/3281366.3281367
12. Boero, R., Morini, M., Sonnessa, M., Terna, P., Terna, P.: Introducing the swarm-like agent protocol in python (SLAPP). Agent-based Model. Econ. Theor. Appl. 31–54 (2015). https://doi.org/10.1057/9781137339812_3

13. Boissier, O., Bordini, R., Hubner, J., Ricci, A.: Multi-Agent Oriented Programming: Programming Multi-Agent Systems Using JaCaMo. Intelligent Robotics and Autonomous Agents series, MIT Press, Cambridge (2020). https://books.google.com.br/books?id=GM_tDwAAQBAJ

14. Boissier, O., Bordini, R.H., Hübner, J.F., Ricci, A., Santi, A.: Multi-agent oriented programming with JaCaMo. Sci. Comput. Program. **78**(6), 747–761 (2013). https://doi.org/10.1016/j.scico.2011.10.004

15. Bordini, R.H., Wooldridge, M., Hübner, J.F.: Programming Multi-Agent Systems in AgentSpeak Using Jason. John Wiley & Sons, Hoboken (2007)

16. Briola, D., Micucci, D., Mariani, L.: A platform for P2P agent-based collaborative applications. Softw. Pract. Exp. **49**(3), 549–558 (2019). https://doi.org/10.1002/spe.2657

17. Cardoso, R.C., Ferrando, A.: A review of agent-based programming for multi-agent systems. Comput. **10**(2), 16 (2021). https://doi.org/10.3390/computers10020016

18. Cardoso, R.C., Ferrando, A., Dennis, L.A., Fisher, M.: An interface for programming verifiable autonomous agents in ROS. In: Bassiliades, N., Chalkiadakis, G., de Jonge, D. (eds.) EUMAS/AT -2020. LNCS (LNAI), vol. 12520, pp. 191–205. Springer, Cham (2020). https://doi.org/10.1007/978-3-030-66412-1_13

19. de Castro, L., Borges, A.P., Alves, G.V., Grossa, C.P.: Developing a smart parking solution based on a holonic multiagent system using JaCaMo framework. In: Proceedings of the 12th Workshop-School on Agents, Environments, and Applications, Fortaleza-CE, Brazil (2018)

20. Collier, R.W., O'Neill, E., Lillis, D., O'Hare, G.M.P.: MAMS: multi-agent microservices*. In: Amer-Yahia, S., et al. (eds.) Companion of The 2019 World Wide Web Conference, WWW 2019, San Francisco, CA, USA, 13–17 May 2019, pp. 655–662. ACM (2019). https://doi.org/10.1145/3308560.3316509

21. Collier, R.W., Russell, S., Lillis, D.: Reflecting on agent programming with AgentSpeak(L). In: Chen, Q., Torroni, P., Villata, S., Hsu, J., Omicini, A. (eds.) PRIMA 2015. LNCS (LNAI), vol. 9387, pp. 351–366. Springer, Cham (2015). https://doi.org/10.1007/978-3-319-25524-8_22

22. Costantini, S., Tocchio, A., Verticchio, A.: Communication and trust in the DALI logic programming agent-oriented language. Intelligenza Artificiale **2**(1), 39–46 (2005)

23. Dennis, L.A.: The MCAPL framework including the agent infrastructure layer an agent java pathfinder. J. Open Source Softw. **3**(24), 617 (2018). https://doi.org/10.21105/joss.00617

24. Dennis, L.A., Fisher, M., Lincoln, N., Lisitsa, A., Veres, S.M.: Practical verification of decision-making in agent-based autonomous systems. Autom. Softw. Eng. **23**(3), 305–359 (2016). https://doi.org/10.1007/s10515-014-0168-9

25. Dennis, L.A., Fisher, M., Webster, M.P., Bordini, R.H.: Model checking agent programming languages. Autom. Softw. Eng. **19**(1), 5–63 (2012). https://doi.org/10.1007/s10515-011-0088-x

26. Dhaon, A., Collier, R.W.: Multiple inheritance in agentspeak(l)-style programming languages. In: Boix, E.G., Haller, P., Ricci, A., Varela, C.A. (eds.) Proceedings of the 4th International Workshop on Programming based on Actors Agents & Decentralized Control, AGERE! 2014, Portland, OR, USA, 20 October 2014, pp. 109–120. ACM (2014). https://doi.org/10.1145/2687357.2687362

27. Durfee, E.H., Garrett, L.H., Johnson, A.: Promoting independence with a schedule management assistant that anticipates disruptions. J. Heal. Inform. Res. **4**(1), 19–49 (2020). https://doi.org/10.1007/s41666-019-00060-5

28. Engelmann, D.C., Ferrando, A., Panisson, A.R., Ancona, D., Bordini, R.H., Mascardi, V.: RV4JaCa - runtime verification for multi-agent systems. In: Cardoso, R.C., Ferrando, A., Papacchini, F., Askarpour, M., Dennis, L.A. (eds.) Proceedings of the Second Workshop on Agents and Robots for reliable Engineered Autonomy, AREA@IJCAI-ECAI 2022, Vienna, Austria, 24th July 2022. EPTCS, vol. 362, pp. 23–36 (2022). https://doi.org/10.4204/EPTCS.362.5

29. Ferrando, A., Papacchini, F.: StreamB: a declarative language for automatically processing data streams in abstract environments for agent platforms. In: Alechina, N., Baldoni, M., Logan, B. (eds.) Engineering Multi-Agent Systems. EMAS 2021. LNCS, vol. 13190, pp. 114–136. Springer, Cham (2021). https://doi.org/10.1007/978-3-030-97457-2_7

30. Ferris, J., Hosseini, H.: MatchU: an interactive matching platform. In: The Thirty-Fourth AAAI Conference on Artificial Intelligence, AAAI 2020, The Thirty-Second Innovative Applications of Artificial Intelligence Conference, IAAI 2020, The Tenth AAAI Symposium on Educational Advances in Artificial Intelligence, EAAI 2020, New York, NY, USA, 7–12 February 2020, pp. 13606–13607. AAAI Press (2020). https://ojs.aaai.org/index.php/AAAI/article/view/7090

31. Giltri, M., Bandini, S., Gasparini, F., Briola, D.: Furthering an agent-based modeling approach introducing affective states based on real data. In: Bazzan, A.L.C., Dusparic, I., Lujak, M., Vizzari, G. (eds.) Twelfth International Workshop on Agents in Traffic and Transportation Co-located with the the 31st International Joint Conference on Artificial Intelligence and the 25th European Conference on Artificial Intelligence (IJCAI-ECAI 2022), Vienna, Austria, 25 July 2022. CEUR Workshop Proceedings, vol. 3173, pp. 124–136. CEUR-WS.org (2022). http://ceur-ws.org/Vol-3173/9.pdf

32. Gutierrez, J., Najib, M., Perelli, G., Wooldridge, M.: EVE: a tool for temporal equilibrium analysis. In: Lahiri, S.K., Wang, C. (eds.) ATVA 2018. LNCS, vol. 11138, pp. 551–557. Springer, Cham (2018). https://doi.org/10.1007/978-3-030-01090-4_35

33. Gutierrez, J., Najib, M., Perelli, G., Wooldridge, M.J.: Automated temporal equilibrium analysis: Verification and synthesis of multi-player games. Artif. Intell. **287**, 103353 (2020). https://doi.org/10.1016/j.artint.2020.103353

34. Howden, N., Rönnquist, R., Hodgson, A., Lucas, A.: Jack intelligent agents - summary of an agent infrastructure. In: Proceedings of the 5th ACM International Conference on Autonomous Agents (2001)

35. Hübner, J.F., Sichman, J.S., Boissier, O.: Developing organised multiagent systems using the moise+ model: programming issues at the system and agent levels. Int. J. Agent Oriented Softw. Eng. **1**(3/4), 370–395 (2007). https://doi.org/10.1504/IJAOSE.2007.016266

36. Kampik, T., Nieves, J.C.: JS-son - a lean, extensible JavaScript agent programming library. In: Dennis, L.A., Bordini, R.H., Lespérance, Y. (eds.) EMAS 2019. LNCS (LNAI), vol. 12058, pp. 215–234. Springer, Cham (2020). https://doi.org/10.1007/978-3-030-51417-4_11

37. Kurpiewski, D., Mikulski, L., Jamroga, W.: STV+AGR: towards verification of strategic ability using assume-guarantee reasoning. In: Aydogan, R., Criado, N., Lang, J., Sanchez-Anguix, V., Serramia, M. (eds.) PRIMA 2022: Principles and Practice of Multi-Agent Systems. PRIMA 2022. LNCS, vol. 13753, pp. 691–696. Springer, Cham (2022). https://doi.org/10.1007/978-3-031-21203-1_47

38. Kurpiewski, D., Pazderski, W., Jamroga, W., Kim, Y.: STV+reductions: towards practical verification of strategic ability using model reductions. In: Dignum, F.,

Lomuscio, A., Endriss, U., Nowé, A. (eds.) AAMAS '21: 20th International Conference on Autonomous Agents and Multiagent Systems, Virtual Event, United Kingdom, 3–7 May 2021, pp. 1770–1772. ACM (2021). https://doi.org/10.5555/3463952.3464232, https://www.ifaamas.org/Proceedings/aamas2021/pdfs/p1770.pdf

39. Mascardi, V., Weyns, D., Ricci, A.: Engineering multi-agent systems: state of affairs and the road ahead. ACM SIGSOFT Softw. Eng. Notes **44**(1), 18–28 (2019). https://doi.org/10.1145/3310013.3310035

40. Mazzoli, M., Morini, M., Terna, P.: Rethinking Macroeconomics with Endogenous Market Structure. Cambridge University Press, Cambridge (2019)

41. Melo, L.S., Sampaio, R.F., Leão, R.P.S., Barroso, G.C., Bezerra, J.R.: Python-based multi-agent platform for application on power grids. Int. Trans. Electr. Energy Syst. **29**(6), e12012 (2019)

42. Minar, N., Burkhart, R., Langton, C., Askenazi, M., et al.: The swarm simulation system: a toolkit for building multi-agent simulations. Santa Fe Institute Working Paper (1996)

43. Müller, J.P., Fischer, K.: Application Impact of Multi-agent Systems and Technologies: A Survey, pp. 27–53. Springer, Berlin, Heidelberg (2014). https://doi.org/10.1007/978-3-642-54432-3_3

44. Nilsson, N.J.: Teleo-reactive programs for agent control. J. Artif. Intell. Res. **1**, 139–158 (1994). https://doi.org/10.1613/jair.30

45. Ombuki, B.M., Burguillo, J.C.: Self-organizing coalitions for managing complexity. Genet. Program. Evolvable Mach. **21**(1–2), 263–264 (2020). https://doi.org/10.1007/s10710-019-09372-2

46. Parizi, M.M., Sileno, G., van Engers, T.M.: Seamless integration and testing for MAS engineering. In: Alechina, N., Baldoni, M., Logan, B. (eds.) Engineering Multi-Agent Systems. EMAS 2021. LNCS, vol. 13190, pp. 254–272. Springer, Cham (2021). https://doi.org/10.1007/978-3-030-97457-2_15

47. Parizi, M.M., Sileno, G., van Engers, T.M., Klous, S.: Run, agent, run! Architecture and benchmarking of actor-based agents. In: Castegren, E., Koster, J.D., Schmidt, T.C. (eds.) AGERE 2020: Proceedings of the 10th ACM SIGPLAN International Workshop on Programming Based on Actors, Agents, and Decentralized Control, Virtual Event, USA, 17 November 2020, pp. 11–20. ACM (2020). https://doi.org/10.1145/3427760.3428339

48. Pigazzini, I., Briola, D., Fontana, F.A.: Architectural technical debt of multi-agent systems development platforms. In: Calegari, R., Ciatto, G., Denti, E., Omicini, A., Sartor, G. (eds.) Proceedings of the 22nd Workshop From Objects to Agents, Bologna, Italy, 1–3 September 2021. CEUR Workshop Proceedings, vol. 2963, pp. 1–13. CEUR-WS.org (2021). http://ceur-ws.org/Vol-2963/paper13.pdf

49. Quigley, M., et al.: ROS: an open-source robot operating system. In: Workshop on Open Source Software at the International Conference on Robotics and Automation. IEEE, Japan (2009)

50. Rao, A.S.: AgentSpeak(L): BDI agents speak out in a logical computable language. In: Van de Velde, W., Perram, J.W. (eds.) MAAMAW 1996. LNCS, vol. 1038, pp. 42–55. Springer, Heidelberg (1996). https://doi.org/10.1007/BFb0031845

51. Ricci, A., Piunti, M., Viroli, M., Omicini, A.: Environment programming in CArtAgO. In: El Fallah Seghrouchni, A., Dix, J., Dastani, M., Bordini, R.H. (eds.) Multi-Agent Programming, pp. 259–288. Springer, Boston, MA (2009). https://doi.org/10.1007/978-0-387-89299-3_8

52. Christie V, S.H., Chopra, A.K., Singh, M.P.: Bungie: improving fault tolerance via extensible application-level protocols. Computer **54**(5), 44–53 (2021). https://doi.org/10.1109/MC.2021.3052147

53. Christie V, S.H., Chopra, A.K., Singh, M.P.: Deserv: decentralized serverless computing. In: Chang, C.K., et al. (eds.) 2021 IEEE International Conference on Web Services, ICWS 2021, Chicago, IL, USA, 5–10 September 2021, pp. 51–60. IEEE (2021). https://doi.org/10.1109/ICWS53863.2021.00020

54. Christie V, S.H., Chopra, A.K., Singh, M.P.: Hercule: representing and reasoning about norms as a foundation for declarative contracts over blockchain. IEEE Internet Comput. **25**(4), 67–75 (2021). https://doi.org/10.1109/MIC.2021.3080982

55. Christie V, S.H., Chopra, A.K., Singh, M.P.: Mandrake: multiagent systems as a basis for programming fault-tolerant decentralized applications. Auton. Agents Multi Agent Syst. **36**(1), 16 (2022). https://doi.org/10.1007/s10458-021-09540-8

56. Christie V, S.H., Smirnova, D., Chopra, A.K., Singh, M.P.: Protocols over things: a decentralized programming model for the internet of things. Computer **53**(12), 60–68 (2020). https://doi.org/10.1109/MC.2020.3023887

57. Vidali, A., Crociani, L., Vizzari, G., Bandini, S.: A deep reinforcement learning approach to adaptive traffic lights management. In: Bergenti, F., Monica, S. (eds.) Proceedings of the 20th Workshop From Objects to Agents, Parma, Italy, 26th–28th June 2019. CEUR Workshop Proceedings, vol. 2404, pp. 42–50. CEUR-WS.org (2019). http://ceur-ws.org/Vol-2404/paper07.pdf

The Entity-Operation Model for Practical Multi-entity Deployment

Andrei Olaru$^{(\boxtimes)}$(iD), Gabriel Nicolae, and Adina Magda Florea(iD)

Department of Computer Science and Engineering, University Politehnica of
Bucharest, 313 Splaiul Independentei, 060042 Bucharest, Romania
{andrei.olaru,adina.florea}@upb.ro, gabriel.nicolae2907@stud.acs.upb.ro

Abstract. In the world of multi-agent system (MAS) frameworks, developers are many times forced into a fixed and reduced array of abstractions, with limited options in expressive modeling of all the components of a MAS. For instance, in JADE, the most popular agent framework, developers are limited to using agents as sole abstraction for all elements of the MAS. These limitations hinder interoperability, the deployment of open, heterogeneous systems, and the use of agents in complex scenarios involving a great variety of elements such as physical devices, context managers, services, and communication infrastructures.

We introduce the *entity-operation model* for multi-agent systems, as an approach to integrate all elements in the MAS deployment as first-class entities in the MAS model, to support heterogeneity and flexibility in the implementation, and to achieve context-aware access control to the functionalities offered by entities.

We present a formalization of the model, together with mechanisms for authorizing operations and for routing operation calls in the MAS. We discuss the entity-operation model in relation to other existing MAS frameworks, and we give insight into implementation challenges which arose when integrating the model with the FLASH-MAS framework.

Keywords: Multi-agent systems · Multi-agent frameworks ·
Communication infrastructure interoperability

1 Introduction

Agents and multi-agent systems (MAS) are used in a great variety of domains, including cloud computing, networks security and routing, social networks, robotics, the Internet of Things (IoT), Ambient Assisted Living (AAL), smart cities, smart grids, and complex systems modeling and simulation [1,6,8].

This work was supported by a grant of the Ministry of Research, Innovation and Digitization, CNCS - UEFISCDI, project number PN-III-P1-1.1-TE-2021-1422, within PNCDI III. This work has been partially funded by UEFISCDI project Cornet (1/2018, PN-III-P3-3.6-H2020-2016-0120).

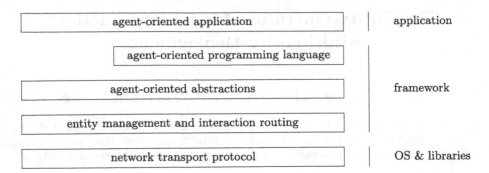

Fig. 1. A view on the layers existing in a MAS framework. Agent-oriented abstractions are entities accessible by the developer, such as agents, artifacts, and nodes.

A MAS framework is meant to save the developer from the task of implementing several functionalities such as inter-agent communication, resource discovery, agent mobility, internal agent event processing and internal agent organization, as well as deployment, control and monitoring of agents.

There are several frameworks which facilitate the design, modeling, and simulation or deployment of MAS [6,19]. Among them there are JADE, SPADE, JIAC, JACK, JaCaMo, PLACE, FLAME, MASON, Repast, of which some allow the deployment on distributed networks of devices, whereas others (such as the last three) are Agent-Based Modeling Simulation (ABMS) platforms, which enable high-performance simulation of large numbers of agents on a single machine or on a computing cluster. Some frameworks, such as SARL and MET4FoF [9,23], support both high-performance local simulation and distributed deployment.

A MAS framework normally offers to the developer an API that allows the creation and management of various agent-oriented abstractions (such as nodes, agents, artifacts), the definition of various aspects of the environment (such as a physical space, tools agents can use, services available), as well as the interaction between all those elements. For instance, JADE [3] offers agents as sole abstraction for the persistent components in a MAS agentification, with containers available as references to the nodes in the deployment. JaCaMo implements the Agent & Artifacts (A&A) model and offers artifacts as abstractions for any aspect of the environment [22]. ABMS frameworks generally split the modeling between event-driven agents and a space-based environment model.

In terms of the infrastructure for communication and services, it is fixed in most frameworks, some, such as SARL and JaCaMo, offering the choice between local and network-distributed message or event routing. Figure 1 shows a perspective on the layers of a MAS framework: the MAS application is built on top of agent-oriented abstractions offered by the framework, and potentially an agent-oriented programming language (e.g., Jason or SARL); the framework deals with the management of entities and with the interaction between entities.

This approach has some important limitations. First, any new type of entity that the developer may need to model must be built on top of the abstractions offered by the framework, adding complexity and leading to two levels of modeling: the agent-oriented model of the framework and the agent-oriented model of the application. For instance, if the developer of a distributed AOP application implemented in JADE wishes to model artifacts, artifacts would have to be implemented as agents, leading to having "agent" agents and "artifact" agents. The alternatives are either to use JaCaMo, forcing the developer to use Jason for agents, or to interoperate CArtAgO with JADE, which brings a different framework into the mix. Similarly, in JaCaMo, organizations are managed via artifacts, such that an organization is not a first-class entity in itself. Other entities may be needed, such as context managers – entities managing an activity or a smart space – which need to perform some proactive actions, such as sending notifications or checking for overlaps, but do not have mental states, making them different from both agents and artifacts.

The second limitation relates to communication infrastructures in distributed network deployments, which are also related to discovery of resources. Most frameworks have the communication infrastructure fixed, and it is impractical to change it. In a complex distributed deployment, using different communication infrastructures in different parts of the system brings challenges in modeling and forces the developer into creating multiple models for multiple frameworks, incurring overhead in interoperating them.

In this paper we introduce a model for the entity management and interaction routing layer of a multi-agent system framework, which relies on a uniform representation of entities and their operations. We call it the *entity-operation model*. In this model, any persistent component in the multi-agent system is modeled, at the most basic level, as an *entity*, and any of its functionality is accessible, at the most basic level, as an operation, which can have arguments and restrictions. The entity-operation model lives below the abstractions which are offered to the developer, as a uniform technical foundation, but it is accessible if desired. The model only specifies how entities can be accessed from outside, leaving total freedom for their internal implementation.

This way, the model of the MAS can contain, as first-class entities, not only agents, artifacts, or organizations, but also communication infrastructures, directory services, context managers, entities at the sub-agent level (components of agents, such as behaviors), and any other type of entity the developer may need. All of these would be accessible to other entities by means of a uniform underlying interface, while allowing each type of entity its own set of specific operations. By using a uniform approach to model any entity, a deployed system can welcome, at runtime, new entities of new types.

Abstractions that make up existing agent-oriented models can be implemented directly on top of the entity-operation model, which is very thin. For instance, instead of implementing organizations via artifacts (as in JaCaMo), an organization can be implemented directly as an entity in its own right, potentially distributed over several nodes. A developer using an agent framework can use "traditional" entity types and interactions (e.g., agents, artifacts, etc) without needing to know about entities and operations, but also has the possibility to create new types of entities, to access other entities via operation calls, and to use the full capabilities of any of the entities in the framework. The entity-operation model is interoperable with other agent-oriented models but supports a flexible approach to the underlying model of individual entities.

A natural addition to the entity-operation model was a means to control the access to operations. We have created a context-based access model, where access is authorized to entities having specific relations to other, known, entities.

We have successfully implemented the entity-operation model in FLASH-MAS[1] [17], reusing existing blocks and models and implementing a scenario demonstrating how the entity-operation model can be used for context-based access to elements in a smart environment.

We have devised an ambient intelligence scenario which we will use throughout the paper, in which a person interacts with entities in a smart building: Andreea is a master student at the Department of Computer Science and Engineering, also working as a teaching assistant for undergraduate students. It's the middle of January and Andreea is going to teach an Operating Systems lecture on a Monday morning in the new smart building in the campus. To reduce the energy bill, the heating is turned off over the weekend and it must be started by an authorized person when needed. Andreea lives quite far from the university, and it takes her about an hour to get there. Before leaving her home, she uses the mobile app to check the temperature of the classroom and she remotely turns on the heating. When she arrives in the building, she uses her smartphone to unlock the door to the lecture room and to turn on the lights. As master student, Andreea has a cloud computing class in another room in the same building later on. She has a desk in Room 308 so she prints some notes using the printer there and then goes to her class. This time as a student, she won't be able to perform the same actions as before – she can temporarily receive control of the projector in the room, but she will not be able to unlock the room.

A second use-case that we address is a platform in which agents are able to exchange pre-trained machine learning (ML) models, evaluate or train them further, and exchange information about their experiences. In this scenario, ML models and their descriptions are first-class abstractions, and act as sub-agent entities that agents can use in their activity and that agents can send or receive. They have a reactive aspect – answering to queries – but also a pro-active (but not autonomous) aspect, as they can report on the status of their training process or report problems with their functionality.

The paper is organized as follows. In the next section we discuss existing frameworks and models for distributed multi-agent systems. After the presentation of the model in Sect. 3 and implementation challenges in Sect. 4, we discuss the advantages and appropriateness of using the entity-operation model for multi-agent frameworks in Sect. 5. The last section draws the conclusions.

---

[1] The Fast and Lightweight Multi-Agent Shell. The source code is available at https:// github.com/andreiolaru-ro/FLASH-MAS.

2   Related Work

Pal et al. [19] survey the current state of framework development, detailing both the application domains of frameworks and their implementation language, as well as their development status and distribution license. An important distinction is between open-source and commercial platforms. A related work lists only 16 projects as in-development general-purpose platforms, combining platforms for distributed deployment, platforms for ABM simulation, and AOP languages. Kravari and Bassiliades [14] survey the development status, license, adherence to standards, ease of deployment, and security for several agent frameworks, concluding that JADE remains the most popular framework. They observe that when choosing a framework for deploying MAS, developers and researchers must select and be limited by application domain, programming language, and learnability. This is why our intention is to develop a more general, easy to use MAS framework.

Agent-based simulation tools are surveyed by Abar [1], Rousset [24] and Lorig [15]. The most popular and giving a high level of performance are the Repast suite and D-MASON. JADE is shown to have very little applicability for ABMS, because of the lack of support for synchronization and for HPC-specific communication. More flexibility in the interaction model could have made JADE a valid option for AMBS.

Cardoso and Ferrando [6] provide a fresh systematic literature review on AOP languages, which are many times related to their respective frameworks. Most languages are based on AgentSpeak [20] (ASTRA, Jason and related languages) or on JADE.

JADE [3] is, by far, the most popular framework for distributed deployment of multi-agent systems. It offers communication, directory and discovery services, agent migration, and a specific, behavior-based structure for agents. In terms of communication, it relies on TCP/IP by default, but other communication methods are available at deployment time, with agent code changes necessary [7]. JADE offers no abstraction other than the agents (potentially offering services), with the framework also abstracted as standard agent instances. Nodes, communication services, and directory services are accessed in different manners – nodes via direct methods, communication via methods in the agent, and directory services via FIPA-ACL messages with specific content [10]. Many other frameworks are based on or inspired by JADE and strive to be FIPA-compliant. Jadex [5] adds support for BDI agent modeling. SPADE [13] is developed in Python and uses XMPP/Jabber as a communication method, featuring a GUI for monitoring agents, giving the advantage of easier interoperation with ML libraries. PADE [16,26] is also implemented in Python and uses Twisted for communication, hence supporting multiple protocols. JACOSO is a JADE-based implementation of the ACOSO Methodology for the development of IoT systems [11]. Apart from Smart Objects, which it agentifies as JADE agents, it builds additional abstractions for other elements in IoT scenarios, such as tasks (as sub-agent entities), events, and a variety of managers and adapters whose properties do not fit in

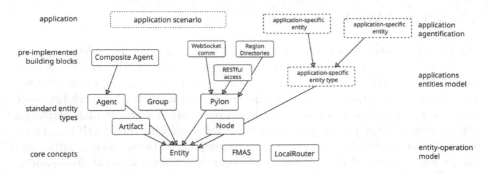

Fig. 2. A view on the object-oriented class hierarchy in a scenario using the entity-operation model. There are several layers of abstraction, with the most abstract at the bottom. See also Sect. 3.2. Dotted borders are used for application-specific models and entities defined by the MAS developer.

the agent model, showing the need to integrate new abstractions in the agent framework without the need to create additional layers.

JaCaMo [4] is another popular MAS framework, which combines the Jason AOP language, based on AgentSpeak and Prolog, with the CArtAgO implementation of the Agents & Artifacts (A&A) model for the environment, and with the MOISE implementation for roles and organizations. JaCaMo rests on strong theoretical foundations and can be deployed both locally and in JADE-based distributed setups. The distinction made between agents and artifacts is very strong, and their development paths diverge from modeling phase. Workspaces exist as virtual entities spanning multiple nodes, but do not have an embodiment with its own code. No new abstractions can be created in JaCaMo, without basing them on existing entities. Initial steps have been taken towards making JaCaMo BDI compatible with ABM simulation, via JaCaMo-SIM [21].

Janus [12] is a language-independent platform but targeted mainly at executing the SARL [23] AOP language. It supports event-driven interaction, and in deployments over a local computer network (via the Janusnode variant) it broadcasts these events to all agents. While combining the A&A approach with the distributed approach, it is not adequate for message-based applications, nor does it offer services such as directory or service discovery.

Met4FoF [9] is a recent, in-development Python MAS framework oriented towards streaming data from sensors. It offers specialized modules for stream management, buffering, and redundancy. It offers only agents as abstractions for persistent entities, with additional data- and stream-related abstractions.

3   The Entity-Operation Model

When implementing complex scenarios using an agent-based approach, a question that is raised frequently is *"what should this be modeled as?"*. This is somewhat related to the question that arises in an open system when a new entity is introduced and the other entities in the system ask questions like "*what is this? how should I interact with this?*". When using a MAS framework, the set of possible entity types is fixed to what the framework offers. New entity types will have to be implemented via existing entity types.

A framework using the entity-operation model does not restrict the developer in this way and allows the deployment of any type of entity as a first-class entity. The framework itself is very *thin* – it only specifies an interaction model, with all the rest being modules that can have various implementations.

Entities. The model that we propose posits that all persistent elements in a MAS are represented as *entities*. The central principle is that entities are *persistent*. Secondly, entities need, in general, to be *accessible*; as such, they expose *operations*, which other entities may *call*; not every operation is available to any entity, as we will detail further on. Third, entities are *autonomous*, in that they can decide how they react to operation calls. All entities should have a unique identifier. In a complex deployment, although mechanisms for name shortening and caching can be used, any entity should be uniquely identified by its *URI*.

Entities may be *local* to (running inside) a physical node, or may be *distributed* across multiple nodes. Distributed entities must have a local *embodiment* on each node where they are present. For instance, in JADE, containers are the embodiment of the JADE platform.

Our goal is to use this model to describe all elements in a running, deployed MAS. That means that, beside agents and components representing aspects of the environment, elements such as nodes and communication infrastructures should also be implemented as entities; similarly, any interaction between entities, be it an interaction between two agents, but also an interaction between an agent and a node, or an agent and an organization, should be performed via operations. Communication infrastructures are also accessed via operations, allowing for more uniformity and for flexibility in the implementation of communication mechanisms.

We do not model in any way the *inside* of entities. We look for interoperability and mutual understanding, but an entity may work in various manners on the inside. Of course, one has the possibility to model the inside of an entity using other entities, as for instance some agents in FLASH-MAS are composed of shards, which are also modeled as entities. FLASH-MAS offers an implementation for *composite agents*, whose behavior is modeled by the shards that are added to the agent [17].

Using entities does not mean we forfeit existing models based on agents or on agents and artifacts. Rather, we offer a uniform underlying model (or meta-model) that underpins the actual model used by the application. This brings unity to the technical implementation of the entities and the opportunity to easily switch between different approaches to modeling.

In our scenario, we model as user's agent as an agent entity, the smart lock, the smart light, the heating appliance, and the temperature sensor as artifacts, and the entities managing the room and the two teaching activities as context managers – non-autonomous agents with a more complex behavior.

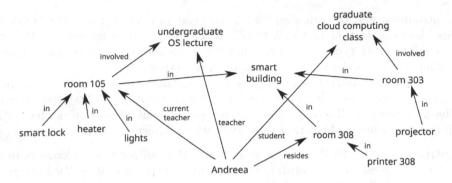

Fig. 3. A perspective on the relations in the running scenario, at the moment when Andreea teaches the undergraduate class on operating systems.

Operations. The model that we propose posits that any interaction between two entities is performed via *operations*, with one entity *calling* an operation of the other entity. Moreover, any interaction between a core element of the framework and an entity should be performed via an operation of the entity.

Entities are expected to have a `list` operation, which returns a description of all the operations available to any other entity. While this can, in the future, be used to semantically search for an appropriate operation, it can currently be used to *duck type* an entity, based on its available operations.

In keeping with the concepts in the A&A and web services models, operations can also have *return values*, which are returned to the initiator of the operation call.

In our scenario, the user's agent can query the temperature sensor to find the temperature in the room, can instruct the smart lock to unlock the room, and can connect to a wireless projector. All of these, of course, if the user is authorized to perform the operations. For instance, the `print` operation of the printer in Room 308 may be available to people who are physically in the room, or are in general residing in that room.

Relations. Access to operations can be *restricted* by using *relations*. Relations link entities in a similar manner to semantic triples in RDF[2]. Relations can express, for instance, that a certain device is in a particular room, or that a user has a role in a particular activity, or that a service runs on a particular node. Once initiated, relations must be accepted by entities at both ends, and can be canceled by any of the two entities.

Relations can be used to restrict which entities are allowed to call a given operation. For instance, a door for a room in a smart building can only be unlocked by the personal agent of a user who is teaching the lecture taking place in that room in that given interval.

In our example, relations describe the placement of devices, the location of the user, and the role of the user in the current context. See Fig. 3 for a

---

[2] Semantic triple https://en.wikipedia.org/wiki/Semantic_triple.

perspective on the relations in the scenario, at the moment when Andreea teaches the undergraduate class.

Context Tokens. An entity calling an operation which has restrictions must *prove* that it indeed has the required relations to other entities. As such, we introduce the idea of *context tokens* – tokens which are a proof of context. Each token is a document containing the statement of a relationship, the timestamp of the document, and an expiration time. To ensure authenticity, tokens can be required by the callee to be cryptographically signed by an authorized entity involved in the relationship.

An entity will receive context tokens periodically from other entities, proving their relationship. As a caller of an operation, it will send, in the operation call, all relevant tokens, proving that it is indeed authorized to call the operation. The tokens must still be valid for successful authorization. The expiration period of context tokens is related to the nature of the relation and is proportional to the time a relation is expected to last. The quality of being employed by an organization can be re-certified (by the emission of a context token) once every month, whereas the property of being in a given room should be recertified once every minute. It is the entity managing a given context that decides the expiration period of context tokens.

For instance, in our scenario, there is a printer in Room 308. When a user with a device enters the room, a relation is created by the local access point between the user's agent/device and the entity managing the room. While the user remains in the room, the user's agent receives, periodically, a context token proving the relation. When the user wishes to call the `print` operation, the user's agent will know that the operation is restricted to users in the room, so the operation call that is sent will also contain the most recent context token proving that the user is in the room; the token is signed by the room manager. The printer already has the public key of the room manager, since one of the restrictions on one of the operations of the printer involves the room manager. It can check the context token and approve the operation.

In the example with Andreea unlocking the door as a teacher, the smart lock entity lists an operation `unlock`, with the restriction that the caller must have the role *current_teacher* in the current room and at the current time. In a different exchange, the entity managing the lecture informs the room who will be teacher in the current time slot. The entity managing the room creates a *current_teacher* relation with the agent of the user, periodically sending to the user a context token proving the relation. When calling the `unlock` operation, this context token will be included, and it will be verified by the smart lock.

3.1 Formalization Sketch

From an omniscient point of view, we define a fully modeled multi-entity system, using the entity-operation model, as a tuple $\langle EE, RR \rangle$, where EE is the set of *entities* and RR is the set of *relations*. We have:

$$EE = \{E \mid E = \langle ID_E, Operations_E \rangle\}$$

$$RR = \{\langle from, relation, to \rangle\}, \text{with } from, to \in EE$$

An *operation* $O \in Operations_E$, with $E \in EE$, is defined as:

$$O = \langle Name_O, Description_O, Arguments_O, Result_O, Restrictions_O \rangle$$

The tuple contains the name of the operation, its description, the description of the arguments, return value, and restrictions on the entities which may call it. The description of the operation can have any form, but a semantic description is more suitable. The description of the arguments is of the form $Arguments_O = \{\langle Name, Description \rangle\}$. In the simplest implementation of the model, the *Description* can be as simple as the type of the argument, and the description of the result the type of the returned value.

The restrictions on an operation are defined as a logical operation on relations. Take, for example, the printer located in Room 308 in our running scenario. It has one operation (print), which should be available to any entity E in the same room ($E \prec_{located} Room308$, and to anyone who is a resident in that room ($E \prec_{resides} Room308$). So, for an entity E to be allowed to call the print operation, it should be true that $E \prec_{located} Room308 \vee E \prec_{resides} Room308$.

The restrictions can be formalized as a disjunctive normal form on positive literals, each literal representing a relation, but replacing the formula $E \prec_{()} E1$ with the pair $(\prec_{()}, E1)$. That is, for an operation O:

$$Restrictions_O \subseteq \{Conjunction \mid Conjunction \subseteq \mathcal{R} \times EE\}, \text{with}$$

$$\mathcal{R} = \{relation \mid \langle *, relation, * \rangle \in RR\} - \text{ the set of all relation names}$$

As such, the print operation has a restriction that looks like: $\{\{(\prec_{located}, Room308\}, \{(\prec_{resides}, Room308)\}\}$

Of course, no single entity in a distributed system has an omniscient view on all other entities (or else it would be a bottleneck and a single point of failure), so, in practice, the system is formed of the set of entities EE, each entity keeping track of its relation to other entities:

$$\forall E \in EE . E = \langle ID_E, Operations_E, Outgoing_E, Incoming_E \rangle, \text{with}$$

$$Outgoing_E = \{(relation, E_{to}) \mid \langle E, relation, E_{to} \rangle \in RR\}$$

$$Incoming_E = \{(relation, E_{from}) \mid \langle E_{from}, relation, E \rangle \in RR\}$$

An *operation call* is an object containing the *caller*, the *callee*, the name of the operation, the arguments for the operation, relevant information about the relations of the caller, and whether a return value should be sent back to the caller (if the operation supports it):

$$call = \langle E_{Source}, E_{Destination}, Name_{Op}, \{Arguments\}, \{Tokens\}, send\text{-}result \rangle$$

where $E_{Source}, E_{Destination} \in EE$, $Name_{Op}$ is an identifier for the operation, *Arguments* are the argument values for the operation, *send-result* is a boolean value, and *Tokens* are the *context tokens*.

3.2   Predefined Entities and Relations

As stated in the Introduction, a developer does not need to create new types of entities or to call operations directly. A layer of predefined entities may prove sufficient for many MAS applications (see also Fig. 2). This has several advantages: (1) a framework based on the entity-operation model can be used exactly like a "normal", existing framework; (2) given enough predefined entities, a framework based on the entity-operation model can be used like *any* of the standard frameworks; and (3) is needed, the developer can still define new types of entities or new implementations of existing entities. Entities in existing MAS models can be represented in the entity-operation model as follows.

An **agent** has a `receive` operation, which allows it to receive messages from any other entity. The implementation of agents can define a `send` method which constructs an operation call directed at another agent. In the A&A model, the implementation can also contain methods for accessing artifacts and operations to allow notifications from artifacts. As there are many approaches to what an agent is, multiple "agent" entity types can be defined depending on the application, each with its own set of operations, defining what an agent is in that approach.

An **artifact** works just as in the A&A meta-model, exposing operations to any entity in the appropriate workspace. Workspaces are distributed entities, and entities are bound to workspaces by means of dedicated relations.

A **pylon** that is the embodiment of a *communication infrastructure*, can receive `route` operation calls from any entity, and it can attempt to route the operation call to its target entity, which may be on a different machine.

A **pylon** that offers directory and discovery services presents the `register` and `search` operations.

A **node** offers a `load&start` operation to any entity which *executes* on the node or which has *authority* over the node. Nodes supporting migration offer a `receive_agent` operation which enables agents to migrate to that node.

Sub-agent entities, for instance **shards** in FLASH-MAS [17], must have a fast two-way means of interaction with their container agent. As such, a shard must offer a `signal_agent_event` operation to receive events from the agent, and an agent supporting shards must offer a `post_event` operation to receive events from its shards. The same mechanisms can be used to build holonic systems. In a model similar to Jade, behaviors could also be modeled as sub-agent entities.

Machine learning models (pre-trained) can be represented as entities having a `get_result` operation. As sub-agent entities, they can be sent from one agent to another, they can be cloned, or they can migrate with an agent from one node to another, using the same migration mechanism as agents. They can have a pro-active aspect which allows them to notify other entities about the status of the training process.

Entities are expected to have a `list` operation, which returns the names and descriptions of operations available to other entities.

Any entity should offer a set of operations which allows it to interact easily with the framework, while also abiding to the model. These operations – `start`,

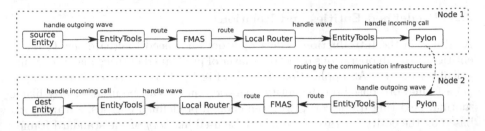

Fig. 4. The path taken by an operation call between entities situated on different nodes.

`stop`, and `isRunning`, should only be available to entities authorized to *control* that entity (e.g., the node on which the entity is executing, or the *owner* of the entity).

4   Implementation Challenges and Results

We have implemented the entity-operation model in FLASH-MAS, a Java-based framework which offers tools for the deployment of complex, distributed multi-agent scenarios, in which the implementation of any entity is customizable. We have re-written the core code of FLASH-MAS so that all entities use the entity-operation model. As such, some challenges arose, and we will present in this section how we solved them.

To abide to the entity-operation model, any object which represents an entity must implement the `EntityAPI` interface, which specifies a minimal number of methods:

- `connectTools` gives the entity a reference to the `EntityTools` instance which will connect it to the framework. Using the `EntityTools` instance, the entity can register (or obtain) and ID with the framework.
- `getID` returns the ID of the entity.
- `handleIncomingOperationCall` is called whenever an operation call is sent to the entity. The method is called by the `EntityTools` instance associated with the entity, which has previously checked if the operation is correctly accessed.
- `handleRelationChange` is called by the `EntityTools` instance whenever a relation involving this entity is created or destroyed.

While representing all persistent things in a MAS as entities, and since entities can be implemented in any way by the developer, there is a need for something to bind the entities together, help manage them, and ensure that operation calls reach their intended destination. Hence, on any JVM where FLASH-MAS is running there is a singleton object called FMAS, representing the framework. To ensure correct encapsulation and to restrict access to powerful FMAS functionality we take example from the internal implementation of JADE and create, for each entity integrated into the system, an instance of the `EntityTools` class, which helps entities interface with the framework. The `EntityTools` instance manages the list of the entity's operations, the access to those operations, and the relations incoming to or outgoing from the entity.

Entities interact via operation calls. There are, however, other types of interactions, which are not direct interactions between entities, and cannot be represented as operation calls. These are: the return value sent as a result of an operation call; the initiation or removal of a relation between two entities; and the acceptance or rejection of a new relation between entities. All these interactions have a destination and a source or a return path, so we can model them collectively as a concept that we call *wave*.

Waves must be routed so that they reach their destination, sometimes across the local network or the Internet. In keeping with the flexibility offered by FLASH-MAS, there is no restriction on the communication method used, as long as the communication infrastructure can deliver a wave to the node where a destination entity is located. In line with the principles of the entity-operation model, interaction infrastructures are embodied by pylons, which are also entities. Routing waves between pylons on the same node is handled by an entity which is directly linked to the FMAS instance, called the *Local Router*.

To route a wave, the Local Router uses the following algorithm:

- if the destination is registered with the local FMAS instance, the wave is routed directly to its destination (via the EntityTools instance associated with the destination);
- otherwise, the list of local entities which offer the route operation is used to look for an appropriate router;
- the wave is sent via the first of these entities that executes the route operation successfully.

A detailed view of this process is shown in Fig. 4. While the wave passes through several entities, the only decision points are in the *Local Router* instances, the rest being only method calls. The advantage of this process is, however, that routing waves can be done using no matter which communication infrastructure. Currently, FLASH-MAS has implementation for communication via WebSocket, RESTful web services, distributed region-based mesh, and ROS. Having an implementation for entities which is agnostic to the communication mechanism opens the path towards using the same codebase for performing high-performance simulations and deploying entities in a distributed setup. In FLASH-MAS we have already performed experiments with using MPI-based communication.

In FLASH-MAS we have strived not only to have the ability to select the communication infrastructure at deployment, and make agent (and, in general, entity) code agnostic of the mechanism used for communication, but also to be able to support the deployment and interoperation of multiple communication infrastructures in the same system. This is also possible in the entity-operation model. Following the principles in previous work [18, 25], *bridge* entities can offer the route operation, the same as pylons of communication infrastructures. A bridge will register in two (or more) communication infrastructures and will act in each one as a sink for the other(s), ensuring waves can travel between any two nodes in a transparent manner for the other entities.

Some MAS frameworks, including JADE, support mobile agents, which can migrate from one node to another. This poses a particularly difficult challenge to the framework, as the agent needs to interrupt its activity, get serialized, transferred to another node, deserialized, and resume execution. In FLASH-MAS, entity mobility needs support from both *inside* and *outside* the entity. The entity must ensure that it suspends its activity correctly, and serialization is also done inside the entity. Once serialized, the entity sends the package as the argument of an operation call to the destination node, which, if it supports migration, deserializes the entity and registers it with the local FMAS instance, leaving to the entity to resume its activity in the correct manner.

It is arguable that, when using cryptographically signed context tokens, checking the tokens can incur a significant performance penalty. We have developed, however, a mechanism to avoid this penalty for the cases where performance is essential. First, many scenarios do not require at all that access to the most used operations is controlled, for instance in a scenario using agents which exchange messages. Secondly, the most important performance penalty is brought when operation calls are routed inside the same node. This is particularly of issue in the case of sub-agent entities (shards in FLASH-MAS) to which only their container agent has access, but which are expected to exchange calls with their agent frequently. Let us take the example of a shard which should post an event to its agent. The shard calls the agent's operation and attaches a context token proving that the shard belongs, indeed, to that agent; but the context token has been generated by the agent, on the same node. This means that the local FMAS instance can check the token only by hashing it and comparing the result against a list of active tokens and their hashes, without needed to verify the signature. Full verification is still needed, however, when calls are exchanged between different network nodes.

We have validated the viability of the entity-operation model by implementing the scenario presented in the Introduction. Our goal was to verify that we can use the entity-operation model to implement all the described processes and to perform functional testing of the context-based access model. This stage of validation was successful.

In the implementation of the scenario, we have created agents for Andreea and other students, context managers for the two lectures, for the smart building, and for the three rooms, and artifacts for the various devices – smart lock, heater, lights, and printer. Relations have been created, especially the ones representing the role of Andreea as a teacher for one course and as a student for the other course. When, in simulated time, Andreea's lecture as a teacher approached, a relation was created by the course manager between Andreea and the room manager. She was now authorized to control some of the devices in the room. When a relation was created between Andreea and the smart building, the `unlock` operation of the smart lock became available to her. After the lecture, her relation with the room was removed, so the operations became unavailable again.

The implementation shows that, indeed, a variety of entities can be implemented using the proposed model, more properly than just implementing them all as "agents". It showed that the context-based access model can be used to limit the availability of operations.

5   Discussion

The idea of having objects distributed across the network, offering operations that can be called, is not new. However, our model is directed specifically towards autonomous entities. Compared, for instance, to Java RMI, the entity-operation model, and the various implementations for actual communication between nodes, increases flexibility as it avoids reliance on a single interaction mechanism.

Having entities and operations is similar, and can be replicated by, having agents which send messages from one to another. It offers, however, a lot more expressivity in modeling the entities in the system, reserving the agent abstraction for truly pro-active, autonomous entities, without abusing them to implement any of the persistent entities in a deployment.

Especially when using web service communication, a deployment using the entity-operation model can be likened to a set of web-services offering various operations. Our approach, however, allows various interaction methods, some of which can be more lightweight than deploying a web server on every node.

Essentially, what we strive to offer with the entity-operation model is choice and expression power. A MAS developer should not be forced into making the choice of implementing an entity as a framework-offered abstraction that is not appropriate for that entity, and this choice should not lead to a development path that is so far from the other types of abstractions that it is difficult to return to the decision point. The developer should be able to choose from a wide array of available abstractions and, when needed, to be able to create their own first-class abstractions, and then use that set of abstractions for the entities in the applications. Let us take a few examples.

A *context manager* handles the interactions between other entities and a smart space or a smart activity [2]. For instance, a context manager keeps track of the entities which are a part of that context, e.g., which are physically in that space, or are part of that activity. In our scenario, the context manager of the room keeps track of the users in the room, or users authorized to control the room devices; the context manager of the course (as an activity) sends updates to the entities involved in the activity. A context manager is not a proper agent, in terms of an entity which has goals, and which achieves goals by executing actions in a plan; it rather manages aspects of the environment. However, it cannot easily be implemented as an artifact (in the sense of the A&A model) because an artifact cannot create relations between it and agents proactively, because agents need to first *focus* on the artifact. When the teacher (or some faculty staff) adds students to a course, some agent would have to send a message to the students' agents, and then the agents would have to focus on the context manager. In the entity-operation model, a context manager entity is able to create relations to agents (that they can approve or not), even if it is not modeled as an agent.

A *broadcast group* (similar to a mailing list) relays messages sent by one of its members to all the other members in the group. Again, a broadcast group would not be properly modeled as an agent. However, it cannot be modeled as an A&A artifact either – artifacts can notify agents only of observable properties or via signals. For a broadcast group, members of the group would not receive the messages in the group as signals, not as messages, needing a different processing path inside the agent. In the entity-operation model, a broadcast group is implemented as an entity which agents can `join` and then it can simply call the `receive` operation of agents each time it needs to broadcast a message.

While the initial question of "What should this be modeled as?" remains, using the entity-operation model as a uniform underlying model reduces some of the stress associated with having to decide on the type of abstraction from the start, makes changing the type of abstraction later on easier, and helps interoperation with new types of entities as they are added to the system.

6   Conclusions and Future Work

We introduce the entity-operation model as a practical approach to the uniform implementation of the various abstractions offered by a MAS framework. The model has been created with the desire to both offer to the MAS developer an array of available abstractions, but also to allow the developer to change previous choices regarding the modeling of the scenario, and to create new types of abstractions, if one needs it. The model is enriched with a context-based access model for operations.

Using the entity-operation model brings a series of advantages, like the possibility to interact with all types of abstractions in a MAS and to model explicitly the communications and services infrastructures. Another advantage is the ability to create sub-agent or supra-agent entities, such as shards and organizations, respectively, or to create holonic structures.

A current development direction is to fully integrate machine learning models as sub-agent entities, while interoperating, using the principles of the entity-operation model, with ML frameworks written in Python. In terms of model development, we must make decisions on whether waves are a technical element or are fundamental to the model.

The next steps in this research are to build entity implementations that use the entity-operation model and are compatible with JADE, JaCaMo, and other popular MAS frameworks. Our short-term goals are to be able to run JADE agent code on other communication infrastructures, to use various agent implementations with the JADE communication infrastructures, to support Jason as an AOP language, and to interoperate with CArtAgO and MOISE. A further goal is to have a common approach when deploying a MAS as an ABMS and when deploying it as distributed over a network, easing the transition from simulation to real-life deployment while preserving the implementation of entities.

References

1. Abar, S., Theodoropoulos, G.K., Lemarinier, P., O'Hare, G.M.: Agent based modelling and simulation tools: a review of the state-of-art software. Comput. Sci. Rev. **24**, 13–33 (2017)
2. Baljak, V., et al.: S-CLAIM: an agent-based programming language for Am I, a smart-room case study. In: Proceedings of ANT 2012, The 3rd International Conference on Ambient Systems, Networks and Technologies, 27–29 August, Niagara Falls, Ontario, Canada. Procedia Computer Science, vol. 10, pp. 30–37. Elsevier (2012). https://doi.org/10.1016/j.procs.2012.06.008, http://www.sciencedirect.com/science/article/pii/S1877050912003651
3. Bellifemine, F., Poggi, A., Rimassa, G.: JADE - a FIPA-compliant agent framework. In: Proceedings of PAAM, vol. 99, pp. 97–108. Citeseer (1999)
4. Boissier, O., Bordini, R.H., Hübner, J.F., Ricci, A., Santi, A.: Multi-agent oriented programming with JaCaMo. Sci. Comput. Program. **78**(6), 747–761 (2013)
5. Braubach, L., Pokahr, A.: Jadex active components framework-BDI agents for disaster rescue coordination. Softw. Agents Agent Syst. Appl. **32**, 57–84 (2012)
6. Cardoso, R.C., Ferrando, A.: A review of agent-based programming for multi-agent systems. Computers **10**(2), 16 (2021)
7. Curry, E., Chambers, D., Lyons, G.: A JMS message transport protocol for the jade platform. In: IEEE/WIC International Conference on Intelligent Agent Technology, 2003. IAT 2003, pp. 596–600. IEEE (2003)
8. Dorri, A., Kanhere, S.S., Jurdak, R.: Multi-agent systems: a survey. IEEE Access **6**, 28573–28593 (2018)
9. Dorst, T., Eichstädt, S., Schneider, T., Schütze, A.: Propagation of uncertainty for an adaptive linear approximation algorithm. SMSI 2020-System of Units and Metrological Infrastructure, pp. 366–367 (2020)
10. FIPA: FIPA ACL message structure specification, December 2002. http://www.fipa.org/specs/fipa00061/SC00061G.html
11. Fortino, G., Russo, W., Savaglio, C., Shen, W., Zhou, M.: Agent-oriented cooperative smart objects: from IoT system design to implementation. IEEE Trans. Syst. Man Cybern. Syst. **99**, 1–18 (2017)
12. Galland, S., Rodriguez, S., Gaud, N.: Run-time environment for the SARL agent-programming language: the example of the Janus platform. Futur. Gener. Comput. Syst. **107**, 1105–1115 (2020)
13. Gregori, M.E., Cámara, J.P., Bada, G.A.: A jabber-based multi-agent system platform. In: Proceedings of the Fifth International Joint Conference on Autonomous Agents and Multiagent Systems, pp. 1282–1284 (2006)
14. Kravari, K., Bassiliades, N.: A survey of agent platforms. J. Artif. Soc. Soc. Simul. **18**(1), 11 (2015)
15. Lorig, F., Dammenhayn, N., Müller, D.-J., Timm, I.J.: Measuring and comparing scalability of agent-based simulation frameworks. In: Müller, J.P., Ketter, W., Kaminka, G., Wagner, G., Bulling, N. (eds.) MATES 2015. LNCS (LNAI), vol. 9433, pp. 42–60. Springer, Cham (2015). https://doi.org/10.1007/978-3-319-27343-3_3
16. Melo, L.S., Sampaio, R.F., Leão, R.P.S., Barroso, G.C., Bezerra, J.R.: Python-based multi-agent platform for application on power grids. Int. Trans. Electr. Energy Syst. **29**(6), e12012 (2019)
17. Olaru, A., Sorici, A., Florea, A.M.: A flexible and lightweight agent deployment architecture. In: 2019 22nd International Conference on Control Systems and

Computer Science (CSCS), Bucharest, Romania, 28–30 May 2019, pp. 251–258. IEEE (2019). https://doi.org/10.1109/CSCS.2019.00048, https://ieeexplore.ieee.org/abstract/document/8744845/

18. Olaru, A., Florea, A.M.: A framework for integrating heterogeneous agent communication platforms. In: Proceedings of ACSys 2015, the 12th Workshop on Agents for Complex Systems, in conjunction with SYNASC 2015, the 17th International Symposium on Symbolic and Numeric Algorithms for Scientific Computing, Timisoara, Romania, 21–24 September, pp. 399–406. IEEE Xplore (2015). https://doi.org/10.1109/SYNASC.2015.66

19. Pal, C.V., Leon, F., Paprzycki, M., Ganzha, M.: A review of platforms for the development of agent systems. arXiv preprint arXiv:2007.08961 (2020)

20. Rao, A.S.: AgentSpeak(L): BDI agents speak out in a logical computable language. In: Van de Velde, W., Perram, J.W. (eds.) MAAMAW 1996. LNCS, vol. 1038, pp. 42–55. Springer, Heidelberg (1996). https://doi.org/10.1007/BFb0031845

21. Ricci, A., Croatti, A., Bordini, R., Hübner, J., Boissier, O.: Exploiting simulation for MAS programming and engineering-the JaCaMo-sim platform. In: 8th International Workshop on Engineering Multi-Agent Systems (EMAS 2020) (2020)

22. Ricci, A., Viroli, M., Omicini, A.: Give agents their artifacts: the A&A approach for engineering working environments in MAS. In: Proceedings of the 6th International Joint Conference on Autonomous Agents and Multiagent Systems, p. 150. ACM (2007)

23. Rodriguez, S., Gaud, N., Galland, S.: SARL: a general-purpose agent-oriented programming language. In: 2014 IEEE/WIC/ACM International Joint Conferences on Web Intelligence (WI) and Intelligent Agent Technologies (IAT), vol. 3, pp. 103–110. IEEE (2014)

24. Rousset, A., Herrmann, B., Lang, C., Philippe, L.: A survey on parallel and distributed multi-agent systems for high performance computing simulations. Comput. Sci. Rev. 22, 27–46 (2016)

25. Suguri, H., Kodama, E., Miyazaki, M., Kaji, I.: Assuring interoperability between heterogeneous multi-agent systems with a gateway agent. In: 7th IEEE International Symposium on High Assurance Systems Engineering, 2002. Proceedings, pp. 167–170. IEEE (2002)

26. Tom, R.J., Sankaranarayanan, S., Rodrigues, J.J.: Agent negotiation in an IoT-Fog based power distribution system for demand reduction. Sustain. Energy Technol. Assess. 38, 100653 (2020)

Remote Deployment of a JADE Agent in Docker

Dennis Maecker[✉] [iD], Henning Gösling[iD], and Oliver Thomas

German Research Center for Artificial Intelligence (DFKI), Osnabrück, Germany
{dennis.maecker,henning.goesling,oliver.thomas}@dfki.de

Abstract. This work presents a technical introduction into the implementation process of a containerized multi-agent system. More specifically, the JADE framework is used as a middleware for the development of software agents. With the goal of achieving high modularity and enhancing usability, the system will be containerized in Docker. To model an application-oriented scenario, the containerized agent-system is deployed on a headless remote server. The goal of this paper is to provide a comprehensive solution to help overcome the technical difficulties encountered in accessing the graphical user interface of agents from an end device. A procedural guide to the implementation process is provided, including the preparation of the JADE-based multi-agent system, creation of Docker containers, and deployment of the containerized multi-agent system on a remote server.

Keywords: Multi-agent system · JADE · Docker · Containerization

1 Introduction

Recently, the novel concept of a *Smart Managed Freight Fleet* was introduced [5], focusing in particular on multi-agent systems applied to supply chains in the transport market. Representing a promising framework for multi-agent systems, the Java Agent Development Framework (JADE) [3,4], already applied in real-world telecommunication applications [8], was chosen as a candidate for the implementation process. As a Java-based middleware, JADE is used to incorporate functionalities of multi-agent systems and follows the standards of the Foundation for Intelligent Physical Agents (FIPA). In the scenario of a large-scale freight-fleet management system, it is crucial to ensure not only the interoperability of the agents, but also compatibility with different platforms, for instance remote servers or fleet assets (e.g., delivery robots), and facilitate the software deployment. For this objective, the container virtualization technology of Docker [1] was chosen. This enables the deployment of self-contained software containers without the need for any configurations on the remote server. In the progress of adapting the multi-agent system for the use in Docker containers, several technical issues emerged. So far, deploying JADE agents in Docker containers was only sparsely investigated or documented at the time of writing. Thus, this paper

A. Ciortea et al. (Eds.): EMAS 2023, LNAI 14378, pp. 271–277, 2023.
https://doi.org/10.1007/978-3-031-48539-8_18

documents the basic procedure in order to make a multi-agent system (MAS) available through Docker containers on an arbitrary machine. Furthermore, the deployment of containerized agents on a remote server is explained, with a focus on the accessibility of the graphical interface by local machines.

2   Pre-requirements

2.1   Implementation of a JADE-Based Multi-agent System

A JADE-based multi-agent platform typically consists of one main container and additional agent containers, each including an arbitrary number of agents. Agent containers can register at the main container, which acts as an adminis-tration instance of the multi-agent platform. In the implementation process, a universal `Container` class was set up. By passing arguments (`MainContainer` or `Agent`) to the execution call of this class, it can be determined whether the instance acts as a JADE main container or an agent container. For a main con-tainer, the IP address of the hosting machine is required as an argument, while an agent container necessitates the agent's name and an existing main container's IP address. In the latter case, the `Container` class then initializes a predefined agent instance within the agent container. As the implementation of the MAS in Java depends on auxiliary libraries (e.g., the JADE framework) it is crucial to ensure dependency resolution with the aim of a portable software. This can be achieved by packing the compiled Java classes in a Java archive (i.e., a `.jar` file). A `META-INF` folder with the meta-information file `MANIFEST.MF` must be generated, as depicted in Fig. 2a. This file specifies the project's main class, `Container`. The packing process of the Java archive file can be undertaken in various ways, depending on the development environment that is being used. After the cre-ation, the `.jar` file can be executed for testing purposes in the console by the fol-lowing command (assuming a locally installed Java environment) considering the local IP of the host machine: `java -jar SmartTransport.jar MainContainer 192.168.0.125`. Conversely, the command `java -jar SmartTransport.jar Agent agent1 192.168.0.125` ensures that the instance of the `Container` class acts as an agent container by passing the argument `Agent`, instantiating an agent with name `agent1` and connecting to the main container with the corresponding IP address given in the argument.

2.2   Setting Up an X Server

As the common interface of a Docker container is console-based, this section addresses the necessary steps for accessing the graphical interface of Docker containers on the host machine. This can be achieved by setting up an X server on the host machine, which manages the graphical output of the Docker container. Depending on the operating system, several solutions are possible, such as X.Org for Linux, VcXsrv[1] for Windows, or XQuartz[2], based on X.Org components, for

---

[1] Available at: https://sourceforge.net/projects/vcxsrv/.
[2] Available at: https://www.xquartz.org/index.html.

MacOS. In either case, after the X server is started, the Docker container merely needs the local IP address of the host machine as an environment variable in order to forward the graphical interface to the X server. This is explained in further detail in the next chapter. Moreover, it is important to allow access to the X server on the host machine. In the case of VcXsrv, this can be accomplished in the program's settings. Considering the X.Org server on Linux, it is sufficient to enter the following command in the console: xhost +. It is important to note, that this procedure opens the X server for all participants in the network. In high security environments, this approach is not recommended.

3   Agents on a Remote Server

The containerization of the agent system is split into two parts. First, a base image is set up in a Dockerfile. In a separate docker-compose.yml file, the establishment of the Docker-related network setup takes place. Also, two containers will be specified, one which runs a JADE main container and one running a JADE agent container. As the host of the Docker containers (i.e., the headless remote server) has no support for graphical output by itself, it has to be ensured that the graphical user interface can be accessed from an end device through a Secure Shell (SSH) connection to the server.

3.1   Accessing the User Interface of Remotely Deployed Agents

First, the remote server is accessed by an SSH connection. It is possible to run graphical applications on the remote server and have the graphical output displayed on the local machine utilizing the X server running on the local system. This can be achieved by passing an -X argument to the call of the SSH connection as follows: ssh -X user@remote-server. Alternatively, when using SSH-clients such as PuTTY, it is possible to configure the forwarding task to the X server in the application settings [7]. However, passing the graphical output of an agent application inside a Docker container through the remote server to the end device requires a more elaborate solution. The most promising approach for forwarding the user interface of the containers to the end device will be further described and can be summarized by the installation of a Virtual Network Computing (VNC) server in the Docker container. When connecting to the remote server via SSH it is possible to connect to the Docker container using a VNC client installed on the server. The graphical output of the VNC client is then tunneled via the SSH connection and displayed on the local end device. This concept is depicted in Fig. 1. The substantial advantage of this approach is that the application continues its operation even under interruptions of either the SSH or the VNC connection. Additionally, as the graphical output is tunneled through the SSH connection to the end device, there is no need for additional ports being accessed on the remote server, hence contributing to the data security of the system.

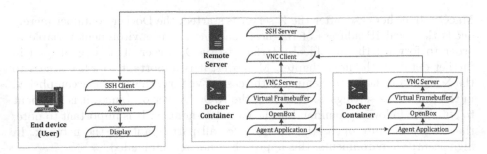

Fig. 1. Data flow of the graphical information (solid lines) as well as data exchange in between the agent applications (dashed line).

3.2   Setting up the Docker Container

The `Dockerfile` for the Docker image used in this part is shown in Fig. 2b. The base image used for this system is an `openjdk:18-jdk-slim` image (line 1) that is a minimal, Debian-based environment containing a pre-installed Java distribution. Subsequently, in line 2 the `.jar` Java archive for the Java agent application is copied to the `home` directory of the Docker image. As stated before, the `.jar` file can be started with different arguments, thus launching either a JADE main container or a JADE agent container. Hence, the Docker image which is created here can be used for both types of JADE containers.

In line 3, the installation of basic packages related to the connection to the X server along with a VNC server (`x11vnc`) and a minimal desktop environment (`openbox`, `tint2`, `xterm`, `lxterminal`) takes place. Lines 4-6 set up the desktop environment. This process is inspired by the descriptions in a publicly available repository [6]. The last command in line 7 refers to the `docker-entrypoint.sh` script that is executed when the container is launched. The content of this `docker-entrypoint.sh` file is shown in Fig. 2c and is responsible for the initialization of the desktop environment and the window manager. Finally, the Docker image can be built using the following command: `docker build -t dfki/agents`. By using the argument `-t`, a tag name for the Docker image, here `dfki/agents`, can be set, which is then further used as a base image in the `docker-compose.yml` file in Fig. 2d.

3.3   Integration in a docker-compose.yml File

The `docker-compose.yml` file describes the setup of a main container and an additional agent container, both based on the JADE framework. In lines 2-9 of the file, a network gateway is defined. Thus, it is possible for each Docker container to possess its own IP address within this separate network. This ensures portability of the Docker system, as the IP addresses do not have to be adapted to the address of the respective host machine. Beginning in line 11, the configuration of the Docker container running the JADE main container is specified. Lines 12 states the base image as the one described by the Dockerfile in Fig. 2b. In line

1: Manifest-Version: 1.0
2: Main-Class: smartTransport.Container

(a) Content of the MANIFEST.MF file.

1: FROM openjdk:18-jdk-slim
2: COPY ./out/artifacts/SmartTransport/
   /home/
3: RUN apt-get update && apt-get -y install
   iproute2 x11-apps libxi6 libxtst6
   libxrender1 lib32z1 xvfb openbox tint2
   x11vnc xterm lxterminal
4: ADD config /opt/config
5: RUN chmod +x
   /opt/config/docker-entrypoint.sh
   /opt/config/openbox/autostart
6: RUN rm -rf /etc/xdg/openbox && cp -R
   /opt/config/openbox /etc/xdg/openbox &&
   (rm -rf /etc/xdg/tint2 || true) && cp -R
   /opt/config/tint2 /etc/xdg/tint2
7: CMD "/opt/config/docker-entrypoint.sh"

(b) **Dockerfile** for containerization of
the multi-agent system intended to be deployed on a remote server.

1: #!/bin/bash -xe
2: xvfb-run -s "$DISPLAY" -s '-screen 0
   1024x700x24 -ac' openbox-session

(c) **docker-entrypoint.sh** file.

1: version: "2.4"
2: networks:
3:   agent_network:
4:     driver: bridge
5:     ipam:
6:       driver: default
7:       config:
8:       - subnet: 192.168.56.0/24
9:         gateway: 192.168.56.1
10: services:
11:   container:
12:     image: dfki/agents
13:     networks:
14:       agent_network:
15:         ipv4_address: 192.168.56.10
16:     ports:
17:     - 1099:1099
18:     - 7778:7778
19:     - 5900:5900
20:     working_dir: /home
21:     environment:
22:       DISPLAY: :99
23:   agent1:
24:     image: dfki/agents
25:     networks:
26:       agent_network:
27:         ipv4_address: 192.168.56.11
28:     ports:
29:     - 1100:1099
30:     - 7779:7778
31:     - 5901:5900
32:     working_dir: /home
33:     environment:
34:       DISPLAY: :99

(d) **docker-compose.yml**-file used for
launching one JADE main container and
one JADE agent container in dedicated
Docker containers.

Fig. 2. Contents of relevant files used in this work.

15, the IP address of this container is set. Following, lines 16-19 define the ports
of the Docker container which are mapped to the ports of the host machine. In
addition to the ports relevant for the JADE communication (7778 and 1099),
port 5900 is opened to allow a VNC connection by the remote server, i.e., the
host of the Docker container. The display environment variable in line 22 is set
to :99, ensuring that the graphical output is sent to the VNC server. The part
after line 23 represents the setup of a second Docker container, dedicated to a
JADE agent container. The configuration procedure is analogous to that of the
first container. However, the setting of the IP address in line 27 and the port
mapping in lines 28-31 differ. The ports need to be altered for this container
as the initial ports on the host machine are already used by the first container.
If more containers for other agents are intended to be launched than there are
specified here, the respective ports have to be altered accordingly (e.g., 1101,
7780, 5902). The file can be built using the following command on the remote

host: `docker-compose up`. After this, the two docker containers are running on the remote host.

3.4 Launching the JADE Agent System

The previous section described how to start the two Docker containers containing the `SmartTransport.jar` that can launch either a JADE main container or an agent container. However, at the time of writing this paper, no solution has been found yet to run the agent application automatically when the Docker containers are starting. Rather, it is necessary to connect to the running Docker containers via a VNC client and to manually start the agent application. After setting up the SSH connection and enabling graphical forwarding to the local X server, the VNC client (e.g., vncviewer) can be launched on the remote host, displaying the VNC software user interface on the end device (see data flow in Fig. 1). In the user interface of the VNC client, the IP and the port of the respective Docker container can be entered, in this case either `192.168.56.10:5900` or `192.158.55.11:5901`. In the following, the Docker container with the IP `192.168.56.10` is used to launch a JADE main container, while the other Docker container with the IP `192.158.55.11` is dedicated to the JADE agent container. A successful connection will exhibit the respective Docker container's desktop environment within the VNC client's interface. In the environment of the Docker container, it is possible to launch a terminal instance (here `lxterminal`, see installation setup in Fig. 2b). A JADE main container can be started by entering the following command: `java -jar SmartTransport.jar MainContainer 192.168.56.10`. When the main container is started, the graphical user interface of the JADE framework can be accessed in the interface of the VNC client. Subsequently, a VNC connection to the second Docker container can be established from the remote server. In a terminal instance, a predefined agent named `agent1` can be started in a JADE agent container by following command: `java -jar SmartTransport.jar Agent agent1 192.168.56.10`. As described before, by passing the IP address of the JADE main container as an argument to the call of the JADE agent container, it is possible that the JADE agent container connects to the JADE main container. Hence, an arbitrary number of agents can connect to the JADE main container to form a MAS. The agent applications stay active, regardless of whether the VNC connection to the Docker containers or the SSH connection to the remote server is active.

4 Conclusion and Further Work

In this paper, we have presented an introduction to how to combine the well-known JADE middleware for MAS with Docker focusing on the deployment on a remote server. To the best of the authors' knowledge, a comprehensive introduction to this topic, as presented here, has not yet been published. Future developments in this regard can be identified for instance by configuring the JADE message protocol (MTP) to utilize HTTP [2]. Hence, JADE platforms distributed over several networks can be connected by using JADE's feature of remote platform connectivity or by implementing REST interfaces.

References

1. Anderson, C.: Docker [software engineering]. IEEE Softw. **32**(3), 102-c3 (2015)
2. Bellifemine, F., Caire, G., Trucco, T., Rimassa, G., Mungenast, R.: JADE administrator's guide. TILab (2003)
3. Bellifemine, F., Poggi, A., Rimassa, G.: JADE - A FIPA-Compliant Agent Framework, pp. 97–108. The Practical Application Company Ltd. (1999)
4. Greenwood, D., Bellifemine, F.L., Caire, G.: Developing Multi-agent Systems with JADE. Wiley, Hoboken (2007)
5. Heinbach, C., Gösling, H., Meier, P., Thomas, O.: Smart managed freight fleet: ein automatisiertes und vernetztes flottenmanagement in einem föderierten datenökosystem. HMD Praxis der Wirtschaftsinformatik (2022)
6. murer: Virtual X and VNC server docker image with openbox (2020). https://github.com/murer/docker-xvfb-x11vnc-openbox
7. Tatham, S.: PuTTY user manual (2022). https://upload.wikimedia.org/wikipedia/commons/b/b7/PuTTY_User_Manual.pdf
8. Ughetti, M., Trucco, T., Gotta, D.: Development of agent-based, peer-to-peer mobile applications on ANDROID with JADE. In: The Second International Conference on Mobile Ubiquitous Computing, Systems, Services and Technologies. IEEE (2008)

Author Index

Printed in the United States
by Baker & Taylor Publisher Services